LPI
Web Development Essentials
Study Gui

T0094193

LPI
Web Development Essentials
Study Guide
Exam 030-100

Audrey O'Shea

A Wiley Brand

To Rick, I couldn't do what I do without your love and support.
—Audrey

Acknowledgments

It takes many people to create a high-quality book, and the following people added greatly to the quality of this one. A big thank-you to Jan Lynn Neal and Pete Gaughan for answering all those questions and keeping me on track, and of course to the team at Wiley working in the background taking care of editing, artwork, and layout. I would like to extend a special thank-you to Kenyon Brown, for matching my skill set with this project, and for actively promoting women in non-traditional roles. Tanner Souva did a great job as technical editor, catching those late-night errors and making valuable suggestions. And of course, I must acknowledge my husband, Rick, for filling in for me on so many things at home, and my family for enduring my endless apologies because "I have a chapter due on Monday."

About the Author

Audrey O'Shea lives on the shore of Lake Ontario in upstate New York, where she is an instructor at a technical school teaching electronics, computer operating systems, hardware, networking, security, programming, and life in general. She also works as a computer consultant when she isn't writing. Audrey is a member of Phi-Kappa-Phi honor society and Women in Technology International. She holds numerous IT industry certifications, and her lifelong goal is to promote the involvement of other women in the information technology field.

Audrey's other published works include *A Geek Girl's Guide to Electronics and the Internet of Things* (Wiley, 2020) and *CompTIA A+ Complete Practice Tests: Exam Core 1 220-1101 and Exam Core2 220-1102, Third Edition* (Wiley, 2022). She's also served as technical editor for the *A+ Complete Practice Tests, Exam Core 1 220-1001 and Exam Core 2 220-1002, 2nd Edition* (Wiley, 2019) by Jeff Parker and Quentin Docter, and *CompTIA ITF+ CertMike*, by Mike Chapple (Wiley, 2023) books.

About the Technical Editor

Born in Phoenix, Arizona, **Tanner Souva** lived in Phoenix for 2 years before moving to Copenhagen, New York. Tanner graduated from Jefferson Community College for Computer Information Technology with an associate degree.

Tanner originally joined the company Keyes Security/Information Technology in high school as a software engineer intern and then was promoted to a paid position. Keyes was acquired and merged into Level Nine Group, a company that focuses on the security of medical and commercial devices/applications.

Contents at a Glance

Contents

Introduction

Whether on their smartphones or a desktop computer, the majority of people rely on web technologies on a daily basis for information about all sorts of things as well as connection to companies or organizations, and perhaps even friends and family. Linux powers the majority of the world's smartphones, web servers, and supercomputers. Linux is even the operating system of choice for the Space Station, so learning about Linux in any capacity is a smart move for *your* IT career.

The Linux Professional Institute (LPI) Web Development Essentials Study Guide: Exam 030-100 covers the knowledge that a beginner in web development will be expected to know, including how web servers and clients communicate, and front-end and back-end technologies. On the front-end, the part that the users see, the certification focuses on the following development tools:

- Hypertext Markup Language (HTML)
- JavaScript (JS)
- Cascading Style Sheets (CSS)

On the back-end, where data is stored and manipulated, the certification focuses on the following:

- Node.js
- Node.js Express
- SQLite

Together, these provide the foundation you need to get up and running with web development. So, let's get started!

What Does This Book Cover?

This book covers the topics outlined in the LPI Web Development Essentials: Exam 030-100 available at www.lpi.org/our-certifications/web-development-essentials-overview.

Chapter 1, "Web Development Basics" This chapter begins with an outline of the types of website development and developers as well as the types of programming languages. It also explains programming editors and editing environments, along with programming paradigms and version control systems.

Chapter 2, "Client/Server Computing" The information in this chapter explains the relationship between a web client and a web server.

Chapter 3, "Database Management Systems"   This chapter provides an overview of database management systems and relational database concepts. Databases are the backbone of an interactive web page.

Chapter 4, "Client/Server Communication"   Here you learn how the client and server communicate—the communication begins with a request from the client to the server.

Chapter 5, "HTML Introduction"   In this chapter, you learn about the skeleton of an HTML page, which is what all web pages start with.

Chapter 6, "Content Markup"   This is your introduction to "marking up" the content to provide a web page's structure.

Chapter 7, "References and Embedded Resources"   Here you learn how to include images and references to other pages in your HTML page.

Chapter 8, "Creating HTML Forms"   This chapter shows you how to create input forms that enable your web page visitors to provide information and interact with your web page.

Chapter 9, "Introducing CSS"   This chapter introduces you to Cascading Style Sheets (CSS) that provide the formatting of your web page content.

Chapter 10, "Applying CSS Styles"   Here you learn how the styles you created in Chapter 9 are applied to the page and what order they're applied in.

Chapter 11, "CSS Styling Fundamentals"   This chapter focuses on units of measure and common properties like color and font and how to use them.

Chapter 12, "CSS Layout and Box Model"   This chapter introduces you to the CSS box model and how to make text flow as you like between other elements.

Chapter 13, "JavaScript Essentials"   Here you are introduced to JavaScript and what it can do for your web page as well as how to attach your JavaScript file to an HTML file.

Chapter 14, "JavaScript Data"   In this chapter, you learn about the types of data that are used by JavaScript and the difference between variables and constants.

Chapter 15, "Functions and Control Structures"   You learn how to create functions and conditional statements in this chapter as well as examine data coercion and truthy and falsy values.

Chapter 16, "The DOM"   Here you focus entirely on the document object model (DOM), which is a method for specifying what element of the page you would like to use or have a style applied to.

Chapter 17, "NodeJS Basics"   This chapter moves us to the back-end of the website, where you learn how to use Node.js to program a server.

Chapter 18, "NodeJS Express"   Here you learn to use Node.js Express to route and serve files, use templates, and validate user input. You also explore the dangers of cross-site scripting and request forgery.

Chapter 19, "Manipulating SQLite with NodeJS"   In this final back-end chapter, you install and work with SQLite databases by entering, changing, and retrieving data.

Who Should Read This Book

As the title implies, this book is intended for people who have an interest in developing websites. Even if you're not planning to become certified (but you should consider it!), this book introduces you to the technologies that are most commonly used to build and maintain websites, and gives you some tips along the way. The topics covered are ubiquitous in the web development world. HTML, JavaScript, and CSS are the building tools for the front-end and Node.js and Node.js Express provide the runtime and framework for the back-end of websites. Regardless of your career trajectory, this book is an excellent place to start.

You don't need programming experience to work with the exercises in the book; the exercises are intended to explain the process to a novice.

The book assumes you have some experience with Linux operating systems, although even novice Linux users should be able to follow the instructions for installing and working with the tools presented. If you're typically a Microsoft Windows user, there are some suggestions in here for you as well. Working with the front-end technologies isn't much different regardless of the operating system, but you'll eventually want to have a Linux computer to practice with. Luckily Linux is free and will work on even most older computers.

Exam Tips

The LPI Web Development Essentials exam consists of 40 multiple choice/multiple answer questions. You'll have sixty minutes to complete the exam. Unlike some other certifications, this one doesn't expire, so once you've passed it, it's good for your lifetime.

Many of the questions ask you to select more than one answer, so be sure to read the questions carefully. Take your time, but remember that there is a time limit and you must submit the exam before the time runs out.

This exam is all multiple choice, but simulates the preciseness of writing code, so ensure that you know the syntax of the various commands presented in this book. Not only for the exam, but for your work as a web designer.

As with any exam, the sooner you take it after taking the course or reading the book, the more you'll remember. Devote yourself to studying in the week (or weeks) before the exam, but the night before, make sure you get a good night's sleep, and take a few minutes to relax before you go in.

Wishing you success!

Interactive Online Learning Environment and Test Bank

The author has worked hard to create some really great tools to help you with your certification process. The interactive online learning environment that accompanies the LPI Web Development Essentials Study Guide: Exam 030-100 includes a test bank with study tools to help you prepare for the certification exam—and increase your chances of passing it the first time! The test bank includes the following:

Sample tests   All the questions in this book are included online, including the assessment test at the end of this Introduction and the review questions at the end of each chapter. In addition, there is one custom practice exam with 100 questions. Use these questions to assess how you're likely to perform on the real exam. The online test bank runs on multiple devices.

Flashcards   The online text bank includes two sets of flashcards with over 100 questions each. They are specifically written to challenge you, so don't get discouraged if you don't ace your way through them at first. They're there to ensure that you're really ready for the exam. And no worries—armed with the review questions, practice exams, and flashcards, you'll be more than prepared when exam day comes. Questions are provided in digital flashcard format (a question followed by a single correct answer). You can use the flashcards to reinforce your learning and provide last-minute test prep before the exam.

Glossary   A glossary of key terms from this book is available as a fully searchable PDF.

Go to www.wiley.com/go/sybextestprep to register and gain access to this interactive online learning environment and test bank with study tools.

Additional Resources

This text covers all of the objectives of the LPI Web Development Essentials certification, but sometimes you want to know more about a particular command or find lists of things. Some resources that will help you with that follow:

```
www.Nodejs.org
www.Expressjs.com
www.sqlite.org/docs.html
www.w3schools.com/html
www.w3schools.com/css
```

```
www.w3schools.com/js/default.asp
https://developer.mozilla.org/en-US/docs/Web/CSS
https://developer.mozilla.org/en-US/docs/Web/HTML
https://developer.mozilla.org/en-US/docs/Learn/JavaScript
```

LPI Web Development Essentials Exam Objectives

This table lists the sections and the percentage each represents of the exam.

Section	% of examination
031: Software Development and Web Technologies	15%
032: HTML Document Markup	20%
033: CSS Content Styling	20%
034: JavaScript Programming	25%
035: Node.js Server Programming	20%
Total	100%

 Exam objectives are subject to change at any time without prior notice and at Linux Professional Institute's sole discretion. Please visit LPI Web Development Essentials website (www.lpi.org/our-certifications/exam-030-objectives) for the most current listing of exam objectives.

Objective Map

Objective	Chapter(s)
Section 031: Software Development and Web Technologies	
031.1 Software Development Basics (weight: 1)	1
031.2 Web Application Architecture (weight: 2)	1, 2, 3

How to Contact Wiley or the Author

If you believe you've found a mistake in this book, please bring it to our attention. At John Wiley & Sons, we understand how important it is to provide our customers with accurate content, but even with our best efforts an error may occur. In order to submit your possible errata, please email it to our Customer Service Team at wileysupport@wiley.com with the subject line "Possible Book Errata Submission."

The author would appreciate your input and questions about this book! Email Audrey O'Shea at audrey.oshea@cliffjumpertek.com.

Assessment Test

1. Which two programming languages can use the `.c` file extension? (Choose two.)
   A. C
   B. C++
   C. JavaScript
   D. Java

2. What is the word `float` an example of in both JavaScript and C++?
   A. Syntax
   B. Pseudocode
   C. Keyword
   D. Operator

3. What do we call a website whose content is the same regardless of who logs into it?
   A. Client
   B. Dynamic
   C. Single-page
   D. Static

4. What makes creating a web page possible for people with no programming experience?
   A. APIs
   B. Content management systems (CMSs)
   C. JavaScript
   D. Web application packaging

5. What type of database is used when data does not easily fit into rows and columns?
   A. Structured database
   B. Relational database
   C. Unstructured database
   D. SQL database

6. What type of field is used to sort and find specific data?
   A. Key
   B. Primary
   C. Lock
   D. Logical

7. Which of these stores your username for your favorite shopping site?

   A. Cookies

   B. WebSockets

   C. Cache

   D. HTTP

8. Which of these will store information as long as the client is connected to the server?

   A. Virtual host

   B. Private cache

   C. Session cookie

   D. Method

9. What type of cache can be used by multiple people at the same company?

   A. Session

   B. Private

   C. Public

   D. Shared

10. Which of these is the markup language used to create and format documents for a browser to interpret?

   A. HTTP

   B. HTML

   C. HTTPS

   D. Java

11. In what section does the `<title>` tag go?

   A. `<html>`

   B. `<body>`

   C. `<head>`

   D. `<start>`

12. Which tag identifies the person who wrote the web page?

   A. `<meta name= "author" content="Chris Cross">`

   B. `<h1>Chris Cross</h1>`

   C. `<title>Chris Cross </title>`

   D. `<meta name="Chris Cross">`

13. What element is described as one that is structurally above the element being considered, regardless of how many layers are between?

    A. Parent

    B. Child

    C. Ancestor

    D. Descendant

14. Which semantic element is used to identify the bottom of the page where you'll likely find legal and copyright information about the page?

    A. `<footer>`

    B. `<header>`

    C. `<bottom>`

    D. `<main>`

15. What type of URL will include the full path to a web page?

    A. Absolute

    B. Main

    C. Relative

    D. Specific

16. Which tag and attribute are used to embed an image into a web page? (Choose two.)

    A. `<img>`

    B. `<em>`

    C. `alt`

    D. `src`

17. What type of image appears behind the entire web page?

    A. Background

    B. Inline

    C. Page

    D. Source

18. In the code line `<label for=" breed" >Choose a breed.</label>`, what will show when the browser renders the page?

    A. Label

    B. Breed

    C. Choose a breed

    D. The entire line

19. What button type will not be visible on the client's browser output?

    A. Image

    B. Button

    C. Submit

    D. Hidden

20. Which of the following are attributes of `<form>`? (Choose two.)

    A. method

    B. action

    C. POST

    D. GET

21. Which of the following is not a method to enter styles into an HTML file?

    A. Linking to a CSS file

    B. Using the style attribute

    C. Using the style tag

    D. Linking to a file with a `.style` extension.

22. You want the area behind your text to be pink. Which of the following does that for you?

    A. `style="color:pink;"`

    B. `style="background-color:pink;"`

    C. `<p> "background=pink"`

    D. `<p "pink">`

23. Which of these is a type selector?

    A. `p`

    B. `#myList ul`

    C. `name`

    D. `!important`

24. What happens in inheritance?

    A. A parent object inherits from a child.

    B. The style applied to a parent stops there.

    C. A child object inherits a style from a parent.

    D. A child object must be styled the same as the parent.

25. Which of the following properties can cause text to display sideways?

    A. `text-decoration-style:`

    B. `text-align-last:`

    C. `text-emphasis:`

    D. `text-orientation:`

26. Which of the following properties will make text taller?

    A. `font-size: xxx-large`

    B. `border-style: solid`

    C. `font-height: large`

    D. `font-weight: dense`

27. Which type of measurement doesn't change?

    A. Relative units

    B. Absolute units

    C. em

    D. vh

28. Which part of the CSS box model makes a box visible?

    A. Margin

    B. Border

    C. Padding

    D. Stuffing

29. Which of the following will keep an object on the screen even if you're scrolling? (Choose two.)

    A. `position: fixed`

    B. `position: absolute`

    C. `position: relative`

    D. `position: sticky`

30. Which of these does not exist?

    A. CSS box model

    B. CSS flexbox model

    C. CSS grid layout

    D. CSS padding model

31. Which of these is used in JavaScript to create a list of shortcuts to full URLs?

    A. `<defer>`

    B. `type="importmap"`

    C. `type="async"`

    D. `<ul>`

32. Which of these is the variable in the code lines `let x=y;` and `var greeting;`? (Choose two.)

    A. `let`

    B. `x`

    C. `y`

    D. `greeting`

33. Which of the following keywords is used to define a value that does not change?

    A. `const`

    B. `let`

    C. `var`

    D. `def`

34. Which of these data types represents `true` or `false`?

    A. Number

    B. String

    C. Boolean

    D. Binary

35. When a variable is defined outside of function or block of code, what is its scope?

    A. Available

    B. Block

    C. Function

    D. Global

36. What kind of function is `alert( )`?

    A. User-defined

    B. Predefined

    C. Performance

    D. Process

37. You're designing a program that chooses a day based on a day number. Which of these commands is best to use? (Choose two.)

    A. `switch`

    B. `break`

    C. `for`

    D. `while`

38. In web development, what does DOM stand for?

    A. Document Order Model

    B. Document Object Markup

    C. Document Object Management

    D. Document Object Model

39. Which method is used to add a class to a DOM object?

    A. `classList.toggle()`

    B. `setAttribute()`

    C. `classList.add()`

    D. `changeAttribute()`

40. What programming tool uses code almost identical to JavaScript but runs on the server-side of a website?

A. Perl

B. Ruby

C. Node.js

D. PHP

41. Which command will end an REPL session?

A. .break

B. .exit

C. .help

D. .save

42. What folder contains EJS files?

A. /ejs

B. /images

C. /scripts

D. /views

43 Which of these commands creates a new instance of Express?

A. const express=require("express");

B. const app=express();

C. const port=3000;

D. app.get("/" , (req, res));

44. Which of these commands is used to delete a SQLite3 table?

A. DROP

B. DELETE

C. REMOVE

D. UNINSTALL

45. Which of the following query types will retrieve all the records from a database and then apply a query to the records?

A. db.each()

B. db.get()

C. db.all()

D. db.filter()

Answers to Assessment Test

1.   A, B. C and C++ can both use the `.c` file extension. JavaScript uses a `.js` extension and Java uses a `.java` file extension. See Chapter 1 for more information.

2.   C. Keywords are reserved by a programming language because they have a specific meaning. Examples of keywords are `float`, `var`, `short`, `finally`, `goto`, and so on. Each language may have hundreds or more keywords. See Chapter 1 for more information.

3.   D. A website whose content does not change no matter who accesses it is known as a static website. A dynamic website does change based on the visitor. See Chapter 2 for more information.

4   B. Content management systems enable a user to create a website even if they have no programming knowledge. See Chapter 2 for more information.

5.   C. When data doesn't fit easily into rows and columns, it is called unstructured data and is stored in an unstructured database. See Chapter 3 for more information.

6.   A. A key field is one that can be used to sort and find data. See Chapter 3 for more information.

7.   A. A cookie stores information about a client on the client's computer that the website can later read. See Chapter 4 for more information.

8.   C. Session cookies hold information about the user as long as the session is active. See Chapter 4 for more information.

9.   D. A shared cache can be used by multiple people at the same company to make retrieving information faster. See Chapter 4 for more information.

10.   B. Hypertext Markup Language (HTML) is the markup language that is used to create and format documents that will be interpreted and displayed by a browser. See Chapter 5 for more information.

11.   C. You'll find the `<title>` tag in the head section of an HTML page. See Chapter 5 for more information.

12.   A. `<meta name= "author" content="Chris Cross">` is used to identify the author of a web page, assuming Chris Cross is the person who wrote it. See Chapter 5 for more information.

13.   C. An element is an ancestor if it is anywhere in the hierarchy, in the same branch, above the element being considered. See Chapter 6 for more information.

14.   A. A footer appears at the bottom of a page. See Chapter 6 for more information.

15.   A. Absolute URLs include the full path to a URL. A relative URL will refer to a file that's in the same file structure. See Chapter 7 for more information.

16. A, D. Images are embedded using the `<img>` tag and `src` attribute. The `alt` attribute is used for alternative text, and the `<em>` tag makes text bold. See Chapter 7 for more information.

17. A. Background images can appear behind an entire page or for an element. Inline images are mingled in with text. See Chapter 7 for more information.

18. C. Text between the beginning label tag `<label>` and the ending lable tag `</label>` will be displayed. See Chapter 8 for more information.

19. D. A hidden button is still there, but not visible to the page visitor. See Chapter 8 for more information.

20. A, B. The three attributes of form are `method`, `action`, and `enctype`. POST and GET are possible values of the `method` attribute. See Chapter 8 for more information.

21. D. To style an HTML file, you can use the style attribute, the style tag, or an external CSS file. See Chapter 9 for more information.

22. B. To make the area behind a paragraph pink, you need to use the `background-color` property. See Chapter 9 for more information.

23. A. Only p is a type selector. `#myList ul` is a descendant selector of an `id`, `name` is not a selector, and `!important` is a property. See Chapter 10 for more information.

24. C. Just as in real life, a child object inherits its style from a parent; however, the style can be overridden. See Chapter 10 for more information.

25. D. Text orientation can turn text from horizontal to vertical. See Chapter 11 for more information.

26. A. `font-size` is used to make the text bigger or smaller. While `font-height` sounds right, it isn't a valid property. See Chapter 11 for more information.

27. B. Relative units change depending on how and where the website is viewed. Absolute units don't. em and vh are relative units. See Chapter 11 for more information.

28. B. A border is a visible feature of the CSS Box model. See Chapter 12 for more information.

29. A, D. The `fixed` and `sticky` values for the `position` attribute will keep an object from scrolling with the page, although they do it differently. `relative` and `absolute` depend on the original position and the body of a document, respectively. See Chapter 12 for more information.

30. D. The CSS padding model doesn't exist. Padding is one of the components of the CSS box model. See Chapter 12 for more information.

31. B. `type="importmap"` is used to create a list of shorter references to a group of long URLs. See Chapter 13 for more information.

32. B, D. x and `greeting` are both variables. The first is declared by `let`, and the second is declared by `var`. While y is commonly used as a variable, the code may simply be referring to the letter y. See Chapter 13 for more information.

33. A. Constants are values that do not change in a program. They are defined using the const keyword. See Chapter 14 for more information.

34. C. true and false are Boolean values. See Chapter 14 for more information.

35. D. If a variable is not defined inside a block or function, that variable is global and can be used anywhere in the program. See Chapter 14 for more information.

36. B. alert ( ) is a predefined function. See Chapter 15 for more information.

37. A, B. Using switch and break here would likely work best. See Chapter 15 for more information.

38. D. DOM stands for Document Object Model. It's a way of accessing objects in an HTML hierarchical tree. See Chapter 16 for more information.

39. C. The classList.add() method enables you to add a class to the chosen DOM object. See Chapter 16 for more information.

40. C. Node.js is a server-side framework that enables the programmer to create code using JS on the server-side. See Chapter 17 for more information.

41. B. .exit will end a REPL session. See Chapter 17 for more information.

42. D. EJS files must be stored in a /views file. See Chapter 18 for more information.

43. B. The app object contains all the Express functions and is the core of Express. See Chapter 18 for more information.

44. A. DROP deletes a table. DELETE deletes a database. REMOVE and UNINSTALL are not valid SQLite3 commands. See Chapter 19 for more information.

45. C. db.all() will retrieve all the records from a database before running a query. See Chapter 19 for more information.

Web Development Basics

LINUX PROFESSIONAL INSTITUTE, WEB DEVELOPMENT ESSENTIALS EXAM 030-100 OBJECTIVES COVERED IN THIS CHAPTER:

✓ **031 Software Development and Web Technologies**

- 031.1 Software Development Basics: The candidate should be familiar with the most essential concepts of software development and be aware of important programming languages.

  - Key Knowledge Areas:

    - Understand what source code is

    - Understand the principles of compilers and interpreters

    - Understand the concept of libraries

    - Understand the concepts of functional, procedural and object-oriented programming

    - Awareness of common features of source code editors and integrated development environment (IDE)

    - Awareness of version control systems

    - Awareness of software testing

    - Awareness of important programming languages (C, C++, C#, Java, JavaScript, Python, PHP)

- 031.2 Web Application Architecture

  - Key Knowledge Areas:

    - Understand the principles of APIs

The main focus of this chapter is the first subobjective of the Linux Professional Institute (LPI) Web Development Essentials Exam, software development. Along the way, you'll learn about the different types of web development and get a bird's-eye view of how programs are created. We'll compare writing environments and compiled versus interpreted languages, then look at different programming paradigms and what happens after a program is written. Grab your favorite note-taking tool, and let's get started!

Developer Types

Most likely, you already know that web development is the process of creating and maintaining web pages. Web pages can be found on servers across the Internet or on your own corporate server used to disseminate information internally. Regardless of where the site exists, there are different developer roles at work creating and maintaining the site.

Let's look first at the *front-end developer*. Front-end developers work on the parts of a website with which the users interact. It's more than just how the website looks. There are actions to consider, such as what happens when you click a button or mouse over a particular spot. These developers are creating the user experience. You can think of this as an artistic endeavor, but front-end developers also need to be able to program using software such as JavaScript, Hypertext Markup Language (HTML), and Cascading Style Sheets (CSS)—which are all covered in later chapters. Front-end development is a combination of programming skill and artistic design to create a positive experience for whoever visits the website, whether they are on a PC, a Mac, or their smartphone. The front-end of a website is also sometimes called the *client-side*.

Back-end developers are responsible for what's happening behind the scenes in a website; they're responsible for the parts that the user doesn't see but that are extremely important. Consider your favorite website for purchasing gifts. The background of that website most certainly has databases containing information about you, your prior orders, and their available inventory. The back-end is also called the *server-side*.

Finally, there are *full-stack developers*. As you might have guessed, full-stack developers are responsible for the entire process of designing a website, which includes both what the end users experience and the information and functionality that resides with the servers supporting the website.

Creating Software

Software, in a very broad sense, consists of lines of instructions for a processor to follow. That processor can be located in a computer, a smartphone, or even the microcontroller of your favorite Internet of Things (IoT) device. Software allows users to interact with hardware and data. Several different methods for developing software exist, most of which will have several iterations of the process before a program is complete. You may have heard of the Agile, Waterfall, Shell, or Sprint methods, but full-on software development and project management isn't within the scope of this certification, so we'll discuss creating software in more general terms.

Software often starts with *pseudocode*. Pseudocode is in human language, describing what we would like the program to do, for example:

- Ask the user to input their first name.

- Ask the user to input their date of birth.

- Calculate the user's age as of today.

- Print out "Hello %firstname%. I see that you are %age% years old." (% signs indicate something that changes.)

From there, software is turned into *source code*. Source code is still written in a format that humans can understand, if those humans are programmers. Source code is the result when a programmer takes those lines of pseudocode and turns them into instructions that are written in a particular programming language. In the Windows environment, most web browsers will allow you to see the source code of a web page, such as in Figure 1.1, by pressing Ctrl+U.

Just as humans speak different languages, there are different *programming languages*. Programming languages consist of a specific set of rules and words that are used to tell software or hardware to perform tasks. Each language has its own words and rules, similar to human grammar, that distinguish one language from another. Examples of these languages are C, C++, C# (the # is read as sharp,) Java, JavaScript, Python, Ruby, Perl, and PHP, to name a few. Each of these languages will have its advantages and disadvantages, and one may be preferred over another, depending on the project at hand. Some are used more on the front-end (for example, HTML, CSS, JavaScript, jQuery), whereas others tend to be used more on the back-end (for example, C#, Java, Python, PHP, Ruby, SQL).

Each of these languages will have their own syntax. *Syntax* refers to the exact order and presentation of the commands, including spaces, punctuation, capitalization, and so on. For example, in JavaScript, I would declare a variable to store the user's input for their first name with a line that says `var firstName`. The same variable in C++ would be declared as `string firstName`.

FIGURE 1.1   Source code example

```
280        'platform':'web'
281      }
282 };
283
284 var digitalDataMappingKey = "MicrositeLandingPageTemplate";
285 if(digitalDataMapping.hasOwnProperty(digitalDataMappingKey))
286 {
287     populateDigitalData(digitalDataMappingKey );
288 }
289
290 function populateDigitalData(digitalDataMappingKey) {
291     for (var key in digitalDataMapping[digitalDataMappingKey]) {
292         digitalData[key] = digitalDataMapping[digitalDataMappingKe
293     }
294 }
295 </script><script type="text/javascript" src="/_ui/shared/js/analyt
296 <script type="text/javascript">
297 /* Google Analytics */
298
299 var googleAnalyticsTrackingId = 'your_google_analytics_tracking_ic
300 var _gaq = _gaq || [];
301 _gaq.push(['_setAccount', googleAnalyticsTrackingId]);
302
```

Data can be presented in different types such as characters, strings, Boolean, integers, and floats. (These types of data will be discussed more in depth in Chapter 14, "JavaScript Data.") A first name, as in the previous example, would be a string of characters, and var refers to the term *variable*, which is data that may change.

Different programs also use different keywords. *Keywords* are words reserved by a program because they have a specific meaning in that particular program. Some JavaScript keywords are goto, float, short, finally, and char, in addition to many more. C++ also uses the keywords goto, float, short, and char, but has many others that are not the same as JavaScript, such as auto and union. These are just a few of the keywords that are available in various languages. A single language can have dozens to hundreds of keywords.

Keywords can be described as different types depending on what they do. The following are just a few keywords that are used in Python. Keywords can be operators (and, or, not, is), or they can control program flow (if, else), control how many times (iterations) a program does something (for, while), or import data (import, from, as). They can even handle problems (try, except, finally, else). These are just some of the functions available using keywords. Remember, some keywords are used in many programs, whereas others are specific to a particular program. Like learning any human language, once you master one, the others are easier to learn.

Just as different programming languages may share the same keywords, programmers may share their work in *libraries*. At its most basic level, a library is a collection of code that is shared to be reused by others. Programming languages have a standard library that is distributed with the program to provide functionality and solve common problems and needs. Python, for example, has an extensive standard library and thousands of third-party packages (libraries or modules) that can be added to the program. The common assumption is that a library is a collection of packages, and a package is a collection of modules, although all three terms are sometimes used interchangeably.

Libraries may solve a particular problem that many programmers encounter, or an uncommon problem that is annoying for just a few programmers. An example of a common problem is how to work with a particular LCD screen. A programmer will create code to interface with the LCD screen and share it with other programmers as a library. Libraries are essential to programmers and save time because the programmers don't need to re-create the solution. Every programming language will have libraries available for it, and some libraries will work with more than one language.

Regardless of the programming language, libraries need to be imported before they can be used. The exact command to import a library will vary by program. For Python, it's `import` *libraryName*, where you would replace *libraryName* with the actual name of the library. C++ uses `#include` *<packageName>* where *packageName* is replaced with the actual name of the package. Figure 1.2 shows a line of code that includes a library in the Arduino integrated development environment (IDE) for working with an LCD screen.

FIGURE 1.2   Adding a library

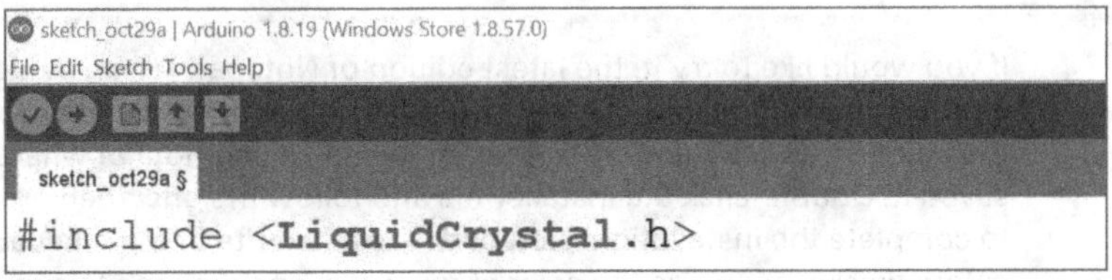

To further complicate the process, source code is not always written in just one programming language. Because each language has different strengths, one language may embed, or call, something written in another language. This happens often with websites that have JavaScript code embedded in an HTML document. Programmers may also use an *application programming interface (API),* which provides a set of rules and protocols that let two dissimilar systems share information, or in this case, two different programming languages. APIs make a programmer's work simpler, and many APIs have been created for various purposes. An API may be private, for use within a single entity, or it may be shared with specific partners or be public and available to anyone to use.

Text Editors and IDEs

Digital devices, such as computers, tablets, and smartphones, are only able to discern if a particular circuit is on or off, so everything in a computer system is represented as either a 1 (the circuit is turned on) or a 0 (the circuit is turned off.) The *binary number system* represents all values using only two digits; 1 and 0. Machines understand binary notation, and although some of us can easily convert short binary numbers to decimal numbers, a document written entirely in binary wouldn't be easily understood by humans. It's amazing to think that a detailed, colorful image or even a symphony playing is just a bunch of 1s and 0s to a computer!

Machine language is binary code that can be read by computing devices but is not readable by most humans. Source code must be converted to machine language *before* the computing device can follow the source code to carry out the programmer's wishes.

You may have wondered what tool you can use to write your own source code. Source code can be written using almost any simple text editor. A *text editor* is a program that allows the user to enter text in a human language or in a programming language, then save it with an appropriate file extension for the language in which the document is written. Examples of text editors are Notepad in Microsoft Windows, or Notepad ++ that works on Microsoft Windows, TextEdit that works with Macs, or Vim that is included in many Linux distributions. In Exercise 1.1, "Hello World," we will use Vim to write your first program. Atom is an open source and cross-platform text editor.

Programs are written in plain text. Some text editors, such as Microsoft WordPad, add formatting characters to the text and are not a suitable choice for writing source code. Other text editors, like Notepad++, use different colors to alert the programmer when something is amiss, such as an error in syntax. Some even provide autosuggestions for completing lines of code.

If you would like to try it, the latest edition of Notepad++ can be downloaded from https://notepad-plus-plus.org/downloads. Download the installer onto a Windows-based machine, taking note of where you saved it. Double-click the installer file and follow the onscreen prompts to complete the installation. Notepad++ is a favorite of mine because the colors quickly show me the error of my ways, enabling me to avoid hours of troubleshooting code.

Each program will have a specific file extension to identify the language that the program is written in. Regardless of which tool you use to create your source code, be sure to save it using the proper extension. A *file extension* is the part of a filename that follows a period, such as `figure1.jpg`. The jpg after the period tells the operating system that this is a JPEG image. The following are some popular programming extensions and the programs they identify:

- `.c`: C and C++
- `.cpp`: C++

- `.cs`: Visual C#
- `.css`: Cascading Style Sheet
- `.htm` or `.html`: HTML files
- `.java`: Java
- `.js`: JavaScript
- `.php`: PHP
- `.py`: Python
- `.sql`: Structured Query Language

Although Structured Query Language (SQL) is the language specifically used to communicate with a database, it makes the list. SQL meets the definition of a programming language because it requires very specific keywords and syntax to communicate between humans manipulating data and a database.

Some source code, such as HTML, can be used as soon as you've saved it from your text editor, and we will do just that in Chapter 5, "HTML Introduction." Other languages require an additional step called compiling. *Compiling* is a process that converts source code to machine language. For those languages that need to be compiled, you need to download additional tools, unless you use an *integrated development environment (IDE)*. An IDE provides the text editor, a compiler, and other tools necessary to convert source code to machine language.

An IDE must support the language that the programmer is writing in. Code::Blocks is a free IDE that supports several languages. Visual Studio Code is cross platform and is very popular and free to try, but continued use requires a subscription. PyCharm is, as you likely guessed, an IDE for the Python language, but it also supports JavaScript and SQL. It has a free version and a full (paid) version as well. Many IDEs have the features of better text editors and may have debugging and testing features as well.

Compiled Languages

A *compiled language* is one that requires the source code to be converted into machine language *before* it can be used. Source code must be compiled into machine code for each platform that it will run on, such as Windows, macOS, or Linux. Remember that machine language is simply 1s and 0s, but they must be arranged in a manner that a processor can use. The GNU Complier Collection (GCC) and Tiny C Compiler (TCC) are both free compilers, although their licensing is somewhat different. The GCC can be used to compile many different languages, including C and C++. Intel also has a C++ compiler, as does IBM, and there are other compilers for use with ARM processors and different programming languages.

Compiled programs take a little longer to create because of the extra compiling step, and they need to be compiled multiple times to be available for multiple platforms. For example, to have the program available to run on Windows, macOS and Linux, it would need to be compiled three times, once for each OS. The advantage of compiled programs is that they tend to run more quickly when executed than programs that are not compiled. C++ and C are typically compiled languages.

Some compilers can also output bytecode. *Bytecode* is the output of a compiler that is intended to be interpreted by a runtime or virtual machine (VM) instead of running directly on a processor. Bytecode is somewhere between source code and machine code. It's a bit slower than running a compiled language, but the advantage of bytecode is that it can be used by multiple platforms—it isn't necessarily compiled for each specific one. A *runtime* provides the environment that bytecode needs to run. Similar to a mini operating system, the runtime provides access to hardware, software, and the user. A Java Virtual Machine (JVM) provides a runtime environment for Java programs. Each platform will have its own JVM that is often installed with the operating system. Python automatically compiles its code into bytecode, so it will run any machine that has a Python interpreter on it. Bytenode is a bytecode compiler for node.js.

Interpreted Languages

You've likely seen real-life language interpreters before. When foreign dignitaries meet, they will need an interpreter to convert the conversation from one language to another, if they speak different languages, one phrase at a time. Interpreted languages are like that. Interpreted languages don't need to be compiled to be used. Python and PHP are examples of languages that are typically interpreted, although like most programs, they could also be compiled. A web browser is an interpreter for HTML pages. A software *interpreter* executes instructions in the source code as it reads them, communicating those instructions to the processor, which understands machine language.

The advantage of interpreted code is that it can be used cross platform, meaning that the same HTML code from your website can be read by a Mac, Windows PC, or a smartphone. The disadvantage of interpreting code is that it tends to run more slowly than compiled code because of the extra interpreting step necessary when the code is run.

Source code is the input to either a compiler or an interpreter. The output from a compiler is either bytecode or a program, while the source code that is read by an interpreter is often called a script, rather than a program. *Scripts*, therefore, are source code that can be executed without being compiled.

Programming Paradigms

You may have heard someone mention a paradigm shift, meaning that they had a sudden change of understanding in the way something exists or is done. *Programming paradigms* are approaches to how programming is done. A program needed to compute a certain value can be written in different paradigms, and the way programming is done will shift, depending on which programming paradigm is being used.

Any paradigm exists in multiple programs and multiple programming paradigms can exist in a single program. Different paradigms are appropriate for different types of programs, and a paradigm may only be used if the language the program is written in supports that paradigm. Let's look at three general paradigms (approaches) to programming.

Procedural Programming

Procedural programming is likely what most people think of when they think of a computer program. A *procedural program* follows a list of instructions that are executed in order, starting with the first line, then moving on to the second line, third line, and so on. The focus of procedural programming is the process that is followed.

Parts of a program that need to be repeated are identified as *procedures*. Procedures, also known as functions, or subroutines, can be predefined and named. When the main program is run, functions and subroutines are called as needed. Although very similar, functions and subroutines are not the same. A *function* is a chunk of code that runs when called and returns a value to the main program, whereas a *subroutine* is a chunk of code that runs but does not return a value to the main program. Because of these named and reused chunks of code, procedural programming has a somewhat modular approach.

Even though procedural programming may use functions and subroutines, those will still be called by a main script that will be followed in sequential order.

Procedural programming can make the task of coding simpler because procedures can be used more than once by simply calling the procedure, instead of entering the code multiple times. This approach reduces the size of the program, and therefore, the memory overhead needed to run it. Procedural programming also mitigates the chance of human error when program changes are needed, because rather than making the same change in many places, it only needs to be changed one time, in the procedure, rather than every place that the procedure is needed.

Figure 1.3 depicts a simple procedural program that calls a function. Under `void setup()`, the line that says `Find_Current();` calls the function. The function is written in the lower section under `void loop()`. In the lower section, the variables `Vin`, `voltage`, `current`, and the constant value `r` are declared. *Variables* are used to store information in a program. Some variables may change as the program runs. *Constants* are variables that will not change while the program is running.

The sample program uses Ohm's law to calculate the current, measured in amps, where the resistance is 1000 and the voltage is read on an analog input pin. However, the output from the pin is a binary value that must be converted to voltage (`voltage=(Vin*5)/1024;`). The resistance is known to be 1000 (`r=1000;`) and will not change. Ohm's law states that current equals voltage divided by resistance calculated in the line `current=voltage/r;`. The last line of the function, `Serial.println(current);`, prints the current as a number. `Serial.println("Amps");` prints the word Amps.

Returning to look at the beginning of the program, `Serial.println("Current is ")` will print the words `Current is` and when the function is called it will read the pin, calculate the current (measured in amps), and print the current as a numeric value followed by the word Amps.

FIGURE 1.3 Simple function call

```
void setup() {
  //print current
  Serial.begin(9600);
  Serial.println("Current is ");
  Find_Current();  //this line calls the function
  }
void loop() {
} //calculate and return current
    float Find_Current()
    {
      float Vin;
      Vin=analogRead(A1);
      float voltage;
      voltage=(Vin*5)/1024;
      float current;
      int r;
      r=1000;
      current=voltage/r;
      Serial.println(current);
      Serial.println("Amps");
```

Object-Oriented Programming

Procedural programming is all about the process, but *object-oriented programming (OOP)* is a programming paradigm centered around data objects and the class to which they are assigned. A *class* in OOP includes the attributes and methods that relate to each data object of that class. *Attributes* are the OOP term meaning a variable, and *methods* are subroutines attached to an OOP class.

The programming shown in Figure 1.1 could also be created using OOP. We could first define a class called current to which we assign objects such as circuit 1, circuit 2, and so on. The class would have attributes called Vin and r, and methods called voltage and current.

An example that's often used to explain object-oriented programming is a class called car. A car will have attributes such as make, model, color, mileage, gas-in-tank, and functions such as drive, brake, fill-up, and so on. We could create an object called Car1, where make=Mercedes, model=C300, color = blue, mileage=50,000, and gas-in-tank=10. If we run the function fill-up, the function may increase the gas-in-tank to 14. If we run the function drive, the mileage attribute would increase by the miles driven. In this way, the methods directly affect the state of data outside of the method. In programming, a *state* refers to the values stored in a program, similar to a snapshot of the program. We could have other cars, each with attributes of make, model, color, mileage, and gas-in-tank describing that car, and the functions defined in the class car would be used to change the attributes of that car.

Classes can also contain other classes. For example, we could have a class called vehicles, and within that class are the classes cars, SUVs, and trucks.

Functional Programming

Functional programming is a programming paradigm that is based solely on functions. In functional programming, a function can be treated as data and passed from one function to another. Unlike procedural programming, which follows a string of commands and where the function can change the state of a program, in functional programming the only effect that the function has is to return a value based on the equations it executes. It will always produce the same output if given the same inputs. By contrast, object-oriented programming interacts with the state of the data, changing the existing data to something new.

Maintaining Software

Once a program has been written, managing and maintaining that program becomes the primary focus. Simple programs might have the entire program contained in a single file, but many programs are very complex and have multiple parts stored in multiple folders and files. For example, open the folder that holds the source code for your operating system and list the files contained there. Storing parts of the program in an organized way, with different logical folders for different parts of the program, will make maintaining the program easier. For example, an accounting program might have a general ledger folder that holds all the files for that section, an accounts payable folder, an accounts receivable folder, and so on. A program could also be sorted by files affecting the front-end (i.e., the user interface) and files affecting the back-end of the program.

   Complicated programs may also have several or hundreds of people who adjust the code to add features or fix problems. Those changes need to be managed, and the way to do that is through a version control system.

Version Control Systems

Version control systems (VCSs) are specialized software used to keep track of changes made to a computer program, when they are made, and who makes them. They can also be used to manage those changes by holding them in a queue and not updating the main source code until others have had a chance to review that change. Version control systems can be centralized or distributed, and can facilitate communication among teams who may be working in different offices or even different parts of the world.

   Version control can be used to avoid problems caused by two programmers working on the same section of source code or lock code that is being edited so that only one person can change it at a time. They can also identify code changes that caused a problem. Software teams can look at the original code and what was changed and more easily revert to prior coding if needed. The features of version control can help programming teams finish a project more quickly and with fewer negative outcomes.

Git is a widely used, distributed version control software. Apache Subversion is a popular centralized VCS, and Mercurial is a popular distributed VCS, but Git is by far the most popular. All three are open source and free.

GitHub and GitLab are VCSs that may sound like Git, but they are owned by different people. Git is open source and maintained by Linux. However, GitHub is owned by Microsoft and is not open source. GitLab is owned by GitLab Inc., and only some of GitLab is open source.

All VCSs need a repository. A *repository* is a place that holds the files for version control. Repositories can be hosted on a local server or online, but the online service must support them. Some online services are free, and some are not.

Software Testing

Whenever software changes are made, it's necessary to test those changes to ensure that they work properly and don't cause any problems with the other parts of the program. If you're using an IDE to create or modify software, the IDE will do some of the testing for you. IDEs can detect errors in syntax, keywords, and functions, but they can't check the logic for you.

Summary

This chapter provided an introduction into the world of web development by discussing developer roles. If you plan to build your career in this field, you need to determine where to start. Will you be a front-end developer or a back-end developer? If you're like me, you just want to know all of it immediately like a full-stack developer, but you still need to pick a place to start.

We examined the process of creating software, going from pseudocode to source code, to bytecode or machine code. Then we examined the different programming languages, each with its own syntax, keywords, and grammar, just like human languages. There are also libraries that house the work of others that we can utilize. Front-end languages have to do with making the user experience pleasant and functional. Examples of these include HTML, CSS, JavaScript, and jQuery, while others are used more on the back-end, on the server to make the whole thing functional. Common languages used there include C#, Java, Python, PHP, Ruby, and SQL. As a practical matter, you'll need to know the file extensions that are used with each of those programming languages.

In order for any programming language to be understood by a computing device, it needs to be either interpreted or compiled. Interpreting is performed by browsers or, in the case of bytecode, by a runtime or virtual machine such as a JVM or a Python interpreter. Code that is interpreted is often called a script rather than a program. When it comes to speed, compiled programs normally run the quickest with the least overhead, then bytecode with scripts running more slowly but being the most versatile in terms of the platforms that a single script can be run on.

Programming paradigms, which is a fancy way of saying the approach that the programmer takes, include functional, object-oriented, and procedural approaches. Each has situations that make it the best or the worst way to program. We dipped our toes into the language of programming by discussing variables, constants, methods, attributes, and classes. And now you know the state of a program is simply a snapshot of how it exists at a given moment in time.

Finally, we looked at the importance of version control systems (VCSs), keeping files organized into logically separate folders (because there will be numerous files), and testing changes before they go live.

Exam Essentials

Know the languages.   Be able to identify languages typically used for the front-end and back-end, including whether those languages are typically compiled or interpreted. Also know the file extensions for those languages. Being able to immediately identify the language of a file by its extension will save you time when you're out there working on a project designed by someone else.

Understand libraries and APIs.   Know what a library is and that they can be a part of the language or a package that someone else has developed. APIs are similar because they are prewritten and save a programmer time, but the difference is that libraries are used for a specific program, whereas APIs facilitate communication between two different systems. It would be worth your time to explore what libraries and APIs are available for a project. Knowing where to look, and looking before you re-create the wheel, will save you countless hours when writing a program.

Compare/contrast compilers and interpreters.   Know the advantages and disadvantages of scripts, bytecode, and programs, and the methods of creating them (interpreting and compiling).

Identify programming paradigms.   Be able to look at a section of code and determine the paradigm used to create it. Know how to discern if it's an OOP, procedural, or functional paradigm.

Explain VCS, file organization, and software testing.   These three concepts are tenets of web development. They'll save you time and frustration, and maybe even your job.

Hello World

Hello World is the first program that most people learn to write. It's a tradition in the programming world, so we will do the same. If you're new to programming, we recommend you use a lab computer that's set aside for this purpose, not the computer you use for your daily work.

We'll use Ubuntu 22.04.1 throughout the book. If you have a different Linux distribution, it might work slightly differently.

First, let's use Vim to write a simple program in C++. If Vim is not installed, the following directions will guide you through that process.

1. Open Terminal.

2. Type **vim hello.cpp** and press Enter. We use .cpp because that is the extension for a C++ file.

   - If you get an error message that states Command 'vim' not found..., then you will need to install it. In that case, type **apt install vim** and press Enter.

   - The package will begin to install and tell you how much space will be used. Type **Y** and press Enter to continue, assuming you have the available space on your drive. After a minute or two, you should be back at the root.

   - Once Vim is installed, type **vim hello.cpp** and press Enter.

3. You should now be in the Vim text editor. Alternately, you can launch the Vim editor by clicking Show Applications at the lower-left corner of the desktop (it's the grid of 9 blocks) and clicking the Vim icon. Pressing F1 will show you help in Vim. Typing **:q** and then pressing Enter will take you back to the Vim Terminal from help. (You'll need to press i to enter Insert mode, where --INSERT-- shows in the lower-left corner.)

4. In the Vim terminal, enter the following lines of code, pressing Enter after each line. Extra line returns are added for ease in reading. Pay attention to capitalization and the different styles of brackets and where they are used.

```
#include <iostream>
using namespace std;

int main() {

        string myvar[]="Hello World!";

        cout << myvar;

        cout <<endl;

        cout <<"This is my first C++ program.";

        return 0;
        }
```

- The first line loads the `iostream` (input/output) library.

- The second line tells the program to use the identifiers from the standard library (as opposed to identifiers from other libraries).

- `int main ()` will be looking for an integer at the end of the program. The last line of the program, `return 0`;, is that integer. Using 0 is the accepted way to say the program has executed successfully. This is the program's exit code.

- The next line creates a `string` variable named `myvar` whose content is "Hello World!"

- `cout << myvar`; tells the program to output that variable to the output device (the monitor), and `cout <<endl`; tells the program to insert a line break.

- `cout <<"This is my first C++ program."`; outputs that line to the monitor.

5. To save the file and exit the Vim editor, first press the Escape key to exit Insert mode. Then type **:wq hello.cpp** and press Enter. This will save your file with the specified file-name and exit Vim. You should be back at a regular terminal.

6. The file should be stored in your user's Home folder. If you need to reopen it, click the folder icon on your desktop and double-click the filename. Remember that if you saved it under the root user, you will only be able to save an edited version if you're in the terminal as root.

7. Now we need to install the compiler. Open Terminal as superuser and enter the following lines of code, pressing Enter after each line:

   ```
   apt install build-essential
   g++ --version
   gcc (Ubuntu 9.2.1-17ubuntu1) 9.2.1 20191102
   ```

8. When the compiler installation is done, it's time to compile the program you wrote. Enter the following line of code:

   ```
   g++ -o hello hello.cpp
   ```

   The first hello in the line is the executable name. The second is the name of the C++ file that we're compiling.

9. To run the program, type **./hello** and press Enter.

Review Questions

1. What is another name for the front-end of a website?

   A. HTML-side

   B. Client-side

   C. Server-side

   D. JavaScript-side

2. What can be described as lines of instruction for a processor to follow?

   A. Software

   B. Data structures

   C. Pseudocode

   D. Back-end development

3. A new programmer writes the following. What is it an example of?

   Ask the user to input their first name.
   When they click on accept, say hello "firstname."
   Show button for continue and return to first page.

   A. Source code

   B. Programming language

   C. Software

   D. Pseudocode

4. Which of the following are instructions written in a specific programming language?

   A. Source code

   B. Programming language

   C. Software

   D. Pseudocode

5. What is the following an example of?

   ```
   Float Vin:
   Vin=analogRead(A1);
   Float voltage;
   Voltage=(Vin*5)/1024;
   ```

   A. Source code

   B. Programming language

   C. Software

   D. Pseudocode

6. Which of the following are languages that are typically used in programming the front-end of a website? (Choose two.)

   A. PHP

   B. CSS

   C. Ruby

   D. JavaScript

7. What term is used to describe the placement of commands, options, special characters, and so on used in a line of code for a particular language?

   A. Keyword

   B. Program

   C. Syntax

   D. Front-end

8. A programmer wants to control how many times a section of code is run. Which of the following keywords might they use? (Choose two.)

   A. and

   B. for

   C. while

   D. times

9. Your friend is a beginning programmer who needs to write some code to use with a sensor. What will you suggest they do?

   A. Look for a keyword to use.

   B. Look for pseudocode to use.

   C. Look for an existing library.

   D. Look for an existing script.

10. You are working on a project, fixing source code someone else wrote that is not working as expected. You're working in HTML, and suddenly come across some code in JavaScript. What will you do?

    A. Delete the code.

    B. Determine if the code is correct.

    C. Replace the code with HTML.

    D. Replace the code with a library.

11. Which of the following refers to code that is written in a language which a computing device can directly understand? (Choose two.)

    A. Machine language

    B. Binary

    C. Source code

    D. Pseudocode

12. What are Notepad, TextEdit, and Vim examples of?

    A. Interpreters

    B. Keywords

    C. Compilers

    D. Text editors

13. A friend has asked you to take a look at some code they wrote and provide any suggestions to make it better. The filename is `funcode.cpp`. What programming language are they using?

    A. C

    B. C++

    C. Python

    D. Perl

14. Which of the following keywords are operators? (Choose two.)

    A. `and`

    B. `for`

    C. `not`

    D. `if`

15. Which of the following can be the output of a compiler? (Choose two.)

    A. Source code

    B. Pseudocode

    C. Bytecode

    D. Machine language

16. You need to write a program that will execute instructions in order but at times call procedures that will be used repeatedly to calculate a value, then return to the string of commands and continue following them in order. What programming paradigm will you be using?

    A. Functional

    B. Object-oriented

    C. Procedural

    D. Reactive

17. What is true of the procedural programming paradigm?

    A. Coding can take less time because you don't need to rewrite code that is repeated.

    B. The focus of the paradigm is the state of the data.

    C. Data is grouped into classes that have attributes and methods.

    D. The purpose of a function is only to return a value, not modify the state of the program.

18. What type of software is used to keep track of program changes so mistakes can be rolled back if necessary?

A. AMD

B. Git

C. OOP

D. VCS

19. Where does a VCS hold files of current and prior program code?

A. Code bank

B. Repository

C. Folder

D. Paradigm

20. What type of programming paradigm is being used in the following example where `Void printcount ()` declares a procedure and the code under `Int main()` causes the code under `printcount` to run?

```
Void printcount()
{ for (int x=0; x<5; x++)
   Cout <<"Hi";
Cout << endl;
}
Int main()
{ printcount();
}
```

A. Functional

B. Object-oriented

C. Procedural

D. Reactive

Chapter 2

Client/Server Computing

LINUX PROFESSIONAL INSTITUTE, WEB DEVELOPMENT ESSENTIALS EXAM 030-100 OBJECTIVES COVERED IN THIS CHAPTER:

✓ **031 Software Development and Web Technologies**

- 031.2 Web Application Architecture: The candidate should understand common standards in web development technology and architecture.

- Key Knowledge Areas:

  - Understand the principle of client and server computing

  - Understand the role of web browsers and be aware of commonly used web browsers

  - Understand the role of web servers and application servers

  - Understand common web development technologies and standards

  - Awareness of single-page applications

  - Awareness of web application packaging

  - Awareness of WebAssembly

  - Awareness of content management systems

- Files, terms and utilities:

  - Chrome, Edge, Firefox, Safari, Internet Explorer

  - HTML, CSS, JavaScript

- 031.3 HTTP Basics: The candidate should be familiar with the basics of HTTP. This includes understanding HTTP headers, content types, caching, and status codes. Furthermore, the candidate should understand the principles of cookies and their role for session handling and be aware of advanced HTTP features.

- Key Knowledge Areas:

  - Understand the difference between static and dynamic content

  - Understand HTTP URLs

  - Understand how HTTP URLs are mapped to file system paths

  - Awareness of commonly used HTTP servers

  - Awareness of HTTPS and TLS

  - Awareness of common HTTP servers

- Files, Terms, and utilities:
  - Apache HTTP Server ("httpd"), NGINX

Whenever there is communication between two computing devices, one of them, known as the server, provides information to other computing devices. By contrast, the client receives information from a server. The client and server share the work of providing information to you, the user. This chapter will explain the basics of client and server communications in a web environment. We'll also examine what an application programming interface (API) is and how APIs help the web work, as well as what each part of a Uniform Resource Locator (URL) identifies.

Client-Side

As you learned in Chapter 1, "Web Development Basics," the part of a website that a user interacts with is known as the client-side or front-end. A *client* is either the hardware or software that is used to connect to a server. A client initiates the interaction with a web server by sending a request asking for information from the server. Most of the time this request is sent via a web browser but not always. This communication is not as simple as you might think. Refer to Figure 2.1.

FIGURE 2.1   Path of a website request

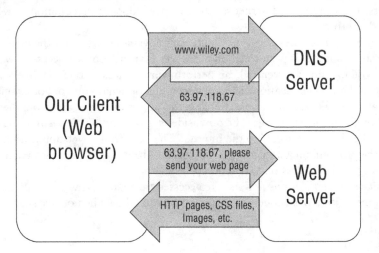

To initiate the exchange, we type a Uniform Resource Locator (URL), a human-readable address such as www.wiley.com/en-us/sybex, into the client. Before our request for this address gets to the web server, the address needs to be put in a language that computer networks will understand, so our request first goes to a *Domain Name System (DNS)* server. DNS servers translate human-readable website addresses to Internet Protocol (IP) addresses. These servers will look at the domain in our request (wiley.com) and reply with the IP address of the domain server, such as 63.97.118.67. When the client receives the IP address, it sends its request to the web server, which considers the request and, if it is valid, responds with the necessary files for the client to render the website. The files may consist of Hypertext Markup Language (HTML) pages, JavaScript programming, Cascading Style Sheets (CSS) files, image files, and so on. When the client receives the files, it will interpret them and display the information for us. This information may or may not be in the form of a website.

The communication between client and server is facilitated in part by an application programming interface (API). APIs are provided by a server to a client to define the types of requests that the client can make and how to properly format them so that the server can properly respond to the client's requests. The client has the programming that it needs to interact with the user, but it must request data files from the server so that it can interpret the information for presentation to a user.

Types of Clients

We often think of web browsers when we think of clients, but not all clients are web browsers. A client is any application that runs on your local computing device and accesses resources from a local server or one across the Internet. It's important to understand the distinction between the web and the Internet. *The Internet* is a vast array of servers that are connected for sharing information. The web uses the Internet to provide its users with a graphical user interface (GUI) based on HTML files provided by a server. The Internet not only provides access to HTML pages via the web, but also access to remote files and email servers. There are many Internet servers that are hidden from common view and not accessed with a browser.

A *web application* accesses data and programming via a browser, but the majority of its work (programs running) is performed on the server that the browser accesses. With a web application, you log into a server and can perform various actions on it. Unlike a web page, the content on the web application changes, depending on what you do. For example, my insurance carrier works this way. I use a browser to access their site, and from there I can pay my bill or change my coverage. The downside of a web application is that they won't work unless the user is connected to the Internet. The benefit of a web application is that changes to the programming and content only need to be made in one place regardless of the platform being used to access that content.

Progressive web applications (PWAs) are accessed through a browser but can also function offline. With PWAs, code will be downloaded and installed on a system.

By contrast, a *native application* is downloaded from an app store and installed on a device. If it will run on multiple platforms, multiple versions of the application must be available. If updates are made, they must be made separately for each of the operating systems that are supported. Native applications can access information on a server, but they typically are able to run offline and access the systems hardware. An example of this is a camera application that works locally but will update photos on a server when the device is connected again. Other examples might include a star-gazing app (depending on its programming) or map applications that download the map to your device and then use your device's GPS or fixed beacons that send out a signal identifying their location so that the software on your device can show you where you are on the map. In those cases, no Internet connection is required.

Hybrid applications are downloaded from an app store, but the work is performed on a back-end server to which they connect. The advantage to the programmer is that although there must be individual native clients for each platform, the bulk of the code is online and shared regardless of the client used to access it. Consider an application on a cell phone, such as the restaurant app that we use to order sandwiches and salads. The client application resides on my cell phone but connects via the Internet to the restaurant's server, which provides the menus and saves my order in a database. The server then spits my order out of a printer or onto a monitor in the kitchen for the sandwich makers. The client provides the GUI that I interact with, but the work is done on a server, using programs that may not have a GUI at all. The app appears the same whether it is on an Android or an iPhone, and they access a common server. I'll bet you have a favorite shopping app on your phone that you use to order items for home delivery. It likely works the same way, providing you with a listing and pictures of items available for sale, their price, and how long delivery will take. You place your order using the client app, but the inventory information and order are stored on the server and data is manipulated there. A client application might also be a game. The game runs on your smartphone or PC, not using a browser, but connecting to the Internet all the same so that you can play against people half a world away. Many mobile clients work this way, but these programs may be on a desktop computer as well.

Other, more serious applications such as Microsoft Teams can be accessed via a client on your computer, and clients on the computers of the team with which you're working. It's a cloud-based application that's part of the Microsoft 365 suite, so there is a server somewhere running the server component.

Also consider Apple's App Store and Microsoft Store, which both enable you to find and download apps without using a browser. Contrast with Google's Play Store, which is accessed via a browser, but also enables you to download other applications. All these have client and server components and use the Internet but may or may not use the World Wide Web.

The Internet can also be accessed through a terminal by typing commands. Some File Transfer Protocol (FTP) servers are accessed this way. The Linux package manager is a command-line tool that enables you to install programs via Linux packages, which are downloaded from an Internet server. In these cases, the client is the terminal running on your computer, and the server is the computer that is supplying the files that you want.

Web Browsers

Common web browsers include Microsoft's Edge browser, which is included in Microsoft's recent operating systems, and Apple's Safari, which works on Apple devices. Firefox is included in most Linux distributions and is free and cross-platform. Other popular cross-platform (and free) browsers include Google's Chrome and the Opera browser by the company of the same name. Figure 2.2 shows the Edge and Firefox browsers.

FIGURE 2.2   Edge and Firefox browsers

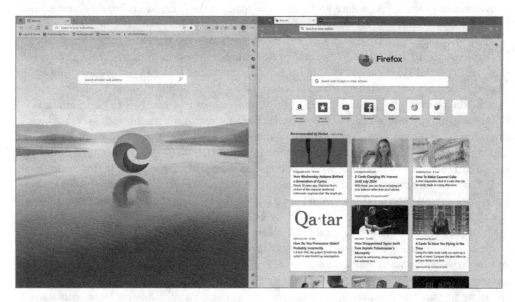

Internet Explorer was the browser included with older versions of the Windows operating system. While most browsers are designed so that any website can be rendered by any browser, Internet Explorer was less cohesive and required special programming for websites to work properly with it. Perhaps that's why Windows 10 and 11 use Microsoft Edge.

Rendering engines are used by web browsers to interpret files and present information on a screen for the user. Today, just three rendering engines are used by most browsers, and they are open source so the community develops them together. These three must be very similar in how they convert the HTML, CSS, and JavaScript of a web page into the interface that you as a user interact with so that the web pages the server sends will function the same whether you open them on a Mac, a Windows PC, or your smartphone. The three engines are WebKit (used by Safari), Blink (used by Chrome, Opera, and others), and Quantum (used by Firefox). The community that maintains these rendering engines is also responsible for keeping them standard in nature to ensure compatibility across the web. A JavaScript engine works with each browser engine. The engines do the job of translating machine code or byte-code into human-readable form.

Browsers typically include tooling. *Tooling* refers to the developer tools for processes such as debugging and testing code. *Minification* is a tool that makes code smaller by removing whitespace and extra characters, so the code takes fewer resources to store, download, and render. Minification is part of *front-end optimization (FEO)*, also known as content optimization, which is the process of improving a website so that it will load more quickly for the user. Other tools called *linters* examine code based on a set of rules and alert you to errors by highlighting your code wherever the rules aren't followed. And finally, libraries and frameworks are tools that help developers create sites more quickly and efficiently.

As mentioned in the previous section, web applications are programs that use a browser to access resources online. Moments ago, I finished a Zoom meeting during which my computer was running the Zoom client via a browser plug-in, as was the organizer of the meeting at their location. There was also a server application running somewhere on a Zoom server. (Zoom also provides a client that works outside of a browser.) We had the user interface running on our browsers, while the server was doing the work of getting our images and voice from one place to another.

Contrast that with applications such as FileZilla, which is an open source application for sharing files using the FTP protocol. FileZilla has a client application and a server application. It doesn't use a browser. Figure 2.3 shows the FileZilla client application running on a desktop, connecting to a server. Some other applications that use the Internet but not necessarily the World Wide Web or a browser are mentioned in the previous section "Types of Clients."

FIGURE 2.3   Client application on a desktop

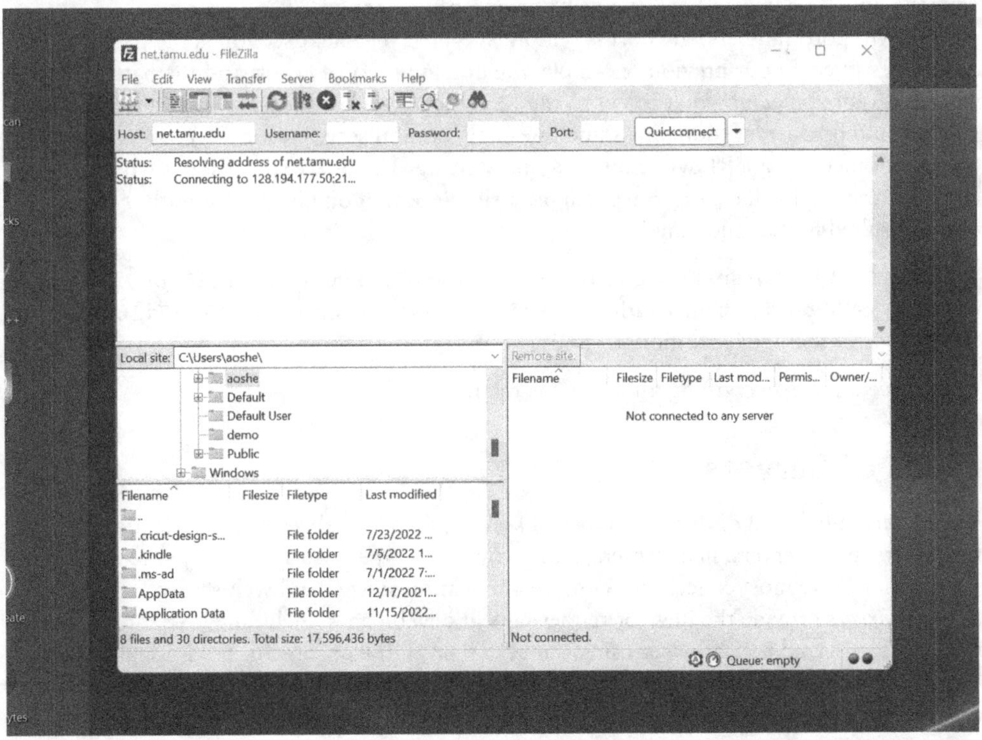

Server-Side

A *server* is computer hardware or software that provides access to resources. Sometimes when we say "server," we are referring to the hardware that houses the information. Other times, when we say "server," we may be speaking of the software that is used to control access to that information. For a client to be of any use, it must connect to a server.

The way we connect to that server changes, depending on the type of client we're using. If we're using a terminal, we'll need an IP address or FTP address. If connecting with a browser, all we need is a URL, as mentioned in the beginning of this chapter.

An example of a URL is `www.wiley.com/en-us/Sybex`. A URL is always formatted the same way and can be broken down into its parts, as shown here: `scheme://host:port/path?query`. The scheme identifies the protocol (rules for communication) that will be used to access the website, either HTTP or HTTPS. *Hypertext Transfer Protocol (HTTP)* is the protocol used to facilitate communications between a web browser and a server. *Hypertext Transfer Protocol Secure (HTTPS)* encrypts HTTP communications between a browser and server using the Transport Layer Security (TLS) protocol. Previously, this protocol was known as the Secure Sockets Layer (SSL) protocol. Often in writing it's common to drop the protocol from the beginning, however if you type `Wiley.com` into a browser, you'll see that the URL the browser shows includes the scheme (https). The `://` separates the scheme from the next section, which is the domain name (host). If a port is specified, it will be located after the domain name and a `:`, but as `http` and `https` are
well-known port numbers, the port is seldom specified. The next section is the path to the desired resource. In our previous example, the domain is `wiley.com` and the path is `/en-us/Sybex`, meaning that to get to the `/Sybex` page, the request will traverse `/en-us`, which could be a server (domains sometimes have several server resources) or a folder on a server. Sometimes a URL will contain a query string. The query string starts with a `?` and contains term and value pairs. Surprisingly, a simple search on Google for **author audrey o'shea** resulted in the following URL:

```
www.google.com/search?q=author+audrey+o%27shea&rlz=1C1CHBF_
enUS999US999&oq=author+audrey+o%27shea&aqs=chrome..69i57j33i160l2
.4987j0j15&sourceid=chrome&ie=UTF-8
```

In this example, everything after the `?` is the query.

Types of Servers

You've certainly heard of different types of servers, such as web servers, application servers, file servers, print servers, mail servers, and so on. Each type of server has a job to do. The servers that we're most concerned with are application servers and web servers.

Web servers provide the files for rendering static web pages, including text and images that are transferred to a browser using the HTTP or HTTPS protocol. Traditionally, web servers provide static information that doesn't change regardless of who logs in or what they click, while *application servers* provide the business logic that is used to generate dynamic web content using various protocols and scripting languages. An application server runs in the background, largely unseen by its users. In the insurance carrier app discussed in Chapter 1, the application server is housing the database that contains information about me, my vehicle, coverage, and payment methods. It also has the code used to process that information, depending on my input and the business needs of the insurance company. A web server can be a component of an application server.

Popular Server Software

A web server needs web server software to communicate with the client's browser, and several popular server software applications exist. Apache HTTP Server and NGINX each support a large share of the web servers worldwide, together comprising approximately 60 percent of all web server installations. Microsoft Internet Information Services (IIS) is used on a much smaller share of the total web servers. Cloudflare Server, node.JS, and LiteSpeed are other popular web server software, but they are not the only ones available.

Apache HTTP Server and NGINX are both free and open source, which means they are supported by a community of users, and anyone can install and use them for free. IIS is a feature of the Microsoft Windows operating system that can be turned on as desired.

Apache HTTP Server is also known as HTTPD. The "D" stands for daemon, which simply means software that always runs in the background, listening for something to wake it up. In this case, the daemon listens for HTTP requests to which the server will then respond.

Popular Web Page–Creating Software

Perhaps you have wondered how it all works so well together—communication protocols, code, IP addresses and domain names, and browsers and rendering engines. The web wasn't always as compatible and cooperative as it is now. Entities such as the Internet Engineering Task Force (IETF), the World Wide Web Consortium (W3C), International Organization for Standardization (ISO), and the Internet Assigned Numbers Authority (IANA), among others, have created standards to define how components of the web interact and keep the web functioning. Of course, those standards need to be updated periodically, but one of the tenets of the Internet is "Don't break the web," meaning that anything new that is created should be compatible with what already exists so that the web will keep working smoothly.

The standards consist of white papers, which are each called a request for comments (RFC). The comments are presented, considered, and accepted or not. The W3C also publishes recommendations that impact HTML/XHTML, CSS, and various image formats.

Most web pages are created using *Hypertext Markup Language (HTML)*, which is a standard system of identifying how text and images in a text file should appear on a page. It is used to define paragraphs and headings, in addition to adding lines, embedded images, and tables. It can also define aspects such as color, size, font, and placement although those aspects are more often defined in related CSS files. You'll learn more about HTML in Chapters 5 through 8. *EXtensible Hypertext Markup Language (XHTML)* is a stricter form of HTML that facilitates working with different data formats and forces the code to be more correct, rather than ignoring errors and trying to present the page as would be done with HTML.

Cascading Style Sheets (CSS) is a language that is used to describe how elements are formatted on HTML pages. A style sheet can define colors, backgrounds, fonts, and the like. CSS can save a programmer countless hours, because instead of re-creating code each time you want to format an element in the same manner as other elements, you can simply refer to the style sheet. You'll learn more about CSS in Chapters 9 through 12.

JavaScript is a scripting language that adds functionality to what would otherwise be boringly static web pages. JavaScript can perform actions based on what the user is doing on the page, such as showing a picture or description when the mouse hovers over a spot, or performing an action when something is clicked. JavaScript makes HTML pages more interactive.

These three languages together—HTML, CSS, and JavaScript—are used to create modern web pages. Of course, whenever you create a web page, you'll want to test it out in multiple browsers to ensure that it looks and functions as you, the programmer, expect it to.

WebAssembly is a new standard being developed by the W3C that will use a low-level but human-readable language (similar to C or C++) and work with JavaScript to improve performance of applications running in a browser. WebAssembly is still being developed, but the plan is for it to consist of a virtual machine (VM) to run a web page's code and WebAssembly APIs that will be used to improve performance of the application.

Another web concept you should be familiar with are single-page applications. A *single-page application (SPA)* rewrites only the content that changes on a web page when data is updated from the server, rather than reloading a whole new page. Pages appropriate for use as single-page applications have the majority of their information remaining static and some pieces of information that periodically are updated by a server. Perhaps the simplest example of a single-page application is email. When you're reading email, most of the page stays the same, but what changes as you scroll down are the email listings, and if you use it, the preview pane. SPAs use APIs to speed their processes.

Content management systems (CMSs) are programs or web applications that allow a user to create a web page without knowing how to code. Some popular CMSs are Squarespace and Wix. Hosting sites such as HostGator that have their own website builder provide you with a CMS. Many other CMSs are also available.

So, you've used your programming skills and created the perfect web application. How do you get the client to the user? *Web application packaging* means putting everything that's required to install and run a client into a single, downloadable compressed (ZIP) file. Each package should include a file that explains how the application and host runtime need to be configured when the application runs. The package also needs to contain files that will exist on the client, such as style sheets, code, images, and so on. Your goal is to make the installation and use of the program as simple as possible for the end user. Application packaging isn't just for websites. They can also be used within an organization to make updating a client easier.

Summary

In this chapter, we examined the relationship between clients and servers, and discovered that they each have two meanings. We identified different types of clients and their characteristics, namely browsers, web applications, PWAs, hybrid applications, and native applications. We listed the most common browsers and explained the role of rendering engines, and then listed the ones that are currently used. Clients are responsible for initiating the conversation with the server.

On the server-side, we dissected a URL and explained that the HTTPS protocol adds TLS security to HTTP. We also explained the differences and relationship between web servers and application servers. Finally, on the server-side we identified the most common HTTP servers. NGINX and Apache HTTP Server together control about 60 percent of web servers. Windows IIS controls less than 10 percent, and various other web servers control the remainder.

In the last section, we examined how HTML, CSS, and JavaScript work together to create the vast majority of web pages. WebAssembly is an upcoming technology being developed with the intent of improving web page performance. Single-page applications (SPAs) are web pages used on many websites, where only a small amount of the content is updated, rather than loading an entire new page. Content management systems (CMSs) are programs that make creating a website user-friendly, because you don't need to know how to code to use them. Web packaging means including all the necessary files for a client in a single package, which can then be downloaded over the Internet or on a corporate network to make installing clients easier and faster.

Throughout this chapter, we've been discussing web development technologies and the standards that are used to manage them.

Exam Essentials

Understand the relationship between clients and servers.   Be able to explain the relationship between clients and servers and how that connection is initiated. Know the types of clients and their characteristics. Know the names of the most common HTTP servers. This is foundational knowledge that will help you in your career and to pass the exam.

Understand URL syntax.   Make sure you know the parts of a URL. Know what each part is called and what information resides there. There will be times when knowing the path to a resource is helpful, and that the parts of a URL are testable information.

Know web technologies.   Make sure that you can identify the technologies that are used to keep the web working, such as HTTP and HTTPS, programming languages used to create web pages, and what an API is. Make sure you can explain the relationship between HTML, CSS, and JavaScript.

Be familiar with standards and who creates them. Be able to explain what a standard is and why they are necessary. Make sure you're familiar with the organizations that create standards related to the web.

EXERCISE 2.1

Turn On Microsoft IIS

In this exercise, we'll turn on Microsoft's IIS feature. It's surprisingly easy to turn your Windows computer into a web server. This feature is available on Windows versions from XP to Windows 11. Whenever you're making changes to your system, remember to create a backup first, and please do this on a lab computer that you can make mistakes on and reset, not on a computer that is vital to your work.

The process will vary slightly, depending on the version of Windows you have installed. First, let's locate the Windows Features list.

1. On a computer with a newer Windows operating system, search for "Turn Windows Features on or off" to locate the utility.

2. In older versions of Windows, open Control Panel, click Programs, and select Turn Windows features on or off.

    You may be prompted for an administrator password.

3. Regardless of how you found the Windows Features list, scroll down the list until you see Internet Information Services.

4. Check the box next to Internet Information Services and Internet Information Services Hostable Web Core (if it is there).

5. Click OK. It may take a few minutes to install all the files and apply the changes.

6. When the process is complete, click Close.

That's it! IIS is now installed. Of course, there is configuration that will be needed if you will be using this as a web server. Configuring IIS is beyond the scope of this book, however.

To remove IIS, simply go back to the Features list and uncheck the boxes.

EXERCISE 2.2

Download and Install NGINX

In this exercise, we will install the NGINX software on Ubuntu 20.04. We're starting with a clean installation of Ubuntu, with drivers installed and a Wi-Fi connection already established. Whenever you're making changes to your system, remember to make a backup first, and please do this on a lab computer that you can make mistakes on and reset, not on a computer that is vital to your work

1. Open a terminal.

2. Type `sudo apt install nginx` to install the NGINX server package.

3. When prompted for your password, enter it. The installation should begin.

That's it! There is, of course, more configuration that needs to be done, like setting up your firewall to allow traffic in on the appropriate ports. Configuring NGINX is beyond the scope of this book, however.

Review Questions

1. In client/server computing, where is the client typically found?

   A. On a web server

   B. On a local server

   C. On the local computing device

   D. It can't be found on a computer because it is the computer.

2. In client/server computing, what device initiates the communication between the client and the server?

   A. The server

   B. The client

   C. The DNS server

   D. An API

3. Which of the following are required for communication between a client and a server? (Choose all that apply.)

   A. An application server

   B. An API

   C. A computing device making a request

   D. A web server

4. Which of the following are accessed using a browser? (Choose all that apply.)

   A. PWA

   B. Native application

   C. Web application

   D. Hybrid application

5. What is the most commonly used client for connecting to a remote web server?

   A. Native application

   B. Progressive web application

   C. Browser

   D. Hybrid application

6. Which of the following is the web browser used in most Linux distributions?

   A. Chrome

   B. Edge

   C. Firefox

   D. Internet Explorer

   E. Safari

7. What is used by a web browser to interpret web files and draw them on a monitor?

   A. Rendering engine

   B. SPA

   C. VM

   D. Opera

8. Which of the following rendering engines is used by Safari?

   A. Blink

   B. Quantum

   C. RootKit

   D. WebKit

9. What type of tool is responsible for removing whitespace and unnecessary characters so that the code will take less bandwidth?

   A. Debugging

   B. Frameworks

   C. Linters

   D. Minification

10. What is a server? (Choose all that apply.)

    A. Hardware

    B. Software

    C. Initiates communication

    D. Responds to requests

11. Which of the following provides an API to facilitate communication between client and server?

    A. Browser

    B. Client

    C. Linter

    D. Server

12. In the URL www.cliffjumpertek.com/binary-is-fun, what does the /binary-is-fun section refer to?

    A. Path on the server

    B. Domain name

    C. Scheme

    D. File name

13. What protocol does HTTPS use that HTTP does not?

    A. TCP

    B. FTP

    C. TLS

    D. SEO

14. What type of server provides the business logic (programming) that facilitates interaction on a website?

    A. Application server

    B. Web server

    C. File server

    D. Domain name server

15. Which of the following web server software products together support approximately 60 percent of all active web servers? (Choose two.)

    A. Apache HTTP Server

    B. LiteSpeed

    C. Microsoft IIS

    D. NGINX

16. Which of the following are used to create most modern websites? (Choose all that apply.)

    A. Cascading Style Sheets (CSS)

    B. Hypertext Markup Language (HTML)

    C. Hypertext Transfer Protocol (HTTP)

    D. JavaScript

17. What technology will rewrite only content that has changed on a web page, not the entire page, thereby mitigating the amount of data that must be transferred from server to client?

    A. Content management system (CMS)

    B. Single-page application (SPA)

    C. Web application packaging

    D. WebAssembly

18. In the URL `www.grammarly.com/business/learn/business-communication-etiquette`, what is `https`?

    A. Host

    B. Path

    C. Scheme

    D. Query

19. You've created a website for a client. The website connects to a database on a server and will welcome the user by displaying their name and listing their last purchases. What type of website is this?

    A. Dynamic

    B. Static

    C. Web application

    D. TLS website

20. When a URL such as www.wiley.com is typed into a browser, what device translates that human-readable URL into an IP address?

    A. The server

    B. The client

    C. The DNS server

    D. An API

Database Management Systems

LINUX PROFESSIONAL INSTITUTE, WEB DEVELOPMENT ESSENTIALS EXAM 030-100 OBJECTIVES COVERED IN THIS CHAPTER:

✓ **031 Software Development and Web Technologies**

- 031.2 Web Application Architecture: The candidate should understand common standards in web development technology and architecture.

- Key Knowledge Areas:

  - Understand the principle of relational and non-relational (NoSQL) databases

  - Awareness of commonly used open source database management systems

  - Awareness of REST and GraphQL

- Files, terms, and utilities:

  - SQLite, MySQL, MariaDB, PostgreSQL

  - MongoDB, CouchDB, Redis

✓ **035 NodeJS Server Programming**

- 035.3 SQL Basics:

- Key Knowledge Areas:

  - Understand primary keys

- Files, terms and utilities:

  - CREATE TABLE

  - INSERT, SELECT

Where would we be without databases! You likely interact with them almost daily, unaware. This chapter is all about databases. You'll learn the different ways content can be stored and why it's stored that way. You'll also learn the difference between relational and nonrelational databases and how to create and update them.

What makes databases so important? Without them, we wouldn't be able to buy things online or look up our latest insurance claim online, just to name a couple of their uses. Databases provide the backbone of dynamic web pages and are integral to running a business. If you're a back-end web developer, you'll likely spend a large portion of your time working with databases.

Database Structures and Languages

You've already learned that JavaScript (JS), Hypertext Markup Language (HTML), and Cascading Style Sheets (CSS) provide the code used to create a web page. The structure, content, styling, and functionality of the web page is stored in those file types and likely doesn't change very often. But what if you have a dynamic web page that displays something different depending on who logs in? You'll need a way to store the information that's related to the people who access the site, and the most popular way to do that is using a *database management system (DBMS)*. A DBMS enables storage and management of large volumes of data and sometimes complex, interrelated information.

Database Structures

Databases come in a variety of types and styles for different uses. The simplest form of database is known as a *flat-file database*. These databases consist of a single table, as shown in Figure 3.1. A *record* is information for one entity, whether that entity is a person, an event, or transaction, and is often stored as a single line in a database. In Figure 3.1, pizza, milk, egg, and so on are records. A *field* is a type of information gathered about each record, such as name, city, state, and so on, and is often stored as a database column. In Figure 3.1, Item, Qty, Measure, Calories, Carbs, Fat, and Fiber are fields.

FIGURE 3.1   Flat-file database

	A	B	C	D	E	F	G
1	Item	Qty	Measure	Calories	Carbs	Fat	Fiber
2	Pizza	1	6" slice	237	26	10	1
3	Milk	1	cup	150	12	8	0
4	Egg	1	ea	778	1	5.3	0
5	Lettuce	1	cup	8	1.5	0.1	1
6	oatmeal	1	cup dry	266	58.8	2.1	9.6
7	tofu	1	ounce	41	1.2	2.8	0.2

LibreOffice is a free, cross-platform productivity package that works great with Linux. One of its many features is a spreadsheet (LibreOffice Calc) that you can use to create a flat-file database. It's simple to install, but first let's see if you have it on your machine already. The following assumes you're running a computer with the Ubuntu distribution:

1. Ensure that you're connected to the Internet.

2. Open a terminal.

3. Update your package list by entering **sudo apt update** in the terminal and pressing Enter.

4. Type **libreoffice --version** and press Enter. If LibreOffice is installed, you'll see the version. If it isn't installed, simply follow these instructions:

    a. Install LibreOffice by typing the command **sudo apt install libreoffice** and pressing Enter.

    b. At some point, it will tell you how much disk space will be used and ask you, "Do you want to continue? [Y/n]." Press y and the installation will continue.

    c. Finally, enter **libreoffice --version** to see which version of LibreOffice you just installed.

Far more popular are relational databases. *Relational databases* consist of multiple tables that are connected through keys. Figure 3.2 shows an example of a relational database schema. A *schema* is the structure of a database, including the type of data stored, the format it can be in, the number and names of tables and fields, and how those tables and fields are related to each other. When designing a database, I always map it out on paper first. I know, it's old-school, but it helps me to think clearly about how the database is going to be structured and saves time when creating a relational database in the database management software.

FIGURE 3.2 Relational database

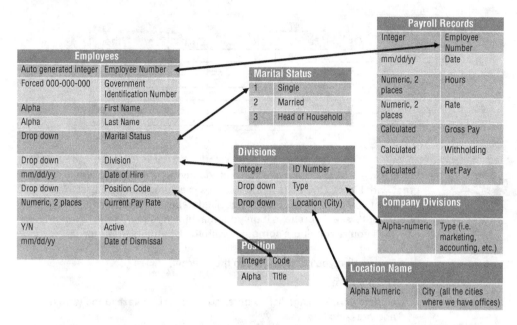

The schema in Figure 3.2 shows a very simplified version of employee records. Excluding the Marital Status table, each table's, left column shows how the data will be formatted or restricted, and the right column shows the field name that will be used. For example, in the Employees table, the employee number will be automatically generated by our DBMS. In this example, the government ID forces database entries in the format of a Canadian ID number. The first and last names will consist of alphabet characters, and entries in the marital status and division fields will be chosen from a drop-down list, and so on. Because the marital status will be a drop-down box and only has three possibilities, it is shown in our schema like a normal table with the columns being the fields and the rows being data. The divisions will also be a drop-down box, but it is more complicated because each will have a division number that references both the type of work and the location where it is being done. The arrows show the fields from each table that will be used to link to other tables. The payroll records database will have multiple records that can be linked to the employee.

So far, the data we've talked about is stored in structured databases. Data can also be unstructured. *Unstructured data* doesn't fit easily into rows and columns. It may have identifiers (fields) that are different from one record to another. Consider a doctor's office that has 50 years of patient records on paper. Some of these records may be images such as an magnetic resonance imaging (MRI), X-ray, or computed topography (CT) scan. Other records for the same patient may be handwritten reports of office visits. In recent years, the medical community has placed their information on systems that can be shared between medical specialists, and each piece likely has some common information such as dates, patient names, and so on, but the bulk of the information defies being stored in database format. Unstructured data lacks a schema but has a great deal of flexibility. Even indexing this data may be difficult and time-consuming. Managing the data (i.e., updating, searching, deleting, and appending), is much more difficult than in a relational database.

Database Languages

Just as there are several programming languages, there are several languages used by databases. Database languages may also be called query languages. First, let's take a look at the categories of database languages:

- *Data definition language (DDL)* is used to control the schema of a database, such as, but not limited to, creating, removing, renaming, and changing databases, tables, and columns.

- *Data manipulation language (DML)* is used to control the actual data in the database, such as adding, deleting, choosing, or changing data.

- *Data control language (DCL)* is used to grant or revoke access to a database or its parts.

- *Transaction control language (TCL)* manages database transactions using statements such as COMMIT to perform a task, or ROLLBACK to return the database to a previous state. As implied, a *database transaction* is an entry or change to a database.

Now that you know the types of language used in databases, let's look at some specific database languages.

Structured Query Language (SQL) is a coding language that enables a user to manage information. It's likely the most-used database language and has been around for a long time. If you're planning on being in data management, you'll want to learn more about SQL. SQL is used by open source databases, such as MySQL from Oracle; MariaDB, a completely free DBMS also from Oracle; and SQLite, which is faster than MySQL but only for smaller database sizes. SQLite is free and open source so anyone can use it. It is also cross-platform; however, SQLite doesn't enforce the integrity of a field's defined data type or enforce references to key fields in other tables (known as *referential integrity*). PostgreSQL is an open source, cross-platform, object-relational DBMS.

SQLite is free, open source, and cross platform, so why not install it? Here are the instructions for installing it on Ubuntu:

1. Open a terminal.

2. Update your package list by entering **sudo apt update** in the terminal and pressing Enter.

3. Install SQLite by typing **sudo apt install sqlite3** and pressing Enter.

4. When it's done running, check the version by typing **sqlite3 --version**. You'll get a long string that should start with 3.31.1 2020-01-27....

Not all databases are SQL. *NoSQL* stands for either not SQL or not only SQL, depending on where your information comes from, and in either case, these are nonrelational databases. They have a flexible schema and don't follow the rules of SQL, but they do have the advantage of being more flexible in storing and retrieving disparate data, and they scale much more easily. Examples of this type of database are MongoDB, Redis, and CouchDB. Some of the data that might be stored in a NoSQL database are images, handwritten documents (stored as images), X-rays, other medical reports, family photos, and so on. Each record in the database would have some identifier that is common, such as a name or record number, but the other data fields that are searchable may be totally different from one record to another.

Relational Database Concepts

As previously mentioned, relational databases start with tables and each table consists of records and fields. Fields may hold information, such as a phone number, address, diagnosis, part number, price, quantity, or any number of other types of data, depending on what the database is being used for. Each table will also have multiple records. Each record is an entry in the database and will have information for each field that relates to that record, as shown in Figure 3.1. The difference is that relational databases have many tables that are connected through key fields. *Key fields* are used to sort, find, or otherwise refer to a record in a field. A *primary key* is a field that will be unique for each record in a table. Examples include a patient number, item number, or simply a record number. A *foreign key* refers to the primary field in a different but connected table. The current table will use the foreign key to connect a record to the information in the other table, as shown in Figure 3.2. In Figure 3.2, the Employee number is a primary key in the Employee table. Division is also a key in the Employee table and links to the ID Number in the Divisions table. This ID Number is a primary key in the Divisions table but is a foreign key in the Employees table.

Connections between databases may be one-to-one, one-to-many, or even many-to-many. Consider a customer database. Rather than store the city, state, and zip code in the same table as the customer name and street address, that information could be stored in a separate table with listings for zip code (or postal code), city, state (or province, or county), and perhaps country. This would be a one-to-many relationship, because one record in the postal code database connects to many records in the customer database. One advantage of using relational databases this way is that the amount of space required to store information is much less. If we have a thousand customers with the same postal code, the location information is only stored one time in our database instead of a thousand times. See Figure 3.3. In this relational database, the primary key in the Customer Information table is Customer Number, and the primary key in the Zip / Postal Code table is Postal Code. Postal Code is also a foreign key in the Customer Information table, which is used to link to a record in the Customer Information table.

FIGURE 3.3 One-to-many relationship

Zip / Postal Code	
Postal Code	City / State / Country
43227	Columbus, Ohio, US
46254	Indianapolis, Indiana, US
77034	Houston, TX, US
46227	Indianapolis, Indiana, US
M1R 0E9	Toronto, Ontario, CA
75001	Paris, France
EH1	Edinburgh, Scotland, UK
24	Dublin, County Dublin, IE
13601	Watertown, NY, US
33435	Boynton Beach, FL, US

Customer Information		
Customer Number	Name	Postal Code
1001000	Jones	46254
1001001	Smith	46254
1001002	Carpenter	M1R 0E9
1001003	Brown	46254
1001004	O'Shea	24
1001005	MacVeigh	EH1
1001006		
1001007		

Content Maintenance and Delivery

Once we have created a database, we'll want to enter, modify, and retrieve information from that database, which is performed using forms, queries, and reports.

Forms are used to enter, view, and modify information contained in one or more databases. To continue our previous example, let's assume that we're entering a new customer record into the database. On the form, when we enter the postal code, the database software looks in the Zip/Postal Code database and automatically links to and displays the city and state associated with that postal code. Figure 3.4 shows a typical input form.

A *query* is a way of searching a database for information. Perhaps we want a list of all the students who attended class on a particular date or a list of everything we ordered in the last month. A query can pull up that information for us. DBMSs usually have a built-in query tool, or you can use SQL to write a query. Two other tools that are available to programmers for retrieving data are GraphQL and REST.

Representational state transfer (REST) is an architecture for creating APIs and is used by a client to request data from a specific URL. The drawback is that the client may get more than just the specific data that they're looking for, known as *overfetching*, or less than they need, known as *underfetching*, in which case they will need to make multiple requests to get all the information they require. Either of these can cause sluggish performance. Enter GraphQL. *GraphQL* is a query language and a runtime for APIs that enables a programmer to define a schema for retrieving specific data. This allows the user of the API to request just what they want to retrieve, instead of everything from a particular URL. It's faster and more specific than using a RESTful API, although GraphQL can also make use of RESTful APIs.

FIGURE 3.4   Input form example

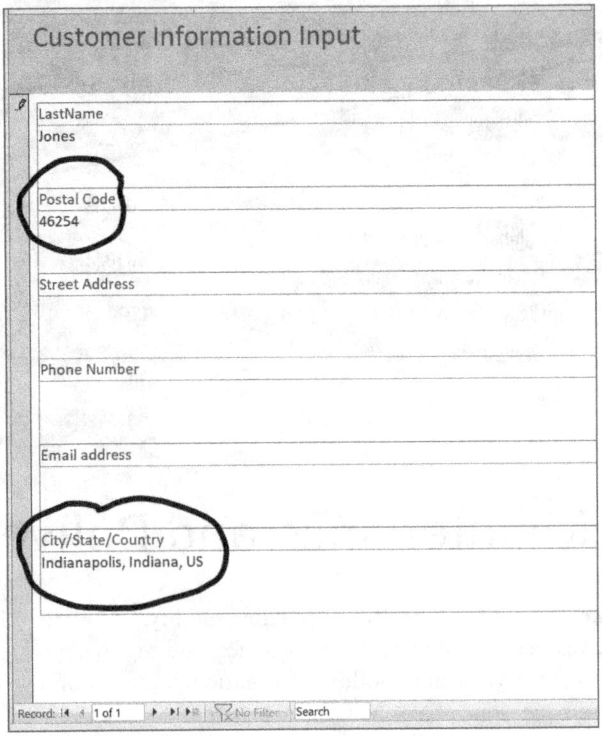

Finally, *reports* allow us to print the information that we want from the database. Maybe what we want are address labels that have the customer name, address, city, state, and zip code on them. A report can do that. Other examples might be quantities of all the ingredients needed for a recipe or grades on all of your assignments for a course. Reports could be printed to a file such as a PDF and viewed on your computing device or printed in hard-copy form from a printer.

When we have multiple users of the same database, we need a way for each of those clients to communicate with the database. You'll learn about that and more in Chapter 4, "Client/Server Communication."

Summary

In this chapter, you learned about databases. Databases can be compared by structure. They can be flat-file or relational, structured with neatly identified and consistent fields, or unstructured (nonrelational) with various types of documents and images in the same database. Structured databases use SQL; unstructured databases are NoSQL. We identified open source DBMSs that are SQL and those that are NoSQL.

You also learned about the four types of coding languages: DDL, DML, DCL, and TCL. The type depends on whether we're changing the schema, managing the information in the database, controlling who has access to that data, or controlling the state of a database transaction.

Finally, we examined how the data is structured in a typical relational database, and how to add, manipulate, or retrieve information from our database, including the difference between REST and GraphQL, and that GraphQL can make use of RESTful APIs.

Exam Essentials

Compare SQL and NoSQL.   Know the difference between SQL and NoSQL databases. Identify what SQL stands for and which specific database management systems are either SQL or NoSQL.

Be able to name the open source DBMSs.   This is a specific exam objective, so make sure you can name them.

Explain relational database concepts.   Understanding relationships in databases will be necessary if you want to pursue a career as a back-end developer. What you've learned here won't make you an expert, but it will enable you to understand these concepts better going forward when you see these terms again.

Compare and contrast REST and GraphQL.   Make sure you understand the difference between REST and GraphQL. They are listed as a separate item on the objectives.

EXERCISE 3.1

Creating a Nonrelational Database

In this exercise, we'll use a spreadsheet to create a simple flat-file database.

If you don't already have LibreOffice installed on your Ubuntu computer, now might be a great time to install it! (See the tip in this chapter.) LibreOffice is free and cross-platform. It includes a spreadsheet, LibreOffice Calc, which we will use to do this exercise.

EXERCISE 3.1 *(continued)*

1. In Ubuntu, go to apps and open LibreOffice Calc. The active cell should be A1. If not, click in the A1 cell.

2. Type **First** in A1, then press the Tab key to go to B1.

3. Type **Last** in B1, then press Tab to go to C1.

4. Type **Birth** in C1, then press Enter.

    First, Last, and Birth are your database's fields. You should now be in cell A2.

5. Type *your first name* in A2, then press Tab.

6. Type *your last name* in B2, then press Tab.

7. Type *your birth date* in C2, then press Enter.

The information you entered about yourself is a record. Feel free to enter as many records as you like.

EXERCISE 3.2

Creating a Relational Database

In this exercise, we'll create a very simple relational database, enter data, then retrieve that data. If you don't already have SQLite installed, check the tip earlier in this chapter for installation instructions.

1. Begin by opening a terminal.

2. Type **sqlite3 birthdays.db** and press Enter. You'll get a message that tells you to "Enter 'help' for usage hints." You've just created a database named birthdays. The prompt should now be sqlite>.

3. Create a table similar to the table in Exercise 3.1. Our database will have the following fields: Name, Month, Day, and Year. The following entry will create the table. We'll also use NOT NULL so that fields are required. Enter the following line:

    ```
    CREATE TABLE birthdays(name text NOT NULL, birthmonth integer NOT NULL, day
    integer, year integer);
    ```

    The semicolon must be there. Press Enter when you finish typing. This should return you to the sqlite> prompt.

4. Let's enter some data. Enter the following lines, pressing Enter after each, making sure the text entries are entered in quotes as shown and ending with a semicolon:

```
INSERT INTO birthdays VALUES ("John", 1,2,1990);
INSERT INTO birthdays VALUES ("Sarah", 9,12, 2010);
INSERT INTO birthdays VALUES ("Ahsan", 6,15, 2022);
INSERT INTO birthdays VALUES ("Meera", 2,14, 1980);
```

5. To see what's in your table, type **SELECT * FROM birthdays;** and press Enter.

   You should see the following output:

```
John|1|2|1990
Sarah|9|12|2010
Ahsan|6|15|2022
Meera|2|14|1980
Sqlite>
```

6. To select just some data, enter what you want such as **SELECT * FROM birthdays WHERE name IS Ahsan;** and press Enter. The output will be Ahsan|6|15|2022.

   When you're using SELECT, you're querying the database. * means all values.

7. Now, we'll create our second database and link it to the first. First, create the second table by entering the following lines. Press Enter after each.

```
CREATE TABLE months (month integer NOT NULL, name text NOT NULL);
INSERT INTO months VALUES (1, "January");
INSERT INTO months VALUES (2, "February");
INSERT INTO months VALUES (3, "March");
```

   Continue entering data until all months have entries. If you want to see the contents of the Months table, type **SELECT * FROM months;** and press Enter.

8. To join the two tables based on the month number, enter the following:

```
SELECT * FROM birthdays INNER JOIN months on birthdays
.birthmonth=months.month;
```

   Your output should be as follows, showing the joining of the two tables:

```
John|1|2|1990|January
Sarah|9|12|2010|September
Ahsan|6|15|2022|June
Meera|2|14|1980|February
Sqlite>
```

EXERCISE 3.2 *(continued)*

9. To see all the September birthdays, enter the following:

    ```
    SELECT *FROM birthdays INNER JOIN months on birthdays.birthmonth=months
    .month WHERE months.name="September";.
    ```

    The output should be Sarah|9|12|2010|September.

10. Press Ctrl+D to exit the sqlite> console.

    There is much more you can do with SQLite, but that remains for another book!

Review Questions

1. You need a way to store and manage large amounts of data about your customers, including their account information and their multiple orders. What will be the best tool to do this?

   A. DBMS

   B. Non-relational database

   C. Schema

   D. GraphQL

2. Your customer is looking at a database in a spreadsheet and wants to know the name of the columns that show the same type of information for each product, such as SKU number and price. What will you tell them that they are called?

   A. Records

   B. Fields

   C. DBMS

   D. Entries

3. Which of the following would you use to catalog family images and documents so that you could search electronically for them later?

   A. Filing cabinet

   B. SQL database

   C. NoSQL database

   D. GraphQL

4. Which of the following are open source database management systems? (Choose all that apply.)

   A. PostgreSQL

   B. GraphQL

   C. MySQL

   D. SQLite

5. You're working with Table 1 of a relational database. A field in Table 1 called ID is matched to a field in Table 2 called Customer. What is the field called Customer to you at this point?

   A. Key field

   B. Primary key

   C. Relational field

   D. Foreign key

6. What is the name for a database consisting of multiple tables linked together through common fields?

    A. Flat-file database

    B. Nonrelational database

    C. Relational database

    D. Schema

7. You're creating a document to help a new programmer understand how the tables in your database work together and how the data in each field must be formatted. What are you creating?

    A. Schema

    B. Relational database

    C. SQL database

    D. Open source database

8. Which of the following are used to sort and find records based on a field in the database? (Choose all that apply.)

    A. Primary key

    B. Key field

    C. Foreign key

    D. Main key

9. You want a query to pull all the information from a specific URL. What will you use?

    A. GraphQL

    B. SQL

    C. REST

    D. DBMS

10. Visitors to your website can leave their name and email address by submitting them on a form. When they do, they're entering them into a database. What is the information about each individual user known as?

    A. Field

    B. Schema

    C. Record

    D. Data definition language

11. Databases use different languages, depending on what the user is doing with the database. As the backside developer in charge, you need to remove someone's access to a database. What language are you using?

    A. DDL

    B. DML

    C. DCL

    D. TCL

12. You're the data manager for an online store, and it's your responsibility to ensure that the data being entered maintains its integrity. The power fluctuated and happened to prevent a transaction from being completely entered, where the sale was entered, but the customer was not charged. What is used within a database to avoid situations like this?

A. DDL

B. DML

C. DCL

D. TCL

13. You're building a database and have two tables. One contains customer's names, addresses, and account numbers, and a second table contains account numbers, invoice numbers, and a list of items sold. Each customer has multiple transactions in the second table. The two tables are connected by the customer's account number What is the relationship between Table 1 and Table 2?

A. One-to-one

B. One-to-many

C. Many-to-many

D. Primary-to-secondary

14. An employee takes phone calls and enters data into a database. What does the employee use to do this?

A. Form

B. Query

C. SQL

D. Reports

15. Which DBMS is open source and faster than MySQL but doesn't guarantee referential integrity?

A. MariaDB

B. PostgreSQL

C. Access

D. SQLite

16. You're creating a database for a doctor's office that includes handwritten documents, lab reports, and images. What will you use? (Choose two.)

A. Structured

B. Unstructured

C. CouchDB

D. SQLite

17. A person in your office needs a hard copy of a report from a structured DBMS. What will they use to achieve this?

    A. Form

    B. Report

    C. Query

    D. NoSQL

18. Which two of the following are DBMSs for unstructured data? (Choose two.)

    A. SQLite

    B. MongoDB

    C. MariaDB

    D. Redis

19. A client has information where they want to record the same type of information about each record. What type of database will they create to store and retrieve that information?

    A. Structured

    B. Unstructured

    C. Modified

    D. NoSQL

20. Which of the following can act as a runtime for an API?

    A. A query

    B. A report

    C. REST

    D. GraphQL

Client/Server Communication

LINUX PROFESSIONAL INSTITUTE, WEB DEVELOPMENT ESSENTIALS EXAM 030-100 OBJECTIVES COVERED IN THIS CHAPTER:

✓ **031 Software Development and Web Technologies**

- 031.3 HTTP Basics: The candidate should be familiar with the basics of HTTP. This includes understanding HTTP headers, content types, caching, and status codes. Furthermore, the candidate should understand the principles of cookies and their role for session handling and be aware of advanced HTTP features.

- Key Knowledge Areas:

    - Understand HTTP GET and POST methods, status codes, headers and content types

    - Upload files to a web server's document root

    - Understand caching

    - Understand cookies

    - Awareness of sessions and session hijacking

    - Awareness of web sockets

    - Awareness of virtual hosts

    - Awareness of network bandwidth and latency requirements and limitations

- Files, terms, and utilities:

    - GET, POST

    - 200, 301, 302, 401, 403, 404, 500

This chapter provides a brief introduction into the world of Hypertext Transfer Protocol (HTTP). First, we look at what happens on the client-side and the server-side of HTTP communications. Then we examine the role of caches and cookies and finish with security concerns when using HTTP.

HTTP

Hypertext Transfer Protocol (HTTP) is a communication protocol that works on the application layer of the Open Systems Interconnection (OSI) networking framework. Virtually all networks follow the OSI framework, which allows for easier communication between networks because they're all built with the same basic structure and rules. A *protocol* is a set of rules, and in order to communicate, both the sending and receiving computers must follow the same set of rules.

HTTP relies on other parts of the OSI model to move requests and information from one place to another. The network layer of the OSI model includes the Internet Protocol (IP). *IP addresses* identify a computer and network where a request or response should be sent, and are part of the Transmission Control Protocol/Internet Protocol (TCP/IP) suite comprised of many protocols that are the backbone of the Internet.

TCP is a communication (transport layer) protocol that guarantees delivery of information. The information sent via TCP can be encrypted using the Transport Layer Security (TLS) protocol, (sometimes also called secure sockets layer (SSL) as this is the encryption protocol that TLS superseded), and includes digital signatures for requests and responses. This encryption and digital signing is the difference between HTTP and Hypertext Transport Protocol Secure (HTTPS).

HTTP and HTTPS are the rules that clients and servers agree upon when sending information and requests back and forth. Both HTTP and HTTPS have components on the client-side and the server-side that assist in transferring information between a web client and a web server.

HTTP Client-Side

As you learned in Chapter 2, "Client/Server Computing," the client initiates communication with a web server by sending a request for files that constitute a particular web page. This communication is often initiated using a web browser such as Firefox or Chrome, but there are other clients that are not browsers. For a refresher on those, refer back to Chapter 2.

Once a communication channel has been established between the client and the server using the TCP/IP suite, the client can send its request. Figure 4.1 shows a request header that was generated by typing www.wiley.com in a browser's search box. A request header contains information about the client's request to a server such as the protocol (HTTP or HTTPS), the method, the name of the host server such as Wiley.com, the user agent that is the software or browser making the request, the type of data that the requester can accept, and possibly a path to a script on the server to run or a username or email address. A request may have other items as well.

FIGURE 4.1   Web page GET Request

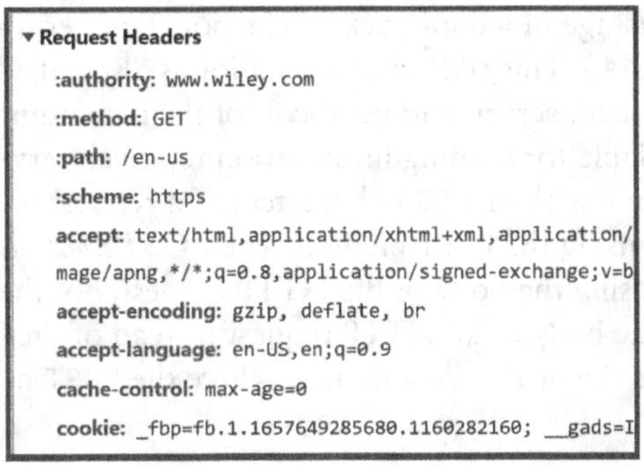

```
▼ Request Headers
   :authority: www.wiley.com
   :method: GET
   :path: /en-us
   :scheme: https
   accept: text/html,application/xhtml+xml,application/
   mage/apng,*/*;q=0.8,application/signed-exchange;v=b
   accept-encoding: gzip, deflate, br
   accept-language: en-US,en;q=0.9
   cache-control: max-age=0
   cookie: _fbp=fb.1.1657649285680.1160282160; __gads=I
```

Let's break this request down.

authority—The domain name that information is being requested from.

method—One of two methods, either GET or POST. GET tells the server that we're looking for information. POST sends information from us to the server.

path—The location of the resource that we want.

scheme—States whether we're connecting with HTTP or HTTPS.

accept—The content types the client can understand or accept.

accept-encoding—May be gzip, compress, deflate, or br to identify the type of encoding that the client can understand.

accept-language—The language or locale that the client can accept such as en-US for United States English, fr for French, or de for German as on the International Organization for Standardization (ISO)'s Language Codes list.

cache-control—Instructions that determine whether and what is cached.

cookie—A list of the cookies that the server previously sent to this client.

A header can also contain a combination of an IP address and the protocol's port number that is being used, such as 192.18.16.99:443, where the part before the colon is the requester's IPv4 address and the part after the colon is the protocol's port number. Port numbers can range from 1 to 65,535. A *port number* is used by a router or other network appliance to identify the protocol or application being used by a network connection. It identifies a logical place that both computers can reference. The network appliance uses this information to either grant or deny passage of a data packet. The port number for an HTTP request is 80 and an HTTPS request is 443. This IP:Port combination is also called a *socket*. The socket identifies the endpoints (client, server, and protocol) of the communication session.

Two methods are available for sending information to a web server. The *GET method* is used for HTTP requests of less than 1,024 characters. If a request is long or needs greater security, it should be sent using the POST method. The *POST method* sends larger data than the GET method by using the body of the HTTP request, not the header. When the information is stored in the body of an HTTP request instead of the header, it is called a *payload*. Figure 4.2 shows the header of a request where the POST method is being used.

FIGURE 4.2   Web page POST request

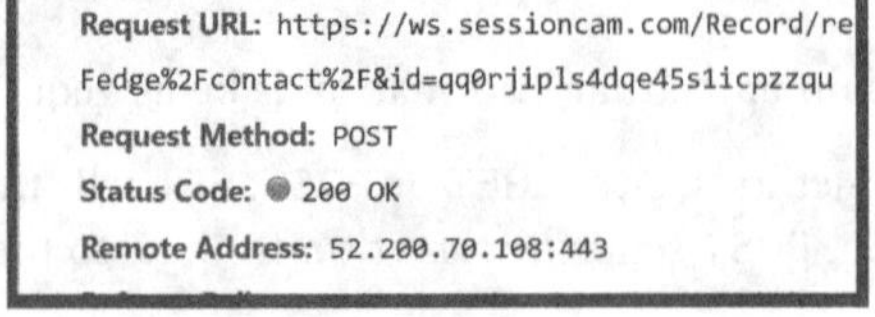

```
Request URL: https://ws.sessioncam.com/Record/re
Fedge%2Fcontact%2F&id=qq0rjipls4dqe45s1icpzzqu
Request Method: POST
Status Code: ● 200 OK
Remote Address: 52.200.70.108:443
```

The POST request shows some familiar information: the request URL, the method (POST), and a web socket. More of this request is shown in Figure 4.3.

FIGURE 4.3   Additional POST header

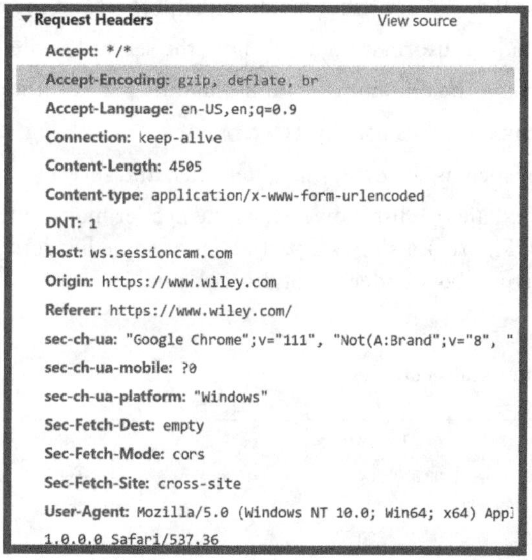

▼ **Request Headers**   View source
    Accept: */*
    Accept-Encoding: gzip, deflate, br
    Accept-Language: en-US,en;q=0.9
    Connection: keep-alive
    Content-Length: 4505
    Content-type: application/x-www-form-urlencoded
    DNT: 1
    Host: ws.sessioncam.com
    Origin: https://www.wiley.com
    Referer: https://www.wiley.com/
    sec-ch-ua: "Google Chrome";v="111", "Not(A:Brand";v="8", "
    sec-ch-ua-mobile: ?0
    sec-ch-ua-platform: "Windows"
    Sec-Fetch-Dest: empty
    Sec-Fetch-Mode: cors
    Sec-Fetch-Site: cross-site
    User-Agent: Mozilla/5.0 (Windows NT 10.0; Win64; x64) Appl
    1.0.0.0 Safari/537.36

Notice in Figure 4.3 that this request shows the content length, which tells us there are 4,505 bytes in the payload. Content type identifies the format of the request. More information about the POST and GET methods can be found in Chapter 8, "Creating HTML Forms."

Web browsers have a way for you to view their code. The process may vary, though, depending on the browser you're using. In Chrome, the process is as follows:

1. Open the desired web page, right-click, and choose Inspect to open the developer tools.

2. Locate and select the Network tab.

3. Reload the page and the HTTP requests should show on the left. Click one to view its contents on the right.

HTTP Server-Side

The server-side will respond to the client's request. The response header will have the following:

- The protocol (HTTP or HTTPS) that matches the protocol of the request
- A status code providing information about how the server handled the request
- Information regarding the amount of data it contains and what it can accept
- The content-type (which is usually text/html)
- Other information such as the date, time, identifier, and server

This is far from an exhaustive list, however, as the header may contain many other pieces of information as well. Figure 4.4 shows a partial list of some headers generated by a website request. Notice the numbers under the Status column.

FIGURE 4.4   Header status codes

Name	Status	Type	Initiator	Size	Time
ATVPDKIKX0DER:144-1286599-0921908:B...	204	text/plain	(index):2247	75 B	44 ...
ATVPDKIKX0DER:144-1286599-0921908:B...	200	gif	(index):58	149 B	51 ...
ATVPDKIKX0DER:144-1286599-0921908:B...	200	gif	(index):58	148 B	43 ...
com.amazon.csm.csa.prod	(pending)	ping	(index):289	0 B	Pen...
com.amazon.csm.csa.prod	200	xhr	(index):289	592 B	240...
com.amazon.csm.csa.prod	200	ping	(index):289	592 B	60 ...

You've likely seen some of the status codes generated by servers such as the dreaded 404. Here is a quick rundown of the main categories of server status codes:

- **1XX**—Information codes
- **2XX**—Success codes
- **3XX**—Redirection codes
- **4XX**—Client Error codes
- **5XX**—Server Error codes

The other two numbers of the code (shown previously as XX) provide more information about the status. For example, in Figure 4.4, one of the status codes is 204. The 2 means that the request was successful, and the 04 means that although the request was processed successfully, there is no content.

The following codes are specifically listed in the exam objectives, so let's take a closer look at them:

- **200: OK**—This is the normal response for an HTTP request.
  - If it's from a GET method, then the requested information is located in the URL that was sent.
  - If it's from a POST method, then the result of the POST is located in the message body.
- **301: Moved Permanently**—The requested resource was moved to a new URL permanently.
- **302: Found**—The requested resource was found at a different URL where it will be located temporarily.
- **401: Unauthorized**—The server doesn't know the client requesting information. The client needs to be authenticated to the server.
- **403: Forbidden**—The server knows the client requesting the information, but they don't have permission to access the resources they're requesting.
- **404: Not Found**—The resource isn't where it's supposed to be and it can't be found. There is no redirect information. (You don't want your website visitors to receive this error.)
- **500: Internal Server Error**—The server can't honor the request for one of many possible reasons.

When an HTTP server receives a request, depending on the server software being used, it may look for the file where it normally keeps its HTML files. However, not all servers will automatically look there. Many will use JavaScript or other server software such as PHP, Python, Ruby, Java, and C# to handle request processing.

Virtual hosts (vhosts) are another service available on some server software like Apache. Using *virtual hosts* allows a single server or system to host more than one domain (company1.com, company2.com, and so on.) This is beneficial because it cuts down on hardware and software cost and maintenance efforts. Virtual hosts can be achieved by using a separate IP address for each host or one IP address and multiple domain names. Virtual hosts can also be dynamic where the host information is added to the header of the response. A drawback with virtual hosts is that some older browsers may not support the HTTP version required for virtual hosts to work.

WebSocket API

The *WebSocket API*, also known as WebSockets, is a protocol and an API similar to but with advantages over HTTP. Like HTTP, it uses the TCP/IP suite of protocols and the OSI framework to facilitate communication over the Internet. Also like HTTP, WebSockets has a secure version called WebSocket Secure, but that's where the similarities end.

Unlike HTTP, WebSockets communicates in full duplex, meaning that both client and server can send information at the same time. With WebSockets, the communication link between the client and server remains open until it is closed by either WebSockets or the client, and the server can push notifications down to the client when something happens. WebSockets is event driven, which means that it works well for real-time data like weather apps, ride-share services, and social media that constantly update. For example, when something happens on the weather app's server end such as a storm blowing in, the app's server pushes that information to their clients.

By contrast, HTTP is more suited to static data like a web page because the request for information is initiated by the client, and an HTTP connection terminates after each request/response cycle is completed. HTTP is half-duplex, meaning that only one participant can send information at a time. HTTP communication is similar to a walkie-talkie, but WebSocket's communication works like a telephone call.

Caches and Cookies

Caches and cookies are two information repositories used by web servers to help load pages faster and provide a better user experience.

Caches store information locally so only the information that has changed on a web page needs to be downloaded to the client, not the entire page each time. That's why subsequent visits to a website may seem to load faster than the first visit. Note, caches can be shared or private.

A *shared cache* is used by more than one client. For example, if I'm supporting a network for a customer who has numerous employees that download large files like video, audio, or computer-aided design (CAD), I would establish a server with a shared cache for all the employees. The large files would be downloaded one time, and everyone at the company could use the file from the shared cache without having to download the file from or across the Internet again. This is beneficial because it improves data acquisition speed (so there is less latency) and decreases bandwidth use.

A *private cache* is one that is used by only one client computer. When a website is visited the first time, all of the necessary files are downloaded. When the same client makes subsequent visits to the website, it only downloads information that has changed. The result is the same as with a shared cache: performance increases and bandwidth use decreases.

Cookies are bits of information that a web server stores on a client computer's drive. Although cookies may seem like an intrusion, they are integral to a website's ability to work with you and meet your needs. They can remember your username when you log into a site, and greet you by your given name, which enhances the user experience. They may even take you to a different login page if you've visited before. Beyond that, they are the reason that when we place multiple items in our shopping cart at our favorite online vendor the items will still be there the next time we visit. They retain our login information as we traverse the website from one page to another, so we don't need to continually log in. They can also store our contact information for future orders and payment information (although personally, I always decline to let them retain my credit card number).

Cookies come in two flavors: session cookies and persistent cookies. *Session cookies* retain our information in a browser until it is closed. With this type of cookie, you'll need to put your information in each time you revisit the website.

Persistent cookies remain available to a browser until a predetermined time elapses or the user deletes the cookies. You can close the browser and the website will remember you and what you left in your cart the next time you visit. The website might even tailor what you see based on what you were shopping for the last time you visited.

HTTP Security Concerns

HTTP is everywhere, but there are some security concerns to consider when using it.

Data sent via HTTPS is encrypted, but data over HTTP is not. The lack of encryption makes HTTP susceptible to on-path attacks (also known as man-in-the-middle attacks), where data is intercepted by a malicious party who may change the payload, delete it, or simply use it for some other purpose like corporate spying.

Another vulnerability is session hijacking. In *session hijacking*, the hijacker reads your session cookie and places it on their own computer, giving them access to a website as if they were you. If you log into Wi-Fi at a hotel or coffee shop and get a message that your communications may not be secure, then you're not using HTTPS or WebSocket Secure to communicate. Without the Secure Sockets Layer/Transport Layer Security (SSL/TLS) protocols, your session cookie could be read by someone other than you. They may then be able to use it to access your accounts and shop using your credit cards or take money out of your bank account.

A session cookie can stay active as long as the browser is open, which is why it's always a good idea to close your browser when you've been shopping or banking and never shop or bank when you're on an unsecured network.

Finally, password information should never be sent in a GET request, because the request content becomes part of the URL string and can be intercepted or stored in the browser history, causing a security vulnerability.

Summary

In this chapter, you learned about communication protocols that are used to communicate across the Internet. The communication using HTTP is initiated by the client, and the server responds. We examined some communications headers and common (but not all) information that can be found there. We took a look at the GET and POST methods and which one has a payload.

On the server-side, we explored what those status codes mean, including the dreaded 404: Not Found status code. We took a quick look at virtual hosts, just to ensure that you're aware of them and what they are.

WebSocket API is similar to HTTP, but it's better if you're working with real-time data and need the server to push information to the client.

We examined the role of caches and cookies. While they're two very different repositories of information, both are designed to speed up communication. There are also shared caches and private caches, session cookies, and persistent cookies.

We wrapped up this chapter with a discussion about the security concerns of HTTP and what session hijacking is. Remember, never share important information like bank account numbers and passwords if the network you're on isn't secure!

Exam Essentials

Identify the status codes.   You need to know these for the test, but also so you'll know what is happening with your website to ensure the best experience for your visitors.

Understand what's in a header.   Knowing what is typically found in an HTTP header and how to interpret what you find there can help with troubleshooting problems when they arise.

Know the types of caching.   Knowing the types of caching helps you determine where to look when there's a problem.

Understand what cookies are and how they are used.   Understanding how cookies are used can help you design your website. Cookies are necessary but can also present a vulnerability to your website, so you must be aware of what should and should not be stored in a cookie.

EXERCISE 4.1

Examine Cookies

In this exercise, we open and view cookies in Google Chrome. Although we use Google Chrome as an example, virtually all browsers have a way for you to view the websites that are placing cookies on your computer and to clear cookies if they're presenting problems or concerns. Let's get started:

1.   Open Google Chrome.

2.   Click the ellipsis (three dots) at the top right of the screen, next to your user avatar.

3.   Choose Settings ➢ Privacy and security ➢ Cookies and other site data, then select See all site data and permissions.

4. Those steps bring you to a screen listing the sites that have placed cookies on your computer. Click the arrows on the right to see progressively greater detail for each website about specifically what is blocked and what is allowed, how many cookies are stored, and how much space they're taking.

5. You always have the option to clear all the data for any or all websites. Remember that if you choose to clear data, the website won't recognize you the next time you access it.

EXERCISE 4.2

Examine Cache Storage

In this exercise, we view the cached pages for a website. We'll use Google Chrome as an example again, but, as before, virtually all browsers have a way for you to see what pages are cached.

1. Open Google Chrome. In the search bar in the middle of the page, type a web page URL preceded by `cache:`—for example: `cache:www.wiley.com/en-us`—and press Enter.

   The screen may briefly flash another screen telling you that it's opening a cached page, or it may change pages so quickly that you don't even see it. However, the browser should show something like `http://webcache.googleusercontent .com/search?q.......`This is how you know you're looking at a cached page.

2. To clear cached pages, follow these steps:

   a. From Chrome, click the ellipsis at the top right to open the context menu (sometimes called Kebob).

   b. Click More tools, then click Clear browsing data.

   c. At the top of the screen that opens, choose a time range or All time to clear everything.

Review Questions

1. What is HTTP? (Choose two.)
   A. A communication protocol
   B. A markup language
   C. Hypertext Transfer Protocol
   D. A security protocol

2. What initiates the HTTP communication between a web server and a client? Choose the *best* answer.
   A. The client
   B. A web browser
   C. A web server push notice
   D. A third party

3. Which of the following status codes indicates a client error?
   A. 200
   B. 302
   C. 404
   D. 500

4. What feature allows a single server to host more than one domain?
   A. WebSocket API
   B. Virtual hosts
   C. HTTPS
   D. HTML

5. Which of these is WebSocket API most similar to?
   A. HTML
   B. SSL
   C. TLS
   D. HTTP

6. Which of these keep the connection link open until it is closed by either party, enabling real-time updates? (Choose two.)
   A. HTTP
   B. HTTPS
   C. WebSockets
   D. WebSockets Secure

7. You're visiting a website for a second time and note that the first time it took much longer to load. What is likely the reason it's loading faster this time?

   A. Private cache

   B. Session cookies

   C. Persistent cookies

   D. WebSockets

8. Which of the following is a communication protocol susceptible to on-path attacks, where a hacker intercepts a communication before passing it on to its intended recipient?

   A. HTML

   B. SSL

   C. TLS

   D. HTTP

9. Which part of a request header would identify the type of information that is being sent/received?

   A. Authority

   B. Accept

   C. Method

   D. Scheme

10. Which of these status codes will a server respond with when the resource has been permanently moved and it can be found?

    A. 200

    B. 301

    C. 401

    D. 402

11. Which of the following provide a secure connection? (Choose two.)

    A. HTTP

    B. HTTPS

    C. TLS

    D. TCP

12. Which of the following would not likely be found in an HTTP request header?

    A. Authority

    B. Method

    C. Scheme

    D. Server status code

13. A person you've hired to test your website's user experience tells you they've received a 404 error when trying to access your website. What does this mean?

    A. They're accessing the site successfully.

    B. They've been redirected to another URL.

    C. The web page can't be found.

    D. They aren't authorized to access the website.

14. What are the advantages of virtual hosts? (Choose two.)

    A. Cuts down on hardware and software costs.

    B. Cuts down on maintenance effort.

    C. Works well with older browsers.

    D. Virtual hosts are not dynamic.

15. Which of these communicate in full duplex and is secure?

    A. HTTPS

    B. HTTP

    C. WebSocket API

    D. WebSocket Secure

16. Which of the following types of request should never include password information?

    A. GET

    B. POST

    C. Status code

    D. TLS

17. Which of these has the advantage of using less bandwidth and having a lower latency? (Choose two.)

    A. Shared cookies

    B. Shared cache

    C. Private cache

    D. Virtual host

18. Which of the following is the port number for HTTP?

    A. 22

    B. 80

    C. 443

    D. 995

19. Which of the following is an encryption protocol?

    A. HTTP

    B. HTTPS

    C. TLS

    D. OSI

20. Which of the following is the port number for HTTPS?

    A. 22

    B. 80

    C. 443

    D. 995

HTML Introduction

LINUX PROFESSIONAL INSTITUTE, WEB DEVELOPMENT ESSENTIALS EXAM 030-100 OBJECTIVES COVERED IN THIS CHAPTER:

✓ **032 HTML Document Markup**

- 032.1 HTML Document Anatomy: The candidate should understand the anatomy and syntax of an HTML document. This includes creating basic HTML documents.

  - Key Knowledge Areas:

    - Create a simple HTML document

    - Understand the role of HTML

    - Understand the HTML skeleton

    - Understand the HTML syntax (tags, attributes comments)

    - Understand the HTML head

    - Understand meta tags

    - Understand character encoding

  - Files, terms, and utilities:

    - <!DOCTYPE html>

    - <html>

    - <head>

    - <body>

    - <meta>, including the charset (UTF-8), name and content attributes

- 032.2 HTML Semantics and Document Hierarchy: The candidate should be able to create HTML documents with a semantic structure.

  - Key Knowledge Areas:

    - Create markup for contents in an HTML document

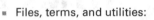

- Files, terms, and utilities:

  - `<h1>`, `<h2>`, `<h3>`, `<h4>`, `<h5>`, `<h6>`

  - `<p>`

  - `<b>`

Welcome to the world of Hypertext Markup Language (HTML). In this chapter, you'll create a web page and set up an HTML skeleton for future projects. We'll get into the basics of creating an HTML page—nothing pretty yet, but rather the bits you need to know so that your page will work on the web. You'll also learn how to put comments in your code so you'll remember why you created a part of the page in a particular way. Roll up your sleeves and let's get started!

What Is HTML?

Hypertext Markup Language (HTML) is the markup language that is used to create and format documents to be rendered by a browser. HTML often incorporates other tools such as Cascading Style Sheets (CSS) and JavaScript (JS). Its most recent version is HTML5, but HTML is a living standard, and as such, it evolves over time. The World Wide Web Consortium (W3C) and the Web Hypertext Application Technology Working Group (WHATWG) agreed in 2019 to work toward a single standard, which is now maintained in a standard document by WHATWG. WHATWG was founded in 2004 by several leading browser companies.

Markup languages use a standard set of symbols to control the formatting and structure of a text document, so an HTML page will have the text to be displayed and the markup text. Markup languages must be interpreted by something else to be useful like a browser or printer. Other markup languages used in web development are Extensible Markup Language (XML) and Extensible Hypertext Markup Language (XHTML), but there are several other markup languages for various purposes.

The HTML Skeleton

In HTML, *tags* are used to identify HTML elements. A tag will be encased between a greater than (>) and less than (<) symbol. The *HTML skeleton* consists of the same basic tags used to start all HTML pages, as shown in Figure 5.1. Strangely enough, a web page will open if you use only the `<title>` tag, but this isn't recommended because leaving out the other skeleton tags could cause some browsers to crash when the page is opened.

FIGURE 5.1   The HTML skeleton

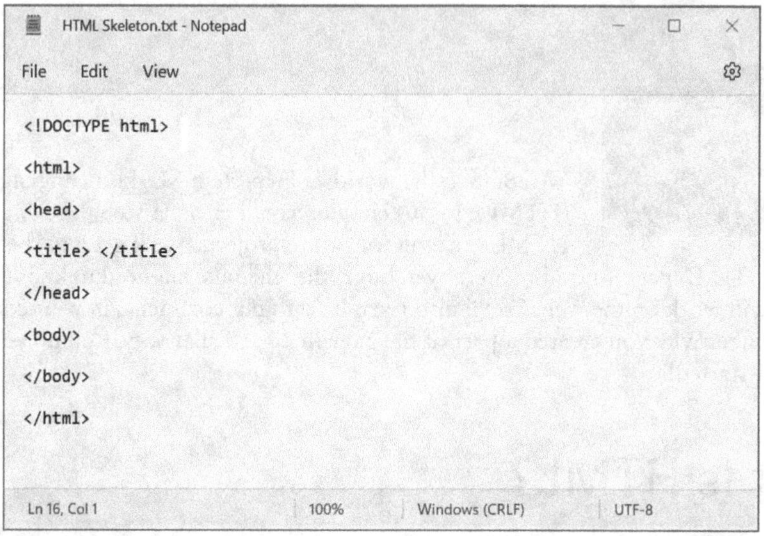

```
HTML Skeleton.txt - Notepad                                    —    □    ×

File    Edit    View                                                    ⚙

<!DOCTYPE html>

<html>

<head>

<title> </title>

</head>

<body>

</body>

</html>



Ln 16, Col 1              100%        Windows (CRLF)         UTF-8
```

Now let's look at what each entry in the skeleton is for. `<!DOCTYPE html>` is a declaration, not a tag, used to tell a browser what type of document it is. When it simply says `html`, then HTML5 is being used. WC3 recommends that you always declare the document type.

HTML *start tags* are used to identify the beginning of an HTML element. (There will be more about elements in the next section and in Chapter 6, "Content Markup.") The `<html>` tag tells the browser that this is the start of our HTML document. At the bottom of Figure 5.1, you'll find the `</html>` tag, or what is known as an end tag. *End tags* start with a forward slash and tell a browser that it's the end of an element, so `</html>` is an end tag that ends the HTML page. All the content of our HTML page and any links to resources will be included between these two tags. Not all tags require end tags, but most of them do. *Empty elements* are those elements that don't have any content, such as `<hr>`, which puts a horizontal line on the page. Sometimes, these are called self-closing elements.

The `<head>` tag identifies the header of our document. Information in the `<head>` element isn't displayed by a browser, and although it is possible to put displayable content in that section, doing so is strongly discouraged. An important tag inside the head section is `<title>`. Whatever is between `<title>` and `</title>` will show in the browser's top bar and is used in search engine searches, so choose carefully. See Figure 5.2. The HTML text document is on the right, and it's open in our browser on the left, displaying the title. HTML can be coded in most text editors, but files must be saved with an `.htm` or `.html` extension so browsers will know they are HTML files to be interpreted.

I like to have a browser with my web page open on half of my screen and what I'm coding on the other half. As I make changes, I can save the text file (with an `.html` extension) and reload the page in the browser to see the results of my changes.

FIGURE 5.2 The `<title>` and `</title>` tags

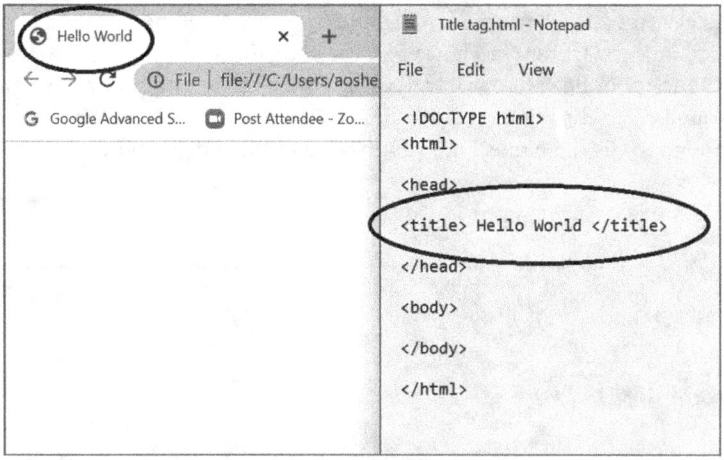

Nesting occurs whenever an element is placed inside another element. The `<head>` and `<title>` tags each have an end tag, and both the start and end `<title>` tags are located inside the head element. When one element is completely inside another element we say that it is *nested*. The `<title>`elementis nested inside the `<head>`element.

Next up are the `<body>` and `</body>` tags. All the text, links, and much of the formatting for our web page happens between these two tags.

Finally, we see the `</html>` tag, which tells the browser that this is the end of our web page. In Exercise 5.1, you'll create your own HTML skeleton and save it to use in your future projects. But before that, you need to learn more about HTML syntax. You learned what syntax is in Chapter 1, "Web Development Basics."

HTML Syntax

Like any language, HTML has its own syntax. Unlike some other languages, capitalization isn't important, although W3C recommends that only lowercase letters be used for tags. Lowercase letters are easier and faster to type, and they're what developers normally use, so it's easier for everyone to read and understand what you're coding when you use lowercase letters. Your code will still work if you enter it in uppercase, but the generally accepted way to code HTML is to type it in lowercase.

HTML elements consist of a start (or opening) tag, element content, and an end (or closing) tag. An example is `<title> Hello World </title>`, where `<title>` is the element's start tag, `"Hello World"` is the element's content, and `</title>` is the element's end tag. Refer back to Figure 5.2.

What if you wanted an element's content to be bold or colored blue? These are considered attributes of the element. *Attributes* provide more information or change the formatting of the element that they are in. Attributes are entered in name:value pairs and are always included in the start tag. In Figure 5.3, the code line

`<h2 style="background-color:LightGray;">This background is gray.</h2>`

sets a background color for the level 2 heading `<h2>`. The attribute in that line is `style`, `"background-color` is the name, and `:LightGray;"` is the attribute value.

FIGURE 5.3   HTML attributes

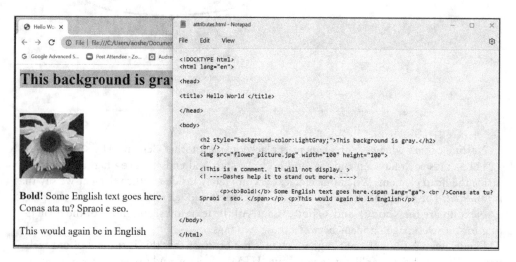

The attribute and its name:value pair are separated by an equal sign, and although it isn't required, it's recommended that attribute values be set in quotes. The code will work without the quotes, but values are quoted to be consistent with what programmers commonly do; it makes the code easier for others to understand. If the attribute value contains a space, such as between flower and picture in `<img src="flower picture.jpg">`, then the value must be quoted for the code to work. This is another good reason to get in the habit of always quoting attribute values.

Just like tag names, attribute names should be set in lowercase. In Figure 5.3, the attribute name `style` is in all lowercase, but `"background-color:LightGray;"` is an attribute value, not an attribute name. Here uppercase letters are used to make the color more readable.

In the header 2 element, there is a space after `<h2` but nowhere in the rest of the element. The code would work if there was a space before and after the equal sign, but it's easier to read and code when spaces are left out, and again, this is how it is conventionally coded.

The color is identified by name (`LightGray`), but colors can also be identified by their HEX color values for red, green, and blue in the format #rrggbb, where the two-character color numbers can be any hexadecimal number between 00 and ff. For example, 550055 would be purple because it combines red and blue. The number 000000 is black, and ffffff is white. To get a pink background for the heading, we would enter:

```
<h2 style="background-color:#FF6080;">This background is pink.</h2>
```

If there is more than one attribute for an element, the attributes are separated by spaces. This often happens with images, for example `<img src="flower picture.jpg" width="100" height="150">`. Here, `src`, `width`, and `height` are all attributes of `img`.

The `<b>` tag sets whatever follows it to a bold font. In our example, `bold!` is made bold. Notice that the `<b>` tag is closed after the word `bold!`, and that's all that is bolded in the output. This is another example of nested tags. The `<b>` tags are nested inside the `<p>` tags. The `<p>` tags are for identifying paragraphs. `<p>` tags move the content that follows down to the next line and insert an empty line between paragraphs.

The break element `<br>` in Figure 5.3 is one of those empty elements we discussed earlier. It doesn't need an end tag; however, it's a good idea to put a / in the element to close it (as `<br />`), because XML and XHTML will expect it to be there in any empty element, and XML or XHTML may interact with your page someday. The `<br>` tag inserts a carriage return, like pressing the Enter key in a Word document. In the example, the first `<br />` tag puts an extra empty line between the gray line and the image that follows. Lower down in the document, it moves the text that follows it to the next line.

The second line that appears in a web page is in the `<html>` tag. By specifying this code `<html lang="en">`, you are declaring that the language used to process the page is English. By knowing whether the language of the page is a specific language such as Chinese(ze), French (fr), Navajo (nv), or Irish (ga), the browser will be able to properly execute features like spell-check, choose default fonts, and text to speech. *Language codes* are the two-character codes that identify nearly 200 different languages that can be used in HTML, as listed in the ISO 639-1 Language Codes standard.

Regional dialects can also be specified such as `<lang="en-US">` or `<lang="es-419">` to specify American English or Latin-American Spanish, respectively.

When writing in a language such as Spanish, you'll need some special characters such as the n with a ~ above it. To display these in HTML we can use escape codes, like &#241, which would be written as `Espa&#241ol`. This displays as Español.

There may be times when you need different languages for different sections of the text. The `lang` attribute is used for this as well with the `<span>` tag, such as `<span lang="ga" > Conas ata tu? Spraoi e seo. </span>` in Figure 5.3, which the browser would know to read aloud in Irish (Gaelic) using text to speech, while the rest of the document would be read in English, as specified in the `<html lang="en">` tag.

Please note that all text on the HTML page is enclosed between tags. Text should never be left on a page without being between two tags.

You may notice in Figure 5.3 code that there's a blank line between the `<body>` and `<h2>` tags. The empty space has no effect on how the page is presented by the browser, but it does make the code easier to read. If there were many lines of code and nothing to break it up, it would be very difficult to read and troubleshoot later. Indenting is also a common practice to make certain sections of code stand out. Again, they don't change how the code behaves—they are just an organizational feature. Make certain you use the spacebar, not the Tab key, when indenting. Sometimes, the Tab key adds formatting characters to your HTML file that may cause undesired results or cause the code to not work at all. I can tell you from experience that hitting that Tab key and the code not working may take hours of your time to figure out what you did wrong. The code will look correct, but it just won't work. The only way I've found to remedy the situation is to delete the affected lines of code and reenter them.

Occasionally, you'll take a great deal of time to figure out how to code something. In those instances, you'll want to put comments in your HTML code to help you remember why you wrote it the way you did. The comment tag starts with an exclamation point, such as `<!-- Working in HTML is fun. -->`. Notice in Figure 5.4 that there are two comment lines added, and neither shows up on the web page. I like to use dashes to make the comment stand out more. The second comment line is much easier to pick out of the code than the first one is. If you have problems with your code and need to fix something, you'll want to find those comment lines easily. Please note that comments should never be nested inside other tags.

FIGURE 5.4   HTML comments

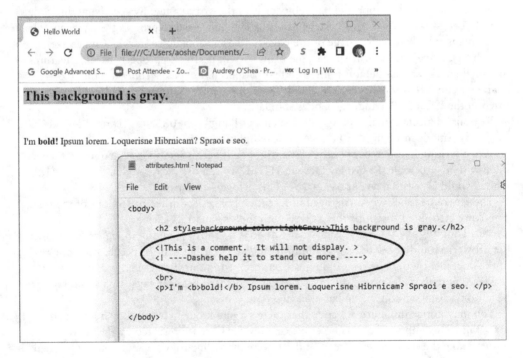

HTML Head

You've already seen that the `<title>` tag resides in the HTML head, but the head section does so much more. The other elements that are found in the head are `<base>`, `<link>`, `<meta>`, `<script>`, and `<style>`. Elements in the head provide information about the HTML page as a whole.

The `<base>` element sets a default address for page links. The `<link>` element links to another resource such as a CSS style sheet. (We'll talk more about this in Chapter 9, "Introducing CSS,") The `<script>` element is for embedding JavaScript or other executable code. (We'll explore this more in Chapter 13, "JavaScript Essentials.") And the `<style>` element is used to define attributes like color and font, but the preferred way to do this is using a CSS style sheet, which you'll learn more about in Chapter 10, "Applying CSS Styles." What we'll focus on in this chapter is the `<meta>` element.

Metadata as a general term means data about data, so the HTML *meta tag* identifies data about an HTML file. Meta tags reside in the `<head>` section of an HTML file and are useful for providing information to browsers and for search engine optimization (SEO), which can help to drive more traffic to a site, among other things.

Meta Tags

The `<meta>` tag has four attributes: `name`, `content`, `http-equiv`, and `charset`. Each of these attributes serves a specific purpose.

The meta `name` attribute describes what information is included in the `content` attribute that follows such as
`<meta name="description" content="Learning flower identification.">`.
So, in this instance, `"Learning flower identification"` is the description of the page. The description name helps a search engine understand what this page is all about. The meta description is often what you see in search results.

Here is what a head area might look like:

```
<head>
    <title>What flower is this? Identifying flowers.</title>
    <meta charset="utf-8">
    <meta name="description" content="Learn how to identify popular flower
species.">
    <meta name="keywords" content="flowers, petals, floriculture" >
    <meta name="robots" content="noindex">
    <meta name="author" content="Audrey O'Shea">
    <meta name="viewport" content="width=device-width, initial-scale=1.0">
</head>
```

The `keywords` value identifies important information that's on a page, but it has been abused in the past, so `keywords` has been depreciated by Google and has not been used for page ranking and SEO for some time.

The `robots` value is used to tell search engines how to treat the page. If robots says "noindex", then web crawlers are being asked not to index the contents of the web page, so they won't be able to provide search results based on its contents. You might want them to index only your landing page and not all the other pages to save bandwidth.

The `author` value is exactly as it sounds—it identifies the author of a page.

The `viewport` value is important to include because "width=device-width" adjusts a page for optimal viewing whether the page is viewed on a smartphone or a laptop. This tag should *always* be included in your HTML code.

Other values of the `name` attribute are `copyright`, `contact`, `application-name`, and `generator`. Know that `application-name` names the metadata, and `generator` describes the program used to create a website such as Adobe Dreamweaver or Wix.

The `http-equiv` attribute enables you to refresh the page after a time. The code looks like this: `<meta http-equiv="refresh" content="60">`, and it would refresh the page after 60 seconds. And if you've been on a website that redirects you to another page after a time, it might be using refresh a different way, for example, `<meta http-equiv="refresh" content=60; url=http://wiley.com>`, which would redirect you to `Wiley.com` after 60 seconds.

The `http-equiv` attribute can also be used to manipulate what happens with cookies on the website: `http-equiv="set cookie"`.

Character Encoding

Beneath the title is `<meta charset="utf-8">`. The `charset` attribute declares the character set to be used with the HTML page. It should always be included and should be UTF-8. The `charset` attribute should be as close to the beginning of the HTML file as possible, because the character set affects the rest of the document. Characters are the letters and numbers that you're familiar with, but also include others such as - . \ , + and letters with accents, umlauts, characters used in different languages, and so on. *Character encoding* means using a binary value to represent each individual character. *UTF-8* is the most popular character encoding set used on web pages. It is one of several that are used to represent *Unicode*, which is a standard that identifies over 1.1 million characters. Each character is called a *codepoint*.

UTF-8 needs 1 to 4 bytes to represent all the Unicode characters. UTF-16 uses either one or two 16-bit values to represent characters, and UTF-32 matches a 32-bit value to each character. It should be obvious that UTF-8 encoding would take less space than the others, which likely explains its popularity.

Specifying UTF-8 at the beginning of an HTML page helps browsers to understand how to read your page, but the document also needs to saved with this encoding. Look back at Figure 5.1 and you will see a small UTF-8 on the bottom right of the image, telling us that this document (written in Notepad) is using UTF-8. Each text editor will be different in how you set this value, but most likely default to it.

Summary

In this chapter, you learned what HTML and markup languages are. We examined the HTML skeleton's parts and defined start and end tags. Next, we looked at elements, which consist of a start tag, contents, and an end tag.

Then you learned the proper syntax for providing more information about a tag, or formatting for its contents, by using tag attributes. Some of the specific attributes we discussed were color, style, src, height, width, and lang. You learned how to enable a browser to read your page in multiple languages and how to include more than one attribute in an element.

Tags included the skeleton tags <!DOCTYPE html>, <html>, <head>, <title>, and <body>; other tags <h2>, <img>, <b>, <p>; and the empty elements <hr> and <br>. You also learned when to nest and not nest tags or elements inside others.

We examined the importance of spacing and comments in our code, even though they don't display in the rendered page.

Finally, we examined what tags need to be placed in the header of the web page, including metadata for the page and character encoding.

In the next chapter, you'll learn even more about how to make your web pages look the way you want them to.

Exam Essentials

Know the parts of the HTML skeleton. You'll use the skeleton in every page you create, so you need to know its outline, what each part of it is for, and how to create a skeleton.

Use proper syntax. If you don't use proper syntax, including tags, attributes, and comments, your code won't work the way you want it to.

Know the HTML head. Make sure you know what's in the HTML head and what the various meta tags are used for. The standards for the exam specifically mention the charset (UTF-8), name, and content attributes.

Be able to explain encoding. You need to understand what encoding is, and which one should be used in most cases (i.e., UTF-8).

EXERCISE 5.1

Create and Save Your HTML Skeleton

This skeleton will be the starting point for all your HTML pages. Once you create and save it, you can repeatedly use it.

1. In Ubuntu, click Show Applications (located at the bottom left). On the second page should be the text editor. Click it to open it.

2. Adjust the text editor so that it takes up about half of your display.

3. In the text editor, enter the following code:

```
<!DOCTYPE html>
<html>
<head>
  <title> Title goes here </title>
</head>
  <body>
  </body>
</html>
```

4. Click Save.

5. Click Create Folder and give the folder a name of your choosing, such as **HTML activities**.

6. Name the document **"skeleton.html"** and click Save.

7. Click Files. Navigate to the folder you created.

8. Right-click the file you created and choose Open With Firefox Web Browser.

9. Adjust the browser so that it covers the other half of your screen. You should see Title Goes Here on the browser tab and an otherwise blank page. Now you're ready to start writing code!

10. Click the Home folder to close it. Your screen should look similar to Figure 5.5 .

FIGURE 5.5 HTML skeleton file

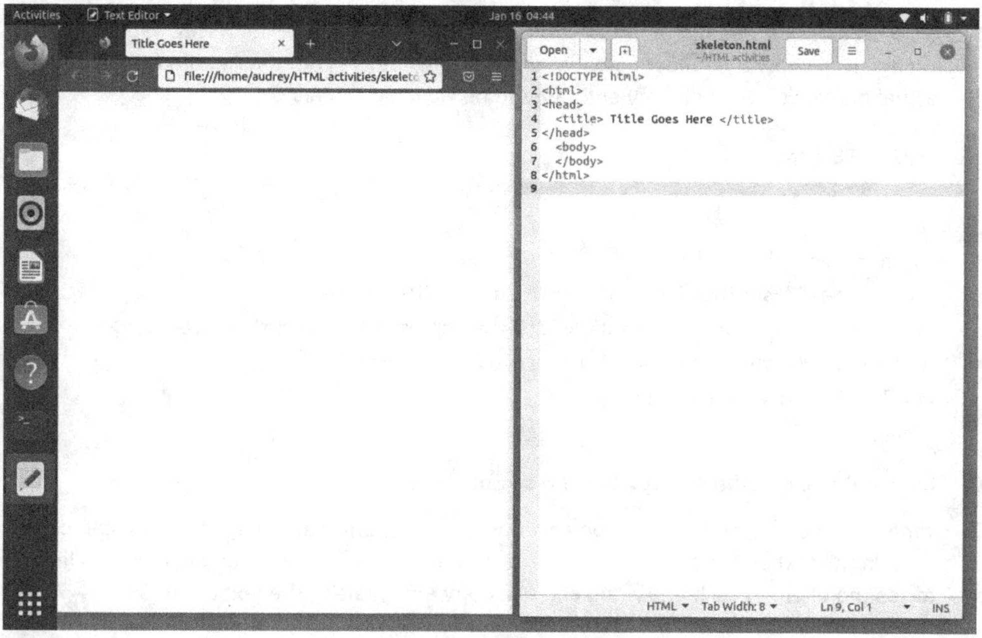

Create and Revise a Simple HTML Document

In this exercise, we'll take our HTML skeleton file from Exercise 5.1 and add some common tags, attributes, and comments. You'll also learn how to monitor it as we're making changes, so if something doesn't come out exactly as we hoped it would, we'll know right away and can adjust the code as needed.

1. Set your screen up as in the previous exercise (or continue from where you were).

2. On skeleton.html in the text editor, click the three lines to the right of Save and choose Save As. Enter **Exercise 5.2.html** in the Name box and click Save.

3. In the browser's search box, type the path and filename to your new file. For me, it is **file:///home/audrey/HTML activities/Exercise 5.2.html**. Press Enter.

4. To ensure that you have the right folder open, in the text editor change the title of the HTML page to **My First Page** or something similar. Click Save. In the browser, click the Refresh button and the web page title should change to the new title you entered.

EXERCISE 5.2 *(continued)*

5. Now, let's have some fun entering code. Go to the beginning of the HTML page and change it to show the following code, changing **"insert your name here"** to your actual name. For example, my entry would be **"Audrey O'Shea"**:

```
<!DOCTYPE html>
<html lang="en">
<head>
<meta charset="utf-8">
<meta name="description" content="My first HTML page">
<meta name="viewport" content="width=device-width, initial-scale-1.0">
<meta name="author" content="insert your name here">
<title> My First Page </title>
</head>
```

6. Click at the end of the <body> line. Press Enter twice.

7. Type the following code in the body section, pressing Enter after each line. You can click Save in the text editor, then click the Refresh button in the browser as often as you like to see the effect of each entry. You can use copy and paste in the text editor.

```
 <p>Here is some text in the body section.</p>
<h1> Heading Level 1 </h1>
<h2> Heading Level 2 </h2>
<h3> Heading Level 3 </h3>
<h4> Heading Level 4 </h4>
<h5> Heading Level 5 </h5>
<h6> Heading Level 6 </h6>
<p style="background-color:LightGreen;"> This line's background is
light green.
<b> And this is bold nested inside the paragraph.</b> Pressing enter
in the middle of the line has no effect on the output.
But putting in a break <br/> does change it.
Putting in a paragraph tag </p> <p> also changes it. </p>
<p style="background-color:#90EE90;"> This is also light green. </p>
<!--- Here is a comment that will not show. --->
<p> This paragraph is in English except where it is in Spanish as follows:
<span lang="es">Esto es Espa&#241ol.</span> … and English again. </p>
```

Your desktop should look similar to Figure 5.6 except that your colors will show as shades of gray if you're using the printed book. They should show in color online.

FIGURE 5.6 HTML practice file

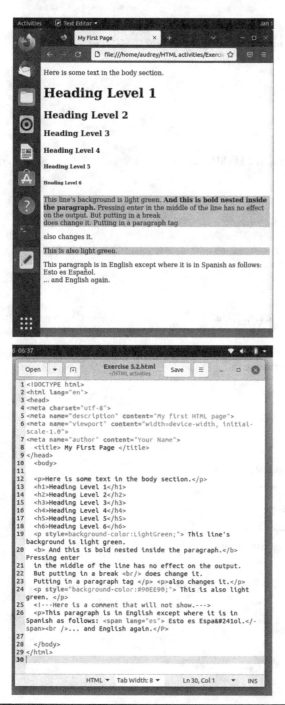

Review Questions

1. Which of the following can be used in Linux to create code for an HTML file? (Choose two.).

   A. Firefox

   B. Text Editor

   C. Vim

   D. Notebook++

2. Which of the following tags is not a part of the HTML skeleton?

   A. `<body>`

   B. `<head>`

   C. `<title>`

   D. `<meta>`

3. Which of these is a declaration and not a tag?

   A. `<!DOCTYPE html>`

   B. `<title> Hello World </title>`

   C. `style="background-color:LightGray;"`

   D. `<b>`

4. In `<meta charset=UTF-8>`, what is `charset`?

   A. Attribute

   B. Tag

   C. Contents

   D. Element

5. Which of the following is a properly nested statement?

   A. `<title> This is my page </title>`

   B. `<p> My text <b>is bold.</p></b>`

   C. `<p> My text <b>is bold.</b></p>`

   D. `<title> This is <!--enter your name--> 's page. </title>`

6. What are the attributes in
   `<img src="mountains.jpg" width="400" height="500">`? (Choose two.).

   A. `img`

   B. `src`

   C. `width`

   D. `mountains.jpg`

7. Which of the following statements is proper coding to produce a background color? (Choose two.).

   A. `<h2 style="background-color:FF6080;">`

   B. `<h2 style="background-color:#FF6080;">`

   C. `<h2 style="background-color:#LightGreen>`

   D. `<h2 style="background-color:lightgreen;">`

8. You're writing an HTML file and you need to have some content move onto the next line when the page is displayed, without inserting a blank line. What should you do?

   A. Press Enter in the HTML text file.

   B. Use the `<br>` tag.

   C. Use the `<p>` tag.

   D. Use the `<enter>` tag.

9. You're explaining to a new hire what a meta tag is used for. Which one of these is not an important use of a meta tag?

   A. Sets the site's displayed date and time

   B. Used as SEO

   C. Identifies copyright information

   D. Identifies the character encoding to use

10. You're formatting elements of a website by adding color, bold, or otherwise making the contents look different. What are you using? (Choose two.)

    A. HTML

    B. HTTP

    C. A markup language

    D. A programming language

11. What is used to identify the beginning of an HTML element?

    A. Start tag

    B. Empty element

    C. `</start>`

    D. `</html>`

12. You're using the `<br>` tag in a document. Which of these are true about the `<br>` tag? (Choose two.)

    A. It inserts a blank line.

    B. It inserts a carriage return.

    C. It is an empty element.

    D. It is an incomplete element.

13. Which two of these groups were or are involved with maintaining the HTML standards?

   A. CompTIA

   B. WHATWG

   C. Intel

   D. W3C

14. A new hire is working on a website and they want to set a heading as large as possible. Which of the following would achieve this?

   A. `<h1>`

   B. `<h6>`

   C. `<h6><span=largeFont>`

   D. `<h5 large>`

15. In the code that follows, what would be considered a value?

`<script type="module" src="new_page.js"></script>`

   A. `script`

   B. `type`

   C. `module`

   D. `src`

16. You're editing someone else's code and have noticed some errors. Which of these will you tell them should always be located on the ends of an element?

   A. Start tag and end tag

   B. Value

   C. " and "

   D. Empty element

17. You want to put a line across your page to visually separate sections. Which of the following is an empty tag that you can use for this purpose?

   A. `<p>`

   B. `<hr>`

   C. `<br>`

   D. `<area>`

18. You're setting up the head section of an HTML document. Which of these should not be there?

   A. `<title>`

   B. `<meta charset="utf-8">`

   C. `<meta name="viewport" content="width=device-width, initial-scale=1.0">`

   D. `<!DOCTYPE html>`

19. Which of the following is the only entry that will display something in a browser, even though all of them are on an HTML document?

   A. `<html lang="en-US">`

   B. `<!DOCTYPE html>`

   C. `<!-- anything here-->`

   D. `<p>Color=blue.</p>`

20. What part of a line of HTML code provides additional information to the browser about that code?

   A. Attribute

   B. Comment

   C. Element

   D. Tag

Content Markup

LINUX PROFESSIONAL INSTITUTE, WEB DEVELOPMENT ESSENTIALS EXAM 030-100 OBJECTIVES COVERED IN THIS CHAPTER:

✓ **032 HTML Document Markup**

- 032.2 HTML Semantics and Document Hierarchy: The candidate should be able to create HTML documents with a semantic structure.

  - Key Knowledge Areas:

    - Create markup for contents in an HTML document

    - Understand the hierarchical HTML text structure

    - Differentiate between block and inline HTML elements

    - Understand important semantic structural HTML elements

  - Files, terms, and utilities:

    - <h1>, <h2>, <h3>, <h4>, <h5>, <h6>

    - <p>

    - <ul>, <ol>, <li>

    - <dl>, <dt>, <dd>

    - <pre>

    - <blockquote>

    - <strong>, <em>, <code>

    - <b>, <i>, <u>

    - <span>

    - <div>

    - <main>, <header>, <nav>, <section>, <footer>

The previous chapter focused on the HTML skeleton, but in it we introduced a bit of content markup, specifically the `<p>`, `<b>`, `<span>`, `<hr>`, `<br>` tags and, in Exercise 5.2, the `<h1>` through `<h6>` tags. This chapter continues to introduce HTML markup tags. You'll learn why headings are important, how to distinguish between block and inline elements, and what hierarchical structure means. You'll also learn about lists and styles and about semantic and non-semantic elements. So, grab your note-taking tool of choice and let's get started.

The Basics

All of the elements that we'll be learning about in this chapter change how information is presented in the `<body>` section of an HTML document or help to organize that information. Identifying the structure of a web page, the sections to be formatted a particular way, and the relationship between sections of text is the essence of HTML.

An important concept in HTML is the parent/child relationship. If there is an `<h1>` tag under the `<body>` tag, then the `<body>` element is the parent and the `<h1>` element is the child. A *parent element* is one that is structurally above (and includes) other elements known as child elements. *Child elements* are those that are subordinate and attached to parent elements. A single element can be a parent to other elements *and* a child of one element. An *ancestor* is any element that is structurally above the element being considered, regardless of how many layers above it is. Finally, a *descendant* is any element that is structurally beneath and within another element.

Refer to Figure 6.1, which shows parent and child elements. Both of the `<h1>` headings are child elements to the `<body>`. Both of the `<h2>` elements are children of the `<h1>` element on the left. The `<h1>` element on the left is a parent to the `<h2>` elements and a child of the `<body>` element. The left `<h2>` element, the `<h1>` element above it, and the `<body>` element are all ancestors to the two paragraphs on the left, and the two paragraphs are descendants of the `<body>`, left `<h1>`, and left `<h2>` elements.

Now, let's examine other ways that elements can be categorized.

FIGURE 6.1   Parent and child elements

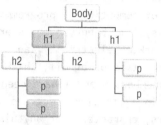

Block and Inline Elements

Block and inline elements each change the way an HTML document looks when the browser renders it, but they are essentially opposites. *Block elements* always start on a new line, add a space above and below the element, and take up as much width as possible. *Inline elements* do not start a new line or add space above or below, and they only take the space that they need within the line in which they exist.

The horizontal rule <hr> element is an example of a block element. It draws a line from left to right across the screen. The nested bold element in the line
<p>This is bold!<p> is an example of an inline element. It only affects the word *bold*.

Block Elements

Like the horizontal rule <hr> element, heading elements (<h1> through <h6>) are block elements. Refer to Figure 6.2, which shows the browser output of three different heading levels.

The <blockquote> tag is used to identify content that's quoted from somewhere else. The blockquote includes a cite:URL attribute that identifies the URL of the alternate resource. The text is usually indented automatically by the browser. Figure 6.2 shows an example of content produced using a <blockquote> tag in the following code:

```
<body>
<h1>  This is a level 1 heading. It is a block element. </h1>
<hr>
<h2> This is a level 2 heading.  </h2> <p> Block elements take the whole line
and insert spaces above and below themselves. But, the break element
<br> is an inline element and doesn't. </P>
<h3> This is a level 3 heading. </h3> <p> As heading levels go higher,
the font gets smaller.</p>
```

```
<h1>Here is a blockquote example: </h1>
<blockquote cite="https://www.cliffjumpertek.com/binary-is-fun">
If you're new to the world of computing or programming, then you many not have
heard of the binary number system. Binary numbers are what makes the computer
world go round. Computers work on electricity, and the only thing they "know"
is whether a particular circuit is on or off, which means that they only have
two states to work in. The numbers 0 and 1 have been assigned to the off and on
states, respectively.  Multiple circuits are grouped together to make larger
numbers or represent letters, characters, or anything else you see on the
screen. This is done using a code. In some computer systems, the ASCII code is
used. ASCII stands for American Standard Code for Information Interchange. In
other computer systems Unicode is used. Unicode is more versatile than ASCII,
and has characters from languages other than English. </blockquote>
</body>
```

FIGURE 6.2   Block elements

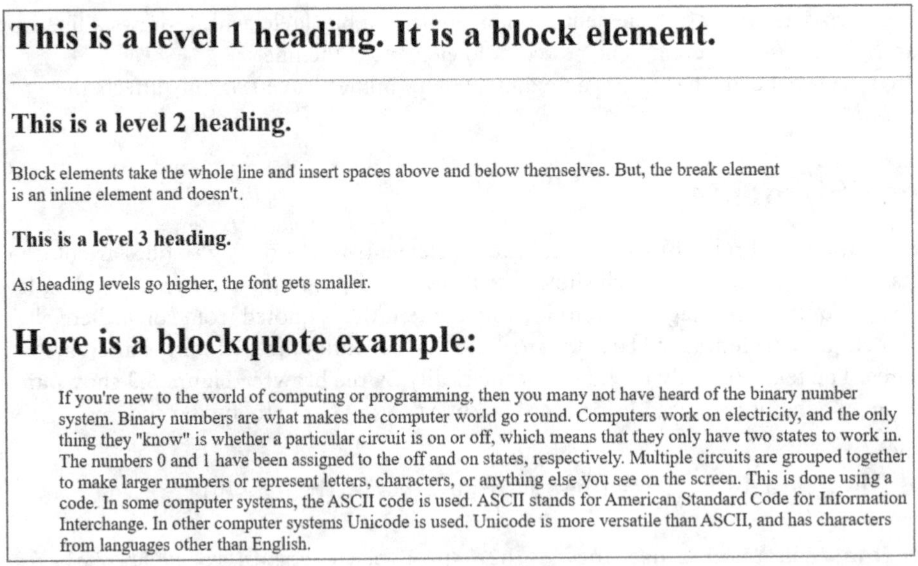

The `<div>` tag is used to identify a section of a document, usually for the purpose of applying a formatting style. For example, if you have two paragraphs that you want styled the same way, they can both be placed within the `<div>` element. Just remember that being a block element, `<div>` will add a break before and after. Figure 6.3 shows the `<div>` element being used.

The <pre> tag is also shown in Figure 6.3 and is used to identify preformatted text that will be displayed with all the spaces, line breaks, and so on, as it is entered in the HTML document. One use of this would be for preserving a poem in its format. The default for the <pre> tag is monospaced, but it can be changed using Cascading Style Sheets (CSS). The following code produces the output shown in Figure 6.3:

```
<body>

<h1> This is my heading level 1 </h1>
  <p> Here is a paragraph with some text. </p>
<div style="background-color:#D3D3D3">
  <p> This is the first paragraph. </p>
  <p> This is the second paragraph in the division. </p></div>
<p> This is another paragraph. It's not in the division.<b><br>
Notice that the two paragraphs within the division have a gray
background.</b></p>
<pre>
This is       P R e f o r m a t t e d    text.
It's preserving my spaces and line breaks.
Without having to enter code to do so.

Have a nice day.   </pre>
</body>
```

FIGURE 6.3   Division and preformatted elements

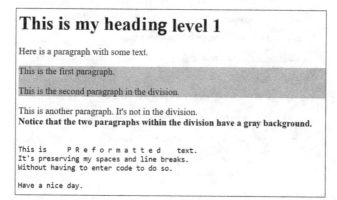

Inline Elements

Chapter 5, "HTML Introduction," discussed the <b> (bold) and <span> inline elements. Some other inline elements, the <em> and <i> tags, can both be used to italicize text. There are also two tags used to create bold text: the <b> tag and the <strong> tag.

The `<u>` tag underlines text, and the `<big>` tag will make the font one size bigger, but neither is supported in HTML 5. It's recommended that CSS be used instead.

Other tags that can be used to change the way text looks are the `<tt>` (teletype) tag and the `<kbd>` (keyboard) tag. The `<tt>` tag monospaces the text but is depreciated in HTML5, so you should use `<kbd>` instead. The last inline element we'll look at here is `<samp>`, which is intended to show computer output. These are only a few of the inline elements available.

The following code shows examples of these inline elements, and Figure 6.4 shows what the browser would render:

```
<body>
<p> Paragraph text <code>[inline code text] </code> is for showing code in a
different font. </p>
<p> We can make text <b> bold </b> using the bold or <strong> strong </strong>
tags.</p>
<p> We can <u> underline </u> or <i> italicize </i> or <u><i> both
</i></u>.</p>
<p> The emphasis tag will also <em> italicize. </em></p>
<p> The <tt> Teletype Text Element </tt> will monospace text like a teletype
machine would. </p>
<p> The keyboard tag is used to identify <kbd> Keyboard Input </kbd> on a
page. </p>
<P> The <big> BIG tag </big> is used to make the font one size bigger. </p>
<p> The samp tag is for showing <samp> [computer output].</samp></p>
</body>
```

FIGURE 6.4   Inline elements for text

Paragraph text `[inline code text]` is for showing code in a different font.

We can make text **bold** using the bold or **strong** tags.

We can <u>underline</u> or *italicize* or *<u>both</u>*.

The emphasis tag will also *italicize.*

The `Teletype Text Element` will monospace text like a teletype machine would.

The keyboard tag is used to identify `Keyboard Input` on a page.

The **BIG** tag is used to make the font one size bigger.

The samp tag is for showing `[computer output].`

Hierarchical Structure

Hierarchical structures exist wherever the relationship between something's parts (or people) could be diagrammed into a pyramid shape, with a main idea or leader at the top, and increasingly larger subordinate layers beneath. Consider this book. The title describes the book, which is broken down into chapters for the big ideas, and then each chapter is further divided into sections for each topic and paragraphs, each with its own concept. Hierarchical structure helps us to make sense of something large, whether it's a book, a document, a network, or a large corporation. Hierarchical structure helps us find the information we need.

Websites are structured the same. Figure 6.1 shows the hierarchical structure of a sample website. People scan websites in a few seconds relying on headings to determine if the page has what they need. Knowing that, the wording you choose for a website's headings becomes very important.

Structuring website content makes it easier and more pleasant to read, but it also helps search engines index the page better, which means better search engine optimization (SEO), bringing the right people to your website. Search engines use heading content as keywords, so although you could use formatting to make text look like headings, you shouldn't. It's important to use the <h1> through <h6> headings that search engines are looking for.

Level 1 headings are the largest, and therefore, most important, with each larger heading number creating a smaller font heading. Although there are six heading levels available, best practice dictates that you should only use three levels on a single page and that there should be only one level 1 heading per page. If you find that you need more heading levels, consider whether the content should be broken into multiple pages.

Lists

Sometimes you'll simply want to list items on a page. Lists may be unnumbered (unordered) lists, numbered (ordered) lists, or perhaps even a glossary of terms and definitions. HTML tags exist to do all of that.

Unordered lists <ul> and ordered lists <ol> contain list items <li>. As with other tags, unordered list <ul>, ordered list <ol>, and list item <li> must have end tags.

Unordered lists have bullet points to identify list items. Imagine you're building a website for a company that posts recipes including their product. The following code section could be used for one of the recipes on their page:

```
<hr>
<h1> Old Fashioned Custard </h1>
<hr>
<ul> <h2><b> Ingredients <b></h2>
  <li> 6 large eggs from O'Shea Farms </li>
  <li> 3 cups milk< /li>
  <li> 1 teaspoon vanilla< /li>
  <li> 1 cup of sugar </li>
  <li> 1 cup craisins </li>
  <li> 1-1/2 cups of cooked rice, any variety </li>
  <li> dash of salt </li>
  <li> cinnamon and nutmeg to sprinkle </li>
</ul>
```

And the code's output would look like Figure 6.5.

FIGURE 6.5   Unordered list

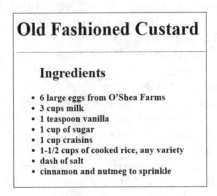

Ordered lists are those that use numbers to identify items. Let's assume we have a numbered list of steps for making the recipe in Figure 6.5. The code could be written as follows, with two unordered lists nested within the ordered list. Pay close attention to when the <li> are ended. If an unordered list is nested in the ordered list, then the parent <li> isn't ended (</li>) until after the <ul> is ended.

```
<ol><h2><b>  Instructions  <b></h2>

<li> Preheat Oven to 350 degrees. </li>
<li> Butter an 8 x 8 baking dish. </li>
<li> Crack the eggs into the baking dish and lightly whisk. </li>
<li> Add the following items and stir until well incorporated:
   <ul>
     <li> milk </li>
     <li> vanilla </li>
     <li> sugar </li>
   </ul>
</li>
<li>Add the following ingredients and stir in lightly:
   <ul>
     <li> craisins</li>
     <li> rice </li>
     <li> salt </li>
   </ul>
</li>
<li> Sprinkle cinnamon and nutmeg on top to taste. </li>
```

```
<li> Set the baking dish inside a larger dish and fill the larger <br> dish
1/2 full of water. </li>
<li> Bake for 1 hour and 45 minutes or until knife inserted <br> in the center
comes out clean. </li>
</ol>
```

The code's output is shown in Figure 6.6

An HTML *description list* is a list of terms with their relative descriptions. As mentioned, a glossary can be created in HTML. It's accomplished by using description list <dl>, description term <dt>, and description definition <dd> tags. An example of description list code follows, and the output is shown in Figure 6.7.

```
<dl>
  <dt> Panthera </dt> <dd> A genus of large wild cats in the Felidae family.
</dd>
  <dt> Tiger <dt> <dd> A panther with stripes. </dd>
  <dt> Lion </dt> <dd> A panther with a large mane. </dd>
  <dt> Leopard </dt> <dd> A panther with spots. </dd>
</dl>
```

FIGURE 6.6   Ordered list with nested items

Instructions

1. Preheat Oven to 350 degrees.
2. Butter an 8 x 8 baking dish.
3. Crack the eggs into the baking dish and lightly whisk.
4. Add the following items and stir until well incorporated:
   ○ milk
   ○ vanilla
   ○ sugar
5. Add the following ingredients and stir in lightly:
   ○ craisins
   ○ rice
   ○ salt
6. Sprinkle cinnamon and nutmeg on top to taste.
7. Set the baking dish inside a larger dish and fill the larger dish 1/2 full of water.
8. Bake for 1 hour and 45 minutes or until knife inserted in the center comes out clean.

FIGURE 6.7   Description list

Panthera
    A genus of large wild cats in the Felidae family.
Tiger
    A panther with stripes.
Lion
    A panther with a large mane.
Leopard
    A panther with spots.

Styles

Styles are groups of formatting applied to HTML content by using CSS to define the visual settings such as text color, size, and font. (The CSS side of this process will be explained in Chapter 9, "Introducing CSS.") HTML marks up the text with tags such as `<h1>` and `<p>`, while all the styles used on an HTML page are typically held in the associated CSS file.

In HTML, two ways we can define the area to be styled are by using the `<div>` block element and the `<span>` inline element. Figure 6.3 shows the `<div>` element being used. The `<span>` element is used similarly, but it is an inline element, and as such, it won't take the entire width of the page or put an empty line before or after it is used. The following code shows how each might be used:

```
<div><p> Here is some text to be formatted.  It is inside a block
element so it will take the entire width available and insert
spaces before and after.
</p>
<p> It can even be used to style more than one paragraph at a time </p>
</div>

<p> The span element is similar and could be used to style multiple
paragraphs, but because it is an inline element, it can be used to style
<span> just this piece </span> without affecting the rest of the paragraph.
```

Semantic and Non-Semantic Elements

Semantics deals with meanings. Therefore, *semantic elements* are those elements where the element name describes the meaning of the information related to it. *Non-semantic elements* do not convey any information about their content with their name.

Examples of semantic elements are `<mark>`, which highlights (or marks) content, and `<p>`, which tells the browser and anyone reading the code that it is paragraph text.

Non-Semantic Elements

Examples of non-semantic elements that we've used in this chapter are `<div>` and `<span>`. Neither of these elements explains what their content is or how it is to be formatted. Their content could be anything, in fact. These elements merely identify areas of content.

Semantic Structural Elements

Some semantic elements are *structural semantic elements*, which identify specific sections of an HTML document and their purpose. For example, when we (or a browser) see the `<nav>` element, we know the content associated with it is for navigating the document. Using semantic elements helps us to make sense of an HTML document, rather than having a plethora of `<div>` or `<span>` tags. Following is a rundown of some of the more popular structural semantic elements:

- The `<header>` element appears at the top of the page and may have a company logo, name, and so on. It may also have `<h1>` elements.

- The `<footer>` element appears at the bottom of an HTML document. A typical footer found on many websites like the one at www.wiley.com/en-us has links to a site map, rights and permissions, a privacy policy, and the terms of use, and shows copyright information.

- The `<nav>` element was mentioned previously. In it, you'll typically find links to other pages or significant parts of a website, perhaps even a related website. The `<nav>` bar across the top of www.cliffjumpertek.com shows Home, About, Books & Courses, Arduino, and some learning resources.

- The `<main>` element identifies the main content and/or ideas of a page. It will not be a descendant of other elements such as articles, sections, or asides. Its parent will be the `<body>` element.

- The `<article>` element identifies content that could stand on its own. It can be reused on its own independently of the rest of the website or web page.

- The `<section>` element is similar to an article, but unlike an article it is not intended to be used independently of the web page or site that it is on.

- The `<aside>` element contains further information on something else, much like the blocks you'll see in the margins of many textbooks. It is related to but not a part of the content near it.

Summary

In this chapter, we looked at different ways that HTML is organized, using parents and children and ancestors and descendants. Elements can be block elements or inline elements depending on how they affect the data related to them. We examined hierarchical structure, why headings are so important, and different types of lists. You learned that styles can be applied using `<span>` or `<div>`, and whether elements are semantic or non-semantic depending on whether the element name conveys meaning.

Twenty-five new tags were introduced in this chapter.

Exam Essentials

Know the markup tags.   Practice using them and remember what they're for. It will help you as you code, and it will help you pass the certification exam!

Explain hierarchical structure.   Understanding the hierarchical structure, why it's important, and how to use it will make your coding more efficient and effective and help you avoid mistakes.

Be able to identify block and inline elements.   If you know whether an element is block or inline, then you'll know how it will affect the finished page.

Know the semantic elements.   Using semantic elements is a best practice when designing your website.

Create an HTML Page to Demonstrate Hierarchy

This exercise will give you practice working with parent and child elements.

1. Use your text editor to open the HTML skeleton that you saved from Exercise 5.1, Create and save your HTML Skeleton, in Chapter 5, and save it as **exercise 6_1.html**. Right-click the saved `exercise 6_1.html` file, choose Open with, and select your browser. Set the browser to one half of your screen and place the text editor on the other half. Now you're ready to code and check the results as you go along.

2. Enter the following lines of code so your file is as follows:

```
<!DOCKTYPE html>

<html lang="en-us">

<head>

  <title> Parents and Children </title>
  <meta charset="utf-8">

</head>

<body>
<h1> Learning hierarchy.  Only one level 1 heading should be on a page.
Every line below me is a descendant. Body is my parent. </h1>

  <h2> (First h2)  I am a child of "Learning hierarchy" and body is my
ancestor. </h2>
    <p> (P1)  I am a child of "First h2" above.  </p>
    <p> (P2)  I am also a child of "First h2" above </p>

  <h2> (Second h2) I am a child of "Learning hierarchy" and body is my
ancestor. </h2>
    <p> (P3)  I am a child of "Second h2" above.  </p>

    <h3> (First h3)  Even though I am a heading, I'm a child of "Second
h2" above.
```

```
    "Learning hierarchy" and "body" are my ancestors. I am <em>not</em>
    a descendant of "First h2."</h3>

        <p>(p4) I am a child of "First h3" and a descendant of "First h3",
    "Second h2", "Learning hierarchy" and "body"</p>

        <p>(p5) I am a child of "First h3" and a descendant of "First h3",
    "Second h2","Learning hierarchy" and "body"</p>

        <p>(p6) I am a child of "First h3" and a descendant of "First h3",
    "Second h2","Learning hierarchy" and "body"</p>

</body>

</html>
```

3. Save your HTML file, then refresh your browser and view the result.

4. Create a hierarchy document for this page, like the one shown in Figure 6.1, labeling each block with numbers such as (p5) as shown in the code.

5. See the Answer section to view the browser output and the hierarchy diagram.

ANSWER:

The browser should show Figure 6.8.

FIGURE 6.8   Exercise 6.1 Browser output.

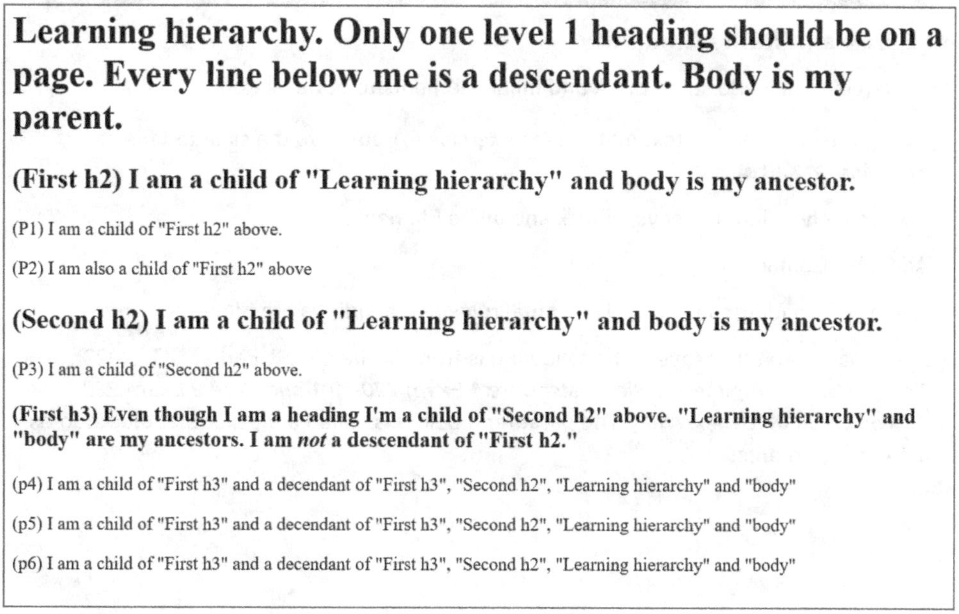

Learning hierarchy. Only one level 1 heading should be on a page. Every line below me is a descendant. Body is my parent.

(First h2) I am a child of "Learning hierarchy" and body is my ancestor.

(P1) I am a child of "First h2" above.

(P2) I am also a child of "First h2" above

(Second h2) I am a child of "Learning hierarchy" and body is my ancestor.

(P3) I am a child of "Second h2" above.

(First h3) Even though I am a heading I'm a child of "Second h2" above. "Learning hierarchy" and "body" are my ancestors. I am *not* a descendant of "First h2."

(p4) I am a child of "First h3" and a descendant of "First h3", "Second h2", "Learning hierarchy" and "body"

(p5) I am a child of "First h3" and a descendant of "First h3", "Second h2", "Learning hierarchy" and "body"

(p6) I am a child of "First h3" and a descendant of "First h3", "Second h2", "Learning hierarchy" and "body"

EXERCISE 6.1 *(continued)*

The hierarchy diagram should look like Figure 6.9.

FIGURE 6.9 Exercise 6.1 Hierarchy diagram.

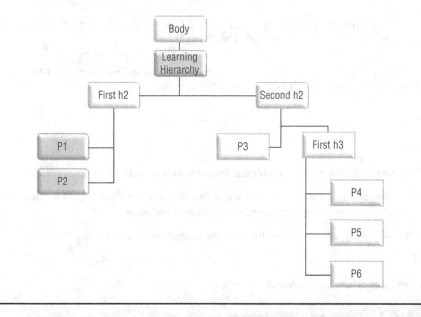

EXERCISE 6.2

Add Block and Inline Elements

In this exercise, we'll add some block and inline elements to our skeleton.

1. Set up the browser and text editor as in Exercise 6.1 but save the skeleton file as **exercise 6_2.html**.

2. Add an h1 heading that says, "Block and Inline Elements."

3. Add a horizontal rule.

4. Add an h2 heading that says, "Horizontal rules and headings are block elements."

5. Add a paragraph that says, "The following is from O'Shea, A., & Parker, J. T. (2022). *CompTIA A+ Complete Practice Tests: Core 1 Exam 220-1101 and Core 2 Exam 220-1102* (3rd ed., p. 600). Sybex/Wiley. The paragraph below is called a blockquote. Blockquotes are block elements."

6. Add a blockquote citing "(O'Shea & Parker, 2022, p. 600)."

The contents of the blockquote are "There are two places to configure a VPN in Windows 10 and 11. Go to Control Panel ➢ Network and Sharing Center, and select Set Up A New Connection Or Network, or go to Settings ➢ Network & Internet, and select VPN. The Windows Mobility Center has settings for mobile devices, and Personalization enables the user to change background, lock screen, and color schemes."

7. Put the following two paragraphs in a division. Set the background color of the division to light blue. The HTML Hex code for light blue is ADD8E6.

Add a paragraph that says, "This paragraph is part of a division."

Add a paragraph that says, "It encompasses two paragraphs."

8. Add a horizontal rule.

9. Add a paragraph that says, "The quoted poem that follows is called 'The Road Not Taken' written by Robert Frost in 1915."

10. Use the preformat code to enter the following poem snippet, observing where each line ends.

"Two roads diverged in a yellow wood,

And sorry I could not travel both

And be one traveler, long I stood

And looked down one as far as I could

To where it bent in the undergrowth;"

Add a horizontal rule.

11. Add a paragraph that says, "Inline elements don't take the entire line they are on. Instead they only take as little space as they need." Use inline elements to make "entire" italicized, "only" underlined, and "little" bold.

12. Add another paragraph that says, "This is computer output. This is keyboard input. The big tag makes text one size bigger." Use the appropriate tag to make each sentence look like computer output, keyboard input, and one size bigger.

13. Save your file, then check your code and output in the Answer section. To conserve space we'll only show the body section of the code.

ANSWER:

The browser output should be that shown in Figure 6.10, but remember that colors will show as different shades of gray in the printed version.

FIGURE 6.10 Exercise 6.2 Browser output.

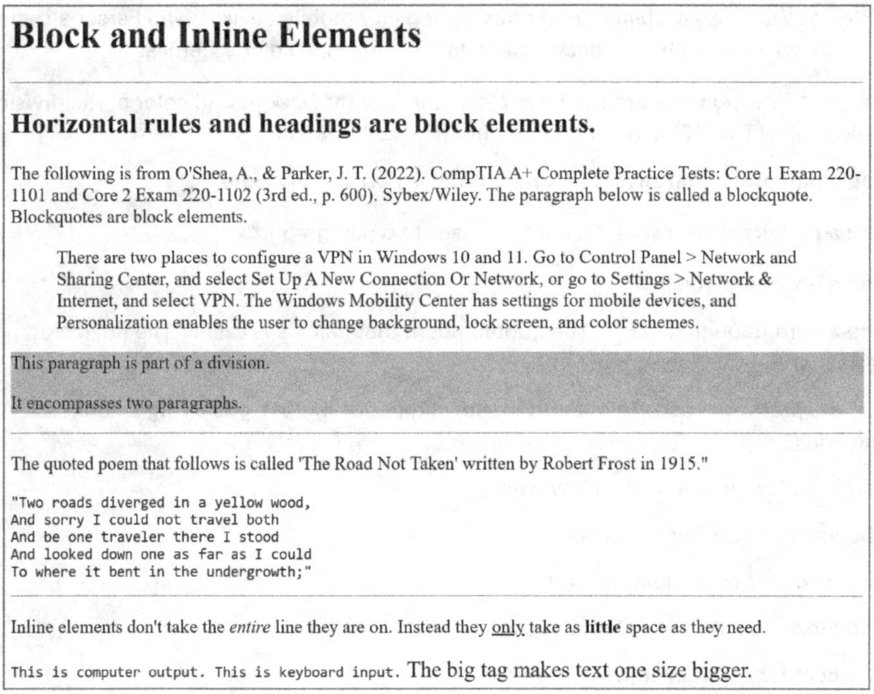

Block and Inline Elements

Horizontal rules and headings are block elements.

The following is from O'Shea, A., & Parker, J. T. (2022). CompTIA A+ Complete Practice Tests: Core 1 Exam 220-1101 and Core 2 Exam 220-1102 (3rd ed., p. 600). Sybex/Wiley. The paragraph below is called a blockquote. Blockquotes are block elements.

> There are two places to configure a VPN in Windows 10 and 11. Go to Control Panel > Network and Sharing Center, and select Set Up A New Connection Or Network, or go to Settings > Network & Internet, and select VPN. The Windows Mobility Center has settings for mobile devices, and Personalization enables the user to change background, lock screen, and color schemes.

This paragraph is part of a division.

It encompasses two paragraphs.

The quoted poem that follows is called 'The Road Not Taken' written by Robert Frost in 1915."

```
"Two roads diverged in a yellow wood,
And sorry I could not travel both
And be one traveler there I stood
And looked down one as far as I could
To where it bent in the undergrowth;"
```

Inline elements don't take the *entire* line they are on. Instead they <u>only</u> take as **little** space as they need.

`This is computer output.` `This is keyboard input.` The big tag makes text one size bigger.

The code should be as follows:

```
<body>

  <h1> Block and Inline Elements </h1>
<hr>
  <h2> Horizontal rules and headings are block elements.</h2>
<p> The following is from O'Shea, A., & Parker, J. T. (2022). CompTIA A+
Complete Practice Tests: Core 1 Exam 220-1101 and Core 2 Exam 220-1102
(3rd ed., p. 600). Sybex/Wiley.  The paragraph below is called a blockquote.
Blockquotes are block elements.
</p>
```

```
<blockquote cite="""(O'Shea & Parker, 2022, p. 600)">
There are two places to configure a VPN in Windows 10 and 11. Go to Control
Panel > Network and Sharing Center, and select Set Up A New Connection Or
Network, or go to Settings > Network & Internet, and select VPN. The Windows
Mobility Center has settings for mobile devices, and Personalization enables
the user to change background, lock screen and color schemes.

</blockquote>

<div style="background-color:#ADD8E6">
<p>This paragraph is part of a division.</p>
<p> It encompasses two paragraphs.</p>
</div>

<hr>

<p> The quoted poem that follows is called 'The Road Not Taken' written by
Robert Frost in 1915."</p>
<pre>
Two roads diverged in a yellow wood,
And sorry I could not travel both
And be one traveler there I stood
And looked down one as far as I could
To where it bent in the undergrowth;"
</pre>
<hr>

<p> Inline elements don't take the <em>entire</em> line they are on.
Instead they <u>only</u> take as <strong>little</strong> space as they need.
</p>
<p><samp>This is computer output.</samp><kbd> This is keyboard input.
</kbd><big>  The big tag makes text one size bigger.</big>
</p>

</body>
```

EXERCISE 6.3

Add Lists

It's time to practice creating ordered, unordered, and description lists.

1. Set up the browser and text editor as in Exercise 6.1 but save the skeleton file as
   exercise 6_3.html.

   To make this exercise a bit easier, we'll use content that you can copy and paste to
   save time.

EXERCISE 6.3 *(continued)*

2. Create an unordered list of the following items. Make the list title "Unordered Lists" with a heading level 3.

   Block Elements

   Inline Elements

   Semantic Elements

3. Create an ordered list of the same items, but make the title "Ordered List" with a heading level 3.

4. Under the block elements in the ordered list, insert a list of three block elements as a nested list.

5. Create a description list of the previous items, adding a description of each term—for example, an unordered list is "a bulleted list of items."

6. Save your HTML file, then open it in a browser. Check your code and output in the Answer section. To conserve space, we'll only include the body section of the code.

ANSWER:

The browser output should be that shown in Figure 6.11.

FIGURE 6.11 Exercise 6.3 Browser output.

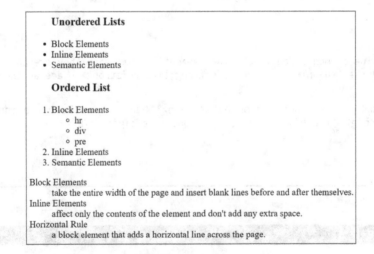

The code should be as follows:

```
<body>

<ul><h3> Unordered Lists </h3>
  <li> Block Elements </li>
  <li> Inline Elements </li>
  <li> Semantic Elements </li> </ul>

<ol><h3> Ordered List </h3>
  <li> Block Elements
    <ul>
        <li> hr </li>
        <li> div </li>
        <li> pre </li>
    </ul></li>
  <li> Inline Elements </li>
  <li> Semantic Elements </li> </ol>

<dl>
<dt> Block Elements</dt><dd> take the entire width of the page and insert
blank lines before and after themselves. </dd>
<dt> Inline Elements</dt><dd> affect only the contents of the element and
don't add any extra space. </dd>
<dt> Horizontal Rule </dt><dd> a block element that adds a horizontal line
across the page. </dd>
</dl>

</body>
```

EXERCISE 6.4

Use Semantic Elements to Structure a Web Page

In this exercise, we'll create a page with navigation and other semantic elements.

1. Set up the browser and text editor as in Exercise 6.1 but save the skeleton file as **exercise 6_4.html**.

2. In the body section, enter the following code, making sure to save your file when finished:

```
<body>
<hr>
<a name="top">
```

EXERCISE 6.4 *(continued)*

```
<header>Working with Semantics </header>
<hr>
<nav>
<p><b>Navigation:</b></p>
<a href="#bottom"> Go to Bottom </a>
</nav>
<hr>

<main>
The main section will contain all the content of my webpage. In this chapter
we looked at different ways that HTML is organized. There are parents and
children, ancestors and descendants. Elements can be block elements or inline
elements depending on how they affect the data related to them. We examined
hierarchical structure, why headings are so important, and different types of
lists. We learned that styles can be applied using span or div, and finally
whether elements are semantic or non-semantic depending on whether the element
name conveys meaning. <br>
Twenty-five new tags were introduced in this chapter.

</main>
<hr>
<section> A section is similar to a division. It can't stand alone like an
article. </section>
</hr>

<a name="bottom"><footer> My legal stuff goes here. I need to put several
lines of text so that I can tell when my page jumps here.
<a href="#top">Top of Page</a>
</footer>


</body>
```

3. Open the HTML file in your browser. Adjust the browser window so that you can only see about half (vertically) of the browser page at a time. At the top of the page, click Go To Bottom. This will take you to the footer of the document.

4. From the footer, click Top Of Page to go back to the top of the document.

Review Questions

1. In the code snippet that follows, which item is a parent of the heading that says "Here is a blockquote example"?

```
<body>
<h1>  This is a level 1 heading.  It is a block element. </h1>
<h2> This is a level 2 heading.  </h2>
<p>Block elements take the whole line and insert spaces above and
below themselves. But, the break element <br> is an inline element and
doesn't </P>
<h3> This is a level 3 heading.  </h3> <p> As heading levels go higher,
the font gets smaller.</p>

<h2>Here is a blockquote example: </h2>
<blockquote cite="https://www.cliffjumpertek.com/binary-is-fun">
If you're new to the world of computing or programming, then you may not
have heard of the binary number system. </blockquote>
```

   A. This is a level 1 heading.

   B. This is a level 2 heading.

   C. This is a level 3 heading.

   D. body.

2. What type of element is horizontal rule `<hr>`?

   A. Inline

   B. Child

   C. Block

   D. Ancestor

3. You are working on a web page that keeps separating a paragraph into two parts, and you don't want it that way. In the paragraph, you've used an `<h6>` tag to make part of the paragraph bold. Why isn't your page working as you want it to? (Choose two.)

   A. The `<h6>` tag adds a line break.

   B. You can't make just part of a paragraph bold.

   C. The `<h6>` tag is an inline element.

   D. The `<h6>` tag is a block element.

4. Given the following code, why are `third thing` and `fourth thing` indented on the browser output? (Choose two.)

```
<ol> List name
  <li> first thing
  <li> second thing
<ul> Unordered list
```

```
<li> third thing
<li> fourth thing
```

   A. The list items are not ended.

   B. The ordered list is not ended.

   C. They are nested.

   D. Unordered lists are always indented.

5. You want to apply the same style to multiple paragraphs. Which of the following options are best to use? (Choose two.)

   A. `<span = <b><i>> content here. </span>`

   B. `<span<p>Text here. </p><p> Another paragraph here. </p></span>`

   C. Use CSS.

   D. `<div> <p>Text here. </p><p> Another paragraph here. </p></div>`

6. You have some content that is complete in itself, and you want other people to be able to refer to it on its own. Which of the following tags is the most appropriate to use to identify that content?

   A. `<article>`

   B. `<main>`

   C. `<section>`

   D. `<aside>`

7. Which of the following is *not* an inline element?

   A. `<b>`

   B. `<br>`

   C. `<p>`

   D. `<samp>`

8. Which of the following tags will *always* be an ancestor to other tags that are used in creating website content?

   A. `<body>`

   B. `<h1>`

   C. `<p>`

   D. `<a>`

9. Which of these are block elements? (Choose two.)

   A. `<h1>`

   B. `<div>`

   C. `<span>`

   D. `<tt>`

10. Which term means that the structure can be diagrammed into a pyramid shape with multiple layers?

   A. Semantic

   B. Structured

   C. Hierarchical

   D. Ordered

11. Which of these do you need for a list that is numbered? (Choose two.)

   A. `<li>`

   B. `<ol>`

   C. `<ul>`

   D. `<dt>`

12. What is the preferred place to define styles of formatting?

   A. At the paragraph level

   B. On each line

   C. HTML

   D. CSS

13. What semantic structural element would you use to include information on a website that is indirectly related to the website's content?

   A. `<nav>`

   B. `<main>`

   C. `<aside>`

   D. `<note>`

14. Which of the following elements moves the content after it to the next line and inserts a blank line?

   A. `<p>`

   B. `<div>`

   C. `<br>`

   D. `<hr>`

15. What should you consider doing if you have more than one `<h1>` heading on a page?

   A. Break the page into multiple pages.

   B. Renumber your headings.

   C. Use more heading levels like 4, 5, and 6 to break up the content.

   D. HTML won't let you put more than one `<h1>` heading on a page.

16. You want to identify an area of text to be styled. The text includes more than one paragraph. Which of the following is the *best* tag to use?

    A. `<h1>`

    B. `<span>`

    C. `<div>`

    D. `<p>`

17. You're going to quote another content creator on your website. What tag allows you to indent the entire quote and cite the author?

    A. `<cite blockquote=""https://www.mysite.com">`

    B. `<quote>`

    C. `<indent quote>`

    D. `<blockquote cite="https://www.mysite.com ">`

18. You want your headings to stand out so that visitors can scan the major topics easily. Which is the *best* option?

    A. Use `<b>` and `<big><big><big>`.

    B. Use the appropriate heading levels based on the content.

    C. Use CSS to style the headings.

    D. Use the `<samp>` tag.

19. Which of these heading levels produces the largest font?

    A. `<h6>`

    B. `<h4><b>`

    C. `<h2><big>`

    D. `<h1>`

20. Which of these can have nested items? (Choose two.)

    A. `<dl>`

    B. `<ol>`

    C. `<ul>`

    D. `<q>`

Chapter

7

References and Embedded Resources

LINUX PROFESSIONAL INSTITUTE, WEB DEVELOPMENT ESSENTIALS EXAM 030-100 OBJECTIVES COVERED IN THIS CHAPTER:

✓ **032 HTML Document Markup**

- 032.3 HTML References and Embedded Resources: The candidate should be able to link an HTML document with other documents and embed external content, such as images, videos and audio in an HTML document.

  - Key Knowledge Areas:

    - Create links to external resources and page anchors

    - Add images to HTML documents

    - Understand key properties of common media file formats, including PNG, JPG and SVG

    - Awareness of iframes

  - Files, terms, and utilities:

    - id attribute

    - <a>, including the href and target (_blank, _self, _parent, _top) attributes

    - <img>, including the src and alt attributes

This chapter is a relatively short but very important one. If you want to make your web pages dance and sing, you need to know how to embed all sorts of media files and link to both internal and external resources. In addition, you'll need to know how to change the attributes of those files. In this chapter, you'll also learn what purpose iframes serve.

Page Anchors

If you did Exercise 6.4, "Use Semantic Elements to Structure a Web Page," you have used an anchor. The *anchor tag <a>* defines a hyperlink whether it's on the same page, a different page of the same website, or an entirely different website.

Linking to a place on the same page is a two-step process. First, you must use the global *id attribute* to identify a section of text where you intend the hyperlink to take the user. Then you must create a hyperlink in the document where the user will click to go from that spot to the section identified with the id attribute. *Global attributes* such as id, style, and title are attributes that can be applied to all HTML elements.

To illustrate page anchors, let's pretend this chapter is your web page. Perhaps we want a hyperlink to each section. First, you name the sections using the id attribute such as `<h1><a id="title"> References and Embedded Resources </a></h1>`. This id attribute identifies the topmost header of the page as title. You would also set up an id for each section where it begins. For example, for the first section you'd set up `<h2><a id="page-anchors"> Page Anchors</a></h2>`, then the next section `<h2> <a id="section2"> External Resource Links </a></h2>`, and so on.

Often sections are identified with section numbers, but if each section has a title, using that title will be less confusing. (Both are illustrated in the previous paragraph.) If you were simply linking to another location without a header, then you could simply use an anchor such as `<a id="bottom"> </a>` without any text in the element.

To use the anchors that you created in the previous paragraph, you must create a hyperlink reference. The href attribute of the anchor tag creates a hyperlink to another resource. At the top of the page, you could create a navigation bar using the semantic elements you learned about in Chapter 6, "Content Markup." For example, you could place the following code as the first item in the body:

```
<nav>
 <a href="#title">[Go to Title]</a>
 <a href="#page-anchors">[Go to Page Anchors]</a>
```

```
<a href="#section2">[Go to Section2]</a>
<a href="#bottom">[Go to Bottom]</a>
</nav>
```

The previous code results in the navigation bar located at the top of the image in Figure 7.1. Note that the square brackets are not a part of the code. They are simply there to help visually separate the hyperlinks. The words `Go to` could also be omitted because they are only there to enhance readability. Clicking any hyperlink at the top of the page will take you to that section of the text.

FIGURE 7.1   Navigation bar

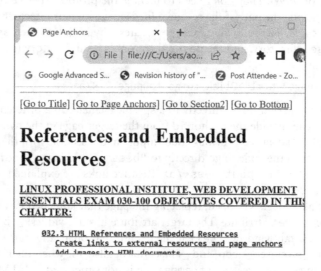

In the first paragraph `id` (`id="page-anchors"`), there is a dash between the words. An `id` must *not* contain empty spaces. You can use a dash or underscore instead, but dashes are preferred because Google and other search engines see them as word separators. Underscores are not treated as word separators.

A second rule to note is that the `id` is case-sensitive. If you use the anchor `<a id="bottom">` and then try to link to it with `<a href="#Bottom">Go to Bottom</a>`, your hyperlink will not work.

Now that you know how to create a hyperlink to other places in the same document, let's create hyperlinks to resources that are not located on the same page.

External Resource Links

External resource links bring our reader to another page on the same website or another website. As with hyperlinks on the same page, you'll use the `<anchor>` tag and `href` attribute. For external links, there's no need to create an anchor on the external resource. In fact, if the resource is on another website, you might not have access to create an anchor there. For example, the following code creates a hyperlink to the list of eTextbooks and courseware on `Wiley.com`:

```
<a href="http://wiley.com Explore textbooks and courseware on Wiley.com</a>
```

The Uniform Resource Locator (URL) in the previous line of code is considered an absolute URL. *Absolute URLs* point to an entirely different website than the one you're on and contain the full path to that resource. The parts of a URL were identified in Chapter 2, "Client/Server Computing."

Code like the following is called a relative URL. *Relative URLs* point to a file that is on the same website or server. They don't need to include the protocol (HTTP or HTTPS), but they do need to include the path if the resource file is in a different directory than where the current page is located. The following example creates a hyperlink to the `page2.html` file that is in the `pages` directory, and the `pages` directory is a subdirectory (child) of the one we are currently in:

```
<a href="pages/page2.html">Click to go to page 2.</a>
```

If you want the hyperlink to go directly to a specific element on a different page of your website, you can include the anchor `id` from the target page in the hyperlink. For example, if `page2.html` in the previous code snippet had a section with the anchor `id` of `<a id="bees">`, then the code to go directly to `"bees"` would be `<a href="/pages/page2.html#bees">All about Bees</a>`. Relative links are explained more in the sections that follow.

By default, a linked page will open, replacing the page that launched it. This can be changed with the `target` attribute. The target attribute has five values: `_blank` opens the linked page in a new tab/window; `_self` is the default that opens the frame in the same tab; and the last three, `_parent`, `_top`, and `_framename`, all work when the browser window is divided into frames. However, the `<frames>` tag is not supported in HTML 5, so what you need to remember is that if you want the linked page to open replacing the current page, you don't need to do anything. If you want the linked page to open in a separate tab, you must use the `_blank` value of the target. In that case, your code might look like this: `<a target="_blank" href="page2.html"> Open Page 2</a>`.

Using Images

Let's admit it. A web page would be boring without some images or graphics to enhance the page's story. Readers expect to see some images on your page, not just text. When you add an image to a page, the image is said to be *embedded* in the page. An *embedded image* is an image that becomes a part of a web page.

The *img* Tag and Its Attributes

Images are easy to add to your web page using the image `<img>` tag and source (`src`) attribute. The image tag does not need to be closed. You'll also want to use the alternate (`alt`) attribute to include some alternate text so that browsers that don't support your image type or that can't open it for any reason will display some descriptive text to users (for example, `<img src="scribble.jpg" alt="Picture of a scribble.">`.) Figure 7.2 shows the result of a *broken link*, which occurs when the web page can't find or open a file.

FIGURE 7.2   A broken link

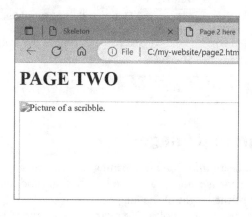

We can also specify how large we want this image to appear by including height and width attributes like this: `<img src="scribble.jpg" alt="Picture of a scribble." height="400" width="600">`. The width and height are expressed in pixels.

You'll want to use relative links when adding images to a web page so that the links will still work when you copy the web page onto another local machine or a web server. The exact way to use a relative link depends on where the image is relative to the page you're working on. Figure 7.3 shows the various configurations of relative links to a file named `lake.jpg`.

The `<a>` tag and `href` attribute can be used with an image, turning the image into a clickable link. A *clickable link* is any text or image that when clicked executes a hyperlink to another page or a place in the same page. To use an image as a clickable link, simply nest the image between the two `<a>` tags. The syntax is
`<a href="link address"><img src="image to use"></a>`.

In the following example, we're using a picture of a lake that's in the `images` subfolder of our web page, to click and take the user to a website for making camping reservations. Alternate text and size for the image are also included.

```
<a href="https://newyorkstateparks.reserveamerica.com">
<img src="/images/lake.jpg" alt="Picture of a lake" width="400" height="300">
</a>
```

FIGURE 7.3   Relative links

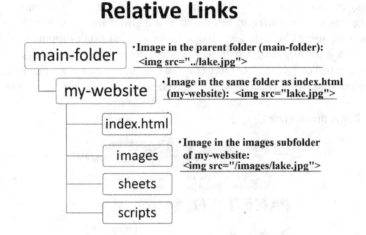

Inline or Background Images

An embedded image can be an *inline image*, meaning that the image is literally on the same line as the text where its code is entered, or it can be a background image. If an image is inline, then the line will be the height of the image (e.g.: `<p> This is an image of Lake Ontario. <img src="lake-ontario .jpg"> It is inline with the text. </p>`).

In HTML, you can change the position of the image by placing it anywhere in the line of text. A better method, though, is to "float" the image to the left or right side of the page, using CSS. (You'll learn about CSS in Chapters 9 through 12.) Figure 7.4 shows inline images in HTML. The code that produced Figure 7.4 follows:

```
<p><img src="left.png" width="100" height="50"> This image is inline at the left.</p> <br>
<p> Any line will take the full height of an inline image. <br>This image is inline <img src="middle.png" width="50" height="50"> in the middle of the line. </p>
<p>This image is inline at the right of the line.  <img src="right.png" width="100" height="50">
```

Background images can be specified for an element or for the entire page and appear behind the element's text. To specify a background image, use the `<style>` attribute. The following example uses a picture of food as the background for a paragraph:

```
<p style="background-image: url('food.jpg');">
```

Then enter the paragraph text and end the paragraph as normal with the `</p>` tag.

FIGURE 7.4   Inline images

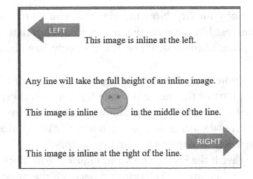

To specify the background for the entire page, the `<style>` for the body is entered in the heading as follows. Figure 7.5 shows the result, which includes an image of Lake Ontario behind the `<body>` text.

```
<head>
<title> Background Images </title>
<style>
  body, html {
    background-image: url("lake-ontario.jpg");
  }
</style>
</head>
<body>
Body text goes here.
</body>
```

FIGURE 7.5   Background image

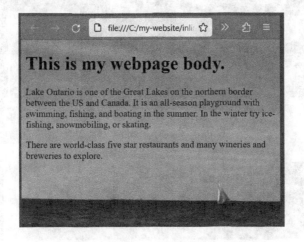

Image Maps

Imagine if you will, a map of your city. Now imagine that you go to a website that has that map showing points of interest like a movie theater or a museum that, when you click them, tell you more about that point of interest. Have you ever wondered how that is done? You're about to find out.

Image maps are images where objects in the image have been named and linked to some resource so that when that part of the image is clicked, the user is taken to the resource. The HTML <map> and <area> tags enable a programmer to choose areas of an image and make them clickable links. The <name> attribute is used to identify the sections of the map. The <usemap> attribute connects the image and the image map.

Assume you're working with the image shown in Figure 7.6, and its filename is inventory.jpg. First, you'll create the relationship between the image and the image map with <img src="inventory.jpg" alt="Items" usemap="#inventory-map">.

FIGURE 7.6   Clickable image with marked points

Now you need to create the image map using the name attribute to link it to the <img> line of code. The entry is <map name="inventory-map">.

Next, you need to identify the clickable areas of the image. The image is 890 pixels wide by 980 pixels high. You'll need software that will enable you to see a grid of your picture or otherwise provide coordinates. The clickable areas must be defined by the coordinates on the image and by shape. The available shapes are circle, which identifies a circle; rect, which identifies a rectangle; poly, which identifies a polygon; and default, which identifies the entire image.

If you're working in Windows, the software paint can show the image in pixels. Coordinates of where your mouse is will appear on the bottom-left of the screen. If you're working in Linux, try using GIMP, Geegie, or pinta (sudo apt-get install pinta). I prefer to use pinta. The coordinates of your cursor appear on the top right.

Let's start with a circle. First, we need to know the coordinates (x, y). In Figure 7.6, a woven basket is located toward the bottom of the image. It's not exactly a circle but close. The center coordinates are 248, 895 and the radius is 100 pixels. Our clickable area will be slightly larger than the basket due to its shape. Look at the white circle surrounding the basket in Figure 7.6. To identify the basket, enter the following code to mark the shape, position, alternate text, and, of course, what clicking it will open, whether it's a website, another page, or another place on this page. In our example, it opens another file called basket.html:

```
<area shape="circle" coords="248, 895, 100" alt="Woven Basket"
href="basket.html">
```

Rectangles are equally simple. Consider the book on the bottom right in Figure 7.6. The top-left coordinates are 658, 627 and the bottom-right coordinates are 849, 858. To make it clickable, we could use the following code:

```
<area shape="rect" coords="658, 627, 849, 884" alt="Heide Erdrich book"
href="Heide Erdrich book.html">.
```

Figure 7.6 uses a white rectangle to identify the clickable area for the book.

The polygon shape is used for those that require multiple coordinate points. If we want to make the woven bowl in the figure more precise, we can use multiple points for each edge. We could also use poly for the art piece located above the books, but that would require 144 sets of coordinates—one for each corner of each piece of wood. For the sake of brevity, we'll examine the bowl. The bowl's coordinates in the figure are marked with white dots, starting from the top left and going clockwise around the bowl, and they provide a much more precise clickable area than the circle does. If you were going to use the polygon shape for your basket, you would not use the circle code as well; you'd choose one or the other. The code then would be:

```
<area shape="poly" coords="154,848,171,833,199,829,229,824,255,822,293,823,
321,826,354,845,350,883,334,895,310,906,269,917,227,918,186,915,157,903,
145,874" alt="Woven bowl" SPihref="basket.html">
```

The `poly` shape draws straight lines between the coordinates. There is no need to repeat the first coordinate at the end either. Of course, our reader would not see the points around the clickable items—they would only see the image.

File Formats

Being familiar with the types of graphic files and knowing their advantages and disadvantages will save you time and perhaps some frustration when creating a website. You'll know what type of file you have based on the file extension. (File extensions were explained in Chapter 1, "Web Development Basics.")

Image files can be either raster or vector type. *Raster files* are designed to work at a specific resolution and don't scale up or down well. Raster images that are scaled up or down can be blurry or lose their crispness. *Vector files* can be scaled up or down easily because their data is stored as text. No single file type is good for every situation. Every graphic file type has its advantages and disadvantages, which are explained next.

Portable Network Graphic (PNG) files are raster files that support transparent backgrounds and can take advantage of over 16 million colors. PNG files don't lose any of their detail when compressed. On the downside, they are much larger than GIF or JPG file types, so they have slower page-loading times when used on web pages. They also don't transfer well to print. They are a popular choice for logos because of their transparent background support.

Joint Photographic Experts Group (JPG or JPEG) files are raster files and are universally recognized and compatible with a wide range of uses and tools. Like PNG files, they can take advantage of over 16 million colors. JPG files are a smaller size than PNG files, though, so they don't suffer slower loading times like PNG files do. Unlike PNG files, however, some of the quality of JPG files is lost when they are compressed.

Graphics Interchange Format (GIF) files are another type of raster file. The biggest advantage of GIF files is that they can be animated. Another advantage is that they don't lose detail when compressed. The downside of GIF files is that they only have 256 available colors, which means images might be low resolution or look blurry. They are certainly not good for use in high-resolution photography. On a slower Internet connection, they could look particularly bad.

Scalable Vector Graphics (SVG) files are vector files, so they can be easily scaled up or down without the loss of quality. SVG files use points and mathematical formulas to draw images. They store files as text, not shapes, which means that search engines can read them and that might help boost your search engine optimization (SEO). A downside of SVG files is that they can only use 147 colors.

The *<iframe>* Tag

An inline frame `<iframe>` tag is used to specify a rectangular frame that will be used to display another HTML document in the current HTML document. The document displayed can be another page of the same website or an external resource such as a YouTube video or another website. Here again we need to be conscious of whether we're using relative or absolute URLs.

Global attributes and event attributes are both supported by the `<iframe>` tag. *Event attributes* enable an HTML element to react to what the user is doing, such as `onclick`, which reacts to a mouse click. You'll learn more about event in Chapter 16, "The DOM."

A typical `<iframe>` element might be something like `<iframe src="page2.html" title="What it's about" width="200" height="150" style="border:3px solid black;">`.

By default, an `<iframe>` has a thin border. The `style` attribute is used to change the border. We can also specify no border by using `style="border:none;"` in the element.

Just like there is alternate text for an image, we'll want text to display if the browser won't open our frame for any reason. Instead of using the `alt` attribute, simply nest the text into the iframe: `<iframe src="page2.html" width="300" height="200"> <p> iframe not supported</p></iframe>`.

Figure 7.7 shows an example of `<iframe>` in use. It shows the default border. There are scroll bars on the side and bottom because the page doesn't fit completely in the `<iframe>` window. The code used to create that frame is `<iframe src="page2.html" width="300" height="200">`.

FIGURE 7.7   An iframe in a page

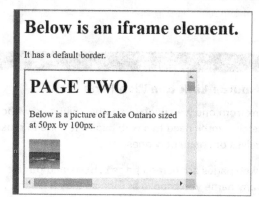

Summary

In this chapter you learned how to create a hyperlink to a different place on the same page, another page, or another website using the anchor `<a>` tag. You also learned what global and event attributes are, and how to use the hyperlink reference `href` and `id` attributes.

The `target` attribute changes how a resource opens, and the `<iframe>` tag can be used to create a window on your page to display a linked resource.

We added images and backgrounds using the image tag `<img>` and source `src` attributes, then examined the different types of image files and the advantages and disadvantages of each. The `alt` attribute is used to provide alternate text for those times that an image can't be opened or when using a browser reader. We also turned an image into a hyperlink and created an image map to put several clickable image links into a single image.

Exam Essentials

Know how to link to other documents. Websites are seldom single-page affairs, so it's important for you to know how to link one page to another.

Know how to link within documents. People are going to expect shortcuts to get to other parts of your page if it's more than one screen long.

Be adept at adding images. What is a web page without any images? Probably not very exciting. Make sure you know how to add images to your web page.

Understand file formats and iframes. Different file formats are for different purposes. Make sure you're familiar with the common file extensions for all multimedia and how to use iframes.

EXERCISE 7.1

Add an External Resource Link to a Web Page

In this exercise, you'll link from one web page to another, with and without opening a new browser tab. For this exercise you'll need two web pages. It's fine to reuse ones that you've created in previous exercises or create new ones.

1. We'll assume your web pages are named page1.html and page2.html, but of course they can be any name you choose as long as they have the .html extension. Make sure there is some different content at the top of each page so you can easily tell which one you're in, and ensure that page1.html and page2.html are in the same folder on your computer.

2. Open page 1 and page 2 in a text editor.

3. In page1, add this hyperlink: `<a href="page2.html">Click to go to page 2.</a>`.

4. In page 2, add this hyperlink: `<a href="page1.html">Click to go to page 1.</a>`.

5. Open page 1 in a browser. You should see a clickable link that says, "Click to go to page 2."

6. Click the link to page 2. Page 2 should replace page 1 in the browser.

7. In page 2, there should be a clickable link that says, "Click to go to page 1." Click the link to return to page 1.

Next, we'll add a hyperlink to open page 2 in a separate tab of the browser.

8. Open page 1 in a text editor. Add a new hyperlink including the `target` attribute as follows: `<a target="_blank" href="page2.html">[Page 2 tab]</a>`.

9. Open page 1 in a browser and click the `[Page 2 tab]` link to verify that page 2 opens in a new browser tab.

ANSWER:

The clickable link on page 1 should take the reader to page 2 in the same tab. The clickable link on page 2 should take the reader to page 1 in the same tab. The second hyperlink on page 1 should open page 2 in a new tab.

EXERCISE 7.2

Add Page Anchors to a Web Page

In this exercise you'll use the anchor tag and `href` attribute, but this time we'll add the `id` tag to move to a different place on the same page. For this exercise you'll need a web page that has at least two paragraphs that are fairly long so that you can see when you jump from one to the other. Either use an existing page or create a new one.

1. Open your web page in a text editor.

2. At the top of the page, in the `<body>` section, enter the following code: `<h1> <a id="top">This is the top of the page </a></h1>`. Ensure that the tags are nested properly.

3. At the beginning of the first paragraph, add the following code to name the paragraph: `< a id="section1"></a>`. Remember that there must be no blank spaces in your `id` name.

4. At the beginning of the second paragraph, add the following code to name the paragraph: `< a id="section2"></a>`.

5. At the bottom of the page, still within the `<body>` section, enter the following code: `<h3> <a id="bottom"> Thank you for visiting my page! </a><h3>`.

6. Above the `<h1>` heading, enter a hyperlink reference to the bottom of the page:
    `<h3><a href="#bottom"> [Bottom of Page]</a><h3>`.

7. Somewhere near the top of the first paragraph, choose a word to use as a link to paragraph 2. For example, if paragraph 1 is about bees and paragraph 2 is about bee hives, you may have a sentence that says, " Bees live in bee hives." You could link to paragraph 2 by entering the following code on that line:
    `Bees live in <a href="#section2">bee hives.</a>`. Bee hives will be a different color and clickable.

8. Create a hyperlink at the top of the second paragraph that goes to the bottom of the page.

9. Create a hyperlink at the bottom of the page that goes back to the top.

10. Test all the hyperlinks to ensure that they work as expected.

    ANSWER:

    The last two hyperlinks should be similar to the following:

    Top of second paragraph: `<a href="#bottom">some text here.</a>`

    Bottom of page: `<a href="#top">[Top of Page]</a>`

All hyperlinks when clicked should take the reader to their respective places.

Add Images to a Document

In this exercise we'll add inline images to a document and put a background on an element. For this exercise you'll need at least two images with a `.jpg` or a `.png` extension. One of them should be fairly light in color so the text can be seen on it.

1. In a text editor, either open an existing web page or open your skeleton and create a new one.

2. In the `<body>` section of the page, enter the following lines, replacing the filenames `left.png`, `middle.png`, `right.png`, and `picture.jpg` with the filenames of your images.

```
<p> <img src="left.png" width="100" height="50"> This image is inline at the
left.</p> <br>
```

```
<p> Any line will take the full height of an inline image. <br>This image
is inline <img src="middle.png" width="50" height="50"> in the middle of the
line. </p>
```

```
<p>This image is inline at the right of the line. <img src="right.png"
width="100" height="50">
```

3. Next, create a short paragraph of text, perhaps like this:

```
<p> This is the paragraph of text <br>that I'm putting a background behind.
<br>    I enjoy working with HTML</p>.
```

4. Now, modify the first paragraph tag to embed the background behind the paragraph:

```
<p style="background-image: url('picture.png');">This is the paragraph of text
<br>that I'm
```

putting a background behind.
 I enjoy working with HTML.</p>

ANSWER:

The first section should look like Figure 7.8.

The embedded background paragraph should look similar to this graphic:

FIGURE 7.8   Text with image behind.

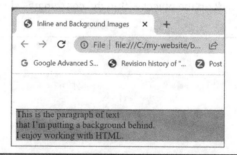

EXERCISE 7.4

Create and Use an Image Map

In this exercise we'll create an image map. For this exercise you'll need an image that has objects or regions that can be identified visually by some boundary (like a picture of a box, a drawing of several shapes) and software that will show the measurement of the object in pixels. You'll also need at least one resource that you want the click to open, such as page2.html. This activity assumes that all your files are in the same folder. Ensure that the image you're using will fit in your web page. If it's too big, resize the image before you start. If you change the size in your HTML file by specifying **width=** and **height=**, then the coordinates you see in your graphics program won't match the image in the HTML file.

1. Start with your skeleton file, opened in a text editor.

2. Insert an image into the file using the following command but replace *my.png* with your image file's name:

    ```
    <img src="my.png" usemap="#my-map">
    ```

3. Link the image to the map with the following command:

    ```
    <map name="my-map">
    ```

4. Use your graphics program to identify the coordinates of an item in the image that you want to make clickable. I suggest you start with a rectangular image. Jot down the coordinates at the top left of the rectangle, such as 8,106. Jot down the coordinates at the bottom right of the rectangle, such as 61,147. When you have the coordinates, enter the following line in your HTML file, replacing my coordinates (8, 106, 61, 147) with the ones for your image, and *page2* with the resource you want the click to open:

    ```
    <area shape="rect" coords="8, 106, 61, 147" href="page2.html">
    ```

5. Save your HTML file and open it with a browser. Test the page by clicking the link to ensure it will open the requested resource.

ANSWER:

Answers will vary, but a click on the object within the coordinates should open the requested resource.

Review Questions

1. Which tag defines a hyperlink?

    A. `<a>`

    B. `<id>`

    C. `alt`

    D. `href`

2. You need to create a hyperlink from your website to a website on a different domain. What type of URL will you use?

    A. Absolute

    B. Domain

    C. Relative

    D. Semantic

3. What attribute must always be used with the `<img>` tag?

    A. `width`

    B. `height`

    C. `alt`

    D. `src`

4. You want to make objects on a picture into clickable links. The name of the picture file is `projects.jpg`. What two of the following lines will be needed first? (Choose two.)

    A. `<img.src="projects.jpg" alt="projects" usemap="#project-map">`

    B. `<map name="project-map">`

    C. `<a href="project.jpg">Projects</a>`

    D. `<map id="project.jpg">`

5. Which of these file formats is not a raster type of file?

    A. GIF

    B. JPG

    C. PNG

    D. SVG

6. Which tag is used to specify a window to another HTML page or resource within the current HTML page?

    A. `<href>`

    B. `<style>`

    C. `<iframe>`

    D. `<window>`

7. You want a background image to appear behind the text on your entire web page. In which section will you put the line of code `background-image: url("myimage.jpg")`?

    A. `<head>`

    B. `<title>`

    C. `<body>`

    D. `<html>`

8. What are attributes that can be used with any element called?

    A. Absolute

    B. Global

    C. Relative

    D. Semantic

9. In this code

```
<a href="pages/page2.html">Click to go to page 2.</a>
```

where is `page2.html` in relation to the `pages` folder?

    A. `page2.html` is within the `pages` folder.

    B. The pages folder is a parent to the folder `page2.html` is in.

    C. The pages folder is a child to the folder `page2.html` is in.

    D. pages is the name of the website that `page2.html` is on.

10. Which two attributes of the `<img>` tag have a value expressed in pixels? (Choose two.)

    A. `alt`

    B. `height`

    C. `src`

    D. `width`

11. You need to create an image map. Which of these is not an element required to create an image map?

    A. `area`

    B. `href`

    C. `img`

    D. `map`

12. Which of these file formats support over 16 million colors? (Choose two.)

    A. GIF

    B. JPG

    C. PNG

    D. SVG

13. You're creating a web page and want to put a picture at the end of a line of text. Which of the following are true? (Choose two.)

    A. You can't put a picture on the right unless you use CSS.

    B. You would insert **<img src="image.png">** at the end of the line of text.

    C. You must set the image as a background image to get it there.

    D. The line of text will take the full height of the image, not flow around the picture.

14. What attribute of the <img> tag determines where an embedded external link will open?

    A. `href`

    B. `frames`

    C. `target`

    D. `pages`

15. You need code that will allow you to click a link and go to paragraph 4 of the same web page. Which of the following would be needed to do that for you? (Choose two.)

    A. `<a href="#pageAnchors">[Go to paragraph4]</a>`

    B. `<a href="#paragraph4"> [Go to paragraph4]</a>`

    C. `<a href="#paragraph 4"> [Go to paragraph4]</a>`

    D. `<a id="paragraph4"></a>`

16. You want a hyperlinked page named `Arduino-projects.html` to open in a separate tab of the browser. Which of the following will do that?

    A. `<a href="arduino-projects.html"> [Arduino Projects]</a>`

    B. `<a target="_blank" href="arduino-projects.html">`
    `[Arduino Projects]</a>`

    C. `<a target="_blank" href="arduino projects.html">`
    `[Arduino-Projects]</a>`

    D. `<a target="_top" href="arduino-projects.html">`
    `[Arduino-Projects]</a>`

17. You run a recipe website and want visitors to your site to be able to click on their choice of food pictures and be taken to the menu for that dish. Your images are in a subfolder of the `webpages` folder called `pictures`. The `webpages` folder contains all of your HTML files. Which of the following lines of code will work? (Choose two.)

    A. `<a href="pastarecipe.html" ><img src="/pasta.jpg/pictures"></a>`

    B. `<a href="pastarecipe.html" ><img src="/pictures/pasta.jpg"`
    `alt="Picture of Pasta"></a>`

    C. `<a href="pastarecipe.html" ><img src="/pictures/pasta.jpg"></a>`

    D. `<a href="pastarecipe.html" width="300" height="100"><img src="/`
    `pictures/pasta.jpg"></a>`

18. You're creating an image map. How do you tell the program what part of the image to use as the clickable link area?

    A. Provide coordinates in x,y format.

    B. Use a mouse to circle the area.

    C. Provide measurements in inches.

    D. Chop the image file into several files and assemble it on the screen so that it looks like one image.

19. You're creating a website that needs some graphics. Since there will be many pictures on your page, you're concerned about page load times, but you also want the color to be as rich and detailed as possible. What would be the best file type to use?

    A. GIF

    B. JPG

    C. PNG

    D. SVG

20. What will the code `<iframe src="flowers.html" title="Flowers of the Congo" width="400" height="300">` do?

    A. Puts the current web page into a window of the `flowers.html` web page

    B. Frames an image of flowers in the current web page

    C. Creates a window in the current HTML page that shows the `flowers.html` page and has a 400×300-pixel border around it

    D. Creates a window in the current HTML page that shows the `flowers.html` page and has a narrow, default border around it

Creating HTML Forms

LINUX PROFESSIONAL INSTITUTE, WEB DEVELOPMENT ESSENTIALS EXAM 030-100 OBJECTIVES COVERED IN THIS CHAPTER:

✓ **032 HTML Document Markup**

- 032.4 HTML Forms: The candidate should be able to create simple HTML forms containing input elements of various types.

  - Key Knowledge Areas:

    - Create simple HTML forms

    - Understand HTML form methods

    - Understand HTML input elements and types

  - Files, terms, and utilities:

    - \<form>, including the method (get, post), action, and enctype attributes

    - \<input>, including the type (text, email, password, number, date, file, range, radio, checkbox, hidden) attribute

    - \<button>, including the type (submit, reset, hidden, button) attribute

    - \<textarea>

    - Common form element attributes (name, value, id)

    - \<label>, including the for attribute

- 031.3 HTTP Basics

  - Key Knowledge Areas:

    - Understand HTTP GET and POST methods

In this chapter, you'll learn how to create an input form to capture visitor information, build a mailing list, get feedback, and a host of other common activities that require forms. This chapter covers the front-end, but for many forms there is also work on the back-end of the website, such as code that is run when a button is pressed, or a database that collects and holds information. Follow along and you'll be creating forms very soon!

Anatomy of an Input Form

Input forms go in the <body> section of your web page. An *input form* enables the owner of a website to request information from the website user. The three tags you need to remember are <form>, <label>, and <input>. The <form> tag also has an end form </form> tag and defines the area of your web page that is the input form. It is possible to have multiple forms on a page. The <label> tag tells the system which input box you're giving this label to and tells the user what the input box is for. It also has an end tag. The <input> tag describes and identifies the type of input for which this input box is being used. It doesn't need an end tag.

Figure 8.1 shows the result of the following code:

```
<body>
<h3>Enter your information to receive our newsletter! </h3>
<form>
<label for="first">Your first name is:</label>
<input type="text" name="first" id="first"><br><br>
</form></body>
```

FIGURE 8.1 A simple input form

You'll need to include the `for` attribute in the label line, and `name` and `id` attributes in the input line as in the previous example. The value of `for=" "` in the `<label>` element matches the value of `id=" "` in the `<input>` element to link the label and the input box. The value for `name=" "` is used to identify that piece of data when it's sent to a server, because if you're getting input, you're going to store or manipulate it in some way and you need a server to do that.

The `id` value identifies the element on the page, and the `name` value identifies the element within the form. Each `id` value must be unique on the page, and each `name` value must be unique in a form. The best practice is to use descriptive names instead of numbers here. You'll find that using meaningful names will make the coding process easier.

The input `type=" "` attribute determines how the input area looks and what the input can be. Various types are explained in the next section.

If you have multiple forms on the same page, you may want to name each form by changing the `<form>` tag to include a name `<form name= "sign_up">`. The `<form>` tag supports global and event attributes.

You'll want to put a break—`<br>` (or two)—after each input line so that the description for the next box will go to the next line. This makes your form neater and easier to read.

Commonly Used Attributes

Perhaps the most used attribute of the `<input>` tag is `type=" "`. The *type attribute* determines the data format the user can input, and its value can change the appearance of the input box. Several attributes of `<input>` will be discussed in the following sections, but here we'll examine the `type` attribute and its values along with a couple of other attributes that are often used with it.

The default if no type is specified is a text box, which will look like the one shown in Figure 8.1.

If `<input type="date">`, then a date selection box will pop up when the user clicks the calendar icon on the input box. The data would be in the form of mm/dd/yyyy and the code to produce that line is as follows:

```
<label for="w-date"> Wedding date: </label>
<input type="date" name="wedding_date" id="w-date"><br><br>
```

If the day of month is not important, the input line `<input type="month" id="month_and_year" name="month">` could be used. The text box and date selection box look a bit different. If you wanted to know the week of the year, simply replace `"month"` with `"week"` in the previous line of code. Again, the date selection box will look slightly different, as shown in Figure 8.2, and will provide a week number instead of month/day/year.

FIGURE 8.2 Date options

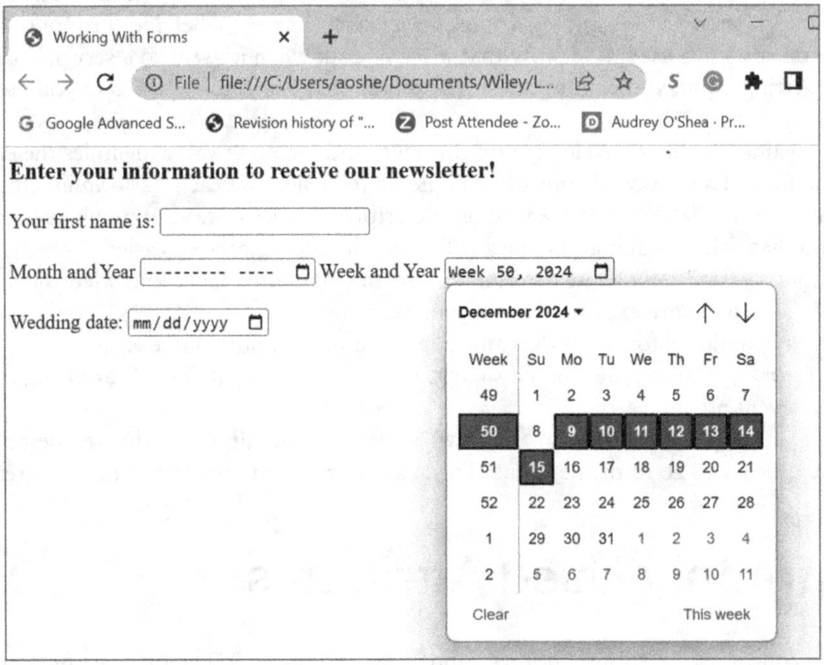

Often when signing up for access to a website, you'll be asked for an email address and password. The email type `<input type="email">` provides a text box for input, but also performs a validation check to ensure that the at symbol (@) is included in the box. Different browsers will handle it differently, but the user might get an error message when they press Enter if they haven't entered an @ symbol or a top-level domain (`.com`, `.org`, `.edu`, and so on) in the text box. To add the ability to enter multiple addresses in the email text box, simply add the `multiple` attribute to the code line. `multiple` is a Boolean attribute that allows for more than one of something, as in the following code:

```
<input type="email" id="email_list" name="email_list" multiple>
```

The text box for an email address looks like any other text box, so you may want a placeholder to suggest to the user what the input should look like. A *placeholder* is part of the input line that will show as grayed text, suggesting to the user what their input should look like. The entry for an email placeholder could be `placeholder="yourname@something .com"` (see Figure 8.3). You may also want to require the user to enter their email or phone number. In that case, add the `required` attribute to the input line. The lines of code to produce the output for the email input section of the form shown in Figure 8.3 are as follows:

```
<label for= "email_list"> What's your email address? </label>
<input type="email" id="email_list" name="email_list"
placeholder="yourname@something.com" multiple required><br><br>
```

Figure 8.3 shows the output of the Chrome browser when the email address is required and it has not been entered when the user submits the form.

FIGURE 8.3   A required email

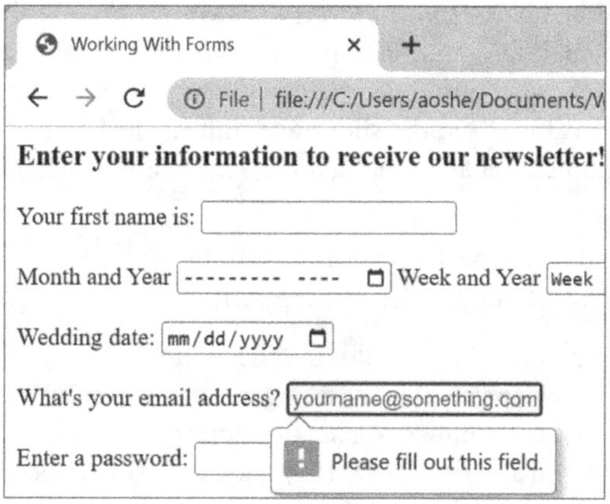

When `<input type="password">`, the text box will hide the input with the familiar dots as the user types.

The `<input type="number">` value specifies that the input for the box is a number. Not only that, but you can specify minimum and maximum values to input, a default value, and a step interval if desired. When the number input box is selected, it will display up and down arrows on the right to select values. A default value can be displayed but overwritten by entering a number or using the scroll buttons (see Figure 8.4). Depending on the device, and particularly on mobile devices, when the focus is set to the number box a numeric keypad might be displayed. Let's assume you want to ask the user to input their age. Your code might be:

```
<label for="user_age"> Your age:</label>
<input type="number" id="age" name="user_age" min="10" max="120"
value="21"><br><br>
```

FIGURE 8.4   Passwords and numbers

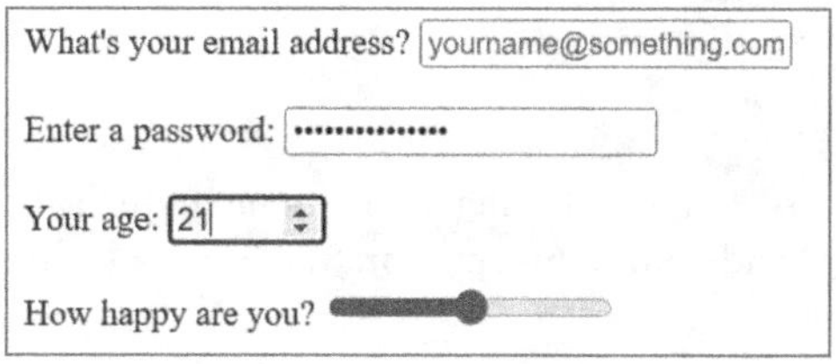

The age would default to 21 but could be overwritten using the scroll arrows or by typing in the box. The lowest value is 10 and the highest value is 120.

Perhaps you would like to display a slider bar for a user to choose from. *Sliders* enable a user to drag a marker on a horizontal bar between a minimum and maximum to the desired value. They work well in situations where a number doesn't need to be precise. Adding a slider is easily accomplished using type="range". Just like the number value, options for the range value can include minimum, maximum, default value, and step interval specified, but when using the range type, you'll need to set the minimum and maximum value for your slider. If no default value is set, the slider will appear in the middle of the range. Let's assume you want a happiness scale. Look again at Figure 8.4. The code for the happiness slider is:

```
<label for="happy"> How happy are you? </label>
<input type="range" id="happy" name="happy" min="0" max="10"><br><br>
```

If you wanted the user to be able to upload a file, you would use the "file" value for input type. A file type can be specified by entering an accept attribute where the values are specific file types separated by commas, such as accept=".jpg, .png", or using image/* means any image file, and video/* and audio/* are any video and any audio file, respectively. As with email, if you want the user to be able to choose multiple files, include the attribute multiple in the code. Adding multiple to the input will cause the Choose File button to change to Choose Files. Clicking the Choose File(s) button will open a file picker window. The following code was used in Figure 8.5. When a file is chosen, the words "No file chosen" will be replaced with a filename.

```
<label for="your_file"> Choose the file to submit. </label>
<input type="file" id="yourFile" name="userfile" accept="image/*"
multiple><br><br>
```

FIGURE 8.5   Files, phones, and hidden elements

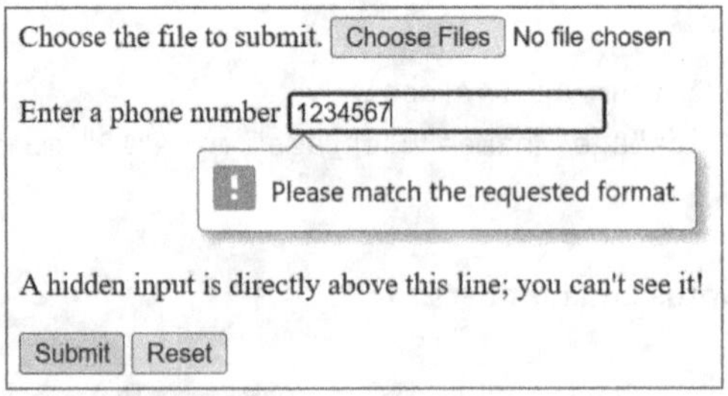

The attribute type="tel" is for entering a telephone number. The line is similar to the others, but if you don't provide more information, the box looks like the default text box.

Again, you could use a placeholder to suggest the format to the user. You can also specify a particular pattern, and the browser will provide an error message to the user if the pattern isn't followed. The following code is for the telephone entry in Figure 8.5, which assumes a U.S. phone number. An incorrect number has been entered to show the error, which will be produced when the form is submitted. You could also require a phone number by adding the `required` attribute as was done with the email entry.

```
<label for="phone" Enter a phone number </label>
<input type="tel" id="phone" name="userphone" pattern="[0-9]{3}-[0-9]{3}-
[0-9]{4}" placeholder="123-456-7890">
```

You might want to have information that is hidden from the user but will be uploaded to the server when the form is submitted. This is done using the `hidden` value for the `type` attribute, as shown in the following code. Note that there is no label with the input line because the input is hidden. It's also important to understand that someone could view the value of the hidden field by viewing the source code (Ctrl+U). The value of the `value` attribute could be determined by some code on the server.

```
<input type="hidden" name="visitorNumber" id="visitorNumber" value="5254">
```

The input boxes for `tel`, `email`, `password`, and `file` all look like a default text box, unless you've entered placeholders. The box isn't different, but they may cause different behavior depending on the browser being used. Using the various type values lets the browser or client-side code know what's expected in that box so that different action will be taken.

Buttons, radio buttons, and check boxes are covered in the sections that follow, but here are a few final values of the `type` attribute you might like to use.

The `color` attribute provides a color picker box. The default value is specified as a hex color number:

```
<input type="color" id="flower1" name="flower1" value="#cbc3e3">
<label for="flower1" >Pick first flower color.</label>
```

The `datetime-local` value enters a date with no time zone:

```
<label for="start" Date and time you started working: </label> <input
type="datetime-local" id="start" name="punchin_time">
```

The attributes `value` and `min` and `max` can also be used.

The `time` attribute is similar to `datetime-local` and is used to enter a time (no date) with no time zone:

```
<input type="time">
```

The `search` attribute creates a search box for your web page:

```
<label for="what"> What do you need to find?</label> <input type="search"
id="what" name="search-site"><button>Search</button>
```

The final type value is for entering a URL. It's one of those that look like a plain text box but provide some validation and can pop up a keyboard on mobile devices:

```
<input type="url" id="url" name="url" placeholder="https://mydomain.com"
pattern="https://.*"><br><label for="url">Enter your URL above.</label>
```

Another attribute of the `<input>` tag that might be useful is `autocomplete`. The `autocomplete` attribute works with `<form>`, `<input>` `<select>`, and `<textarea>` elements. It might require that the last three elements belong to a form. `autocomplete` can be turned on for a form and off for a particular form element, or off for a form and on for an element, depending on where `autocomplete` is entered. Exactly how it functions depends somewhat on the browser being used. It enables a browser or other *user agent* (any software representing the user, such as a browser) to suggest entries based on information that had been entered previously. The two possible values of `autocomplete` are `"on"` or `"off"`. Here is an example using the `autocomplete` attribute:

```
<label for="street"> Street Address </label>
<input type="text" name="street" id=<streetid> autocomplete="on">
```

Button Types

Buttons provide a clickable object on a web page that will perform the action specified. Buttons can be created as a `type` of the `<input>` tag, or they can be created using the `<button>` element. Why do you want buttons? Online forms will usually have a submit button that will send information to the server. They may also have a reset button to clear the input rather than submit it. Figure 8.5 shows the type `"submit"` without any value. The `value` attribute in the following code would change the text that's on the buttons but not the button's functionality. Technically, a submit button isn't needed because pressing Enter after input should automatically submit the information on the form to the resource that is manipulating it.

```
<input type="submit" value="Submit Form">
<input type="reset" value="reset Form">
```

The `<input>` tag can use an image as a submit button using the `src` attribute:

```
<input type="image" id="submit_image" alt="submit your answer" src="answer
.png">
```

The type attribute of the `<button>` tag has four values: button, submit, reset, and hidden. If you simply enter `<button type="submit"> </button>`, a very small but clickable button will appear. Submit and reset will both work this way, but they don't have any words on them until you tell them what to say, such as:

```
<button type="reset"> Click to clear the form. </button>.
```

The button value won't perform any action unless you tell it to. It works with global and event attributes. The button will execute a script when an event occurs. The syntax is `<button type="button" event="script"> Displayed button text </button>`. Mouse events such as onclick, onmouseover, or onmouseout work particularly well with it, and one of the advantages of using `<button>` is that you can change how a button appears with `<em>`, `<i>`, and so on—for example: `<button type="button" onmouseover="alert('Welcome back!')"><em><i> button to click<i></em></button>`. The `<button>` tag can show an image to click instead of or in addition to words. This is accomplished by nesting an `<img>` tag in the `<button>` tag, like this: `<button type="submit"><img src="lake.jpg">Reserve campsite.</button>`.

You might want to hide a button. Like an input box, a button can be hidden with the hidden type: `<button type="hidden"></button>`. The button will still be there but will not be visible to a user.

Figure 8.6 shows the `<button>` tag using the following code and the onmouseover alert:

```
<button type="submit"></button><br><br>
<button type="reset">Click to clear the form. </button><br><br>
<button type="button" onmouseover="alert('Welcome back!')"><em><i>button to click
<i></em></button><br><br>
<button type="submit"><img src="lake1.png"> Reserve campsite.</button><br><br>
```

FIGURE 8.6   Buttons

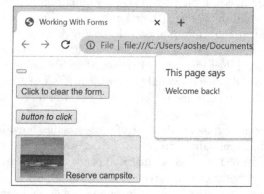

Adding Functionality

Most websites gather some information. Whether it's for sales, building a mailing list for a nonprofit organization, or simply requesting the results of a search, you need that information to be transferred to your server in some way. This functionality is added using the `<form>` tag. The attributes of `<form>` that you'll be examining are name, action, method, and enctype.

The `name` attribute simply assigns a name to your form, such as `<form name="userdata">`. The name is used by the server when referring to data that is uploaded, and it's used by JavaScript, which you'll learn more about in Chapter 13, "Java Script Essentials."

The `action` attribute tells the page what to do when the submit button is clicked or when the web page visitor presses the Enter key. It can send the user to another page: `<form action=/index.html>`. It can open up the user's email app and insert data from your form: `<form action="mailto:info@mydomain.com">`. Or it can send data to a server: `<form action="myDatabaseScript.php">`, where *myDatabaseScript.php* would be a server script that performs some action on the data. It's worth noting that the file for the action follows the same hierarchy rules that you learned in Chapter 7, "References and Embedded Resources." Refer back to Figure 7.3 if you need a refresher.

The `method` attribute has two main values: `GET` and `POST`. The one that you'll use depends on how much data you're going to send to the server. The `GET` method is useful when only a small amount of data is being sent. The `GET` method can put all its information into the header of an HTTP request. In fact, the information in the `GET` method becomes part of the URL being requested. A URL has a limit of only 2,048 characters, so using `GET` with `method` won't get us much. This might be form data, like the contents of a search box.

The `POST` method is used to send larger amounts of data that will be stored in the body of an HTTP request. This can be something like the data from a feedback form or images. It might also be data to update a database on a server or create a new entry like a sales order. Because the data is in the body of the request, the amount of data is not limited. The drawback of using `POST` is that it inherently creates more network overhead because the information is in the body, not in the URL. There are other differences between `GET` and `POST`. The `GET` value will show in the URL and in browser history, so `GET` should not be used with *personally identifiable information (PII)* or any other sensitive information like passwords. Examples of PII are full name, address, and date of birth, which can be used to identify a person and steal their identity. `GET` requests can be bookmarked. `POST requests` are not bookmarked, nor do they show in browser history, but `GET` requests will appear in the browser history. The format in the HTML document would be `<form method="get">` (or `post`).

The encoding type `<enctype>` attribute of `<form>` specifies how the data is to be sent. There are three encoding type values. `application/s-www-form-urlencoded` is the default. It's similar to the `GET` method because it appends the information to the URL. Most of the time it's fine to leave the encoding type at the default.

The `text/plain` encoding type is just as it sounds. It will send data in plain, readable text. There are very few places where this would be used, but, for example, if you were using the `"mailto"` action, you would encode the data in plain text to be transferred to your mail app.

The last `enctype` is `multipart/form-data`. This type is typically only used if the form will be sending a file along with form data.

Putting this all together, a `<form>` line might look something like this:
`<form action="mydatabasescript.php" method="post" enctype=application/ s-www-form-urlencoded>` or `<form action="mailto:info@cliffjumpertek .com" method="get" enctype="text/plain">`.

Radio Buttons and Check Boxes

radio and checkbox are types of the <input> element. Both allow a user to choose item(s) from a list. The radio type provides a circle for a user to click in to select a single item from a list. The checkbox type lets a user choose multiple items from a list. Both need to have an input line and a label line. They use the id, name, value, and for attributes that other input types use. In addition, the <fieldset> element is used to group the control buttons within a form. The <legend> tag is a child of <fieldset> and is used to present a heading for the group. <fieldset> and <legend> aren't just for radio buttons and check boxes. They can be used any time that you want to visually group elements together. The <fieldset> tag draws a box around the desired elements, and the <legend> tag will show as a name inserted in the top of the box. The following code is abbreviated but shows what each line type would be like. The full code produced the browser output in Figure 8.7.

```
<body>
<fieldset>
  <legend>What subject do you like best?</legend>
    <input type="radio" id="literature" name="topic" value="reading">
    <label for="literature">Literature </label>
    <input type="radio" id="history" name="topic" value="art">
    <label for="history"> History </label>
</fieldset><br><br>
<fieldset>
  <legend> What do you like? Choose any that apply.</legend>
    <input type="checkbox" id="literature" name="topic" value="reading">
    <label for="literature">Literature </label>
    <input type="checkbox" id="history" name="topic" value="art">
    <label for="history"> History </label>
</fieldset>
```

FIGURE 8.7   Radio buttons and check boxes

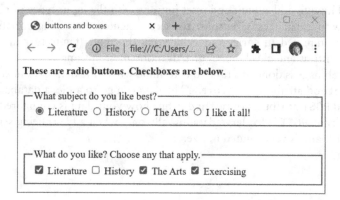

A Form for Reviews

You've likely seen them on many web pages: sections for reviewing what you thought about a product or service. These forms are often created using the <textarea> element. Attributes for <textarea> are id, name, rows, and cols. The id and name attributes function the same as before. The rows and cols values are used to determine a starting size for the <textarea>, but the text box can be expanded by dragging a corner. The following is an example using <textarea>. Figure 8.8 shows the output of this code. Notice the bottom-right corner of the text box where there are diagonal lines that a user can click and drag to expand the box.

<label for="review"> What did you think?</label>

<textarea id="review" name="review" rows="5" cols="20">Please type your review here. Thank you! </textarea>

FIGURE 8.8   A review box

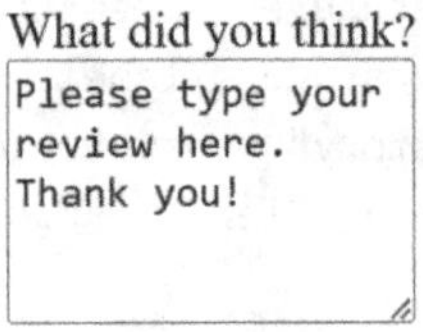

What did you think?

Please type your
review here.
Thank you!

Summary

In this chapter, you learned about creating HTML forms. They start with the same basic tags and attributes, and from there it gets interesting. You examined the type attribute of the <input> tag and all its values. You looked at multiple ways to pick dates and added some common fields like email, password, numbers, and hidden fields.

You learned how to add submit and reset buttons with the input types of submit and reset and how to use images in buttons. You experimented with using onmouseover with a button. You even nested an <img> tag inside your <button> tag to turn an image into a button. Radio buttons and check boxes give us more input options.

When the web page is done, it's time to determine where the data goes next with the action and method attributes of <form>. The data can go to a file, a database, or an email.

The GET and POST attributes of method define how your data is configured when it leaves your website. POST is for large data, usually only when a file is being sent. GET appends the URL and is very limited in size.

The encoding type `<enctype>` specifies how data will be formatted. The default is `application/s-www-form-urlencoded`, but you can also send it in text/plain or multipart/form-data.

The chapter ended with a simple form for reviews using the `<textarea>` element.

Exam Essentials

Be able to create a simple form. Forms are used on almost every website you visit: sign-up forms, email required for access, and providing feedback are three simple examples.

Comprehend form methods. Understand the difference between the GET and POST methods and how to use them.

Know the most common input attributes. Many of the attributes have special effects on how data is input. Make sure you're familiar with the ones covered in this chapter.

Understand how to use radio buttons and check boxes. Radio buttons and check boxes allow you to choose one or more of something from a list. There will be times when these options come in handy. Make sure you know which lets you choose one and which lets you choose many.

EXERCISE 8.1

Create an Input Form

In this exercise, you create an appointment form to practice some of the input types you learned about in this chapter.

1. For this exercise, start with your HTML skeleton.

2. Make the title of the HTML page **Appointments**.

3. In the body of the HTML page, create a form with an `id` of **appointment**.

4. Place a horizontal rule at the top of the form. Indent the horizontal rule and all code within the form by three spaces to show that it is part of the form.

5. Add text that will display **About You!**. You can center this text on the page using `<p align="center">`.

6. Create input fields for first name, last name, email, and phone number with appropriate labels and types. Each label and entry box should be on its own line. The link tying the input box to the corresponding label should be first, last, email, and phone.

7. For the email and phone number, prompt the user on the format that should be used.

8. Make the phone number required.

9. Create another horizontal rule.

10. Create a field for the user to choose an appointment date. Label it **Please choose a date to see us**. Use the text **appointment date** to link the field and label.

11. Save your file as **exercise 8_1.html** and test your form. You will use this file again later.

ANSWER:

The code should be as follows:

```
<!DOCKTYPE html>

<html lang="en-us">

<head>

 <title> Appointments </title>
 <meta charset="utf-8">

 </head>

<body>
<form id="appointment">
   <hr>
   <p align="center"> About You! </p>

   <label for="first">Please enter your first name. </label>
   <input type="text" id="first" name="first"><br><br>

   <label for="last">Please enter your last name. </label>
   <input type="text" id="last" name="last"><br><br>

   <label for="email">Please enter your email address. </label>
   <input type="email" id="email" name="email" placeholder="yourname@
something.com"><br><br>

   <label for="phone">Please enter your phone number. </label>
   <input type="phone" id="phone" name="phone" placeholder="123-456-7890"
required><br><br>

   <hr>

   <Label for="appointment_date"> Please choose a date to see us. </label>
```

```
      <input type="date" id="appointment_date" name="appointment_date"><br><br>

   </form>

   </body>

   </html>
```

Create a Feedback Form

In this exercise, you create a feedback form for your customer. Assume that you have sent the customer an email after their appointment with a link to the feedback form's web page.

1. For this exercise, start with your HTML skeleton.

2. Make the title of the HTML page **Feedback**.

3. In the body of the HTML page, create a form with an `id` of **feedback**.

4. Place a horizontal rule at the top of the form. Indent it and all code within the form by three spaces to show that it is part of the form.

5. Add text that will display `Thank you for visiting us!` and on the next line `Please tell us about your experience:`.

6. Insert a horizontal rule.

7. Add text that will display `Please rate the following on a scale between 1 and 10, where 10 is the best you've seen and 1 is terrible!`.

8. Put two blank lines between the text above and what follows.

9. Create three slider inputs with values ranging from 1 to 10.

10. Label them `Customer Service:`, `Price:`, and `Wait time:`, with `id`s of **service**, **price**, and **wait**, respectively.

11. Use the `<input>` tag to create a reset button that says `Clear the Form`.

12. Next to the reset button, use the `<button>` tag to create a submit button that says `Submit Feedback`.

13. Place a horizontal rule.

EXERCISE 8.2 *(continued)*

14. Enter a label that says **Your phone number: (optional)** and add the appropriate input entry line, ensuring that it isn't required.

15. Finish with a horizontal rule.

16. Edit your `<form>` element so that it will submit the data to a file named `feedback.php`. Be sure to include the appropriate `enctype` and `method`.

17. Save your file as **exercise 8_2.html** and test your form. Note that when you attempt to submit the form, it will try to find the file `feedback.php`, which doesn't exist, so it will produce an error message.

ANSWER:

The code should be as follows:

```
<!DOCKTYPE html>

<html lang="en-us">

<head>

 <title> Feedback </title>
 <meta charset="utf-8">

</head>

<body>
<form id="feedback" action="feedback.php" method="get"
enctype="application/s-www-form-urlencoded">
    <hr>
    <p> Thank you for visiting us! <br>
    Please tell us about your experience:" </p>
    <hr>

    <p>Please rate the following on a scale between 1 and 10 where 10 is the
best you've seen and 1 is terrible!"
    </P><br>

    <label for="service"> Customer Service: </label>
```

```
<input type="range" min="1" max="10" id="service" name="service"><br><br>

<label for="price">Price: </label>
<input type="range" min="1" max="10" id="price" name="price"><br><br>

<label for="wait">Wait time:</label>
<input type="range" min="1" max="10" id="wait" name="wait"><br><br>

<input type="reset" value="Clear the Form">
<button type="submit"> Submit Feedback </button> <br><br><br>

<hr>

<label for="phone">Your phone number: (optional) </label>
<input type="phone" id="phone" name="phone" placeholder="123-456-7890" <br><br>

<hr>



</form>

</body>

</html>
```

EXERCISE 8.3

Create Radio Buttons and Check Boxes

In this exercise, you add choices for our website visitors. For some options, they can only choose one, and for others they can choose as many as they like.

1. For this exercise, open the file exercise 8_1.html.

2. Save it now as **exercise 8_3.html** to ensure that you won't accidentally overwrite exercise 8_1.html.

3. Put a horizontal rule beneath the appointment date.

4. Beneath that but still in the same form, create a line asking
   How do you prefer we contact you? with two choices—email or phone—and make them the type where the visitor must choose one or the other. For id, use **email2** and **phone2**, respectively. For name, use **contact**.

EXERCISE 8.3 *(continued)*

5. Be sure to indent sections as appropriate so they will stand out in your code.

6. Enter a break code to insert a line feed.

7. Create another list where the customer can choose one or all of your services. Make sure this section is labeled **Please choose any or all services you would like.** Pretend this is a salon where services will be shampoo, haircut, manicure, pedicure, lip wax, and an herbal facial. You should have two services per line, with an empty line between lines of services. Use appropriate ids for each and for name use **services**.

8. Under this section, place a horizontal rule. Normally you would have a submit and a reset button here too, but you practiced that in the previous exercise.

9. Save your file as **exercise 8_3.html** and test your form.

ANSWER:

We're not repeating the Exercise 8.1 part here, just the new code that should appear after the Exercise 8.1 code but still be inside the form.

```
<hr>

  <fieldset>
      <legend> How do you prefer we contact you?</legend>

      <input type="radio" id="email2" name="contact" value="email2">
      <label for="email2"> Email </label>

      <input type="radio" id="phone2" name="contact" value="phone2">
      <label for="phone2"> Phone </label>

  </fieldset>
<br>

  <fieldset>
        <legend> Please choose any or all services you would like.</legend>

      <input type="checkbox" id="shampoo" name="services" value="shampoo">
      <label for="shampoo"> Shampoo </label>

      <input type="checkbox" id="haircut" name="services" value="haircut">
      <label for="haircut"> Haircut </label><br><br>

        <input type="checkbox" id="manicure" name="services" value="manicure">
```

```
<label for="manicure"> Manicure </label>

<input type="checkbox" id="pedicure" name="services" value="pedicure">
<label for="pedicure"> Pedicure </label><br><br>

<input type="checkbox" id="lip_wax" name="services" value="lip_wax">
<label for="lip_wax"> Lip Wax </label>

<input type="checkbox" id="herbal-facial" name="herbal-facial" value=
"herbal-facial">
<label for="herbal-facial"> Herbal Facial </label><br><br>
</fieldset>
<hr>

</form>
```

The form should look like Figure 8.9.

FIGURE 8.9   The form

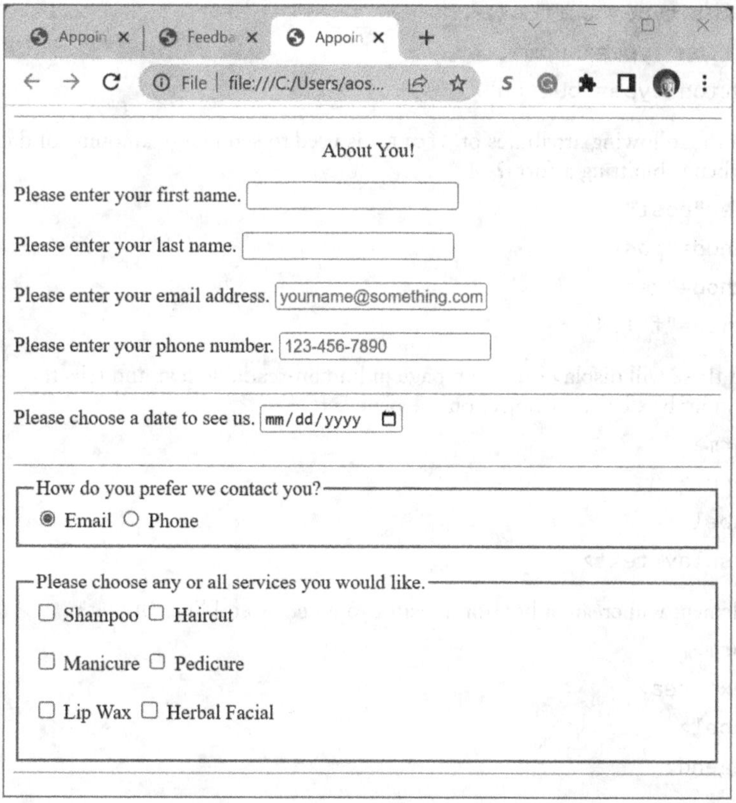

Review Questions

1. Which of the following is used to identify a piece of data when it is sent to a server?

   A. `for=`

   B. `id=`

   C. `name=`

   D. `<label>`

2. For the following code, what will the default entry be unless the user changes it?
   `<input type="number" id="age" name="user_age" min="1" max="120" value="21">`

   A. 1

   B. 21

   C. 120

   D. blank

3. Which of the following will not have any text on the button unless it is specified?

   A. `<input type="submit">`

   B. `<input type="button">`

   C. `<button type="submit">`

   D. `<button type="button">`

4. Which of the following attributes of `<form>` is used to send large amounts of data and/or images when submitting a form?

   A. `type="post"`

   B. `method="post"`

   C. `method="get"`

   D. `action="file"`

5. Which of these will display on a web page in human-readable text and tells the website user what an input box or other object on the page is for?

   A. `<form>`

   B. `<input>`

   C. `<label>`

   D. `<display text>`

6. Which element will create a box for a visitor to enter several lines of text?

   A. `<form>`

   B. `<textarea>`

   C. `<label>`

   D. `<legend>`

7. Your code has the line `<input type="first" name="name" id="firstname">`. Which line of code is correct to include with this input type?

   A. `<label for="first">my label</label>`

   B. `<label for="input">my label</label>`

   C. `<label for="name">my label</label>`

   D. `<label for="firstname">my label</label>`

8. You want a form where information can be completed based on previous information input. Which line do you need?

   A. `<form acton="myscript.php" fillIn="on">`

   B. `<input type="text" name="street" id=<streetid>streetid" autocomplete="off">`

   C. `<form action="myscript.php" autocomplete="on">`

   D. `<input autocomplete="all">`

9. Which of the following will produce a button that will clear the form data on the screen instead of sending it?

   A. `<button="submit">`

   B. `<input type="clear">`

   C. `<button type="button">`

   D. `<button type="reset">`

10. Your `<form action>` is set so the user of your website can email you a question. What value of the enctype attribute should be used?

    A. `enctype="text/plain"`

    B. `enctype="email"`

    C. `enctype="application/s-www-form-urlencoded"`

    D. `enctype="multipart/form-data"`

11. What is the default value for `<input>` type when the type is not specified?

    A. Name

    B. Date

    C. Text

    D. Button

12. You want the information that's entered into a text box in a form field to be obscured with dots as it's typed. What input type will you use?

    A. Obscure

    B. Secret

    C. Text

    D. Password

13. You need to tell the browser to send information to a database on the `cliffjumpertek` `.com` domain. Which of the following commands will you use?

    A. `<method post="cliffjumpertek.com/data/mydatabase.php">`

    B. `<form action="cliffjumpertek.com/data/mydatabase.php"` `method="post">`

    C. `<action post="cliffjumpertek.com/data/mydatabase.php">`

    D. `<form action="cliffjumpertek.com/data/mydatabase.php"` `method="get">`

14. You're creating a questionnaire and want the visitors to choose everything that applies to them from a list. For each option, you'll need a line. What will each line need to start with?

    A. `<input type="choose"`

    B. `<input type="radio"`

    C. `<input type="checkbox"`

    D. `<input type="option"`

15. You're creating an input form that will group several input lines together for a user to choose what colors of flowers they will use. They can choose more than one color. Each color is a line. Which of the following lines will you need to create the options list of this form? (Choose two.)

    A. `<fieldset>`

    B. `<legend>`

    C. `<group>`

    D. `<textarea>`

16. You're creating a website and you would like to have multiple slider bars so users can indicate how interested they are in various topics. Which of the following will give you a slider bar?

    A. `<input method="slider" min="1" max="10">`

    B. `<input type="slider" min="1" max="10">`

    C. `<input type="range" min="1" max="10">`

    D. `<input type="number" min="1" max="10">`

17. You would like your user to be able to upload only PDF documents to a server. Which of the following will allow a user to choose only pdf document(s) to upload? (Choose two.)

    A. `<input type="file" id="yourfile" accept="*.doc, *.docx">`

    B. `<input type="file" id="yourfile" accept="documents">`

    C. `<input type="file" id="yourfile" accept="*.pdf" multiple>`

    D. `<input type="file" id="yourfile" accept="*.pdf">`

18. You want a user to be able to pick a date from a date selection box (calendar) in mm/dd/yyyy format. Which of the following will you use?

   A. `<label for=date> mm.dd.yyyy </label>`

   B. `<input type="date" id="mydate" name="formdate">`

   C. `<input type="month" id="mydate" name="formdate">`

   D. `<input type="week" id="mydate" name="formdate">`

19. Your code line starts with `<button type="hidden"`. Which of the following are true? (Choose two.)

   A. Visitors to your website will not see it.

   B. You can make it take some action when the user's mouse passes over it.

   C. It can only be used for a visitor number.

   D. It can't react to what the user does.

20. You work for a medical claims company and are coding their website to allow users to upload an image of their medical receipt along with data such as their name and ID number. What type of encoding will you use?

   A. `enctype="text/plain"`

   B. `enctype="email"`

   C. `enctype="application/s-www-form-urlencoded"`

   D. `enctype="multipart/form-data"`

Chapter

9

Introducing CSS

LINUX PROFESSIONAL INSTITUTE, WEB DEVELOPMENT ESSENTIALS EXAM 030-100 OBJECTIVES COVERED IN THIS CHAPTER:

✓ **033 CSS Content Styling**

- 033.1 CSS Basics: The candidate should understand the various ways to style an HTML document using CSS. This includes the structure and syntax of CSS rules.

    - Key Knowledge Areas:

        - Embedding CSS within an HTML document

        - Understand the CSS syntax

        - Add comments to CSS

        - Awareness of accessibility features and requirements

    - Files, terms, and utilities:

        - HTML style and type (text/css) attributes

        - <style>

        - <link>, including the rel (stylesheet), type (text/css) and src attributes

        - ;

        - /*,*/

- 033.2 CSS Selectors and Style Application: The candidate should be able to use selectors in CSS and understand how CSS rules are applied to elements within an HTML document.

    - Key Knowledge Areas:

        - Use selectors to apply CSS rules to elements

As you've learned, HTML provides the structure of your web page. Now you're going to move into Cascading Style Sheets (CSS), which makes your web page visually pleasing, and by referencing external files, can make your coding more concise and easier to modify. So, grab your favorite note-taking tool, and let's get started!

Applying Styles to HTML

There are three different ways that you can apply CSS styles to a web page. You can use the `style` attribute or the `<style>` tag, or you can store CSS rules in a separate file. Think of CSS as three layers of customization. First there is the `style` attribute— `<p style "...">`—which applies a style at the element. The next layer is using the style tag, `<style>`, at the page level, and finally using external CSS files to apply to the entire website. The advantage of using a separate file to house your CSS rules is that the same rules file can be applied to multiple HTML pages, giving your website a cohesive look with less effort. It also makes making changes easier, because you make changes in one place, not several. The `style` attribute and the `<style>` tag work well for quick, simple style application within the HTML file.

First, let's examine how to change the appearance using CSS inside the HTML document with the `style` attribute and the `<style>` tag. Then we'll examine using a separate style sheet and external reference to change the website appearance.

The *style* Attribute

To apply the `style` attribute to an element, you place the attribute in the body of the HTML file, in the individual element tag. The `style` attribute is a global attribute, so all HTML elements support it. The syntax for the `style` attribute is `style=property:value`. Let's say you wanted the text of your heading to be red. The code would look like this: `<h2 style="color:red;">This is my h2 heading </h2>`.

The property is the characteristic you want to change, and the value is what you want to change it to. In this case the property is `color`, and we want to change it from the default to red. As mentioned in Chapter 5, "HTML Introduction," the value of the color can be expressed by a name, also known as a keyword, or as a hexadecimal value or red-green-blue (`rgb`) value.

But what if that isn't enough? Red as used previously applies to the foreground of the element, in this case, the font. If you want multiple styles to apply to the same element, you simply list them, ensuring that there's a semicolon between each property:value pair, as follows: <h2 style="color:red; background-color:yellow;"> This is my h2 heading with a yellow background. </h2>. You could add many more property:value pairs, as long as each ends with a semicolon and there is a colon between the property and the value. If this looks familiar, it should. The <style> attribute was used as an example in Chapter 5, "HTML Introduction," where elements and attributes were the topic. The words "name" and "property" are used interchangeably, so you might see either term used to describe what you want to change.

In Chapter 6, "Content Markup," you learned about block and inline elements. Inline elements go from left to right across the page, whereas block elements can be several lines vertically. If you think of everything on an HTML page as occupying a rectangle of space, whether it's a horizontal line or a block, then it's easier to visualize what you'll be changing by using a particular selector, such as <h1> or <p>. The background-color:value of a paragraph will color the entire paragraph, both horizontally and vertically (that is, the whole block). The background color of a heading will be that line. The background color of an inline element such as a single word will be only behind that word. Here we use the <span> tag to isolate a word in a paragraph:
<p> This is an inline <span style="background-color:yellow;"> element </span> with a yellow background to highlight the word element. </p>

CSS Rules and Selectors

What would you do if you had 100 <h2> headings that you wanted all coded in the same way? Coding *that* would be tedious to say the least, and subjects the code to the possibility of more human error. And, what if you decided to change it later? Yikes! A better way to do this is to use CSS rules and selectors.

A *selector* is a value used to link properties and elements in CSS. It can be the type of element, such as <h2> or <p>, or it could be a class, unique ID, and so on. (You learn more about class and unique ID in Chapter 10, "Applying CSS Styles.") A *CSS rule*, also called a declaration, consists of its selector plus its properties (see Figure 9.1). The selector is what you want to change, the property is the characteristic that you want to change, and the value is what you want to change it to. The selector is written without brackets, such as p instead of <p>.

FIGURE 9.1   A CSS rule

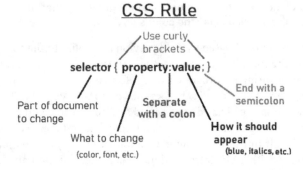

Using CSS rules enables us to modify entire groups of elements at the same time. Instead of coding your one hundred <h2> headings individually, you could code them in one place, at one time. Not only does it make your job easier, but it also cuts down on errors and the time required to maintain the site. It also makes troubleshooting easier because if something isn't looking just right, you can change it in one place and the problem will be corrected throughout the page. This discussion now brings us to the <style> tag.

The *<style>* Tag

The <style> tag belongs in the header section of your web page. It's where you can enter your CSS rules and have them work throughout the page.

The <style> tag has two attributes: type and media.

The type attribute is used to tell the browser what Internet media (MIME) type is being used for the file. The syntax for using the type attribute is <style type="media_type">. The default value of the type attribute is text/css, which specifies that the style is CSS. At present, text/css is the only value available, so it's the default. If it isn't specified, text/css is assumed.

The media attribute specifies what type of media or device the page is optimized for. This could be printers (print), computer screens (screen), and handheld devices (handheld), among several others. The default value is all. The syntax is <style media="value">— for example, <style media="print">. It can also use the Boolean operators and, not, and or, written as a comma, (,), so if the web page were optimized for computer screens and handheld devices the line might read <style media="screens and handheld";>.

As mentioned previously, the <style> tag resides in the <head> of the document and affects the entire document. The style can have many different specifications, such as one for paragraphs and another for level 1 headers, level 2 headers, images, and so on. The settings applied to each selector are found between two curly brackets—{ }—and to keep the code readable, it's common practice to separate each setting on a different line ending in a semicolon. For example, check out the code that follows, which produced the output in

Figure 9.2. If you forget the semicolon, the code may not work. Always double-check that you have a semicolon at the end of each property:value pair.

```
<html lang="en-us">
<head>
<title> Styles & Selectors </title>
<meta charset="utf-8">

<style type="text/css" media="all">

h1{
   background-color:white;
   border-style:dotted;
   height: 5px;
   width:50%;
      }

h2{
   background-color:yellow;
   color:blue;
      }

P {
   color:blue;
   background-color:lightGray;
   font-family:fantasy;
   font-size:18px;
      }


</style>
</head>

<body>
<h1> This is my h1 heading. </h1>
<p> This is my first paragraph <br> It takes two lines. </p>
<h2> This is my heading with a yellow background. </h2>
<hr>
</body>
</html>
```

FIGURE 9.2   Using the `<style>` tag

Notice in Figure 9.2 that the font in the paragraph is different, along with the two different heading styles—one with a box around it and the other with a yellow background, (If you're learning from the printed book, the colors will show as different shades of gray). The h1 and h2 in the `<style>` section of the `<head>` are the selectors that were linked to the content of your web page through the `<h1>` and `<h2>` tags. The style for the paragraph was linked from the p selector in the `<style>` section to the `<p>` tag in the body. Now if you have one hundred `<h2>` tags in the body of your web page, they will all have a yellow background with blue text, without the work of entering the styles again.

Notice, too, how easily you can pick out each selector style using spacing in your code. If you want to temporarily stop one of those styles from being applied, all you need to do is comment it out by placing it between a set of `/*`, `*/` as in the code that follows. The set of `/*` and `*/` tells the browser that what lies between them should be ignored. It's merely a comment. In the output, it will remove the formatting from any `<h1>`, but not the text that is in the body of your page. You can use these characters any time you want to put a comment in your CSS code so you'll remember why you wrote it the way that you did, and what is between will be ignored by the browser.

```
/*
h1{
  background-color:white;
  border-style:dotted;
  height: 5px;
  width:50%;
    }*/
```

CSS Stored in Separate Files

Having your styles stored in the head of a web page is simpler than styling each element, but what if your website has 50 pages? To get a consistent look, you would need to copy the `<style>` section of your document `<head>` to each of the 50 pages, and if you made any changes, you would need to do it again. This sounds quite cumbersome to me! Instead, a better plan is to store the CSS styles in a separate document that can be referenced by each page. Then it only needs to be coded one time, and when changes are made to the CSS file, each of the pages that reference it will also change. Another advantage of using a CSS file is that the CSS file can be cached by the browser, which will make the page load more quickly.

Using an external CSS file requires two steps. One is setting up your CSS file, and the other is linking to it. Just as you would create a separate folder for your images, all CSS files should be in a CSS folder, where they're easy to find. CSS files are saved with a .css extension. The CSS file is not rendered by the browser. It's merely a list of your CSS rules. When you have many CSS rules, putting them in alphabetical order within the CSS file can help you find what you're looking for more quickly.

In each HTML file that will use the CSS file, you remove the styles from the <head> section of the page and replace them with a link to the CSS file. The link states the relationship between the HTML and CSS file, and contains a hyperlink to find the CSS file. It has several available attributes, but the two you're concerned with are rel (relationship) and href (hyperlink reference). The path follows the familiar hierarchical rules. CSS files can be created in a text editor, just like HTML files. Figure 9.3 shows your HTML <link> tag linking to the CSS file and the beginning of your CSS file.

FIGURE 9.3   Linking to a CSS file

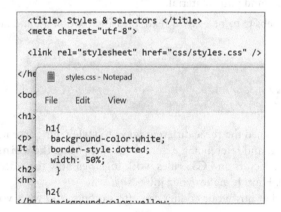

CSS Accessibility Features

You must be aware of how your coding affects the accessibility of a website. *Website accessibility* refers to how easy the website is for anyone to get to or use the site. CSS enables you to use all sorts of different settings for your content, but you need to take care not to go too far from what is expected, because people rely on certain visible or audible clues (in the case of screen-reading software) to use websites. Here are a few tips to keep your page accessible while you're styling with CSS:

- Web pages where the color of the text is too close to the color of the background are difficult to read. That doesn't mean that you need red text on a yellow background, but do use a reasonable amount of contrast. There are several online tools to check the accessibility of your page's color choices and other elements. Search for **accessibility color checker** to find one you like.

- Headings and paragraphs are used to organize your pages. Just as you shouldn't make a single paragraph line look like a heading, you shouldn't make a heading so small that it doesn't stand out. Headings provide visual cues to readers and help them navigate the page, in addition to them being used for search engine optimization (SEO). Use the appropriate sizes and contrast for your headings and configure them with heading tags.

- Whether it's headings, paragraphs, or lists, always use the right semantic elements to identify them.

- Consider what the user will expect when it comes to active and inactive tabs, and how objects look when they're hovered over. People depend on these visible cues to help them navigate web pages.

- Always provide alternate text and/or captions for images and media to help people more thoroughly understand your material.

- You want your website to be easy to read, pleasing to look at, and accessible to your audience.

Summary

In this chapter, you learned the three different ways to style your content: the `style` attribute, the `<style>` tag, and referencing external CSS files using the `<link>` tag.

You learned how selectors and CSS rules work together, how to create a CSS file, and why you would want one. Hint: It makes your job easier.

Finally, you looked at how your coding can affect others, and ways you can make your code more accessible.

Exam Essentials

Know how to embed CSS in an HTML document.   Know the different ways to embed CSS within an HTML document (i.e., the `style` attribute and `<style>` tag, and how to use them). Although an external file is used more often, there are still times when you need these two internal options.

Understand CSS syntax and conventions.   Understand the CSS syntax, but more than that, learn to write your code in the expected manner. It makes your work easier for you and for others to follow what you've done.

Know how to add comments.   Comments in CSS can help you remember what you did and why, and they can be used to temporarily turn code off when you're troubleshooting.

Be familiar with accessibility.   You want everyone to be able to enjoy and use your website, so always keep accessibility in mind when you're coding. Depending on where you live, you could be fined if your site doesn't follow accessibility laws.

EXERCISE 9.1

Use the *style* Attribute in an HTML Page

In this exercise, you use the first method to style a page: the style attribute.

1. Begin with your HTML skeleton.
2. Change the title to **Using the style attribute**.
3. Write two short paragraphs of text.
4. Use the `style` attribute to change the first paragraph to blue with a background color of light gray.
5. Save your file as **exercise9_1.html**.

ANSWER:

```
<!DOCKTYPE html>
<html lang="en-us">
<head>
  <title> Using the style attribute. </title>
  <meta charset="utf-8">
</head>
<body>

<p style="color:blue; background-color:lightGray;">
This is my first paragraph.  It is very short.</p>

<p> This is my second paragraph.  It is also very short. </p>

</body>
</html>
```

EXERCISE 9.2

Use the *<style>* Tag in an HTML Page

In this exercise, you use the second method to style a page: the `<style>` tag.

1. Begin with your HTML skeleton.

2. Change the title to **Using the style tag.**

3. Create a level 1 heading.

4. Create two level 2 headings.

5. After the first level 2 heading, enter some random text.

6. Use the `<style>` tag to configure your level 2 headings to green with a background color of yellow. Place a dashed box around the level 2 headings. Enter the default type and assume the page is optimized for all media types.

7. Save your file as **exercise9_2.html**.

ANSWER:

```
<!DOCKTYPE html>

<html lang="en-us">
<head>

  <title> Using the style attribute. </title>
  <meta charset="utf-8">

  <style type="text/css" media="all">

  h2{
    background-color:yellow;
    color:green;
    border-style:dashed;
    }

  </style>

</head>
<body>
  <h1> This is a level 1 heading. </h1>
    <h2> This is my first level 2 heading. </h2>
```

```
    <p> Some random text would be here. </p>
    <h2> This is my second level 2 heading. </h2>
</body>
</html>
```

Use Separate CSS Files to Change an HTML Page's Presentation

In this exercise, you put your CSS rules in a separate CSS file and link your HTML page to the CSS file.

1. In the folder where your HTML file is, create a folder called **CSS**.

2. In the CSS folder, create a new text file called **styles1.css**.

3. Open the exercise9_2.html file and save it in the same folder you opened it from as **exercise9_3.html**.

4. Create a rule in the styles1.css file to color the <h1> heading purple by using a hex code.

5. Copy the rule for the <h2> headings from the exercise9_3.html file to the styles1.css file. (If the setting doesn't work when you test it, you might need to delete the copied rule and manually type it in.)

6. Delete the <style> </style> section from the exercise9_3.html file.

7. Enter a line in the HTML file that will reference the CSS rules in the styles1.css file. Remember that the path must be correct.

8. Save both files and test the output.

ANSWER

Note, your purple hex code might be different from the answer because there are many shades of purple.

Exercise9_3.html:

```
<!DOCKTYPE html>

<html lang="en-us">

<head>

  <title> Using the style attribute. </title>
```

```
    <meta charset="utf-8">

    <link rel="stylesheet" href="css/styles1.css" />

    </head>

    <body>

    <h1> This is a level 1 heading. </h1>

    <h2> This is my first level 2 heading. </h2>
    <p> Some random text would be here. </p>

    <h2> This is my second level 2 heading. </h2>
    </body>

    </html>
```

Styles1.css

```
    h1{
        color:#800080;
        }

    h2{
        background-color:yellow;
        color:green;
        border-style:dashed;
        }
```

Review Questions

1. Where does the `<style>` tag belong in an HTML document?
   A. `<head>`
   B. `<body>`
   C. At each element you want to style
   D. In a `filename.styles` file

2. Which two of these embed a style into an HTML document? (Choose two.)
   A. `<body><link rel="stylesheet" href="css/styles.css" />`
   B. `<head><link rel="styles.css" href="styles" />`
   C. Using the `<style>` tag in the head of the HTML file
   D. Using the `style` attribute in the opening tag of the element

3. Which of these options are selectors? (Choose two.)
   A. `h1`
   B. `p`
   C. `<style>`
   D. `<select>`

4. Which of the following are used to add comments to CSS?
   A. `//`
   B. `!!`
   C. `*.*`
   D. `/* */`

5. What is missing in the following CSS rule?
   ```
   P {
   color:yellow
   }
   ```
   A. `:`
   B. `;`
   C. `/*` and `*/`
   D. The selector

6. What tag is used to connect an HTML file to a CSS file?
   A. `<style>`
   B. `<link>`
   C. `<css>`
   D. `<stylesheet>`

7. Your file, `whatever.html`, is going to be using a style sheet called `style1.css` that is in the same folder as the HTML file. Which of the following is correct to link to that file?

    A. `<link> rel="stylesheet" href="style1.css" </link>`

    B. `<stylesheet="style1.css" link="whatever.html">`

    C. `<link rel="stylesheet" href="style1.css" />`

    D. `<link rel="stylesheet" href="/style1.css" />`

8. Your friend is working on changing some styles in CSS. They called you because they commented out a style, and now nothing after that is working. What is the problem?

    A. They didn't link the files properly.

    B. They didn't use `/c` to comment.

    C. They forgot to end the comment with `*/`.

    D. They forgot to end the comment with `/*`.

9. Which of these is not important to keep in mind when creating a website because it doesn't affect accessibility?

    A. Color combinations.

    B. Website topic.

    C. Ensuring that alternate text exists for images.

    D. Use semantic elements in building the website.

10. Where should the `<link>` tag be placed?

    A. In the `<title>` section of your HTML file

    B. In the `<head>` section of your HTML file

    C. In the `<body>` section of your HTML file

    D. In the `<html>` section of your CSS file

11. Which of the following is the proper syntax for a CSS rule?

    A. `selector {property:value;}`

    B. `{selector: property;value}`

    C. `selector:{property;value;}`

    D. `property {selector:value;}`

12. When you see the following line of code, what do you know about the HTML file?
`<link ref="stylesheet" href="corporate.css" />`

    A. The styles are stored in the HTML file head.

    B. The styles are created at each appropriate tag.

    C. The styles are in a file called `stylesheet`.

    D. The styles are in a file called `corporate.css`.

13. Which attribute of the `<style>` tag is used to tell the browser what kind of Internet media (formerly called MIME) is being used for the HTML file? (Choose two.)

  A. `type="media_type"`

  B. `type="text/css"`

  C. `src="media_type"`

  D. `href="media_type"`

14. Which of the following lines of code correctly applies a style to part of a page using a selector?

  A. `p { font:italic: }`

  B. `<p> {font:italic;}`

  C. `h2 { bgcolor : lightgray ;}`

  D. `<h2>{apply=bgcolor:beige;}`

15. Which of the following does not pertain to CSS selectors?

  A. They belong in a CSS file.

  B. They belong in an HTML `<head>` section.

  C. They work with the `<style>` tag.

  D. They work with the `style` attribute.

16. Which of these are used to style HTML content internally to the HTML file? (Choose two.)

  A. The `style` attribute

  B. The `<link>` tag

  C. The `<style>` tag

  D. The `href` attribute

17. If you want all of your paragraphs to be styled with a gray background, what will your selector be?

  A. `<p>`

  B. `p`

  C. `<p>=gray`

  D. `paragraph=gray`

18. Which of these is not an advantage of using CSS files to style HTML files?

  A. Using CSS styles saves the programmer time.

  B. A CSS file can be applied to multiple HTML files, providing easy website consistency.

  C. Changes to styles can be done in just one place for many pages.

  D. You need a separate CSS file for each HTML file.

19. What are possible consequences of ignoring accessibility when creating a web page? (Choose two.)

    A. Some people won't be able to interact with your page.

    B. You might be required to pay fines.

    C. Your website will work fine with screen readers.

    D. You'll increase traffic to your site.

20. What are best practices when coding HTML pages? (Choose two.)

    A. Use CSS for formatting.

    B. Use attributes to make the first line of a paragraph look like a heading.

    C. Use colors that are close together like beige on white.

    D. Use semantic elements to identify the parts of your page.

Chapter

10

Applying CSS Styles

LINUX PROFESSIONAL INSTITUTE, WEB DEVELOPMENT ESSENTIALS EXAM 030-100 OBJECTIVES COVERED IN THIS CHAPTER:

✓ **033 CSS Content Styling**

- 033.2 CSS Selectors and Style Application: The candidate should be able to use selectors in CSS and understand how CSS rules are applied to elements within an HTML document.

    - Key Knowledge Areas:

        - Use selectors to apply CSS rules to elements

        - Understand CSS pseudo-classes

        - Understand rule order and precedence in CSS

        - Understand inheritance in CSS

    - Files, terms, and utilities:

        - element; .class; #id

        - a, b; a.class; a b;

        - :hover, :focus

        - !important

In Chapter 9, you learned that you can use elements as selectors to identify which CSS styles should go where. This chapter introduces you to other types of selectors and different ways that CSS determines how styles are applied, including inheritance, pseudo-classes, and order of precedence. Get ready to be creative!

Other Selectors

Type selectors are those that use an element to identify which parts of the page to style. As you learned in Chapter 9, "Introducing CSS," using an element like <h3> as your selector applies the style to every <h3> element on the page. Applying styles this way is great when you want to make major changes to a web page, but what if you want to select something less or more specific? No worries; you have options.

Let's start with the id attribute. You may remember from Chapter 7, "References and Embedded Resources," that an id attribute is intended to identify only one instance of an element in a document. There are two parts to using an id attribute. First, you must specify the id where you want the style to occur in the document; then you must define the style for the id either in the <style> section of the HTML <head> or in a CSS sheet.

For the element, the syntax is <element id="name">.

When specifying the style to use, place a hashtag (#)before the id name, as in the following example. Be sure not to use any spaces between the hashtag and the id name. The following code is an example of using the id attribute, and its results are shown in Figure 10.1.

```
<!DOCTYPE html>
<html lang="en-us">
<head>
 <title> Applying Styles </title>
 <meta charset="utf-8">
 <style>
 #myParagraph {
  color: purple;
  background-color: pink;
  text-align: center;
 }
 </style>
</head>
```

```
<body>
<p id="myParagraph"> This paragraph would be centered with a purple font and
<br> pink
 background. </p>
<p> This paragraph would not be styled like the first one. </p>
</body>
</html>
```

FIGURE 10.1   Using the id attribute to apply a style

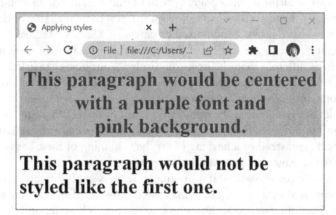

If you wanted two or more ids to have the same style, you can group them by including both in the style, with a comma between the ids. This applies to any number of multiple selectors, as in the following example, where the #pageTop and the #footer are both the same style:

```
#pageTop {
 color: green;
 text align: center;
 }
#specialParagraphs {
  color: purple;
  background-color: pink;
  text-align: right;
  }
#footer {
 color: green;
 text align: center;
 }
```

Code could be written as:

```
#pageTop, #footer {
 color: green;
```

```
   text align: center;
 }
#specialParagraphs {
  color: purple;
  background-color: pink;
  text-align: right;
 }
```

Another way to identify what you want styled is to use classes. A *CSS class* can be used to style any number of elements on a page, instead of one instance of an element. Imagine that you run a museum and your website shows a list of what's available both to see and for purchase. The website shows items sorted by category, such as "Renaissance" or "Victorian," which might equate to the section of the museum they're in. You want items for sale in each section to look different than the items on display. Your items are listed alphabetically in each section, so items for sale and display are intermingled. You're going to use color to identify which ones are for sale and which are not.

CSS class styles are set in either the `<style>` section of the HTML page or in the CSS stylesheet like an `id`; however, the syntax is `.className { property:value; }`. Note the use of a period (`.`) instead of a hashtag (`#`) at the beginning of the `className`.

The element of the page that you want styled uses the syntax `<element class="className">`. If more than one class applies to an element, the classes are separated by a space. The syntax is `<element class= "className className2">`. The following code shows how to use multiple styles and the output is shown in Figure 10.2. In the printed version of the book, the shades of gray make discerning the colors difficult, but if you try this on your computer, you'll clearly see that the Honore Daumier: Painting and Mary Thornycroft: Sculpture lines will be green.

```
<!DOCTYPE html>
<html lang="en-us">
<head>
 <title> Using Classes </title>
 <meta charset="utf-8">
 <style>
  .renaissance {
      font-family: "French Script MT";
      text-align: center;
      }
  .victorian {
      font-family: "Kunstler Script";
      text-align: center;
      }
  .top {
      font-size: 50px;
      }
  .item {
```

```
      font-size: 20px;
      }
  .sell {
      color: green;
      }
  .display {
      color:purple;
      }
 </style>
</head>
<body>
<h2 class="victorian top"> Items from the Victorian Era </h2>
<p class="display item"> Chaise Lounge from the Waldorf Hotel </p>
<p class="display item"> Lady Feodora Gleichen: Sculpture </p>
<p class="sell item"> Honore Daumier: Painting </p>
<p class="display item"> Jean-Baptiste-Camille-Corot: Painting</p>
<p class="sell item"> Mary Thornycroft: Sculpture </p>

<h2 class="renaissance top"> Items from the Renaissance </h2>
<p class="display item"> Leonardo da Vinci: Sculpture </p>
</body>
</html>
```

FIGURE 10.2   Using classes

Coding this way avoids clutter at the elements, helps prevent human error, and saves time when writing and changing code. (Fonts will be explained in more detail in Chapter 11, "CSS Styling Fundamentals.")

 If you're applying a specific font and your page doesn't display with that font, it might be that the font isn't available on your computer. You'll need to download the font and install it. One source for some fun fonts is `https://fonts.google.com`.

As with `ids`, a style can be applied to multiple classes. The following list shows four different ways of specifying selectors based on where you want the style applied. Notice that the `ul` selector is written in the syntax of specifying an element.

`.renaissance {property:value ;}` applies to any element where `class="renaissance"`.

`ul.renaissance {property:value ;}` applies only to `ul` type elements in the renaissance class.

`.renaissance.top {property:value ;}` applies to all items in *both* the renaissance and top classes.

`.renaissance .top {property:value ;}` applies to all items in *either* the renaissance or the top class.

Notice the difference between `.renaissance.top` and `.renaissance .top`. If there is a space between class names, the style is applied to either class. If there is *no* space between class names, the style is applied only when the item is in both classes.

It's also important to keep inheritance and order of precedence in mind when planning your styles. Both considerations are covered later in this chapter.

CSS Inheritance

An element "inherits" from its parent element, just as people do. *Inherited properties* apply the same style to a child element as the parent element had. So, for example, if the `<body>` element is styled with a font color of blue, everything inside the body will have a font color of blue unless you change it. Examples of inherited properties are `color`, `background-color`, `font-family`, `font-size`, and `line-height`.

Another way to achieve the same result is to use a page-wide style. *Page-wide styles* use an asterisk in place of an element name, such as `<h3>`, and apply to everything on the page unless changed by a style applied to a specific element. See the following example of a page-wide style:

```
* {
color:blue;
font-family: "chiller" ;
}
```

Another example of inheritance occurs with lists. <li>s inherit from the <ul> or <ol> element they are part of. This can be changed by specifying a style on a <li>.

If you don't want a child to inherit its parent's style, it can be changed with the !important property. This property overrides any otherwise inherited style. Using your code from earlier, <p class=display> Paragraph text here </p> displays in purple, because that's what the .display class is set to. However, if you entered the line p { color: blue !important; } in the <style> section of <head>, then all paragraphs would print in the color blue, regardless of their class.

Another way to stop inheritance is to apply a descendant selector. *Descendant selectors* apply to elements that are children of the id specified. If you specified #myList {color:yellow;} and applied that in the page to an unordered list, <ul id="myList">, but you didn't want the list items in that list to be the same color, you could place another style in the <style> section, such as #myList ul {color:black;}. In that case, the second style would be applied to the children (list items) of the list whose id="myList". The <ul> text would be yellow, and the <li> text would be black.

Some properties are not inherited. *Non-inherited properties* use the default value of the property; they don't get the property value of their parent. Examples of non-inherited properties are border, height, width, margin, and padding.

Keep inheritance in mind when applying styles and troubleshooting. If something has a style applied that you weren't expecting, you might have to cancel that style by specifying something else on the element.

CSS Pseudo-Classes

Pseudo-classes are special selectors that are based on an object or element being in a specific state or an event occurring, such as when a user's pointer hovers over a button or when an object is in focus. *Focus* means that an element has been selected in some way, such as clicking, tapping, or tabbing to the item.

Although the exam objectives only mention :hover and :focus pseudo-classes, there are many others in several categories. For example, input pseudo-classes include choices like :checked, which selects an object or element when a radio button or check box is clicked on, and :valid or :invalid, which are based on the contents of a user input box. The :lang pseudo-class selects an item based on the language of the content. There are also resource pseudo-classes, :playing and :paused, and time pseudo-classes, :past, :present, and :future. Pseudo-classes can be used to change the color of a link based on whether it has been visited, :link, :visited, or being hovered over, :hover. The caveat when using pseudo-classes for links is that the :hover pseudo-class must be listed last; otherwise the code won't work properly. Other useful pseudo-classes are ;autofill, :enabled, :disabled, and :read-only. The pseudo-classes listed here are only a few of the available pseudo-classes.

The syntax for a pseudo-class is selector:pseudo-class { property: value; }. For example, if you want a link to be blue when it hasn't been visited, red when it has been visited, and have a green background when the website user is hovering over it, the code would be as follows:

```
a:link {
color: blue;
 }
a:visited {
color: red;
}
a:hover {
background-color:green;
}
```

Like other classes, pseudo-classes can be specified in the <style> section of the web page <head>, or in a separate CSS file. The links would be in the <body> of the web page.

CSS Order of Precedence

The final topic for this chapter, but by no means the least important, is the order of precedence. How do you know which style is applied if conflicting styles exist on a particular element? This is where the word *cascading* comes into play with Cascading Style Sheets (CSS). Rules can cascade from several sources down to the individual element on a page.

An element can have none, one, or many rules applied to it. Styles can come from a browser's default style, a CSS stylesheet, the <style> element in the page's <head> section, or by being specified at the element. The browser's style sheet is overridden by styles in a CSS file. If styles are specified in the <style> section of the document's <head>, then they are applied, and the last applied are those at the element. The end result is that styles specified at an element take precedence over those applied elsewhere. For example, if you have
`body {color: "blue"; font-family: "Arial"; }` and
`p {font-family: "Times New Roman"; },`
then the paragraphs will be colored blue because they are part of the body, but they will have the Times New Roman font because a paragraph is a more granular, more precise, part of the web page than the body. The paragraph is inside the body.

Styles applied by an id take precedence over styles applied by a class, because there can be only one instance of an id but several instances of a class on a page. This makes the id style more precise than the class style.

For styles applied in a style sheet, those found at the end of the list take precedence over those at the beginning of the list.

As you can see, the order of precedence is very important when writing styles for your web pages. Keep this in mind when you're troubleshooting a page that just isn't looking as you expected.

Summary

In summary, this chapter explained more about selectors. They can be based on the element, an id, a class, or pseudo-class—that is, based on user actions like :hover, states of being like :focus, or :viewed, along with many others. This chapter also examined inheritance—that child objects inherit from their parents unless you specifically change them, and that the !important property overrides any inheritance. The final section of this chapter explained the importance and order of precedence. The order of precedence dictates that browser styles are applied first, then CSS sheets, then the <style> section of the header, and finally the styles found at the element. In a list of styles, the last in the list takes precedence over the styles that come before it, and when styles conflict, the most specific style takes precedence.

Exam Essentials

Know how to apply styles.   You can apply styles in more ways than by element. Ensure that you know the difference between using an id or a class to define a style and be familiar with pseudo-classes, because interactive web pages are so much more exciting than plain text.

Be conscious of the effect of where styles are applied.   You have options for applying styles. Sometimes it makes more sense to apply them at the element. If you have many styles to apply, you likely want to use an external CSS file to apply them to keep your page cleaner and easier to troubleshoot.

Remember which rules take precedence.   It makes a difference where a style is specified and how specific it is. Knowing the order of precedence can save you time and trouble when building your web page.

Understand inheritance and how to circumvent it.   Sometimes it's convenient to have child objects inherit styles from their parent objects, and sometimes you'll want them to have their own styles.

EXERCISE 10.1

Change a Style When a User Hovers

In this exercise, you create a couple of buttons and make them change color when the user's mouse hovers over them.

1.   Begin with your HTML skeleton.

2.   Change the title to **hover**.

3. Start with the body of the page first. Create a label that says **Enter your first name** and a corresponding input box with the placeholder of **First Name**.

4. Enter two <br> tags.

5. Create a submit button and set its text as **Submit Your Name**.

6. Enter two <br> tags.

7. Create a reset button and set its text as **Clear the Form**.

8. Save the file as **Exercise 10_1.html** and test it. Once you establish that your input box and the buttons are working, move to the next section.

9. Create a <style> section in the head of the HTML document.

10. Enter a style that makes the button's background color yellow and the text color green when the button is hovered over. Remember, the syntax for a pseudo-class is `selector:pseudo-class { property: value; }`, and in this case, the selector is `button`.

11. Test your web page. When you hover over either button, the background should be bright yellow and the words green.

ANSWER:

The code should be as follows:

```
<!DOCTYPE html>
<html lang="en-us"?
<head>
 <title> hover </title>
</head>
 <style>
  button:hover {
  color: green;
  background-color: yellow;
  }
 </style>
</head>
<body>
 <hr>
 <label for="first"> Enter your first name. </label>
 <input type="text" id="first" name="first" placeholder="First Name">
```

```
<br><br>

<button type="submit"> Submit Your Name </button> <br><br>
<button type="reset"> Clear the Form </button>

</body>
</html>
```

EXERCISE 10.2

Identify the Order of Precedence

In this exercise, you observe the order of precedence in action.

1. Open the file named exercise 10_1.html.

2. Save it as **exercise 10_2.html**.

3. In the body of the web page, after the two buttons create two paragraphs with some random text in them.

4. Save the file and open it in a browser to verify that your page works and to make a mental note of how the paragraphs look. This should be the default styling of your web browser.

5. Open another instance of your text editor and create a CSS file that makes the paragraph text purple with a background color of #d8f9ff. Refer back to Chapter 9 if you need a reminder.

6. In the folder where your HTML file is located, create a subfolder called **styles**.

7. Save the CSS file as **styles1.css**.

8. Ensure that you have entered the button style into the CSS file, removed the style section from the HTML page, and created a reference to your styles1.css file in the HTML page's head.

9. Open your HTML file and verify that hover works and that the paragraphs have purple text and a light blue background. The style of the paragraphs is now determined by the style sheet.

10. At the second paragraph in your HTML file, create an **id=special**.

11. In the style sheet, enter a style to set the background color of special to yellow.

12. Save your HTML file.

13. Save your style sheet.

EXERCISE 10.2 *(continued)*

14. Refresh your HTML page in the browser. The second paragraph's background should now be yellow. The yellow setting takes precedence over the blue setting because the id selector is more specific than the paragraph selector is.

15. Save your styles1.css file as **styles2.css**.

16. Save your exercise 10_2.html file as **exercise 10_2a.html**.

17. Edit styles2.css, placing a style at the bottom that sets the paragraph text to white and background color to black. Save the file.

18. Edit exercise 10_2a.html so that it references styles2.css.

19. Save the HTML file.

20. Refresh the browser and observe what happens.

The paragraph style at the bottom of the CSS file takes precedence over the other paragraph entry because it's last on the page. The text in your paragraphs should all be white, but only the first paragraph should have a black background because the id selector on the second paragraph is still more specific than the paragraph selector.

ANSWER:

The code of styles1.css should be:

```
button:hover {
 color: green;
 background-color: yellow;
 }
p {
 color: purple;
 background-color: #d8f9ff;
 }
#special {
 background-color: yellow;
 }
```

The code of exercise 10_2.html should be:

```
<!DOCTYPE html>

<html lang="en-us">

<head>

 <title> Hover </title>
```

```
<meta charset="utf-8">
<link rel="stylesheet" href="styles/styles1.css"/>

</head>

<body>
<hr>
<label for="first"> Enter your first name. </label>
<input type="text" id="first" name="first" placeholder="First Name"><br><br>

<button type="submit"> Submit Your Name</button> <br><br>
<button type="reset"> Clear the Form</button>

<p> This is my first paragraph with some random text. </p>
<p id=special> This is my second paragraph with some random text in it. </p>

</body>

</html>
```

The styles2.css file adds the following lines of code to styles1.css:

```
p {
 color: white;
 background-color: black;
 }
```

The exercise 10_2a file changes the <link> line to:

```
<link rel="stylesheet" href="styles/styles2.css:"/>
```

Review Questions

1. Which type of selector needs a hashtag before it when assigning a style in a style sheet?

   A. Class

   B. Descendant

   C. Element

   D. `id`

2. Which category of selectors use an element to identify the parts of the page to be styled?

   A. Class

   B. Descendant selectors

   C. Non-inherited properties

   D. Type selectors

3. Which of the following apply a style only to elements in both the `special` class and the `first` class?

   A. `.special, .first {property:value;}`

   B. `.special AND first {property:value;}`

   C. `.special .first {property:value;}`

   D. `.special.first {property:value;}`

4. Which of these is not an advantage of using classes and `id`s as selectors?

   A. They make the code less cluttered.

   B. They add complexity, so others won't steal your code.

   C. They help prevent human error.

   D. They save time when making changes.

5. What does the CSS line `a:hover {color: yellow; }` do?

   A. Changes the color of the page when a user is on it

   B. Makes the background of a paragraph yellow

   C. Changes a button color to yellow when a mouse hovers over it

   D. Changes the color of a hyperlink to yellow when a mouse hovers over it

6. Which of the following are pseudo-classes? (Choose two.)

   A. `:hover`

   B. `:focus`

   C. `id="special"`

   D. `#myList`

7. Which of these is correct for specifying a style for an id?
    A. .idName {property:value;}
    B. #idName {property:value;}
    C. #idName {property;value;}
    D. !idName {property:value;}

8. Which of these is not a place where CSS styles are created?
    A. In the <styles> section of the <html> <head>
    B. Using the styles attribute in the <html> <body>
    C. In the <styles> section of the <html> <body>
    D. In a CSS style sheet

9. You want to create a style called mammals that styles a specific paragraph, but not the others. Which of the following do you need? (Choose two.)
    A. <p id="mammals">
    B. .mammals { property:value; }
    C. style.mammals { property:value; }
    D. #mammals { property:value; }

10. You just created a new HTML page. It's the first file you've created for this page. Where does it get the font for the page from?
    A. Your browser.
    B. The associated style sheet.
    C. The parent element.
    D. It will be blank until you specify a style to use.

11. Conflicting styles have been specified for the <ol> element. Where will the <ol> element get its style from if the following exist?
    A. An entry near the top of the style sheet that styles ordered lists
    B. An entry near the bottom of the style sheet that styles ordered lists
    C. An entry that styles the body of the web page
    D. An entry that styles all paragraphs of the web page

12. You want several paragraphs to be styled the same but not all paragraphs. Which two of the following will you need? (Choose two.)
    A. <p class="className">
    B. <p id="idName">
    C. <style> .className {property:value; }
    D. <style> #className {property:value; }

13. Which of these is correct for specifying a style for a class?

   A. `.className {property:value;}`

   B. `#className {property;value;}`

   C. `className {property;value;}`

   D. `!className {property:value;}`

14. Your style sheet contains the following lines:
`body {color: "blue"; font-family:`
`"Arial"; background-color: white;}` and
`p {background-color: yellow; }`. How will the paragraphs be styled?

   A. With an Arial font and a white background

   B. With an Arial font and a yellow background

   C. With the default browser font and a white background

   D. With the default browser font and a yellow background

15. Which of the following make a hyperlink turn red when it has been clicked?

   A. `a:link {color: red; }`

   B. `a:link visited {color: red; }`

   C. `a:hover {color: red; }`

   D. `a:visited {color: red; }`

16. Which of these is the correct way to apply a style to more than one selector?

   A. `p AND #footer {property:value;}`

   B. `p, #footer {property:value;}`

   C. `#special.p {property;value}`

   D. `.special: .p {property;value;}`

17. Which of these will have the same style as is applied to a single `<div>`, if no other styles are applied?

   A. `<body>`

   B. Any element within the `<div>`

   C. Any element that comes after the `<div>`

   D. Only the `<div>` paragraphs will be styled that way.

18. You want to change the background color of an item only when it is the item being examined on the page. What are you using to do this? (Choose two.)

   A. A class

   B. `:focus`

   C. A pseudo-class

   D. `:active`

19. Your CSS page has the following rules:

```
body {
color: blue;
font-family: chiller;
}
p {
color: black;
{
div {
color: green !important;
}
```

What color will the text of a paragraph inside the division be?

A. Blue

B. Green

C. Black

D. Browser default color

20. You're making an ordered list where the division it's in is styled with the `.fun` class, but you want only the list items to be orange. What is the best way to write your style to achieve this?

A. `li.fun {color: orange;}`

B. `.li .fun {color: orange;}`

C. `.fun li {color: orange;}`

D. Enter `<li color="orange">` at each list item.

Chapter

11

CSS Styling Fundamentals

LINUX PROFESSIONAL INSTITUTE, WEB DEVELOPMENT ESSENTIALS EXAM 030-100 OBJECTIVES COVERED IN THIS CHAPTER:

✓ **033 CSS Content Styling**

- 033.3 CSS Styling: The candidate should use CSS to add simple styles to the elements of an HTML document.

  - Key Knowledge Areas:

    - Understand fundamental CSS properties

    - Understand units commonly used in CSS

  - Files, terms, and utilities:

    - px, %, em, rem, vw, vh

    - color, background, background-*, font, font-*, text-*, list-style, line-height

This chapter gets down to the nitty-gritty of website development. The concepts here are so integral to creating a website that several of them have been informally introduced in other chapters. The concepts of absolute or relative units of measure, colors and fonts will be daily considerations when you're developing websites, so be sure to take good notes, highlight important information, or use any other tool that helps you remember the tools you learn in this chapter. Let's get started!

Units of Measure

Depending on where you live (or perhaps your generation), you've learned to measure in inches or centimeters and quarts or liters. Websites, too, have their different units of measure and places where the use of each is appropriate.

You might not realize it, but you've used several units of measure as you've worked through this book. Some that you've used are pixels (px), larger, and em. Some units of measure are absolute units (pixels) and others are relative units (larger, em).

Absolute Units

Absolute units are those that are specific and consistently measurable. They don't change. Examples include centimeters (cm), millimeters (mm), inches (in), pixels (px), points (pt), and picas (pc). In Cascading Style Sheets (CSS), a *pixel* is 1/96th of an inch and is commonly used to describe the size of an image. An inch is always equal to 2.54 centimeters. A centimeter (cm) is always equal to 10 millimeters (mm), and so on. Figure 11.1 should give you an idea of the relationship between the different units of measure. The units won't be exactly as you see them on your device because each device (monitor, smartphone, printer, etc.) may render the image differently, but Figure 11.1 gives you an idea of how they compare.

The small gray box inside the cm box is one mm. The small gray box inside the 1pc box is a pt, and the small gray box inside the 10 px box is a single pixel.

If you prefer to do the math, please refer to Table 11.1. For example, if you know you want text to be 2 inches high and your font needs to be expressed in points (pt), multiply the height in inches (2) by 72 (points per inch). Therefore, 2 inches = 144 points. Conversely, an 18-point font will be 1/4 of an inch (18 divided by 72).

FIGURE 11.1   Comparing absolute measurements

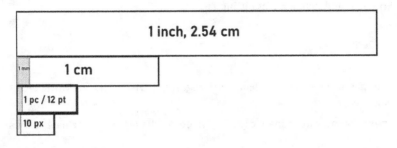

TABLE 11.1   Absolute units

Unit	Equal to
1 inch	2.54 cm, 72 points, 96 px
1 cm	10 mm
1 pc	1/6 of an inch, 12 points
1 pt	1/72 of an inch
1 px	1/96 of an inch

Pixels measurements can be quirky. A pixel in CSS is 1/96th of an inch. A pixel on a computer monitor is a dot of color made by combining red, green, and blue light. Pixel density (or pixels per inch) can vary by monitor, so a 2560×1440 pixel monitor might be the same physical size as a 3840×2160 pixel monitor, but the pixel density is much greater in the second case. When you're working on a website, remember that pixels mean different things depending on what is being discussed.

Relative Units

Relative units are based on some other object's size, so the same relative measurement might be a different physical measurement depending on the value that the unit is related to. The em is compared to an element's font size; for example, 3em is 3 times the current element's font size. So you could define a class using em:

```
.three {
Font-size: 3em;
}
```

You could then use the class to define a paragraph, division, or any other element in web page text, such as:

```
<p> Some text here, but <span class="three"> this text is three times bigger, </span>
and more text here. </p>
```

Other common relative units that you need to know are found in Table 11.2.

TABLE 11.2   Common relative measurements

Relative unit	Equates to
em	A multiple of the current element's font size (that is, 0.5em = 1/2 the font size).
rem	A multiple of the root element size. (In CSS, the root element is the default font size of the HTML element in the browser being used (unless you specify the font size for the HTML element, in which case the specified size will be one rem). One rem is the same throughout a document, but an em may change with the element it relates to.
vw	Relative to 1% of the browser window width (that is, viewport width.) For example, on a smartphone with a 6.9cm width, 10vw is 0.69cm (or 10% of 6.9).
vh	Relative to 1% of the browser window height. For example, on a laptop monitor that is 10 inches high, 20vh would be 2 inches high (or 10×20%).
%	Relative to the size of the parent element. For example, if a parent font is 18 points, 30% would make the selected text 6 points.

Creating your page using relative units is a way to ensure that your page looks consistent regardless of the device it's being viewed on.

Common Properties

There will be properties that you repeatedly use, others that you'll only use once in a while, and still others that you'll think, "I wonder if I can. . ." and then you'll start searching for the right properties to use. In the next section, we look at several of those properties that are used often.

Color

By now, using color in your code should be familiar to you. You've already learned that color can be identified by a keyword (i.e., red, yellow, green, purple, and so on) or by red-green-blue values between 0 and 255, such as rgb(0,255,0) for very dark green, or hexadecimal numbers (also with values between 0 and 255 but expressed in hexadecimal notation where digits 0 through 9 and A through F are used to represent values). The hex value #00FF00, for example, is very dark green. If you want to learn more about the hexadecimal number system, try the tutorial at www.cliffjumpertek.com/hex-is-fun.

Some of the common (rainbow) colors are listed in Table 11.3 and can be found in numerous resources online. An example of specifying a color in each case follows:

```
h1 {
color: orange;
}
h2 {
color: rgb(255,165,0) ;
}
h3 {
color: #FFA500 ;
}
```

TABLE 11.3   Color values

Keyword	rgb value	Hex value
Black	rgb(0,0,0)	#000000
Brown	rgb(165,42, 42)	#A52A2A
Red	rgb(255,0,0)	#FF0000
Orange	rgb(255,165,0)	#FFA500
Yellow	rgb(255,255,0)	#FFFF00
Green	rgb(0,128,0)	#00FF00
Blue	rgb(0,0,255)	#0000FF
Violet	rgb(238,130,238)	#EE82EE
Gray	rgb(127, 127, 127)	#7F7F7F
White	rgb(255,255,255)	#FFFFFF

Another consideration with color is opacity. *Opacity* is a measure of how transparent or opaque (solid) a color is. Opacity is expressed as a number between 0 and 1, where 0 is completely transparent and 1 is opaque. For example:

```
.pale {
opacity: 0.25;
}
.medium {
opacity: 0.5;
}
.opaque {
opacity: 1;
}
```

See Figure 11.2 for a visual of this effect.

FIGURE 11.2   Opacity

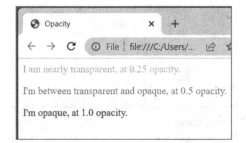

Opacity can also be specified along with an rgb color by using rgba instead, where *a* is the value of opacity. Instead of three numbers between 0 and 255, a fourth number between 0.0 and 1.0 will specify the opacity. For example, rgba(238,130,238,0.5) will result in a color of violet with 50 percent opacity.

Background

The background property has several values that can be specified, such as color, image, position, size, and repeat. In Chapter 5, "HTML Introduction," we used the style attribute with background-color:color-name; to change the color behind a line of text. This same attribute/value combination can be used to change the background of a paragraph, division, or any other element. When used with the <body> element, the background setting affects the entire document.

Often the `background` property is used to place an image behind a document or part of a document. When specifying an image to use in the background, you need to identify the image with **url**("***image path***"). For example:

```
body {
background-image:url("flower.jpg");
{
```

which assumes that `flower.jpg` is in the same folder as the HTML file. Refer back to Chapter 7, "References and Embedded Resources," if you need a refresher on how to properly enter the path to a file.

If the background image doesn't completely fill the screen, it will repeat by default until the screen is filled, starting at the top left and going right as far as the width of the browser screen, then repeating on the next line and so on. To stop it from repeating, add `no-repeat`; to the code like so:

```
body {
background-image: url("flower.jpg");
background-repeat: no-repeat;
}
```

The other options for `background-repeat` are `:repeat-x` (as in x-axis), which will repeat the image horizontally across the screen from left to right, or `:repeat-y` (as in y-axis), which will repeat the image vertically on the screen.

As mentioned previously, the default position for a background image is the top left of the browser screen; however, you can change this with the `background-position` property. The image can be placed with the relative positions of left, right, and center, and top, bottom, and center. If only one value such as `top` is specified, then `center` is assumed for the other value. For example: `background-position: center center`; would put the image centered in the screen both vertically and horizontally. The position can also be specified by using two percentages that indicate horizontal and vertical in that order. For example, `background-position: 0% 100%`; would be the left bottom, `0% 0%` is top left, and `100% 100%` is bottom right of the browser screen.

Finally, the background image can be positioned using absolute values, again with the first value being horizontal position and the second value being vertical. If only one is given, then the other will default to 50 percent. Percent and absolute measurements can be mixed. For example, `background-position: 20px 20%`; would put the image 20 pixels from the left and 20 percent of the total length down the page.

`background` by itself can be used as a sort of shorthand, mixing different properties in the same line. For example:

```
body {
background: blue url("flower.jpg") no-repeat bottom center;
}
```

Borders

We often want to emphasize an image or object by placing a box around it, which is called a *border*. Borders were mentioned in Chapter 7, but we'll go into more detail here. A color can be specified for a border as it is for other attributes, but a border style can also be specified. Figure 11.3 shows the available border styles, and if you're reading this online, you'll see different colors too.

Border width can be specified using keywords of thin, medium, or thick, or by using absolute measurements such as pixels, points, or mm.

A border can have up to four values representing the four sides of the box. If only one style is specified, it will be for all four sides. If two are specified, the first value applies to the top and bottom borders, and the second value applies to the left and right borders. If three are specified, the order is top (1), right and left (2), then bottom (3). If four values are specified, the order is top (1), right (2), bottom (3), and left (4). In the line `border-style: solid, double, dotted;` the top is solid, the left and right borders are double, and the bottom is dotted.

FIGURE 11.3   Border styles

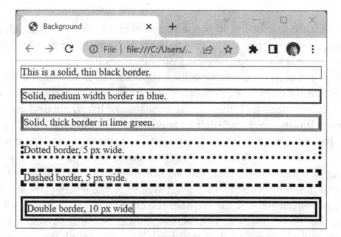

The following is a segment of the code that was used to create Figure 11.3. As it's somewhat repetitive, only the first two styles for border types are shown.

```
<style>
  .b1{
    border-style: solid;
    border-width: thin;
    }
  .b2{
    border-style: solid;
```

```
    border-width: medium;
    border-color: blue;
    }
```

Font

As mentioned previously in Chapter 10, "Applying CSS Styles," if a font isn't found on a computer, it needs to be installed. There's no way to know if your website visitor will have that perfect font that you want to use for your website. If the font isn't there, then the browser's default font is used. Most browsers use a serif font, but there are five generic font styles. *Serif fonts* have "tails" on letters that make the letters flow together visually. *Sans-serif fonts* don't have tails on the letters. In *monospace fonts*, every character takes up the same width. In other fonts, the character width is proportional to the letter. The fourth generic type is *cursive fonts*, which is intended to look like handwriting, and the last is *fantasy fonts*, which are quite unusual fonts that have their own particular flourish, designed to evoke a certain mood depending on the font. See Figure 11.4 to see examples of these generic types. Most browsers will have a serif, sans-serif, and monospace font available.

FIGURE 11.4   Generic font styles

Times New Roman is a serif font.

Arial is a sans-serif font.

Currier New is a monospaced font.

Lucida Handwriting is a cursive font.

Chiller is a fantasy font.

You'll want to specify one of these generic font families so that the web page will look as close as possible to your desired font, if the desired font is not available. A font would be entered as:

```
selector {
font-family:  chiller, papyrus, sans-serif;
}
```

In the preceding code, the chiller font will be applied unless it's not available on the target system, in which case the browser will look for the papyrus font. If that isn't available either, the default font will be applied in the sans-serif style. When multiple fonts are specified as in our example, the browser looks for the fonts in the order that they're specified in the code.

Other font-related properties are as follows:

`font-size`: From xx-small to xxx-large, relative to the default font size used by the browser (example: `font-size: xx-small;`). Font size can also be expressed in the other measurements you've learned such as pixels and points.

`font-weight`: Equates to density/thickness of the font relative to the parent object. Options are normal, bold, lighter, bolder, or a value from 100 to 900. The best way to see these options is to try them in a sample web page/CSS sheet (example: `font-weight: 900;`).

`font-style`: Examples are bold, italic, oblique, or oblique 25deg, where the degree value tells the browser how much to slant (oblique) the font. It's best to use a font family that has options for italic and oblique, but if the currently selected font family doesn't, the browser may attempt to slant the text. Italics is usually finer than oblique. For oblique, allowed values are –90 to 90 (example: `font-style: oblique 40deg;`).

Figure 11.5 shows just some of the font options.

FIGURE 11.5 Font options

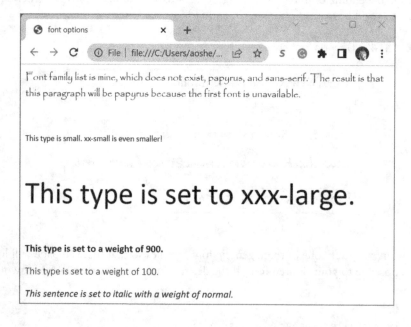

Text

There are a myriad of text-formatting properties, which is why the objectives list them as `text-*`.

You've already learned to format the color of text, such as `body { color:blue; }` using color keywords, rgb values, and hex values, so properties such as `text-decoration-color` are not listed in Table 11.4. Color might be the most used of the text properties. The syntax for any of the following properties is `text-property : value;`. With so many text properties and even more values, we'll use Table 11.4 to show the most popular ones. This is *not* an exhaustive list. The text properties also support global values of inherit, initial, revert, revert-layer, and unset, so those won't be listed each time.

TABLE 11.4   Text properties

Property	What it does	Values	Examples
`text-align:`	Sets the horizontal position of inline text	start, end, left, right, center, justify, match parent	`text-align: center;`

`text-indent:`	Determines how much space to leave to the left of a line of text	em, %, px, mm, and so on, and can include each-line, hanging, or hanging each-line	`text-indent: 5%;`
			`text-indent: 3em;`
			`text-indent: 6em hanging;`

`text-decoration-line:`	Underlines, over-lines, colors a line or section of text	underline, overline, wavy, dotted, blink, color name, size (e.g., px), line through	`text-decoration: wavy underline purple;` `text-decoration: line-through red;`
`text-decoration-style:`	Sets the style of underline	solid, double, dotted, dashed, wavy	`text-decoration-style: double`
`text-decoration`	Allows the programmer to specify line, color, style, and thickness in one entry (shorthand)	Any of the preceding text-decoration-* values	`text-decoration: wavy underline purple 3px;` `text-decoration: line-through red;`
`text-align-last:`	Aligns the last line of a block or line of text before a break	right, center, left, auto, start, end, justify	`text-align-last: justify;` `text-align-last: right;`

`text-emphasis-style`	Sets the character to use for text emphasis	Keywords: filled, open, dot, circle, double-circle, triangle, filled sesame, open sesame, keyboard characters in quotes, and Unicode characters in quotes	`text-emphasis-style: double-circle filled;`
			`text-emphasis-style: "X";`
			`text-emphasis-style: "\220e";`

TABLE 11.4   Text properties *(continued)*

Property	What it does	Values	Examples
text-emphasis	Adds emphasis above selected text, a shorthand for text-emphasis-style and text-emphasis-color	All as in text-emphasis-style plus color keywords and values	text-emphasis: red double-circle filled; text-emphasis: yellow "x";
text-orientation	Sets the orientation of characters in a line, requires use of writing mode	mixed, upright, sideways-right, sideways, use-glyph-orientation	Writing-mode: vertical-rl; text-orientation: mixed
text-shadow	Applies a shadow to specified text	Pixels, colors. Syntax offset-x, offset-y, blur radius, color	text-shadow: 2px 2px 3px limeGreen;

The `text-decoration:` property inherits values, while the `text-emphasis:` property doesn't. `text-emphasis` can affect the height of the line. `text-decoration` doesn't, so if an underline is set very large and the text wraps to the next line, it may be hidden by the underline unless the line height is adjusted. `text-emphasis` puts the chosen characters above the text, while `text-underline` can be above or below the text.

In the `text-shadow` property, the color can be anywhere in the order, but values entered for offsets and blur will be interpreted as `offset-x, offset-y, blur`.

List Style

There are two types of lists that are used on web pages. Lists will either be ordered, meaning numbered or otherwise identified, or lists will be unordered. Unordered lists aren't enumerated, but may be bulleted. Let's start with unordered lists.

Unordered Lists

As with text properties, there are so many list properties that it's impossible to list everything you can do with them here. `list-style` is shorthand for `list-style-image`, `list-style-position`, and `list-style-type`. Perhaps the simplest is `list-style: none`, which eliminates the bullets on an unordered list.

List style types include the keywords disc, circle, square, decimal, and keyboard characters and Unicode values in quotes. This is only a partial list. An example is list-style-type: "*";.

To use an image as a bullet, insert the location into the list-style property such as list-style: url("/images/puppy.gif").

The list-style-position options are inside or outside. The outside option places all text to the right of the bullet, even when the text wraps to the next line. The inside option lets the wrapping text start under the bullet.

Putting them all together, we might have a line like list-style: inside '\2206'; or list-style: outside square;. Make certain that you use the correct quotes if using Unicode. The bullets by default are black. If you want differently colored bullets, the easiest way is likely to create a PNG file that matches the size and color of the bullet that you want.

Ordered Lists

The default style for ordered list is numbers 1. 2. 3. and so on. However, they can be changed using a numbering *type*, or list-style-type: type;. Your options are upper-alpha (A), lower-alpha (a), and upper-roman (I), and lower-roman (i) for Roman numerals. numbers (1) is the default.

To change the numbering style at the <ol> attribute, use <ol type= "i"> for lowercase Roman numerals and so on. Alternately, use list-style-type: lower-roman; in a CSS style class.

Figure 11.6 shows some unordered and ordered list styles.

Relevant parts of the code that made the list in Figure 11.6 follow. The CSS styles are on single lines to save space.

```
<style>
    body {font-family: calibri; }
    ul.a {list-style: inside square; }
    ul.b {list-style: outside '\2206'; }
    ul.c {list-style; inside url("puppy.png"); }
    ol.roman {list-style-type: upper-roman; }
    ol.lower {list-style-type: lower-alpha; }
</style>
</head>
<body>

    <ul class="a"> Unordered List with inside and square.
        <li> First item.  Let's let the text wrap to the next line so you can
see what inside does.  </li>
        <li> Second item.  </li>
        <li> Third item.    </li>
    </ul>

    <ul class="b"> Unordered List with outside and Unicode.
```

```
    <li> First item.  Let's let the text wrap to the next line so you can
see what inside does.  </li>
    <li> Second item.  </li>
    <li> Third item.    </li>
  </ul>

  <ul class="c"> Unordered List with an image.
    <li> First item. </li>
    <li> Second item.  </li>
    <li> Third item.    </li>
  </ul>

  <ol class="roman"> Ordered list with Roman numerals.
    <li> First item. </li>
    <li> Second item.  </li>
    <li> Third item.    </li>
  </ol>

  <ol class="lower"> Ordered list with lowercase letters.
    <li> First item. </li>
    <li> Second item.  </li>
    <li> Third item.    </li>
  </ol>

  <ol type="I">  Ordered list with Roman numerals.
    <li> First item. </li>
    <li> Second item.  </li>
    <li> Third item.    </li>
  </ol>
```

Line Height

line-height comes in handy when using underlines that are big and bold, or when writing a poem or other text where you would like more space between lines. The options are line-height: normal; and line-height: value, where the value is expressed as a multiple of normal, or in other measurements you've learned about earlier such as em, %, and px.

FIGURE 11.6   List style examples

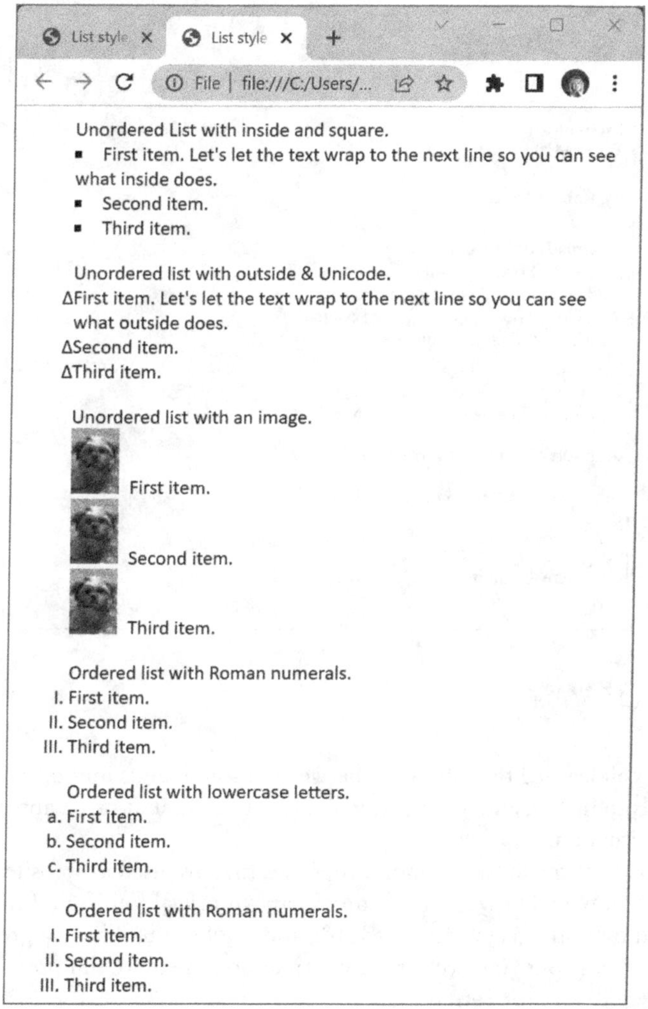

Figure 11.7 shows an example of text with a normal line height for the font and with a line height of 200 percent. The syntax is simply `line-height: measurement;`, and the example in Figure 11.7 is `line-height: 200%;`.

FIGURE 11.7   Adjusting line height

Summary

In this chapter, you learned the difference between absolute units and relative units. You compared pixels to inches, and looked at whether a relative unit or an absolute unit is needed for the situation.

You also looked at the most common properties that are used in websites and the impact they can have. You wouldn't want to use an overly whimsical font for a funeral parlor's website, but beyond that opacity, line-height, and background have a great impact on how visitors feel about your website, not to mention the more fun properties like text-shadow and text-orientation.

Occasionally you'll need a larger line height to accommodate your text and its emphasis, and if you're not happy with the default list bullets, you know how to change those, too, using the list-style property.

The terms and concepts are tools you'll use every day when you're creating or managing websites. Practice using them to hone your skills so when the time comes, you'll be ready.

Exam Essentials

Identify and know the CSS fundamental properties.   If you are coding on a daily basis, you'll be using these properties on a daily basis. You need to know what they are and how to use them.

Choose appropriately between relative and absolute units.   Sometimes using absolute units is best, and other times using relative units is best. You need to understand how each type works and when one or the other is a better choice.

Select the right color properties.   There is more to color than just picking a pleasing palette. You must be able to choose the right opacity for the situation.

Pick the right font and features.   Most of a website relies on the fonts you choose and the features of each. It's important to understand your options and be able to choose fonts that make sense for the material presented and that will be pleasing to your website visitors.

EXERCISE 11.1

Style an Element Using Units

In this exercise, you use relative and absolute units to style an element.

1. Begin with your HTML skeleton.

2. Title the project **Style with units**.

3. Set the font to Calibri or another sans-serif font, ensuring that you include the generic font name.

4. Create a style named **bigRed**. Configure the text to be 1 inch high using points and text color red using a keyword.

5. Create a style named **littleBlue**. Configure `littleBlue`'s font to be size medium and blue color by using an rgb value.

6. In the body of the document, create three paragraphs with some random text. Let the first be normal paragraph style. Style the second with the `bigRed` group and the last with the `littleBlue` group.

7. Save and test your file.

ANSWER:

```
<!DOCTYPE HTML>
<html lang="en-us">
<head>
  <title> Style with units </title>
  <style>
   body {
        font-family: calibri, sans-serif ;
        }
p.bigRed {
        font-size; 36pt ;
        color: red;
        }
p.littleBlue {
        font-size: small ;
        color: rgb(00,00,255);
        }
  </style>
</head>
<body>
<p> Random, normal text. </p>
<p class=bigRed> Here is some red random text. </p>
<p class=littleBlue> Here is some random blue text. </p>
</body>
</html>
```

Use Fundamental CSS Properties to Style an HTML Document

In this exercise, you work with background, borders, text, and ordered and unordered lists.

1. Choose a picture and use your favorite editing tool to make it a small size, such as 1/2-inch square.

2. Now, start with the HTML skeleton and title the project **Exercise 11.2**.

3. Style the body so that it uses the browser's default serif font and the image repeats across the bottom of the page from left to right.

4. Create another style group called **b1** that creates a border that is blue, dashed, and 10px thick.

5. Create another style called **u1** that underlines and overlines the selected text in red (using span to select the text later). Use the `text-decoration` shorthand.

6. Create a fourth style called **s4** that places a wavy, medium, purple line under selected text.

7. Create a style called **shadow** that applies a gray shadow to text with x and y offsets of 1 pixel and a blur radius of 3 pixels.

8. Create a style for an ordered list that uses uppercase Roman numerals.

9. Create a style for an unordered list that uses square bullets outside.

10. In the body of the document, make a paragraph for each of the four styles after the `<body>` style, and apply a different style to each paragraph.

11. Create an unordered list and an ordered list and apply those styles as appropriate.

12. Save and test your file.

ANSWER:

```
<!DOCTYPE HTML>
<html lang="en-us">
<head>
  <title> Exercise 11.2  </title>
  <style>
   body {
      font-family: serif ;
      background-image: url("puppy.png");  /*replace puppy.png with your
file name.*/
      background-position: bottom;
      background-repeat: repeat-x;
      }
    .b1 {
      border-color: blue;
      border-style: dashed;
      border-width: 10px;
      }
    .u1 {
      Text-decoration: underline overline red;
      }
```

```
    .s4 {
        Text-decoration: underline wavy purple;
        }
    .shadow {
        Text-shadow: 1px 1px 3px gray;
        }
    Ol.roman {
        List-style-type: upper-roman;
        }
    ul.osh {
        list-style: outside square;
        }
    </style>
</head>
<body>
  <p class=b1>  This text will have a blue border. </p>
  <p class=u1> This text will have a red underline and overline. </p>
  <p class=s4> This text will have a wavy purple underline. </p>
  <p class=shadow> This text will have a shadow behind it. </p>
  <ol class="roman">
     <li> These will be numbered with </li>
     <li> uppercase roman numerals.  </li>
     </ol>
  <ul class="os">
     <li> These will have an outside square </li>
     <li> as their bullet. </li>
     </ul>
</body>
</html>
```

Review Questions

1. Which of the following are relative units in CSS? (Choose two.)

   A. in

   B. px

   C. em

   D. %

2. Which of the following is *not* a valid value for a shade of blue?

   A. `color: light blue;`

   B. `color: rgb(255.165.0);`

   C. `color: rgb(0,100,255);`

   D. `color: ""#0000FF""`

3. Which of the following contains an invalid entry for the background property? (Choose two.)

   A. `background-size: fit;`

   B. `background-image: url("filename.png");`

   C. `background-repeat: -y;`

   D. `background-position: 100% 0%;`

4. You want to place a box around an element. Which of the following achieves this?

   A. `box-style: solid;`

   B. `box-style: rectangle;`

   C. `border-style: solid;`

   D. `border-style: dashed`

5. You enter the line `font-family: parchment, papyrus, serif;` in your web page body style. When you examine the page you created, the font is Times New Roman. Why? (Choose two.)

   A. The other fonts don't exist.

   B. The other fonts aren't installed on your computer.

   C. Times New Roman is the default serif font for Linux.

   D. Times New Roman is the default serif font for the browser.

6. Which line below places dots above a span of text? (Choose two.)

   A. `text-decoration-style: dotted above;`

   B. `text-emphasis-style: dot;`

   C. `text-emphasis: dot blue;`

   D. `text-decoration-style: dot;`

7. Which of the following lines are correct for unordered lists? (Choose two.)

    A. `list-style: disc blue;`

    B. `list-style: *;`

    C. `list-style: "x";`

    D. `list-style: url("mypic.gif");`

8. You're troubleshooting a website that has the following line: `<ol type="i">`. What will the numbering type be for the list that follows it?

    A. Uppercase alphabet

    B. Lowercase alphabet

    C. Numbers (1, 2, etc.)

    D. Lowercase Roman numerals

9. You're concerned about how your page will look on a smaller screen instead of your desktop monitor. Which of the following units would be helpful in ensuring that images won't take over a smaller screen? (Choose two.)

    A. vw

    B. in

    C. vh

    D. px

10. You have a background image that you don't want to repeat on the page. You want it centered vertically and horizontally regardless of what happens with the rest of the page. Which of the following code lines will do that?

    A. `body { background: "myimage.png" ; }`

    B. `body { background: url("myimage.png") ; }`

    C. `body { background: url("myimage.png"); no-repeat; }`

    D. `body { background: url("myimage.png") 50% 50% ; }`

11. You want to ensure that an element doesn't take over the entire screen when viewed on a smaller device. Which of the following will you use to ensure this?

    A. Absolute units

    B. Relative units

    C. Inches

    D. Pixels

12. You want a color to be more transparent than opaque. Which of the following makes it the most transparent but still have some color?

    A. `.pale { opacity: 0.0; }`

    B. `.pale { opacity: 0.2 }`

    C. `.pale {opacity. 0.2 }`

    D. `.pale {opacity: 0.8 }`

13. Which of the following lines will cause an image to be repeated from left to right on each row, filling the entire web page? (Choose two.)

A. `background: url("image.png");`

B. `background: repeat -y`

C. `background-repeat: l,r`

D. `background: repeat -x`

14. What is the default for an image's position if nothing is specified?

A. Top left

B. Top right

C. Centered vertically and horizontally

D. Bottom left

15. You want a font to be small. Which of the following will achieve this?

A. `font-size: small;`

B. `font-weight: 100;`

C. `font-weight: 900;`

D. `font-style: oblique 10%;`

16. In the line `border-style: double, dotted, solid;` what will the left border be?

A. Double

B. Dotted

C. Solid

D. No border

17. Which of the following styles will be inherited? (Choose two.)

A. `text-orientation:`

B. `text-shadow:`

C. `text-emphasis:`

D. `text-decoration:`

18. In the line `border-style: dashed,dotted;`, which borders will be dashed? (Choose two.)

A. Bottom

B. Left

C. Right

D. Top

19. Which of the following will result in an ordered list identified with uppercase letters such as A, B, and so on? (Choose two.)

    A. `<ol type="I">`

    B. `<ul type="A">`

    C. `<ol type="A">`

    D. `<style> ol.special {list-style-type: upper-alpha;} </style>`
          `<ol class="special">`

20. Which of these is equal to 1/72 of an inch?

    A. 1cm

    B. 1pc

    C. 1pt

    D. 1px

CSS Layout and Box Model

LINUX PROFESSIONAL INSTITUTE, WEB DEVELOPMENT ESSENTIALS EXAM 030-100 OBJECTIVES COVERED IN THIS CHAPTER:

✓ **033 CSS Content Styling**

- 033.4 CSS Box Model and Layout: The candidate should understand the CSS box model. This includes defining the position of elements on a web page. Additionally, the candidate should understand the document flow.

- Key Knowledge Areas:
    - Define the dimension, position and alignment of elements in a CSS layout
    - Specify how text flows around other elements
    - Understand the document flow
    - Awareness of the CSS grid
    - Awareness of responsive web design
    - Awareness of CSS media queries

- Files, terms, and utilities:
    - width, height, padding, padding-*, margin, margin-*, border, border-*
    - top, left, right, bottom
    - display: block | inline | flex | inline-flex | none
    - position: static | relative | absolute | fixed | sticky
    - float: left | right | none
    - clear: left | right | both | none

This chapter is all about how to get HTML elements where you want them on the page, and how those elements will flow through that page. It draws on what you learned in Chapter 5, "HTML Introduction," about the HTML hierarchy, Chapter 6, "Content Markup," about block and inline elements, and Chapter 11, "CSS Styling Fundamentals," about borders. You'll also discover some cool features such as how to make an element stay on the page when the visitor scrolls, and how web designers adjust the same page to different sizes of viewing screens. So, grab your notebook and get ready to have some fun.

The CSS Box Model

The *CSS box model* refers to the layers of space around an HTML element. Each CSS element takes up a certain space that can be visualized as an invisible box surrounding the element. Remember when we talked about inline and block elements in Chapter 6, that block elements go to the end of the line, and inline elements only take up the amount of space that they need. They follow each other in a line from left to right, then start again on the next line at the left, but regardless, everything in HTML exists within a box. Figure 12.1 uses color to show the boxes that exist around block and inline elements.

FIGURE 12.1 Boxes around block and inline elements

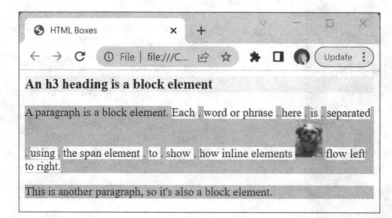

CSS Box Model Parts

The invisible boxes around an element can be surrounded by other boxes. *Margin* is the space between elements. A *border* is a visible box that surrounds the content, and *padding* is added space between the content and the border. In Chapter 11, we put different types of borders around paragraphs and specified border styles and widths. Figure 12.2 shows the box layers that surround an element—that is, our content, and the height and width of the entire element.

FIGURE 12.2   CSS box model layers

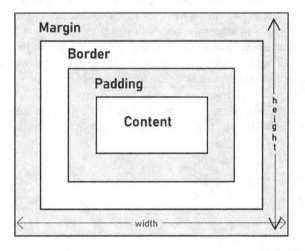

Element Dimensions

The *dimension of an element* is the total height and width of the element, including all its boxes. The height and width of each box related to the element can be specified, just as the borders were specified in Chapter 11.

Some elements have a default margin surrounding them. If not for the default margin for our content, we would need to specify a margin so that the text can be read more easily. Figure 12.1 uses default margins. Theoretically, an element, margin, padding, or border can be any size from zero on up, using absolute or relative measurements as in Chapter 11. Margins can be calculated automatically by the browser, by specifying a style of `margin: auto;`, causing the browser to center a box on a page each time the browser is resized.

Margin, padding, and border should all be specified as a style in a CSS sheet, rather than at the element or in the HTML header, as you learned in Chapter 9, "Introducing CSS." Each side of each box can have its own width or height specified just as they were with borders. If only one value is specified, the same measurement is used all around the box. If two measurements are used, then the top and bottom use the first measurement and the two sides use the second measurement. If four measurements are specified, then they are applied clockwise starting with the top of the box.

Figure 12.3 shows four paragraphs. The first specifies height (40px) and width (100px) of the content, plus a margin and dotted border. The first paragraph is 10px from the top and side of the page. The second paragraph has a margin of 20px, so the distance between it and all sides is 20px. The third paragraph has a zero margin, so the distance between paragraph two and paragraph three comes from the paragraph two setting, and because there is no margin, paragraph three starts flush with the left of the page. The fourth paragraph also specifies a zero margin, so the last two boxes are touching with no space between.

The fourth paragraph also specifies padding of 20px on the top and bottom, and 100px on the sides. The padding moves the content the specified distance from the sides of the box. Notice the difference between where the text is in paragraph three and paragraph four.

The total width of the first element (in this case, a paragraph) can be calculated by adding the width plus left and right margin, plus left and right border: Total width = 100 + 10 + 10 + 2 + 2 = 124px. The total height can be calculated similarly by adding the height plus top and bottom margin and top and bottom border: Total height = 40 + 10 + 10 + 2 + 2 = 64px.

In the body of the HTML page, remember that each paragraph would have an id, such as `<p id="first">` This is my first paragraph. `</p>`. The code for the related CSS sheet follows:

```
#first {
    background-color: lightGray;
    width: 100px;
    height: 40px;
    margin: 10px;
    border: 2px dotted;
    }
#second {
    background-color: yellow;
    margin: 20px;
    border: 0;
    }
#third {
    background-color: lightGray;
    margin: 0;
    }
#fourth {
    background-color:yellow;
    padding: 20px 100px;
    margin: 0;
    }
```

FIGURE 12.3   Padding around an element

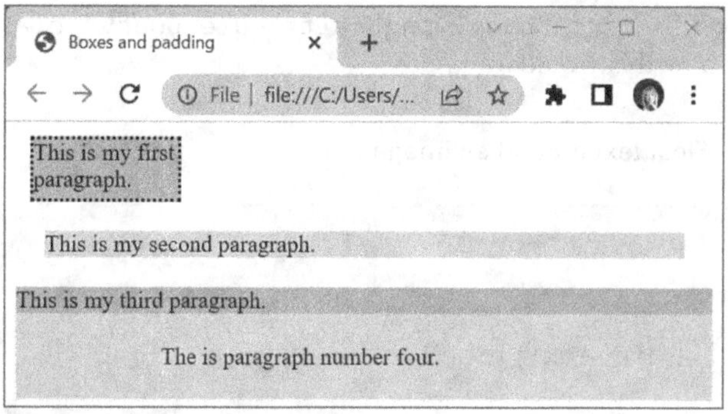

CSS Website Layout

Now that you know what the CSS box model is and how to create boxes, it's time to look at how to position those boxes on an HTML page.

Elements and Their Positions

When considering the position of elements in a page, *normal flow* (also called flow layout) is the default way elements are rendered, following the hierarchy of the web page. This means that block elements are stacked on top of each other, and inline elements flow from left to right, repeating as long as necessary to display the complete content of the inline element. Think of block elements as vertical stacks and inline elements as horizontal flow, and although block elements default to the entire width of the page, the width can be specified as in the first paragraph of Figure 12.3.

Within a web page's hierarchy, boxes can be nested inside other containers such as divisions, ordered and unordered lists, sections, and asides. If there are multiple child elements, such as several paragraphs in a division, then those paragraphs are stacked inside that division. The height of a container depends on the contents of the container, such as the paragraph with an image in Figure 12.1.

All elements will follow normal flow, stacked on each other, unless you specify otherwise.

Text Flow

Text normally flows within its block container (such as a paragraph), but what if you would like text to flow around other elements? You can do that using the `float` attribute. Elements can be floated left, right, but not center. To float an element to the right and have text flow around it, create a class in your CSS style sheet such as:

```
.right {
   float: right;
   padding: 0 0 0 10px;
   }
```

Assigning an image to this class will float it to the right of the paragraph that follows it and add padding for white space to the left of the image. In the HTML document, the line would be similar to `<img src="puppy.png" alt="cute puppy" class="right" />`. Figure 12.4 shows how this would look.

FIGURE 12.4   Float text around an image

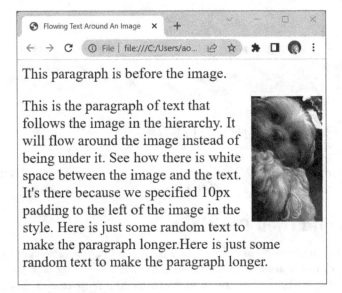

Document Flow

The `float` attribute isn't just for images. It can be used to change the flow of other elements within a web page. If you have three sections and want to move one of them to the left, you would add `class="left"` to your CSS sheet similar to the `class="right"` in the previous section, and then float the section left. When `float` is used, automatic margins are ignored, and instead of being above the next sections, the first section would appear floated to the left, as shown in Figure 12.5. To not float a box, the attribute:value pair `float: none` can be used.

You may be thinking, "Why not just use `text-align`?" `text-align` can't move an entire element. Instead, it aligns the text within the element, so as in Figure 12.5, `text-align` would not be able to move the entire Section 1 to the left and put the other two sections to the right. Similarly floating the object does nothing to align the text within the object (center, left, or right).

If you're floating text, you'll likely want to set the height and width of the section you're floating by adding an entry like width: 30%; to the style. Adding a border or whitespace around the section will separate it visually and keep the text from running together.

FIGURE 12.5   Floating a section left

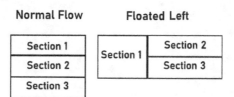

The clear attribute resumes normal flow, and could be entered in a style sheet with a class such as .stop { clear: left; }. Look again at Figure 12.5. If the stop class is applied to Section 4, Section 4 would go beneath Sections 1 through 3, resuming normal flow. The clear: left value skips any boxes floated left, and clear: right will skip any boxes floated right. Other values are clear: both and clear: none.

In addition to floating boxes, static positioning can be used. *Static positioning* follows the normal flow of elements but specifies the position they will be in. Values for the position property are absolute, fixed, relative, static, and sticky. Let's start with the most fun—the sticky value.

When using the sticky value, a box will scroll but stop at a position specified when the page keeps scrolling, so sometimes it's relative and sometimes it's fixed. It could be used to keep a picture or a map on the top of a page, a footer at the bottom, or even a sidebar. In the CSS style sheet, an entry might be h1 { position: sticky; top: 5px; }.

The other values are somewhat simpler. An explanation of each follows:

position:absolute places a box relative to the <body> element or relative to a parent that is not static, so it will follow the parent as it moves.

position:fixed places a box relative to the viewport. The viewport is the window that the page is being displayed in. The viewport changes size depending on whether the user is on a smartphone, a laptop, or other device.

position:relative places a box relative to its original position.

position:static follows the normal flow of the page.

The display property is used to change the way a box behaves. For example, display:inline can be used to make a box act like an inline element, although its use isn't recommended. If you want to hide an element, use display:none. display:block causes the element to be treated as a block element.

Display has another value called flex. The *CSS flexbox model* uses a flex container created when the flex value of the display attribute is used, in which the direct child elements of the flex container behave as if in a table row like inline elements. Elements that would normally be stacked are placed horizontally, not vertically. To use the Flexbox model, create a class using a style entry like .flexible { display:flex; }. Then in the <body> of the page, the flexible class would be assigned to a parent object like the code that follows:

```
<ul class="flexible">
  <li> item 1 </li>
  <li> item 2 </li>
  <li> item 3 </li>
</ul>
```

Figure 12.6 shows the difference between a normal list and a list inside a flexbox.

FIGURE 12.6   Flexbox vs. list

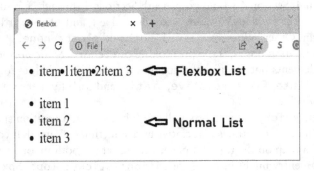

Other Layout Features

Another way to lay out a page that doesn't require floating anything and that gives you more control than a flexbox is the CSS grid layout. In a *CSS grid layout*, a grid container parent element is created with any number of child items arranged in horizontal rows and vertical columns, much like a spreadsheet. A class for the parent item is created like in the flexbox layout, then multiple child elements. Typically, divisions are used for the elements.

The grid-template-columns: attribute is used to set the number of columns desired. It can either be valued in specific units, or auto auto auto auto, which would divide the usable space into four equal columns. To put space between rows and columns use row-gap: unit and space-gap: unit as shown in the following code.

In the CSS sheet:

```
.gridParent {
    display: grid;
    column-gap: 30px;
```

```
    row-gap: 50px;
    grid-template-columns:auto auto auto auto;
    padding: 10px;
    }
.gridChild {
    border: 1px solid green;
    padding: 10px;
    font-size: large;
    text-align: center;
    }
```

In the <body> of the HTML page:

```
<div class="gridParent">
    <div class="gridChild"> 1 </div>
    <div class="gridChild"> 2 </div>
    <div class="gridChild"> 3 </div>
    <div class="gridChild"> 4 </div>
    <div class="gridChild"> 5 </div>
    <div class="gridChild"> 6 </div>
    <div class="gridChild"> 7 </div>
    <div class="gridChild"> 8 </div>
    <div class="gridChild"> 9 </div>
    <div class="gridChild"> 10 </div>
    <div class="gridChild"> 11 </div>
    <div class="gridChild"> 12 </div>

</div>
```

The result is the first grid layout in Figure 12.7. If you want a wider space, you could create a style such as .item6 { grid-column-start: 2; grid-column-end: 4; } and apply that class to Item 6 in the body of the HTML document with the line <div class="gridChild item6"> any content here </div>, which would result in the second grid layout in Figure 12.7. Instead of a number, each box would contain text, images, or whatever you desire on your web page.

Responsive web design is an approach to web development that adapts the page across all types of devices automatically, providing a pleasant user experience. One way to do this is using *media queries*, which cause the browser to detect aspects of the equipment being used to view the web page and respond accordingly. The one you'll explore here detects the size of the viewport and responds by using different code appropriate for that viewport. Media queries can also detect printers and speech recognition. The screen query is used to read the size of the viewport and causes the browser to recalculate each time the viewport changes, so even resizing a browser window could result in the page being displayed differently. For example, in our previous grid layout, using four columns might make each grid square too tiny to see on a smartphone, so we could use the code that follows to change to use four columns only when the viewport is 414 pixels or more wide:

```
@media(min-width:414px) {
   .gridParent {
   display: grid;
   column-gap: 10px;
   row-gap: 10px;
   grid-template-columns:auto auto auto auto;
   padding: 5px;
   } /* ends the class */
   }   /* ends the media query */
```

To see the difference when resizing your browser, use a larger minimum width such as 600 pixels.

FIGURE 12.7   A CSS grid layout container

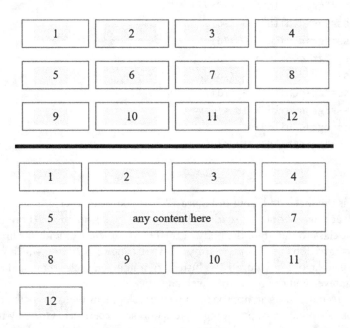

Summary

In this chapter, you learned that each element is inside an invisible box that can be modified by adding any margin, border, or padding. The total dimensions of the element include the width and height added by the margin, border, and padding.

Next, we looked at the normal flow of elements on a website and the normal flow of text, and how both can be changed by using the float attribute. You also learned how to set a floated object apart by using white space around it.

Static positioning follows the normal flow of elements, but can make their position relative to the page, the parent object, or the viewport.

Finally, you learned about the CSS flexbox model and CSS grid layout, and how to use media queries to create a responsive web design.

Exam Essentials

Know each part of the CSS box model.   You need to know what each part of the box model is and does so you can design appealing web pages using them.

Understand what normal flow is.   You need to understand the normal flow of elements and text before you can understand how to modify them to meet your needs.

Recognize the difference between CSS flexbox and grid layouts.   Each of these can be used to modify the normal placement of elements on your page, but you need to know which does what.

Explain what responsive web design and media queries are.   The certification objectives want you to be aware of these and how they work together.

Understand the values of the display attribute.   Whether you want an element's placement to be related to the page, the parent or the viewport will determine which value of the position attribute you'll use to achieve the desired result.

EXERCISE 12.1

Define a CSS Web Page Layout

In this exercise, you practice some of the page design and layout concepts that you've learned in this chapter.

1. Create or find an image that is 1 inch square.

2. Open your HTML skeleton.

3. Title the file **CSS Web Page Layout** and save it with the filename **exercise12_1.html**.

4. Create a style sheet and save it as **exercise12_1styles.css**.

5. Edit your HTML file to link the HTML file to the style sheet.

6. In the style sheet, create the following classes:

    - A class called **left** that will float an element left and place a 20px padding around the top, right, and bottom of the element.

- A class called **right** that will float an element right and put a 20px padding around the top, left, and bottom of the element.

- A class called **stop** that will clear all floats.

- A final class called **keep** that will have a sticky position at the top of the page.

7. Open your HTML file and add a paragraph that will at least be the width of the screen, then insert a line adding your image to the page. Float the image to the left and make it sticky so it will stay at the top when the page is scrolled.

8. Add at least three paragraphs of text to your HTML file, of about equal lengths and long enough that you would need to scroll the page to see all of it.

9. Allow the first of the three paragraphs to float around the image on the left. Make sure the paragraph is long enough to go under the image.

10. Insert another image after the first paragraph and float it to the right.

11. Allow the next paragraph of text to flow around the second image.

12. Use the style you created to stop the next paragraph from flowing around anything. It should take the width of the screen. You might need to make this paragraph longer so the page can scroll.

ANSWER:

When viewing the HTML page, the image on the left should stay at the top of the screen even when the page is scrolled all the way to the bottom of the page. The image on the right should disappear as the page is scrolled. You might need to adjust the browser width to see the effect if the paragraphs are not long enough.

CSS style sheet:

```
.left {
    float: left;
    padding: 10px 10px 10px 0;
    }
.right {
    float: right;
    padding: 10px 0 10px 10px;
    }
.stop {
    clear: both;
    }
.keep {
```

```
    position: sticky;
    top: 0;
    {
```

HTML page: Paragraphs should be much longer than what we are showing here so you will get the proper visual effect.

```
<!DOCKTYPE html>
<html lang="en-us">
<head>
   <title> CSS Web Page Layout </title>
   <meta charset="utf-8">
   <link rel="stylesheet" href="css/exercise12-1style.css" />
</head>
<body>
    <p> The paragraph should be long enough to go all the way across the
page. </p>
      <img src="your-file.png" alt="alt text here" class="left keep" />
      <p> This paragraph should be long enough to wrap around and under the
image on the left. </p>
      <img src="your-file.png" alt="alt text here" class="right" />
      <p> This paragraph will wrap around the image on the right. It should be
flush left. </p>
      <p class="stop"> This paragraph should be under both images, going from
the left to the right of the screen and long enough so you must scroll the
page to see the sticky effect of the left image. </p>
```

EXERCISE 12.2

Create Elements Following the Box Model

In this exercise, you use the CSS box model to change the appearance of text and images.

1. Begin with your HTML skeleton.

2. Title the file **CSS Box Model**, and save it as **exercise12_2.html**.

3. Create a style sheet with four different ids. Naming them **first**, **second**, and so on will make your work easier.

4. In your HTML file, create four different paragraphs with text of your choosing. (I used "This is my first paragraph." and so on.) Assign one of the four ids from step 3 to each paragraph.

5. Back in the style sheet, you'll practice adding the components of a box (margin, border, and padding) as appropriate. In the style sheet, configure the paragraphs as follows:

   ▪ **First paragraph:** Center the element on the page. Add a solid border of 5px wide. Add a box component that will make the space between the content and border 5px wide on the top and bottom, and 50px wide on the sides. Make the content area of the box 200px wide. Make the background color light green.

   ▪ **Second paragraph:** Add a double border 3px wide. Add a box component that will be outside the border and will put a space around this box of 50px. Give the content a background color #d4c1d9.

   ▪ **Third paragraph:** Add a dashed border 3px wide. Add a box component that will make the space between the content and the border 25 pixels on the top, 75 pixels on the bottom, 50 pixels on the right, and 150 pixels on the left. Make the background color yellow. Remove the default margin. Make the content width 100px.

   ▪ **Fourth paragraph:** Make the content width 100px. Set the background color to white. Give it a border that is gray and dotted and 5px wide. Remove the default margin and center the box.

6. Save your style page as **exercise12_2style.css** and create a link to it in the head of your HTML page; then save the HTML page.

7. Test the page by opening it in your browser.

ANSWER:

Style sheet:

```
#first {
    margin: auto;
    border: 5px solid;
    padding: 5px 50px;
    width: 200px;
    background-color: lightGreen;
    }
#second {
    border: double 3px;
    margin: 50px;
    background-color: #d4c1d9;
    }
```

```
#third {
    border: dashed 3px;
    padding: 25px 50px 75px 150px;
    background-color: yellow;
    margin: 0;
    width: 100px;
    }
#fourth {
    width: 100px;
    background-color: white;
    border: 5px gray dotted;
    margin: 0 auto;
    }
```

HTML page:

```
<!DOCKTYPE html>
<html lang="en-us">
<head>
    <title> CSS Box Model </title>
    <meta charset="utf-8">
    <link rel="stylesheet" href="css/exercise12-2style.css" />
</head>
<body>
    <p id="first"> This is my first paragraph.  </p>
    <p id="second"> This is my second paragraph.  </p>
    <p id="third"> This is my third paragraph.  </p>
    <p id="fourth"> This is paragraph number 4.  </p>
</body>
</html>
```

Your web page should look like Figure 12.8. If you have the print book rather than the online version, the colors will show as different shades of gray.

EXERCISE 12.2 *(continued)*

FIGURE 12.8 Answer to Exercise 12.2

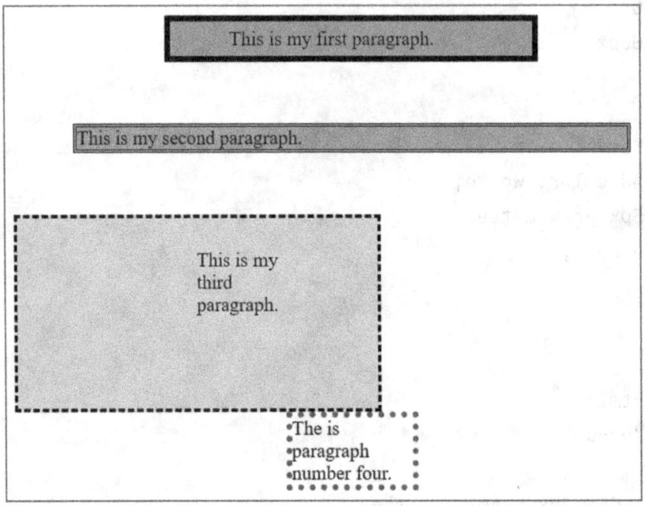

Review Questions

1. Which of the following refer to the layers surrounding an HTML element?

   A. CSS box model

   B. CSS flexbox model

   C. Static positioning

   D. CSS grid layout

2. An element's contents measures 100px high by 100px wide. The padding is 10px, the border is 3px, and the margin is 5px. What is the total height of the element in pixels?

   A. 100

   B. 118

   C. 136

   D. 236

3. Which of the following are needed to center a paragraph on a page? (Choose two.)

   A. `.middle {margin: center; }`

   B. `<p class="middle">`

   C. `<p #middle>`

   D. `.middle { margin: auto; }`

4. What is the position of elements called when block elements are stacked one on top of the next, each taking the entire width of the page, based on the web page hierarchy?

   A. Static positioning

   B. CSS Flexbox model

   C. Normal flow

   D. Text flow

5. Which of the following has the effect of making normally vertically arranged child objects flow horizontally (like text) instead?

   A. CSS Box model

   B. CSS Flexbox model

   C. Normal flow

   D. Text flow

6. Which CSS feature enables easy arranging of content by creating a pattern of boxes in columns and rows?

   A. CSS grid layout

   B. CSS flexbox model

   C. Normal flow

   D. Responsive web design

7. Which of these is not a part of the CSS Box model?

   A. Padding

   B. Border

   C. Content

   D. Stuffing

8. Paragraph 1 has no margin, and Paragraph 2 has a margin setting of 10px. How far apart are the two paragraphs?

   A. 0px

   B. 5px

   C. 10px

   D. 20px

9. Which of the following lines of code would be used to combine two boxes of a grid layout into one so content could be wider?

   A. `#item4 { grid-column-start: 4: grid-column-end: 5; }`

   B. `#item4 { grid-column-start: 4; grid-column-end: 6; }`

   C. `#item4 { combine: 4,5; }`

   D. `#item4 {span: 2 col; }`

10. Which part of the CSS box model would be used to put extra space around a paragraph and the space would have the same background color as the paragraph?

   A. Margin

   B. Border

   C. Padding

   D. Stuffing

11. You see the following line of code in a style sheet: `margin: 20px 30px 40px 10px;`. What is the measurement of the bottom margin in pixels?

   A. 10

   B. 20

   C. 30

   D. 40

12. Which of these describes the size of whatever you're seeing a web page's content in?

   A. Viewport

   B. Browser window

   C. Full screen

   D. Dimension

13. Considering the following code, what will the total width in pixels of the box be for the paragraph?

```
p {
    width: 80px;
    height: 50px;
    margin: auto;
    border: 10px solid;
    padding: 5px;
    }
```

- **A.** 0
- **B.** 80
- **C.** 110
- **D.** Width of the screen

14. Which of these does @media affect? (Choose two.)

- **A.** Search engine optimization
- **B.** Responsive web design
- **C.** Size of the viewport
- **D.** Presentation of a web page

15. You want to ensure that there is adequate space between an image and the text around it. Which of these is the most appropriate to use?

- **A.** Margin
- **B.** Padding
- **C.** Border
- **D.** Float

16. What will the style .new { clear: both; } do when applied to an element?

- **A.** Remove any pictures in the element.
- **B.** Float a picture on both sides of an element.
- **C.** Stop an element from floating on either side of the page.
- **D.** Ignore a float applied to any element above it.

17. You have a parent item that is not fixed on a page, and you want the immediate child item to follow it as it moves on the page. Which value of these do you need to use?

- **A.** position: absolute
- **B.** position: fixed
- **C.** position: relative
- **D.** position: follow

18. How will these list items be presented given the code `.flexible {display: flex; }` in the style sheet and the following in the HTML page?

```
<ol class="flexible">
  <li> first list item </li>
  <li> second list item </li>
  </ol>
```

    A. They will flow around an object.

    B. They will be stacked vertically.

    C. They will be in a horizontal line.

    D. They will only be visible in certain viewports.

19. Which of these lines tells the browser to display the child objects in equally sized columns?

    A. `display: pattern;`

    B. `column-gap: 30px;`

    C. `row-gap: 20px;`

    D. `grid-template-columns: 200 200 200;`

20. Using media queries is a part of what type of design?

    A. Normal flow

    B. Responsive web design

    C. CSS flexbox

    D. CSS box

Chapter

13

JavaScript Essentials

LINUX PROFESSIONAL INSTITUTE, WEB DEVELOPMENT ESSENTIALS EXAM 030-100 OBJECTIVES COVERED IN THIS CHAPTER:

✓ **034 JavaScript Programming**

- 034.1 JavaScript Execution and Syntax: The candidate should be able to execute JavaScript files and inline code from an HTML document and understand basic JavaScript syntax.

    - Key Knowledge Areas:

        - Run JavaScript within an HTML document

        - Understand the JavaScript syntax

        - Add comments to JavaScript code

        - Access the JavaScript console

        - Write to the JavaScript console

    - Files, terms, and utilities:

        - <script>, including the type (text/javascript) and src attributes

        - ;

        - //, /* */

        - console.log

Hypertext Markup Language (HTML), Cascading Style Sheets (CSS), and JavaScript (JS) are the three pillars of web page design. We use HTML to create and organize content, CSS to style the content, and JavaScript to program what happens on a page when a user's mouse hovers, when something is clicked, or when one of a myriad of other conditions is met. In other words, JavaScript makes our page interactive, dynamically updating the content.

In previous chapters, you learned about HTML and CSS. The next chapters teach the basics of using JavaScript. In this introductory chapter, you'll learn how to launch a JavaScript program and you're introduced to the rules for writing JavaScript code.

JavaScript Statements and Syntax

Like any other programming language, JavaScript has specific grammatical rules (syntax) that must be followed. Let's start with a JavaScript statement. A *JavaScript statement* tells the browser what you would like it to do. Statements can contain comments, expressions, keywords, operators, and values. Their types can be declaration statements, expression statements, conditional statements, loop statements, and error-handling statements. Each statement ends with a semicolon.

Let's start with a declaration statement. *Declaration statements* are used to create variables and functions. Consider the following two statements. The first creates a function named `writeGreeting`. The second creates a variable named greeting.

```
function writeGreeting();
var greeting;
```

Expression statements state or assign a value, such as `x = 1;`, which assigns a value, or `4-2;` and `"hello";`, which don't assign a value to a variable but do provide a value. Logical (Boolean) expressions equate to true or false, such as `1=1;` (true) or `500 < 50;` (false).

A *conditional statement* performs an action when a certain condition is met. The words *if* and *else* are used in conditional statements—for example, `if (x < 500) { do this thing ; }`, where *do this thing* is replaced with what you want it to do if the statement x < 500 is true. Think of else as false. So if the statement is true, do this. Else if it's false, do something else. For example:

```
if (x < 500) {
  x + 1;
  } else {
  x = 0;
  }
```

In the previous statement, if x is less than 500, x is increased by 1. Otherwise, if x is 500 or more, the value of x will be reset to 0.

Loop statements repeat an action as long as the condition of the statement is true. For example, consider the following code:

```
let x = 0;
while (x <10) {
  ++x;
}
```

The previous code first assigns the value of 0 to the variable x. As long as x is less than 10, it will increment (++) x by 1. As soon as x is equal to 10 or more, it will stop incrementing and move on to the next piece of code. The code will run 10 times, and on the 11th iteration, x will indeed equal 10 and the code will not increment x by 1. If you replaced let with if, the code would only run once.

Error-handling statements are used to find and define what will happen when an error in code is detected. An example is using try and catch statements when testing code. The syntax is try{ code to test} catch(err) { do this if there's an error in the previous code}.

JavaScript syntax has several rules to follow. The first is that each statement must end with a semicolon like CSS does. If the semicolon is omitted, then a feature called automatic semicolon insertion (ASI) may read the code as correct when the page is parsed (interpreted). If the code entered is:

```
let x=1
let y=2
(x+y)
```

a browser using (ASI) reads it as:

```
let x=1;
let y=2;
(x+y);
```

The code should function as it would with the ending semicolons. However, ASI doesn't always work, so the best course of action is to get in the habit of entering the semicolons.

Here are more JavaScript syntax rules:

- JavaScript is case sensitive. Mine does not equal mine.
- Identifiers can't begin with a number. They can begin with upper- or lowercase letters (A to Z, and a to z), dollar signs ($), or underscores (_).
- No hyphens are allowed in identifiers, such as first-name. Instead of a hyphen, use *lower camel case* where the first word is lowercased and the second word is uppercased to make reading identifiers easier. So, instead of first-name, use firstName. Constructors, which are placeholders for a new object, are often written in upper camel case, where all words start with a capital letter such as FirstName. Camel case is used by convention, not as a requirement.
- JavaScript can use single (') or double (") quotes, but double quotes are used more often. When quotes are nested, you'll need to use both single and double to identify which code goes with which quotes. For example, "Her name was 'Sarah'." Would be used to display: Her name was 'Sarah'.
- Arithmetic operators (+ - * /) are supported for computing values.
- JavaScript supports comparison operators like ==, !=, >=, !==, and so on.
- Arrays are defined using square brackets [ ].
- Functions, classes, and variables are defined with the keywords function, class, and var, respectively.
- Spaces are ignored in JavaScript (unless placed in quotes), so feel free to add them to make the script more readable.

Adding Comments

Comments are similar to comments in other programming languages, with a caveat. /* */ will comment out all that's between the two slashes. A double slash // will only comment out what follows on the same line. This means that /* */ must be used for multiline comments, as shown in the following code:

```
let x = y; // All the text here (after the double slash) is a comment.
Let y = 7; // y will = 7 because it's on a new line; a new statement.

Let x = y; /* Everything between the two slashes will be a comment.
Let y = 7;    And y will not equal 7 because it's part of the comment. */

let x = 10;

/* This is where I can specify that everything between slashes on
multiple lines is a comment.  Sometimes you'll need a long explanation that
will span multiple lines to remember why you coded the line the way that
you did.*/
```

Inserting JavaScript into HTML

For JavaScript to do its work, it must be embedded into your HTML file. All modern browsers include a JavaScript engine so they can run JavaScript in the user's browser, although the exact behavior it exhibits might be affected by the browser that's parsing it.

JavaScript can be added directly into an HTML element. Here is an example, showing only the necessary part of entering JavaScript in the HTML `<body>`, directly into the HTML code:

```
<body>
<h1> Demo embedding JavaScript <h1>
<h2> Directly in the body </h2>
<p> JavaScript can be a part of the body of the HTML page, like in the button on the
 next line. </p>
<button type="button" onclick="someFunction()"> Click here </button>
<p> More HTML content here </p>
</body>
```

JavaScript can be placed between `<script>` `</script>` tags, and any code between the tags will be executed by the browser as it's loading the page. It can be placed in the HTML `<body>` or `<head>`. Here is an example of the `<script>` tag in the `<head>` of an HTML page:

```
<head>
<title> Embedding JavaScript into html code. </title>
<script> alert("Wake Up!"); </script>
</head>
```

If the `<script>` tag is used in the head, the JavaScript is run before the remainder of the page. Any time the `alert` method is used, the user is required to click the displayed OK button before the page continues to load. See Figure 13.1.

FIGURE 13.1   An alert box

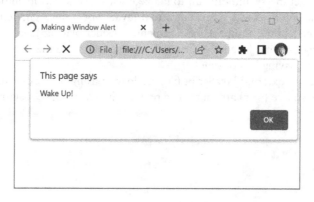

Here is an example of using the `<script>` tag in the body of an HTML page:

```
</head>
<body>
  <script> let who = prompt( "What's your first name?", "Visitor!");
    document.write("Hello " + who);
  </script>
```

The `prompt` method asks for user input. The two arguments between the open and close parentheses,`(` and `)`, are the label and default data. Neither is required. The second line will write the contents of the parentheses (`"Hello "` + who) to the document, changing the HTML page dynamically. `"Hello "` is in parentheses because it's text that will print (including the space), and who is not in parentheses because it is a variable containing a value. If the user does not enter their name but clicks the OK button, `Hello Visitor!` will appear on the HTML page. Note that the `document.write()` method clears everything from the HTML page before writing its contents. It should only be used in testing.

Both the `alert` and `prompt` methods stop the processing of the web page until the user interacts with the message.

Scripts can be placed anywhere in an HTML document, from the `<head>` to the end of the `<body>`. They will be executed in order of the hierarchy of the document, so here are some things to keep in mind:

- Code at the beginning of the HTML file will be run before the rest of the file is loaded. Sometimes this is desirable, and other times it is not. If you need code to run before the rest of the page is loaded, place it in the head. Just remember that the page will be blank until the code loads, which may be off-putting to your web page visitor.

- If the code depends on some other input on the page, be sure to place it after that other input or toward the bottom of the page. Always keep hierarchy order in mind when deciding where to load scripts in a page.

JavaScript as an External File

HTML pages can get messy and difficult to manage with several scripts in the HTML page. The example code you used was short, but actual JavaScript code might actually be very long. To streamline loading and page management, consider placing JavaScript code in an external file. Using external JavaScript files also allows you to use the same script on more than one web page, saving lots of time!

Like internal code, external JavaScript files are loaded using the `<script>` tag, but they require use of the source (`src`) attribute. The path to the script can be relative to the HTML page, or it can exist in another directory or somewhere accessible via a URL. When you enter paths, the manner is the same as shown for CSS external files:

```
<script src="scripts/meaningfulNameScript.js"></script> /* Script file in the
  scripts subfolder of my HTML page's location. */
<script src="https://yourDomain.com/scripts/myScript.js"> </script> /* This is for
a file located somewhere on the web. */
```

Using the `src` attribute causes the browser to ignore any other code that is between the `<script>` tags. If you need to use multiple scripts in multiple places, simply use the `<script>` element with the `src` attribute to call each JavaScript file as needed.

There are two `<script>` attributes that may be helpful. Both download scripts in the background while the page is being parsed, which may help the page to load more quickly.

The first is the `async` attribute. Adding the `async` attribute will run the script immediately after being downloaded, even if parsing the page has not been completed. The second one, the `defer` attribute, won't load the script until the page finishes parsing, and because it's already downloading the scripts in the background, you won't have `async` and `defer` in the same element. The syntax to use `defer` or `async` is `<script src="scripts/myScript.js" async> </script>`.

If neither `async` nor `defer` is specified, then the page loads as explained in the previous section, stopping the parsing to download and run a script each time it encounters one before the remainder of the page loads.

A third but seldom-used attribute of `<script>` is `type`. Seemingly self-explanatory, it tells the browser what type of script is referenced in the element. The type values can be `empty`, `module`, `importmap`, or any other valid MIME value.

The type values `importmap` and `module` work together to find and load scripts that are specified in the HTML file. The `importmap` value must be specified first in the hierarchy and looks like the following, with an `id` for each file on the left (in the example, `jump` and `inputs`) and the path to the resource on the right:

```
<script type="importmap"> {
  "imports": {
  "jump": "https://mydomain.com/scripts/myScript.js",
 "inputs": "/scripts/inputs.js"
 }
 }
</script>
```

Once the map is established, the `ids` can be used to import modules from the map such as:

```
<script type= "module">
  Import { userID } from 'inputs';
</script>
```

Using `<script type = "module">` tells the browser that this is an ECMAScript Sixth Edition (ES6) module. Mappings are ignored by an `src` attribute used in a `<script>` tag to load a JS file, even if a mapping exists with the same name.

Using `<script type= "text/javascript">` or not specifying the type tells the browser that it is a classic JavaScript script. Note that the type attribute is not required in HTML 5.

ECMA International develops standards for the computer, communications, and programming industries. It is a nonprofit organization based in Geneva, but its standards are used worldwide.

The JavaScript Console

The JavaScript console is available in all modern browsers. It enables coders to test and troubleshoot code in real time. To use it, first open the desired page in a browser. Each browser has their own way to access the console through the browser's menu system, and each has hotkeys to do the same. The keys to access it are similar among browsers, replacing the Cmd and Option keys on a macOS keyboard with the Ctrl and Shift keys in Microsoft Windows. For Firefox enter Cmd+Option+K, for Safari enter Cmd+Option+C, and for Chrome enter Cmd+Option+J.

From there you simply execute commands by typing them in the console window. Try it now by opening your preferred browser and accessing the console. In the console pane type **var show = "practice";** and press Enter; then type **console.log (show);** and press Enter. The first statement defines a variable named show whose value is the string `practice` and the second statement tells the browser to display the value of the variable show on the console screen. See Figure 13.2. Notice that the output is the value of the variable defined on the first line. Also notice that the semicolon was omitted in the console of Figure 13.2, but the code worked as desired because of ASI.

Using `document.write` in place of `console.log` writes the value to the console and the web page, but in the process it clears everything else from the web page. It should not be used in the console, except for testing purposes.

FIGURE 13.2   The Chrome console

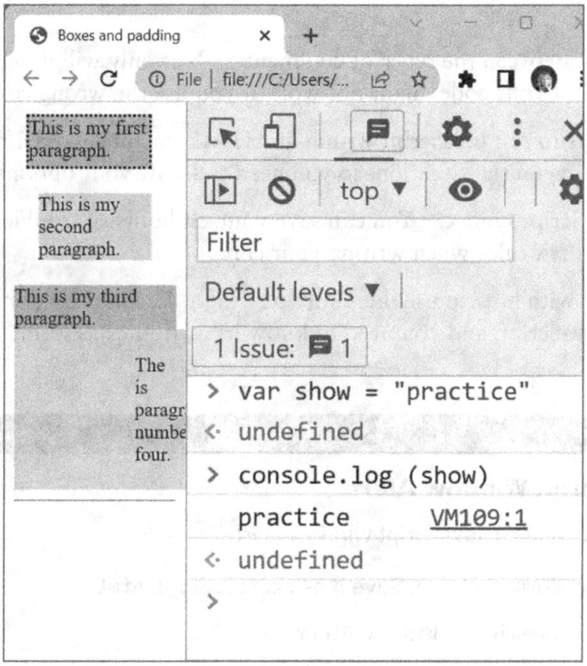

Summary

In this chapter, you learned about the different types of JavaScript statements, and you were introduced to some of the JavaScript syntax, specifically statements and the use of the semi-colon, and the proper use of the comment characters /* */ and //. Other JavaScript syntax rules are that it's case sensitive and identifiers can't start with a number. No hyphens are allowed in identifiers; instead, a common practice is to use camel case where the first letter of a second and subsequent words of the identifier are capitalized, but not the first letter of the first word.

We examined the various ways that JavaScript can be included in an HTML file—by writing it directly in the HTML code, or by using the <script> tag anywhere in the HTML document. Next, you also learned the importance of the order and placement of scripts in the HTML document, and the src, type, async, and defer attributes of the <script> tag.

The chapter wrapped up with a quick peek at the JavaScript console.

Exam Essentials

Know the difference between the types of comments.   Not only will it help you with the certification exam, but your code might not work if you use the wrong comment format.

Understand the ways to run JavaScript within an HTML document.   Different methods are appropriate depending on the situation, so you need to know your options.

Remember the JavaScript syntax.   You can save yourself hours of troubleshooting by remembering the syntax rules when writing your code.

Familiarize yourself with how to use the <script> tag.   Use of the <script> tag is integral to coding in JavaScript, and you need to know its attributes as well.

EXERCISE 13.1

Create a JavaScript Window Alert

In this exercise, you create a JavaScript window alert.

1.   Begin with your HTML skeleton. Save it as **exercise13_1.html**.

2.   Change the title to **Making a Window Alert**.

3.   Insert the following code in the <body> of the HTML document:
    <script> alert("Wake Up!"); </script>.

4.   Create a paragraph with several lines of text in it.

5.   Save your file.

6.   Open the file with a browser to test it.

7.   A window should pop up saying "Wake Up!", and when you click OK, the rest of the page should load.

ANSWER:

Your page should look like Figure 13.1, then after the OK button is clicked, the window should go away and text will appear.

EXERCISE 13.2

Write JavaScript to the Browser Console

In this exercise, you create an external JavaScript file, then enter some code in the browser console.

1. Begin with your HTML skeleton. Save it as **exercise13_2.html**.

2. Enter the following code in the sections indicated:

```
<head>
    <title> External JS file </title>
    <meta charset= "utf-8">
    <script src= "scripts/myScript.js" type= "text/javascript"> </script>
</head>
<body>
    <br>
    <script>
    let who2=prompt( "Enter your name here.", "Friend!");
    document.write( "Hello ", who2);
    </script>
</body>
</html>
```

3. Save the HTML file.

4. In the folder where your exercise13_2.html file resides, create a subfolder called **scripts**.

5. Open your text editor and create a new file called **myScript.js** and save it in the scripts folder. Remember, capitalization is important in JavaScript.

6. Enter the following lines of code into your myScript.js file:

```
let who=prompt( "What is your name?", "Visitor!");
document.write( "Hello ", who);
```

7. Make sure you enter a space after Hello and before the ". Save the file.

8. Open the exercise13_2.html file in a browser window. Click OK at each prompt.

9. Enter the keystrokes to open the browser console. For example, if you're using Chrome, press Ctrl+Shift+J.

10. In the console window, enter the following code. (If the console window is very small, drag the divider bar between the console window and the browser display so that you can see the console entries on a single line.)

```
let x=1;
let y=2+2;
let bogus=x+y;
console.log (bogus);
```

EXERCISE 13.2 ***(continued)***

11. The value of 5 should appear in your console. You might think that entering `document.write (bogus);` would cause it to appear in the browser and it will, but entering `document.write` here will clear the browser of whatever is in it at the time.

ANSWER:

The browser console pane should look like Figure 13.3 that follows, and the browser window will display:

Hello Visitor!

Hello Friend!

FIGURE 13.3 Answer to Exercise 13.2

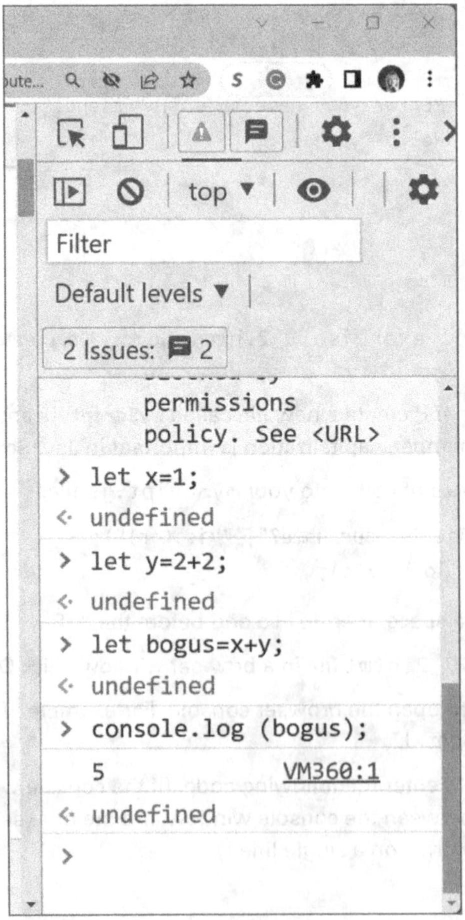

Review Questions

1. You've written an equation in JavaScript code and want to put a short comment in the code on that line. Which of these will you use?

   A. `/* comment text here */`

   B. `?? comment text here`

   C. `// comment text here`

   D. `/* comment text here;`

2. You need to run JavaScript code in an HTML document. Which of these codes is *not* a way that you can achieve this?

   A. `<button type="button" onclick="someFunction()"> Click here </button>`

   B. `<body>`
   `<script src = "scripts/anyName.js"> </script>`

   C. `<script src = "scripts/anyName.js" > </script>`

   D. `<script> src = "scripts/anyName.js" </script>`

3. You would like to specify that the external file being referenced is a JavaScript file. Which of these lines of code will achieve that?

   A. `<script type= "text/javascript">`

   B. `<script type= "text/html">`

   C. `<script type= text/javascript>`

   D. `<script type= "js.module" >`

4. Which of the following are correct JavaScript statements? (Choose two.)

   A. `function writeCurrent ( );`

   B. `var Current`

   C. `x=1;`

   D. `y+1`

5. How many `<script>` tags can be used in an HTML file?

   A. Only one

   B. Two

   C. Sixteen

   D. As many as are needed

6. Which character should be at the end of each JavaScript statement?

   A. :

   B. ;

   C.)

   D. >

7. Which of these are invalid? (Choose two.)

   A. `let 3rdPlace = 3;`

   B. `var first-name;`

   C. `var MyWorld;`

   D. `function writeFirst_name ( );`

8. Which of the following statements is true?

   A. `current = Current`

   B. `First = 1st`

   C. `_flavor = -flavor`

   D. `current = current`

9. What can be done to have a script download in the background while the web page is loading? (Choose two.)

   A. `<script> src="myFile.js" defer> </script>`

   B. `<script> src= "myFile.js" sync> </script>`

   C. `<script> src= "myFile.js" async> </script>`

   D. `<script> src= "myFile.js" background> </script>`

10. Which of these are correct? (Choose two.)

   A. `alert ( "Wake Up!" );`

   B. `alert "Wake Up!" ;`

   C. `alert ('Wake Up!');`

   D. `alert "Wake Up!" ;`

11. You're entering JavaScript into an external JS file. Which of the following is not a correct entry?

   A. `let x=y;`

   B. `<script> let x=1+y; </script>`

   C. `let car_make = prompt ( "Enter the make.");p`

   D. `if (x = y) { z+1; } else { z = 0; }`

12. Which of these are valid ways to get JavaScript from an external file? (Choose two.)

    A. `<script src= "scripts/myScript.js"></script>`

    B. `<script src= https://yourdomain.com/scripts/myscript.js ></script>`

    C. `<script> src= "https://yourDomain.com/scripts/myscript.js" > </script>`

    D. `<script src= "https://yourDomain.com/scripts/MyScript.js" > </script>`

13. You're working in the console and suddenly everything on the HTML page disappeared except the current value. What did you enter?

    A. `console.log`

    B. `document.write`

    C. `clear`

    D. `new`

14. What type of statement is `a = (z - 2); and "Yellow"`?

    A. Boolean

    B. Conditional

    C. Logical

    D. Expression

15. You've added a script near the top of a web page that asks the user to input their account number. This needs to be done before the entire page loads because other elements on the page need the data provided by the user input. Of the choices given, which would be the best entry to achieve that?

    A. `<script> src="myFile.js" defer> </script>`

    B. `<script> src= "myFile.js" sync> </script>`

    C. `<script> src= "myFile.js" async> </script>`

    D. `<script> src= "myFile.js" background> </script>`

16. You've written some JavaScript code that needs a lengthy explanation. Which of the following will you use?

    A. `?? comment text here`

    B. `/* comment text here */`

    C. `// comment text here`

    D. `/* comment text here;`

17. Which type of statement states or assigns a value?

    A. Conditional

    B. Declaration

    C. Expression

    D. Variable

18. Which of these is the correct way to declare a function?

    A. `let myFunction = ( ) ;`

    B. `isFunction = myFunction ( ) ;`

    C. `function myFunction ( )`

    D. `function myFunction ( ) ;`

19. You have a list of URLs that are lengthy and will be used in more than one web page, so you decided to put them in a JS file. Which of the following can you use to create a list of `ids` for the list of URLs?

    A. `<defer>`

    B. `type="async"`

    C. `type= "importmap"`

    D. `<ul>`

20. The following script is in the `<head>` of your `my.html` file:
`<script src= "/myScript.js" > </script>`. How will this page load?

    A. The page will be parsed, stopping to download and run the script when the browser reaches it.

    B. The script will download, then the page.

    C. The script will download in the background while the page is parsing, and the script will run as soon as it's available.

    D. The script will download in the background while the page is parsing, and the script will run after the page is fully parsed.

Chapter

14

JavaScript Data

LINUX PROFESSIONAL INSTITUTE, WEB DEVELOPMENT ESSENTIALS EXAM 030-100 OBJECTIVES COVERED IN THIS CHAPTER:

✓ **034 JavaScript Programming**

- 034.2 JavaScript Data Structures: The Candidate should be able to use variables in JavaScript code. This includes understanding values and data types. Furthermore, the candidate should understand assignment operators and type conversion and be aware of variable scope.

- Key Knowledge Areas:

  - Define and use variables and constants

  - Understand data types

  - Understand type conversion/coercion

  - Understand arrays and objects

  - Awareness of the variable scope

- Files, terms, and utilities:

  - =, +, -, *, /, %, --, ++, +=, -=, *=, /=

  - var, let, const

  - boolean, number, string, symbol

  - array, object

  - undefined, null, NaN

In the previous chapter, you learned the rules and format for writing JavaScript code and including it in your HTML pages. In this chapter, you'll learn about the types of data and how to work with variables and their values. We'll also look at the math operators, some shortcuts, and how to create and use arrays and objects to save time and avoid human error. There's a lot to cover, so let's get started!

Variables, Constants, and Scope

One of the first things I teach my information technology students is that the four main jobs of a computer system are input, output, processing, and storage. It's what programming and computer systems are all about. High-level languages like JavaScript make it easier to tell computers how to accept your input, process it, and create output.

You start with the data that you want to manipulate in some way. Maybe it's sales receipts for a business, actuary tables used to figure out the cost of someone's insurance, or an ingredient list for a recipe that you'll later make in a larger batch. You must input data into a program before the other steps can take place.

Data is gathered and stored in variables and constants. Later in this chapter you'll learn about advanced data structures used to organize data that's been input. In JavaScript and most other programs, variables and constants are declared differently and have different restrictions on their use. Variables and constants have two similarities—the variable or constant must start with an underscore or a letter, and their values are assigned in name=value pairs.

Variables

Variables are so named because the value that they hold is subject to change. Prior to 2015, the only keyword to declare a variable or a constant in JavaScript was the var keyword. Variables are declared in name=value pairs—for example, var spouse="yes";, where spouse is the name of the variable and yes is the value. Another example is var a=10;, where a is the variable name and 10 is the value. If the line a = 10; were written instead, JavaScript will assume you intended a to be a variable. The value of a variable can be changed in a program simply by entering a line such as a=11;. It can also be changed by using an operator, which we'll review soon.

A variable could be used throughout a program, but if the value of the variable is changed anywhere, it is changed everywhere. As you can imagine, that would make programming more complex indeed. To make programming simpler, when ECMAScript 6 (also known as ES6 or JavaScript ES6) arrived in 2015, the let and const keywords were added: let for variables and const for constant values.

The code let a=10; declares the value of a just as var a=10; would, but they are different in the places they can be used. This is explained in the upcoming section "Scope."

Constants

Once upon a time, it was true that constants were variables that didn't change. Now they have their very own keyword to distinguish them from variables. A constant is used for a value that won't change, such as the number of feet in a mile or ounces in a cup. They are declared using the const keyword—for example, const mile=5280; or const cup=8;. Constants aren't always universal truths. A constant can be something specific to our program that won't change, like const b="Building B";.

If you declare mile using the const keyword and then try to change it with mile=5000;, the program will give you an error message. Assume the following code is entered into a file named script.js:

```
const mile=5280;
console.log(mile);
mile=5000;
console.log(mile);
```

In the console log, the first line of code's output is 5280, which is the value assigned to the constant. When the second line of code is added, the error "Uncaught TypeError: Assignment to constant variable at script.js:3:1" results. At the end of the error, 3 is the line where you tried to change the constant and 1 is the line where the constant was declared. When the script reaches an error, it stops running.

If the same value were declared using let or var, then no error message would have resulted, and the value of mile would be changed. Using the const keyword helps prevent human errors caused by changing a value that should not be changed.

Scope

The JavaScript *scope* is the part of a program in which a variable can be used. The types of scope are local, function, block, and global. *Code blocks* are the code between curly brackets—{ }. A *block scope* occurs when const or let is used to declare a value inside a code block, making the constant or variable only available to that block of code. A *function scope*, also called a *local scope*, means that the variable or constant was declared inside a function and is only available to that function. This is true even when the variable is declared with the var keyword. A *global scope* occurs when any variable is declared outside of a function or block. A variable declared with var inside a code block has a global scope. Table 14.1 summarizes the types of scope.

TABLE 14.1   Summary of scope types by keyword

Where declared	const	let	var
Inside a code block	Block	Block	Global
Inside a function	Function	Function	Function
Not in a block or function	Global	Global	Global

Let's look at some examples. The value of x is declared outside of a function or code block as follows:

```
let x = 3;
if (x < 3) {
x+1;
} else {
x = 0;
}
console.log(x);
```

The value displayed will be 0, because x is not less than 3, and because x was declared outside of a block of code or a function, it has a global scope.

If you declare the value inside a code block using let, you cannot use it outside of the code block, as in the following code:

```
{
let x = 3;
}
console.log(x);
```

In this case, the console displays the error "Uncaught ReferenceError: x is not defined at script.js:." Constants declared using the const keyword behave the same way let does.

If you write the same script using the var keyword—{ var x = 3; }
console.log(x);—the console will display the value 3 because var acts as a global function even when declared inside a code block.

Objects and Methods

Objects and methods are the building blocks of object-oriented programming. *Objects* are variables, but unlike other variables objects can contain multiple values. Objects are usually created using the const keyword and the equal sign (=) similar to declaring a variable (e.g., const objectName = {}) and the object's values are assigned within the object using the familiar name:value pair syntax used when assigning values to a property.

The following method is called creating an *object literal*, where the object is defined and properties are created together:

```
const house = {
  listingNumber:123456,
  color:"white",
  yearBuilt:1990
  };
```

The object is house , and the name of each value, listingNumber, color, and yearBuilt, are properties. The values are 123456, white, and 1990.

Object methods are actions that can be performed on the object, defined by a property whose value is a function definition. You must give the property a name, then perform some action on the object. Continuing with the previous example, a method is added as follows:

```
const house = {
  listingNumber:123456,
  color:"white",
  yearBuilt:1990,
  description:function () { return this.listingNumber + " is a " + this.color + "
 home built in " + this.yearBuilt + "."}
  };
```

There are more ways of creating a new object, but the object literal method is less cumbersome, so use that instead. Following are two of them. One is by using const objectName = {}; to create an empty object and then adding its properties as follows:

```
const house = {};
  house.listingNumber=123456,
  house.color="white",
  house.yearBuilt=1990,
  house.listing=function () { return this.listingNumber + " is a " +
this.color + "
 home built in " + this.yearBuilt + "."}
  };
```

Another is by using a constructor function and the new keyword. This method works well when you need to create multiple instances of an object, each with the same properties. First, define the constructor function (house), then use the new keyword to create new instances of the house object. The following code shows creating the function and one instance of the object:

```javascript
function house(listingNumber, color, yearBuilt){
  this.listingNumber = listingNumber;
  this.color = color;
  this.yearBuilt = yearBuilt;
  }
const house1 = new house(1234456, "white", 1990);
```

Data Types

A value's data type determines what can and cannot be done with that data. In JavaScript, there's no need to declare the type of data when it is entered, because JavaScript is a dynamically typed language that automatically determines the variable's data type for you. Although this makes writing code much easier, it can occasionally lead to bugs related to data type when the code is run.

Primitive Types

Primitive data types are built into most programming languages. They are basic in nature and may be used to build more sophisticated data types, as you'll see in the next section. JavaScript has eight primitive data types, shown in Table 14.2.

TABLE 14.2   Primitive data types

Type	Description
Boolean	Logical, true or false, 1 or 0.
BigInt	Big integer, a number beyond what's considered "safe." Cannot be fractional numbers.
Null	Empty, but defined.
Number	Positive floating point (decimal anywhere) numbers between 2^{-1074} and 2^{1024}.
String	Alphanumeric characters not treated as numbers.
Symbol	Creates a unique symbol for a value within a program.
Undefined	The absence of a value—for example, a variable defined without its value (let x;) creates the variable but with no value assigned.

A variable's value type within a JavaScript program can change as its value changes. For example, `let a = "apple";` assigns the string type to variable a. Later in the program, `let a = 10;` will change a's type to number. Changing it again with a statement like `let a = true` returns the variable type of Boolean. If however, you write the statement `let a = "true";` or `let a = "10";`, then a will return the variable type of string. The difference between `a = true` and `a = "true"` is the quotes. The quotes turn the Boolean value of logical true to a text string.

At any time you can tell what type a variable is using the `typeof` command. For example, `let a = "apple"; console.log(typeof a);` outputs `string` on the console log because the quotes tell the program that what's inside is a string.

Data types `null` and `undefined` are special. They might look the same at first glance, but they are not. Neither `null` nor `undefined` is equal to zero. `undefined` means that the variable has been declared, but no value has been assigned. For example, `let b; console.log b;` returns `undefined`.

`null` is a defined value that is empty or doesn't exist. For example, `let s = null; console.log (s);` returns the value `null`. The value is that there is no value. In the case of a number, null does not mean zero. In the case of a string, null is the absence of characters. It's defined but empty.

Arrays

An *array* is a special type of object in JavaScript that holds multiple pieces of data, a list. That sounds somewhat like an object, so what's the difference? An object represents a type of something, and there are many of these things. In the previous example, houses were used. Each instance of an object has different values. An array, on the other hand, is simply a list of values. Imagine that you have a list of available outdoor games. An array in that program might be `const yardGames = ['Croquet', 'Tennis', 'KanJam','Lawn Darts'];`. Arrays make code more concise, because rather than enter a line for each type of yard game, (`let yardGame1= 'Croquet'; let yardGame2= 'Tennis';` and so on), you can enter all of them as a single variable.

You can pull information from an array by identifying the position of the desired item in the list. Like many things in the computer world, numbering starts with the number 0. Croquet is in position 0, Tennis is in position 1, and so on. If you enter `yardGames[1];` in your console, it returns the value `Tennis`. An *index number* identifies the position of an item in an array.

Items can be added to the list using `push( )` or `unshift( )` and removed from the list using `pop( )` or `shift( )`. Push and pop manipulate items at the end of the list, whereas unshift and shift manipulate items at the beginning of it. For example, to add Bocce Ball to the end of the previous list, you would enter the line `yardGames.push('Bocce Ball');`. You can add multiple items at the same time, such as `yardGames.push('Bocce Ball', 'Badminton');`. An array could have numbers as its list rather than strings.

Items can also be added to an array by specifying the next index number, such as `yardGames[4] = ' Bocce Ball';`. If the wrong number is specified, such as `yardGames[5] = 'Bocce Ball';`, then `yardGames[4];` would return undefined.

To remove a specific item(s) from the array, use the `splice( );` method. This method has two parameters. The first number is the index number to be removed, and the second number is how many items to remove. If the second number is left blank, everything after the first number will be removed. For example, to remove the undefined index number 4 from the previous array, you'd enter `yardGames.splice (4,1);`. After that entry, `yardGames[4];` would return the value `Bocce Ball`. If instead you entered `yardGames.splice(4);`, index number 4 and everything after it would be removed.

An array can also store a quantity of something. Imagine that you manage a kids sporting club and need to know how many of each type of game you have. Your array might look like this: `const yardGames = ['Croquet',1, 'Tennis', 2, 'KanJam', 8, 'Lawn Darts',3];`. Notice that all the quantities are odd index numbers and all the games are even index numbers. Now the code `console.log( "We have " + yardGames[5] + " of " + yardGames[4]);` returns `We have 8 of KanJam`.

Strings

Strings, as mentioned previously, are one of the seven primitive data types. There are, however, some special things about strings that you need to be aware of.

String Syntax

Strings can include numbers, spaces, letters, and other characters. A string is always enclosed in single or double quotes. Both work the same, but whatever style quote you use, you'll want to be consistent throughout your program. To place information inside quotes, within a string, use a different style of quote such as
`let city = "We went to the 'windy city' on our senior trip.";`.
Alternatively, this could also be accomplished using the backslash character to treat a quote as part of the string. The previous example could also be written as
`let city = "We went to the \"windy city"\ on our senior trip.";` which would output the line `We went to the "windy city" on our senior trip.` So, if using a backslash makes what follows it part of a string instead of a special character, how would you display a backslash as part of your string? Using two of them, such as
`let sentence = "The \\ symbol is called a backslash.";` would return the line `The \ symbol is called a backslash.`

When writing a contraction within a string, always use `\'`. For example,
`let status = "It's your turn.";` would instead be entered in a string
as `let status = "It\'s your turn.";`.

String Methods and Searches

Strings can use several methods and properties because JavaScript treats them as objects. This is not so with other programming languages. The following are just a couple of things you can do with strings. The `length` property returns the number of characters in a string. `var name = "Audrey O"; let nameLen = name.length; console.log(nameLen);` would return the number 8. Note that the space contained within the quotes counts as a character.

Another useful tool is the `replace()` method, which will find and replace characters in a string. `let fail = "Your son is failing."; let update = fail.replace(/son/, "child");` will result in the new value of `fail` being `Your child is failing.`

A string can be searched for a specified value and that value returned. Like the values in an array, the first character in a string is position 0. In our first example, remember that although there are eight characters, the positions are counted starting with 0, not 1, so to see the position of the letter O, entering `let position=name.search( "O" ); console.log(position);` will return the value 7 and not 8.

In the second example, the position of `"failing"` will be different depending on whether son or child is in the sentence. Before the change, `let failPos=fail.search( "failing" ); console.log(failPos);` will return 12 before the change and 14 after.

Concatenating a string means adding one string to another, and can be done in JavaScript using the `concat()` method or the plus sign (+) sign. Consider the following code:

```
let first = "Audrey";
let last = "O\'Shea";
console.log(first.concat(' ', last));
```

The code returns my name, `Audrey O'Shea`, with a space between the two names. Note the double-ended parentheses on the last line. The first one closes what is added, whereas the second one encloses everything that the console should display. Note the empty space added between the first and last name. The last line could be replaced with `console.log(first + " " + last);` and the result would still be the same.

Operators and Precedence

Because the plus sign (+) was mentioned in the previous section, it's time to consider operators. Most of the arithmetic operators should be familiar to you, but you might not be familiar with the modulus operator, which is written as a percent sign (%). The modulus returns the remainder when one number is divided by another. For example, `14 % 4;` would return 2, as 4 * 3 = 12, and 14 – 12 = 2, so 2 is the remainder of 14 / 4. See Table 14.3 for a list of operators and what they do.

TABLE 14.3   Arithmetic operators and their purpose

Operator	Purpose	Example
+	Add numbers or concatenate strings	a + 1
–	Subtraction	a – 1
*	Multiplication	a * 4
/	Division	a / 2
%	Modulus (division remainder)	a % b (See previous example.)
++	Increment by 1	a++ (If a = 2, the result is 3.)
––	Decrement by 1	a–– (If a = 2, the result is 1.)
**	Exponent	10**3 means 10×10×10

An operator that includes the = sign is an assignment operator (see Table 14.4).

TABLE 14.4   Assignment operators and what they do

Operator	Purpose	Example	Equivalent
=	Assign value or compare	let a = 1, if (a =1);	a = 1
+=	Assign a value to the current value plus another value	a += b	a = (a + b)
*=	Assign a value to the current value multiplied by another value	a *= b	a = (a * b)
-=	Assign a value to the current value minus another value	a -= b	a = (a – b)
/=	Assign a value to the current value divided by another value	a /= b	a = (a / b)

Precedence means the order in which something is done. When referring to arithmetic operators, it's the order in which the calculations are performed. Perhaps you learned PEMDAS in math class? It stands for parenthesis, exponents, multiplication, division, addition, and subtraction. In JavaScript it's essentially the same, with a few twists. Consider the following:

x=(1+2*3-4)

Parentheses are first, but that's irrelevant here. Multiplication happens before addition, so the value is 2*3=6; addition is before subtraction, so 6+1=7; and finally 7-4=3, hence x=3. If you were unaware of the order of precedence you might work from left to right and calculate the wrong answer (1+2=3, 3*3=9, 9-4=5), x=5.

If the statement were written as x=((1+2)*3-4), then the value of x would indeed be 5.

Ensure that you pay attention to the order of precedence in your programming. Other actions such as functions and ++ and -- also have a prescribed order. An excellent online reference can be found at http://w3schools.com/js/js_precedence.asp.

Data Conversions

Data conversion happens when a bit of data starts out as one primitive type but becomes another along the way as it is interpreted by JavaScript. *Data coercion* is another name for data conversion. *Implicit conversions* are conversions that happen automatically due to how JavaScript itself works. *Explicit conversions* are those that you intentionally program into your code. This section explains how implicit conversions work.

Strings to Values

A string such as "10" will be converted to a value when used with the -, /, or * operators. For example:

```
let a = '3' - '2'; console.log(a); returns the number 1.

let a = '3' * 2; console.log(a); returns the number 6.
```

Values to Strings

A numeric value, Boolean value, or undefined or null value used with a string and the + sign will result in a string; for example:

```
a = 5 + '2'; console.log(a); returns "52", not 7.

a = '7' + true; console.log(a); returns the string "7true".
```

Values to Numbers

Non-numeric strings, in equations with -, *, or /, results in NaN, which stands for Not a Number. For example:

a = 7 - 'true'; returns NaN. Here, 'true' is a string because of the quotes surrounding it.

a = 7 - 'flowers'; returns NaN.

A Boolean will be converted to a number when used with a number. The Boolean value true = 1, and false = 0, for example:

a = '7' - true; console.log(a); returns 6.

When used in an equation with a number, null will be converted to 0; for example:

a = '7' - null; console.log(a); returns 7.

a = 4 + null; console.log(a); returns 4.

a = 6 / null; console.log(a); returns infinity.

a = 6 * null; console.log(a); returns 0.

The undefined value used in any equation with a numeric value and operator will result in the NaN value. a = 6 + undefined; returns NaN; however, a = "true " + undefined; returns the value true undefined. But a = true + undefined; returns the value NaN, because the Boolean true is converted to the number 1.

Values to Boolean

Values can be converted to Boolean, but those are discussed in the next chapter in the section "Truthy and Falsy Values."

Summary

In this chapter, you examined the similarities and differences between var, let, and const. Those differences can affect the scope of a variable, depending on where they are created. Constants are declared with the const keyword and variables can be declared with the let or var keyword.

Anything not declared within a function or block of code has a global scope, while anything declared in a function has a local (function) scope. Using const or let inside a block of code will limit it to that block of code, but using var will give the variable a global scope.

You learned that objects are like variables, but they can hold multiple values. You can create many new objects that will have the same type of name:value pairs. An object method is an action that can be performed on the object, like driving miles will change a car's total mileage, if your object is about cars.

You can now list all the primitive data types like number, null, string, and so on, and how they can be converted implicitly (automatically). You also learned that arrays hold multiple pieces of data and how to manipulate and pull data from arrays.

Furthermore, you also learned about strings, their syntax, methods, and how to search for and pull data out of a string. And you learned the list of arithmetic and assignment operators and what they do, like the modulo (%), which returns the remainder of a division operation.

Exam Essentials

Know which keyword to define a variable with.   Using let instead of var might limit you when you want to use a variable in another part of the program.

Understand the different data types and how to enter them.   JavaScript determines the type of data for you without having to declare it. But if you don't enter it correctly, it might treat a number as a string and cause problems with your code.

Recognize the difference between arrays and objects.   Sometimes you need a list of the same type of thing, and other times you need multiple pieces of information about each one of those things.

Consider the nuances of type conversion.   Understanding how JavaScript uses implicit conversion can make the difference between a successful program and hours of troubleshooting.

EXERCISE 14.1

Define and Manipulate Variables and Constants

In this exercise, you create a web page and use the console to see what happens to variables and constants as you work with them.

1. Start with an HTML skeleton and create an HTML file to use with this exercise as follows:

```
<!DOCTYPE html>
<html>
<head>
  <title> Working With Variables </title>
  <meta charset="UTF-8" />
  <style>
```

EXERCISE 14.1 *(continued)*

```
      body {
        height: 1500px;
        background-image: linear-gradient (to top right, #c6c2dc, #744a99);
        }
      h1 {
        font-family: sans-serif;
        text-align: center;
        }
  </style>
  <script src="script14.js"></script>
</head>
<body>

<h1> Here we go! </h1>

</body>
```

2. Save the file as **exercise14_1.html**.

3. Use your text editor to create another file and save it as **script14.js**.

4. Open both files on your desktop. After each entry, you'll make changes in the script14.js file, save it, and then reload the browser window to see the changes made in the JavaScript (JS) file.

5. In the HTML file, open the console.

6. In the JS file, enter **let x=4; console.log(x);** and save the file. Reload the web page and the console should display the number 4 on the left, and on the right script14.js:2. The example uses Chrome, so the result might be slightly different if you're using a different browser, but the output (the number 4) should be the same.

7. Now you'll create a variable outside of a block and use it inside the block. Type the following code in the JS file: **if (x > 3) { x ++; } console.log (x);**. Then press Enter. Reload the web page and observe that the console now displays 4, then 5. Why is the second value 5?

8. In the JS file, enter **let y=0; console.log(y); if (y=0) { y=5; } console.log(y);**. Save the JS file, then reload the web page. Why does the console show 0 0 instead of 0 5?

9. In the JS file, enter **let z=2; if (z=2) { let a=6; } console.log (a);**. Save the JS file, then reload the web page. Why do you get an error saying a is undefined?

10. In the JS file, enter **const mile=5280; console.log (mile);**. Save the JS file; reload the web page.

11. In the JS file, enter **const mile=5000; console.log (mile);**. Save the JS file, then reload the web page. Why do you get an error message?

12. Comment out the section of code created in number 11 by enclosing it in /* */.

13. In the JS file, enter **let b = "10" +1; console.log(b);**. Save the JS file, then reload the web page. How does it calculate 101 instead of 11?

14. In the JS file, enter **console.log(typeof b);**. Save the JS file, then reload the web page.

15. In the JS file, enter **console.log(x); console.log(z) x*=z; console.log(x);**. Save the JS file, then reload the web page. Why does x now = 10?

ANSWER:

(7) The second value is 5 because ++ increments x by 1; also, the variable x was created outside the if statement, so it has a global scope.

(8) y=5 was assigned inside a block, so it has a block scope and can't be used outside the block.

(9) a was defined inside a block, not outside the block, so it can't be used outside the block.

(11) An error message is returned because constants do not change.

(13) JavaScript converts the 1 to a string because it is added to an existing string, so '10' + '1' = '101'.

(15) x = 10 because *= means the first value equals the first value times the second value, so 5 * 2 = 10.

EXERCISE 14.2

Create Objects and Arrays

In this exercise, you create and modify an array, and create two instances of an object.

1. Open the web page and script file used in Exercise 14.1.

2. In the JS file, create an array called **shopping** with the items **milk**, **bread**, and **cheese**. Then enter **console.log(shopping);**. Save the JS file, then reload the web page. Your array should appear.

3. In the JS file, enter **shopping.pop(""); console.log(shopping);**. Save the JS file, then reload the web page. What does the list now display?

4. Enter the code to add **eggs** to the beginning of the list (without retyping the list). Then enter **console.log(shopping);**. Save the JS file, then reload the web page to verify your result.

5. With the same web page and JS file open, create an object using the object literal method, where the name of the object is `car` and the names of properties are `year`, `make`, `model`, and `color`. If you don't know that much about cars, choose something with many types and characteristics like people (firstName, lastName, street, city) or computers (color, RAM, CPU Speed, storage).

6. Create a method (function) in your `car` object that would output
   `year color make model`.

ANSWER:

(3) The list displays (2) `['milk', 'bread']`.

(4) The code should be `shopping.unshift('eggs');` and the list on the console should display (3) `['eggs', 'milk', 'bread']`.

(5) If `car` is the object, then the object literal method would be
`const car = { year:2024, make:Jeep, model:wrangler, color:orange,};`.

(6) Adding a function would be `const car = { year:2024,make:Jeep,`
`model:wrangler, color:orange,listing:function(){return this.year +`
`" " + this.color + " " + this.make + " " + this.model;}};`.

Review Questions

1. Which of the following will define a variable? (Choose two.)

   A. `const m = "miles"`

   B. `let m = "miles"`

   C. `var m = "miles"`

   D. `let const m = "miles"`

2. What will the result of the following code be?

   ```
   const c = 2;
   let d = 3;
   d*=c;
   console.log(c)
   console.log(d)
   ```

   A. An error message

   B. 2,6

   C. 6,2

   D. 9

3. Why will the following code result in an error?

   ```
   a = 3;
   { a++;
     let b = 3*a;
     }
   b++;
   console.log(b)
   ```

   A. a is not declared.

   B. a is declared outside the code block.

   C. The wrong brackets are used.

   D. b has a block scope.

4. What is the term that means data is interpreted by JavaScript as a particular type of data because of the code around it—for example, when a number like 99 is interpreted as a string? (Choose two.)

   A. Data inversion

   B. Data conversion

   C. Data coercion

   D. Data manipulation

5. Which of the following will result in a data string?
    A. `a = "5" - "3"`
    B. `a = "5" + "3"`
    C. `a = 5 * "3"`
    D. `a = 5 + 3`

6. For which of these is the value 0?
    A. `null`
    B. `undefined`
    C. `a = 0 - null;`
    D. `let a;`

7. What is the value of Boolean `true` in an equation with a number?
    A. An error
    B. 0
    C. 1
    D. `"true"`

8. What will the result of the following code be?

    ```
    const c = 2;
    let d = 3;
    c*=d;
    console.log(c)
    console.log(d)
    ```

    A. An error message
    B. 2,6
    C. 6,2
    D. 9

9. What is the result of a = true + "3";?
    A. NaN
    B. undefined
    C. true3
    D. 4

10. What is the result of a = anything - 3; ?
    A. NaN
    B. undefined
    C. 3
    D. anything3

11. What is the value of a = "10" * 5;?

    A. NaN

    B. 50

    C. undefined

    D. 105

12. What is the value of a = true + false + 1;?

    A. null

    B. NaN

    C. truefalse1

    D. 2

13. What is the value of a = null + 1;?

    A. NaN

    B. null

    C. 0

    D. 1

14. What is the value of a = null + "14";?

    A. NaN

    B. null

    C. null14

    D. undefined

15. What is the result of a = "50" / 10;?

    A. 5

    B. NaN

    C. null

    D. 5010

16. What is the value of a = undefined * 3; ?

    A. null

    B. NaN

    C. 3

    D. undefined3

17. Which of these is used to add an item to the beginning of an array?

    A. push( )

    B. pop( )

    C. shift( )

    D. unshift( )

18. You want the letter p to always equal the numeric value of Pi (3.14) in your program. How would you do this?

    A. `let p = 3.14;`

    B. `const p = Pi;`

    C. `const p = 3.14;`

    D. `symbol p = 3.14;`

19. Which of these creates a guaranteed unique identifier for a value within a program?

    A. `null`

    B. `symbol( )`

    C. `let`

    D. `var`

20. You're not sure what primitive data type an equation is resulting in. Assuming the equation starts with x =, which of the following will tell you the primitive data type?

    A. `console.log(typeof x)`

    B. `console.log(primitive x)`

    C. `console.log(x)`

    D. `console.log(type x)`

Functions and Control Structures

LINUX PROFESSIONAL INSTITUTE, WEB DEVELOPMENT ESSENTIALS EXAM 030-100 OBJECTIVES COVERED IN THIS CHAPTER:

✓ **034 JavaScript Programming**

- 034.3 JavaScript Control Structures and Functions: The candidate should be able to use control structures in JavaScript code. This includes using comparison operators. Furthermore, the candidate should be able to write simple functions and understand function parameters and return values.

    - Key Knowledge Areas:

        - Understand truthy and falsy values

        - Understand comparison operators

        - Understand the difference between loose and strict comparison

        - Use conditionals

        - Use loops

        - Define custom functions

    - Files, terms, and utilities:

        - if, else if, else

        - switch, case, break

        - for, while, break, continue

        - function, return

        - ==, !=, <, <=, >, >=

        - ===, !==

Now that you've learned about data and data structures (input and output), it's time to do things with (process) that data. For that you must work with functions and conditional statements. By the end of this chapter, you'll be doing some real programming. You'll learn how to write and call a function, and then see the results of the function. It's fun and exciting, so let's get to it!

Functions

Remember from Chapter 1, "Web Development Basics," that functions are blocks of code used to manipulate the data in your programs by performing some action on data. A function must be called (invoked) before it will run, and it will continue to run until it reaches a return statement. The beauty of functions is that they are chunks of code that can be reused as often as needed, so they save lots of programming time and help you to prevent human error caused when mistakes are made repeating or editing the code in multiple places.

Some functions are *predefined functions*, which are already a part of the programming language. The alert(); function and the prompt(); method are predefined functions that were used in Chapter 13, "JavaScript Essentials." Other functions known as *user-defined functions* are created by the person writing the code. User-defined functions are also called function statements or function declarations.

Methods are functions that are tied to a particular object, but other functions can run anywhere in a program independent of any object.

Function Syntax

Like all things in programming, functions have their own syntax. User-defined functions must start with the function keyword and be given a name. *Function parameters* are values that are passed to the function when it starts, and are listed in parentheses—( )—after the function name. The values are separated by commas, and there can be as many as necessary. The *function body* is enclosed in curly brackets—{ }—and contains the action to be done with the data. See Figure 15.1.

FIGURE 15.1   Anatomy of a function

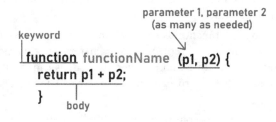

If you wanted a function to calculate the difference between two values, you might define it as follows:

```
function adjust (s,c) {  //my function has two values
   return (s - c);       }   //the function finds the difference between them
```

Starting and Stopping Functions

A function must be called (invoked) before it will run. Functions can be self-invoked, called by some other programming code, or called when something happens to trigger it, such as clicking on a screen or hovering over a button.

A *return* is the result of the actions in the function's body, and the result is returned to the code that called it.

Consider a simple function that would check the temperature in the room and determine how much to turn the heat up if the temperature is too low. Assume you're using an Arduino to read the ambient temperature as a voltage on an analog pin, convert it to a Fahrenheit temperature with a variable name of temp, then pass it to the JavaScript code. First, you'll get the values of your variables and enter your function:

```
let cTemp = temp;
let setTemp = prompt ("Enter desired temperature", " 70 ");
function adjust(s,c) {
   return (s - c);
   }

let a = adjust(setTemp,cTemp);
```

Let's break this example down line by line:

- In the first line, if the temperature sensed by the Arduino board is 68 degrees, then the variable cTemp would also be 68 degrees.

- The second line is a method that asks the user to enter the temperature they would like the room to be. The default temperature is 70. The variable setTemp holds the value.

- The third line names your function adjust and tells it to expect two values (s and c) to be passed to it.

- In the fourth line, `return` tells it to return the result of what is in the body of the function back to the code that called it. Line 4 also tells the function to subtract the second value from the first value.

- In the last line, the `adjust` function is called by the `( )` operator, which contains the values that will be copied and replace the parameters—in this case, the values of `setTemp` and `cTemp` in place of `s` and `c`. When the code is run, `a = 2` (70 – 68), so you know the thermostat needs to be turned up by 2 degrees. The line also assigns the result to the variable `a`.

This may seem like a lot of work, but if you had 100 different places where you wanted one value subtracted from the other, it would save you lots of time. Instead of entering the calculation each time, you would enter the line calling the function, substituting the variable names for the ones in that situation. The function doesn't care what the names of the variables are, only what position each occupies. In fact, instead of using variable names in the `( )`, you could simply enter values.

If somewhere in the same program you entered the line `let b=adjust(100,25)`, then the value of `b` would be 75. While this is a very simplified equation, consider that some calculations may be many lines long. Using functions means typing those many lines only one time. Then each time you want to use that calculation you only need to enter one line to call it.

Functions and Variables

As you learned in Chapter 14, "JavaScript Data," any variable defined inside a function has a local (function) scope. Although the normal way to pull data into a function is by using parameters, variables with a global scope can be used inside a function.

The parameters passed to a function are variables. In your previous example, you were *passing arguments by value*, which means that the value of the variable is copied to use inside the function and what happens in the body of the function will not change the original value of the variables used.

If what you were substituting for the function's parameters was an object or array with multiple values, then the values aren't copied. Instead, the parameters refer to the original object and changes to those values made in the function change the values being referred to, which are the values of the original object or array. This is called *passing by reference*.

Conditional Statements

As you learned in Chapter 13, conditional statements are those that are executed only if the specified conditions are met. `if` statements should be what comes to mind first, but `else if` and `else` statements are also part of that group. The syntax for an `if` statement is:

```
if (condition) {//action to perform;}
```

For example, if (x > 1) {x++;} is a conditional statement. In this case, when x=2 and this statement is encountered, x will be incremented by 1. If x=0 and this statement is encountered, then nothing will happen. x will remain at 0.

But what if you want the program to do one thing if the statement is true and something else if the statement is false? In that case, you use an else or else if statement. Continuing with the previous example:

```
x = 1                //sets the value of x to 1
if  (x > 1) {x++;}  //the condition is false, so x is not incremented
else { x + 10;}    //since the condition is false, we add 10 to the value of x.
```

When more conditions are needed, you use the else if statement:

```
x = 1     // sets the value of x to 1
if (x > 1) {x++;}
else if (x = 0) { x + 2;}
else if (x < 0) {x = "invalid";}
else {x = 1;}
```

The program reads the lines of code in order. If the first if condition (x > 1) were true, then it would perform the action in the curly brackets, { }, and skip the else if and else lines that follow. But because the first condition is false, it will read the else if statement on the next line and follow the instructions. As long as the condition is false, the program will keep executing the else and else if statements. If a condition is true, it will skip all the following else and else if statements and go to the next line.

Rather than writing many else if ( ) statements, sometimes it's more appropriate to use the switch and case commands. A switch statement is evaluated one time and compared to each case. When the case matches the result of the switch statement, the code in that case is executed. The syntax is
switch (what the value is) { case "if it's this" : //code to run; break; ...} continuing with the code until you reach the desired number of options. Confusing? It's OK. The following example should clarify it.

Let's assume that your visitor is choosing the day of the week and you want to convert it to a number to run in your program. The following code is truncated and would, of course, be continued out to all seven days:

```
let day = prompt("Choose a day to start:", "Monday");
switch (day) {
  case "Sunday":
    dayNum = 1;
    break;
  case "Monday":
    dayNum = 2;
```

```
      break;
   case "Tuesday";
      dayNum = 3;
      break;
 }
console.log(dayNum)
```

If the visitor left their choice at the default, Monday, then `console.log` would output 2.

Programs that loop also rely on conditional statements. In Chapter 13, you learned that a loop is a repeating section of code, so that instead of you writing the code multiple times, it will repeat as long as the condition is true. The first loop you'll examine uses the `for` keyword. The syntax is `for (execute one time; condition; afterthought) {//code to run when condition is true}`. Consider the following code to count down from 10 to 1, which produced the output in Figure 15.2.

```
for (let t=10; t > 0; t--) {
   console.log( t + " and counting!");
   }
console.log("Done!")
```

FIGURE 15.2 A looping program

```
10 and counting!                          script15-3.js:2
9 and counting!                           script15-3.js:2
8 and counting!                           script15-3.js:2
7 and counting!                           script15-3.js:2
6 and counting!                           script15-3.js:2
5 and counting!                           script15-3.js:2
4 and counting!                           script15-3.js:2
3 and counting!                           script15-3.js:2
2 and counting!                           script15-3.js:2
1 and counting!                           script15-3.js:2
Done!                                     script15-3.js:4
>
```

Refer to the code directly before Figure 15.2 and the image. Notice that in Figure 15.2, the code is run (`{console.log...}`) before the afterthought (`t--`) is executed, because the first value displayed is the value that t started as. The program stops when the value of t reaches 0 and continues on with the next line of the program. That's because the program told it to loop only as long as t is greater than 0. When the loop condition is no longer true, the program continues to execute line by line.

while can also be used to execute commands as long as a condition is true, but the difference is that the for command executes a single command line, and while can execute multiple command lines. The syntax is
while (condition) {//body with commands;}. For example:

```
let t = 5;
while (t > 0) {t --; console.log(t); }
```

There is also a do-while command that is similar to while; however, the while loop checks the condition before it runs the body commands, and the do-while loop runs the body commands and then checks the condition. The syntax for do-while is do
{ // commands to execute;} while (condition). For example:

```
let t = 5;
do { t--; console.log( t ); } while (t > 0)
```

A break statement will let you exit a loop before the condition equates to false. For example:

```
for (let t=5; t  > 0; t--) {
   if (t === 3) {break;}
   console.log( t + " and counting!");
   }
console.log(Done!)
```

The === is a strict comparison operator that will be explained more toward the end of this chapter. The previous code will display:

5 and counting!

4 and counting!

Done!

because it exited when the value reached 3. If you would like your program to skip a value but keep going, then use continue instead of break.

```
for (let t=5; t  > 0; t--) {
   if (t === 3) {break;}
   console.log( t + " and counting!");
   }
console.log(Done!)
```

The previous code will display:

5 and counting!

4 and counting!

2 and counting!

1 and counting!

Done!

Comparison Operators

Programs are always evaluating things. In particular, the if statement is looking at a condition to determine whether it is true or false. You likely learned the basic comparison operators in a math class, but there are other more complex comparison operators. Table 15.1 contains the list.

TABLE 15.1   Comparison operators

Comparison operator	What it means
==	The values are equal.
!=	Not equal to.
<	Less than.
>	Greater than.
<=	Less than or equal to.
>=	Greater than or equal to.
===	Strict identity equal operator.
!===	Strict identity not equal operator.

Data Coercion

In Chapter 14, you examined how data can be coerced (converted) into a different type of data. For example, "1" will usually be converted in an equation to the number 1. For a refresher of what gets converted when, refer back to Chapter 14.

Most comparison operators perform a loose comparison, meaning that they will coerce the compared values; for example, "1" = 1 will equate to true, because the string "1" will be coerced into being a number 1.

The === and !== comparison operators don't allow for coercion. These are known as strict identity operators. So, "1" === 1 will equate to false, because the string "1" is not the same type as the number 1, but 1 === 1 will equate to true. The !== operator means "not equal," so "1" !== 1 will equate to true, because it is true that the string "1" does not equal 1, and 1 !== 1 will equate to false, because (1 is "not equal" to 1) is a false statement.

Truthy and Falsy Values

Truthy values are not quite true, and falsy values are not quite false, but they will equate to true or false Boolean values. Anything that isn't falsy will be truthy. Only the following values are falsy: `null`, `undefined`, `false` (Boolean false), `NaN`, `0`, `-0`, `0n` (BigInt zero), `""` (empty string), and `document.all` (which is an object). Everything else is truthy.

For example, `[]` is truthy, as is `(5)`. If given as the condition in an `if` statement, the condition equates to true and the body of the `if` statement will be executed, such as `if ([]) {//this will run;}`. Conversely, the condition in the following `if` statement is falsy, so the body would not execute: `if (NaN){//does not execute;}` and the result would be `undefined`. It would be nearly impossible to remember all the truthy values, so just remember which ones are falsy. Everything else is truthy.

Another operator, the logical AND, which in JavaScript is written as `&&`, returns false if the first object is falsy, such as `console.log(NaN && "house")`, and true if the first object is truthy such as `console.log ("I'm a string" && "house")` or `(44 && "house")` will both return Boolean true.

Summary

In this chapter, you learned how to create a function and call it into action, then return the value of the function to the code that called it. You learned that passing arguments by value means using simple values to replace the parameters of a function and that it only changes values in the function. But passing by reference is for more complex structures and changes the original (source) values.

Even though you usually think of conditional statements as *if-then* statements, there are many more types of conditional statements. First, you can add `else` and `else if`. Then there are `switch`/`case` statements, where a value is compared against a list to find the right result.

You then learned about looping programs and how to get out of them using `break` or skip a value using `continue`.

The chapter wrapped up with comparison operators, and the difference between loose and strict comparison using the strict identity operators `===` and `!==`. Finally, we reviewed truthy and falsy values, which equate to true unless they're on the falsy list.

Exam Essentials

Know the falsy values.   It's easier to remember the falsy value list, because if it isn't one of those special characters, then it will equate to true.

Recognize all the comparison operators.   Most of them are somewhat intuitive, but you must recognize them to be able to program properly.

Know the difference between loose and strict comparison. Whether you use =, ==, or ===
in your program can make the difference between a program that works as expected and one
that doesn't, and you need to know that the ! in !== and != means not.

Understand when to use conditionals, loops, and custom functions. Using the right
kind of conditional or creating your own custom functions can save countless hours of
programming.

EXERCISE 15.1

Create Custom Functions

In this exercise you create and call functions.

1. Open your HTML skeleton. Save it as **exercise15_1.html**, and open it in your favorite
   browser. Open the console.

2. Open your text editor and save a file as **exercise15_1.js**.

3. With your HTML file open in a text editor, in the style section of the header refer to the
   script file that you just created. Change the page title to **Exercise 15-1**. Add an <h1>
   heading stating **Exercise 15-1**. Save the HTML file.

4. In your JavaScript (JS) file, create a function named **Celsius** with one parameter, **f**.
   Enter code in the body of the function to return $(f-32)/1.8$.

5. Create a prompt where the variable f equals an input temperature in Fahrenheit.
   (Ask the user to enter the temperature in Fahrenheit.) Enter a line declaring the variable
   C = Celsius(f);. Remember that JS is case sensitive.

6. Enter
   `console.log(f + " degrees Fahrenheit is equal to " + C + " degrees Celsius.");`.

7. Save your JS file and reload your HTML file. It should ask you for a temperature in
   Fahrenheit, then convert it to Celsius and display the result. (If you enter **40**, it should
   return 4.444 degrees Celsius.)

ANSWER

The HTML file should contain:

```
</style>
<script src= "exercise15_1.js" > </script>
<body>
<h1> Exercise 15-1 </h1>
```

The JavaScript file should be as follows:

```
function Celsius (f) {
   return ((f-32) / 1.8);
   }
let f = prompt ("Enter temperature in Fahrenheit", " ");
let C = Celsius(f);
console.log(f + " degrees Fahrenheit is equal to " + C + " degrees Celsius.");
```

EXERCISE 15.2

Write Code Using Conditional Statements

In this exercise you use conditional statements to create a program that will output a sentiment about the weather based on the temperature.

1. Open your HTML file exercise15_1.html. Change the title and the <h1> heading to **Exercise 15-2**. Change the <script = reference to **exercise15_2.js** and save the file as **exercise15_2.html**. Open the file in a browser and open the console.

2. Open your exercise15_1.js file and save it as **exercise15_2.js**.

3. At the end of the existing code in the JS file, enter an if/else conditional statement(s) such that if the temperature is 32 degrees Fahrenheit or less, the value of a variable s will be "It's freezing!". But if the temperature is between 32 and 69 degrees Fahrenheit, the value of the variable s will be "Well, at least it's not freezing!" and if it's 70 or higher degrees, the value of s will be "Nice day!".

4. At the end of the JS file, enter the line **console.log(s)**.

5. Save the file and reload the HTML file to test your program. The program should ask for input and display the lines as in Exercise 15.1, then display the appropriate statement based on the temperature.

ANSWER

The following lines should be added to the JS file for steps 3 and 4:

```
if ( f <= 32 ) { s = "It's freezing!"; }
else if ( f >=70 ) { s = "Nice day!"; }
else { s = "At least it's not freezing!"; }
console.log(s)
```

EXERCISE 15.3

Write Code Using Loops

In this exercise you use the `while` command to create a program loop.

1. Open your HTML file `exercise15_1.html` with your text editor. Change the title and the `<h1>` heading to **Exercise 15-3**. Change the `<script` = reference to **exercise15_3.js** and save the file as **exercise15_3.html**. Open the file in a browser and open the console.

2. Open your text editor and save the file as **exercise15_3.js**.

3. The first line will generate a random number between 1 and 10. Enter
    let x = Math.floor((Math.random() * 10) + 1);.

4. Enter a statement creating a variable n asking the visitor to guess a number between 1 and 10, and set the default number to 0.

5. Create a `while` statement that will display "Sorry, try again." on the console and ask for a new number as long as x != n, but when x= n it will say "Congratulations! You guessed it!" and no longer ask the user for an input number. (Caution: Don't use the strict comparison here.)

6. Save your JS file and test it.

ANSWER

The following lines should be in the JS file:

```
let x = Math.floor((Math.random() * 10) + 1);
let n = prompt ("Enter a number between 1 and 10.", "0");
while (x != n) {
  console.log ("Sorry, try again.")
  n = prompt ("Enter a new number between 1 and 10.", "0");
  }
console.log ("Congratulations! You guessed it!")
```

Review Questions

1. Which of these statements is true?

    A. A function is a method.

    B. A method is a function.

    C. A method cannot be a function.

    D. A custom function starts with the function's name.

2. Which of these contains a truthy value? (Choose two.)

    A. `if (NaN) {"hello";}`

    B. `if (0) {"hello";}`

    C. `if ([]) {"hello";}`

    D. `if (1024) {'hello';}`

3. You want to compare two values and only execute the code if the two values are not equal, and not allow coercion. Which of the following will you use?

    A. `===`

    B. `!==`

    C. `!=`

    D. `<>`

4. You want code to be executed `if (x = y)`, but do nothing if the equation is `false`. Which of these is best to use?

    A. `if (x=y) {//code;} else if {//othercode;}`

    B. `if (x=y) {//code;} else {//code;}`

    C. `if (x=y) {//code;} else {'';}`

    D. `if (x=y) {//code;}`

5. You have the following code in your JavaScript file. What will happen if the user accepts the default of Monday? (Choose two.)

```
let day = prompt ('Choose a day to start', 'Monday');
switch (day) {
  case 'Sunday':
    dayNum = 1;
    break;
  case 'Monday':
    dayNum = 2;
    break;
```

```
   case 'Tuesday':
    dayNum = 3;
      break;
   }
let time = prompt ('What time?', ' ');
```

   A. The code will skip Monday and continue evaluating.

   B. dayNum will equal 2.

   C. The user will be prompted to enter a time.

   D. dayNum will equal 3.

6. In the following code, assume that a = 95 and b = 2 before the code is encountered. Which of the following are true? (Choose two.)

```
while (a < 100)   {c = b * a++};
```

   A. The final value of a will be 100.

   B. The final value of b will be 198.

   C. The final value of c will be 198.

   D. The final value of c will be 200.

7. You want to compare z to a, and only execute the code following if z is equal to or less than a. Which of these operators will you use?

   A. z ==> a

   B. z += a

   C. z <= a

   D. z >= a

8. Which of the following will equate to true? (Choose two.)

   A. 99 !== "99"

   B. 99 == "99"

   C. 99 === "99"

   D. 99 !== 99

9. Which of the following options can invoke this function?

```
function total (par1, par2) {return (par1 + par2);}
```

   A. total(100,5);

   B. function total;

   C. function (100,5);

   D. total(par1 + par2);

10. Which of the following keywords can you use so a program will loop? (Choose two.)

   A. `if`

   B. `for`

   C. `while`

   D. `switch`

11. Considering the `for` statement that follows, which of the following options are true? (Choose two.)

    ```
    for (x=0; x < 10; x++) {console.log(x);}
    ```

   A. The final line that prints says 9.

   B. The final line that prints says 10.

   C. The calculation will be executed 10 times.

   D. x will be reset to 0 each time the code runs.

12. Which of these is the right way to write a `switch/case` statement, assuming `siteNo` is the variable whose value is being compared and `city` is the output value?

   A.
   ```
   switch (siteNo) {

       case 1: city = "New York"; break;

       case 2: city = "Tokyo"; break; }
   ```

   B.
   ```
   switch (siteNo) {

       case 1: city = "New York";

       case 2: city = "Tokyo";

       break; }
   ```

   C.
   ```
   switch (siteNo) {

       case 1; city = "New York"; break:

       case 2; city = "Tokyo"; break: }
   ```

   D.
   ```
   switch (siteNo) {

       case 1; city = "New York": break;

       case 2; city = "Tokyo": break; }
   ```

13. Which of the following is a properly written function that will provide the sum of two values?

   A. `function total (val1 + val2) {return total;}`

   B. `function total (a,b) {return (1+2);}`

   C. `function total (a,b) {return (a+b); }`

   D. `function total (1,2) {return (a+b)}`

14. Given the following code, what will the result be?

```
If ('') {1+4;}
```

   A. `''`

   B. `5`

   C. `null`

   D. `undefined`

15. You want to compare two values and execute a condition if the two values will equate to each other. Which of these operators will you use?

   A. `=`

   B. `==`

   C. `===`

   D. `!=`

16. Considering the following code, what would the value of x be?

```
let y = 100
if (y <100) {x = "fell short";}
else if (y=100) {x = perfect;}
else if (y > 100) {x = "too high";}
```

   A. `fell short`

   B. `perfect`

   C. `too high`

   D. `undefined`

17. You're writing code asking a user to input a donation amount, which can be any dollar value. Depending on the amount they enter, you want to respond with "Thank You" or "Please reconsider" or "Your bonuses will be shipped to you within a day." Which conditional will be best to use?

   A. An `if` statement

   B. An `if, else` statement

   C. An `if, else if` statement

   D. A `switch/case` statement

18. Which of the following functions will calculate the square of an input number when the line that calls it is `let x = mySquare (9);`?

A. `function mySquare(a,b){`

`return a*b ;}`

B. `function mySquare(a){`

`return a*a; }`

C. `function mySquare(x){`

`return =x }`

D. `function mySquare(a){`

`return a*a}`

19. Which of these are calling or invoking a function? (Choose two.)

A. `invoke functionName (1,2,3);`

B. `alert("Wake up!");`

C. `function mine (a,b,c) {return (a+b*c); }`

D. `let a = mine(1,2,3);`

20. Given the following code, which statements are true? (Choose two.)

```
function total (a,b) {return (a*b); }
let x = total(2,4);
```

A. The value of x is 6.

B. The value of x is 8.

C. The function returns its value to the `total` variable.

D. 2 and 4 are parameters for the `total` function.

Chapter

16

The DOM

LINUX PROFESSIONAL INSTITUTE, WEB DEVELOPMENT ESSENTIALS EXAM 030-100 OBJECTIVES COVERED IN THIS CHAPTER:

✓ **034 JavaScript Programming**

- 034.4 JavaScript Manipulation of Website Content and Styling: The candidate should understand the HTML DOM. This includes manipulating HTML elements and CSS properties through the DOM using JavaScript as well as using DOM events in simple scenarios.

  - Key Knowledge Areas:

    - Understand the concept and structure of the DOM

    - Change the contents and properties of HTML elements through the DOM

    - Change the CSS styling of HTML elements through the DOM

    - Trigger JavaScript functions from HTML elements

  - Files, terms, and utilities:

    - document.getElementById(), document.getElementsByClassName(), document.getElementsByTagName(), document.querySelector(), document.querySelectorAll()

    - innerHTML, setAttribute(), removeAttribute() properties and methods of DOM elements

    - classList, classList.add(), classList.remove(), classList.toggle() properties and methods of DOM elements

    - onClick, onMouseOver, onMouseOut attributes of HTML elements

The Document Object Model, or DOM as it's affectionately known, brings together bits and pieces of what you've learned in other chapters. You've learned that HTML provides the content and structure for your website, CSS provides the style, and JavaScript controls how the website behaves. Here you'll learn how to use the DOM to enable JavaScript to access and change parts of your content, to change website behavior, and to switch between different CSS styles.

DOM Structure

The *Document Object Model (DOM)* is a tree structure that follows the hierarchical structure of a website and is used by JavaScript (JS) to identify what element is being acted upon. (You learned about hierarchical structures in Chapter 6, "Content Markup.") The DOM considers the order in which each of the levels occur, what each is a child object of, and its position relative to the parent object (first child, second child, and so on). Each element in the DOM is an object.

Let's use the following HTML code for examining the DOM:

```
<!DOCTYPE html>

<html lang= "en">

<head>

  <meta charset= "utf-8">
  <title> DOM Structure </title>
  <link rel= "stylesheet" href= "style1.css">

</head>

<body>

  <h1> The DOM tree <h1>
    <p> First paragraph </p>
```

```
    <p> Second paragraph </p>

    <ul> This is my list.
      <li> first list item </li>
      <li> second list item </li>
    </ul>

  <h2> More information </h2>
    <p> more info paragraph 1</p>
    <p> more info paragraph 2 </p>

<script src="domScript1.js"></script>

</body>

</html>
```

Notice that the script is at the end of the body, right before the </body> tag. It's there because JS can't read the DOM until after the HTML is loaded. Be certain that you place your script reference there. Remember that although you can put JS code and CSS styles directly into your HTML page, the best practice is to place them in separate files that are accessed by the HTML file. HTML is for structure and content, CSS is for styling, and JS adds behavior to your web page. And although you put your JS file at the bottom of the page, the CSS style sheet needs to be referenced at the beginning of your HTML page. The DOM structure for the previous code would look like Figure 16.1.

HTML Tree Generator

The Chrome browser has an extension called HTML Tree Generator that will show you a graphical representation of your page's HTML Tree.

Search for **HTML Tree Generator**. Click the blue Add to Chrome button. Confirm that you want it by clicking the white Add extension button on the window that pops up. It will add a tree icon to your extensions. Right-click it and choose Manage eextension, then in the list find Allow access to file URLs and click the toggle button at right to turn it on. . Now when you have your website open, left click the extension, and it will show the HTML tree.

Refer to Figure 16.1 as you read this section. You might also want to open a browser and console to work along as you read. Everything in your HTML page, including the HTML element, is encompassed by the document so the HTML page is a child element of the document. The HEAD and BODY elements are siblings to each other, and both are child elements of the HTML page. META, TITLE, and LINK are siblings to each other, and child elements of the HEAD. Likewise, H1, P, P, UL, and H2, P, P, and SCRIPT are child elements of the BODY. H1 is the first child of the body, and SCRIPT is the last child of the body.

FIGURE 16.1   A DOM tree

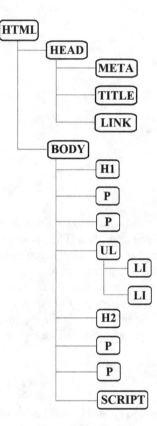

When using the DOM to refer to elements of your HTML page, you use the typical camel case, putting the first word in all lowercase and the first letter of each subsequent word in uppercase to make reading the words easier. The elements are separated by a period.

document.firstElementChild; refers to the entire HTML page because the HTML element is the first child of the document.

document.firstElementChild.firstElementChild; refers to the <head> section. The <head> section is the firstElementChild of the HTML element, which is the firstElementChild of the document.

document.firstElementChild.lastElementChild; refers to the body section. The only direct child elements of the HTML element are the head and body. Everything else belongs to one of those sections.

document.firstElementChild.lastElementChild.firstElementChild; refers to the first thing in the body, which is often an <h1> element.

It's easy to see that the descriptions could get very long before you get to the bottom of your HTML page, so a common practice is to assign variables to the objects rather than write them out each time. For example, `var mainHead = document`
`.firstElementChild.lastElementChild.firstElementChild;` assigns the variable `mainHead` to the `<h1>` heading. The variable `mainHead` is much shorter and easier to refer to than its associated description.

The contents of `domScript1.js` file are as follows:

```
let body = document.getElementsByTagName("body")[0];
console.log(body.innerHTML);
```

The first line assigns the variable body to the body of the document using its tag name. The *tag name* is the type of element such as body, list item (`li`), paragraph (`p`), and so on. When you access the DOM, the return is an array. Because there is only one body, it must be the first element in the array, which is always numbered 0, so the [0] says to retrieve information from the first element of the array.

The last line, `console.log (body.innerHTML);`, displays the contents and HTML markup (`.innerHTML`) of the body variable, which is your entire web page, in the console. Because body is a variable, you can use it to manipulate the entire `<body>`.

In addition to the tag name, we can access parts of the DOM using their `class` or `id`. An `id` is easy to use because `id`s are unique on a web page, but you may not want to assign an `id` to everything. Accessing by `id` or `class` is done using `document.getElementById();` or `document.getElementsByClassName();`. When getting elements by `id`, be conscious about using `Id`, not `ID` or `id`, in the `get` statement, and note that `element` is singular when retrieving elements by `id` (because there can only be one for each `id`), but plural (`elements`) when retrieving elements by class.

Content can also be retrieved using `querySelector()` or `querySelectorAll()`. The first will return the first item by selector and the `All` option will return all the elements that match the selector. Selectors are the same as CSS selectors except that in the DOM they must be in quotes, such as `querySelector("li")`, which would give you the first list item, or `querySelectorAll("li")`, which would give you all of the list items on the page.

But what if you have five list items and want to access number three? Use the `:nth-child()` pseudo-class to find it. For example, `let third = document`
`.querySelector("li:nth-child(3)").innerHTML` would return the content and HTML of the third list item to the variable third. If the selector doesn't find any items, then the value of the variable will be `null`. Note that this works with *child* items. This is why it's desirable to put paragraphs inside a `<div>`, then `("p:nth-child(3)")` would return the third child *if* it is a paragraph. To change the text in the third paragraph in a division, you could enter:

```
document.querySelector("p:nth-child(3)").innerText= "New text here.";
```

If, however, the paragraphs were not in a division, and they were preceded by something, perhaps an `<h1>`, then the preceding code would return the second paragraph, because it is a paragraph and the third child of the body.

Another option is (" p:nth-of-type(2)"), but it may not be as widely supported. This would only look at the paragraphs and choose the second one.

DOM Methods and Properties

In the previous section, you used several methods to retrieve elements from your web page using the DOM, now you'll learn how to manipulate them. As you learned before, properties are characteristics of an object and methods are what you can do with it. DOM objects are the same.

You can tell methods from properties simply by looking for the () at the end. For example, querySelectorAll() is a method, as is getElementsByTagName(). Properties, on the other hand, do not have the parenthesis () at the end. innerHTML, innerText, attributes, and classList are properties.

Adding and Deleting Classes and Attributes

Sometimes it's advantageous to be able to add elements to a particular class. First, to list what's in a class, use the getElementsByClassName() function. The following code assigns a variable named elements, which will contain an array of all the elements with the class name fun:

```
var elements = document.getElementsByClassName( "fun" );
```

If you want to see what classes an element belongs to, you can use the classList property. The following code will return a list of the classes that the element whose id is member belongs to:

```
document.getElementById( "member").classList
```

You can add the fun class to the element in the previous line of code using the classList.add() method as follows:

```
document.getElementById( "member").classList.add( "fun");
```

If you later decide to remove the class fun from the element member, you will use the following code with the classList.remove() method:

```
document.getElementById("member").classList.remove("fun");
```

You can add and delete element attributes using the DOM too. As you learned in Chapter 5, "HTML introduction," attributes provide more information about an element such as size, color, and so on. You'll find attributes inside the tag, such as `<h2 style= "background-color:LightGray;"> heading text </h2>` and `<img src= "flower picture.jpg" width= "100" height= "150">`, where style, src, width, and height are all attributes.

You add and remove attributes using the `setAttribute()` and `removeAttribute()` methods. The syntax is `element.setAttribute( "name", "newValue");`. Let's add an attribute to our `<h1>` heading. It's the only `<h1>` heading, so we can access it using its type. Refer to the code that follows:

```
document.querySelector("h1").setAttribute("class", "important");   //adds the
important class to the <h1> element.
```

When setting a Boolean attribute, if the attribute is there it's considered true; if the attribute is not there, it's false. In the following code, assume that there is a paragraph with the id of `memberP` that you want to display if someone is a member but hide if they are not.

```
const member = document.getElementById("memberP");   /*locates the memberP
paragraph and assigns the variable member to it. */

member.setAttribute("hidden", "" );   //hides the memberP paragraph
```

The empty quotes or the attribute name are often used as the value, and the presence of a Boolean attribute equates to true, so the member paragraph will be hidden. To display the paragraph, `hidden` would need to be false, so it would not be present. To remove it, use the following code:

```
member.removeAttribute("hidden");
```

Retrieving and Setting Values

To change a property, you retrieve the item as explained in the "DOM Structure" section, then specify what you want it to be. Let's assign an id of `"li1"` to the first list item, and `"li2"` to the second list item and add a third item with the id of `"li3"`.

```
<ul> This is my list.
   <li id= "li1"> first list item </li>
   <li id= "li2"> second list item </li>
   <li id= "li3"> third list item </li>
</ul>
```

You could then retrieve the value of the `.innerHTML` property by id and change the contents of the second list item with this line:

```
document.getElementById("li2").innerHTML = "<li> Bananas! </li>"
```

This changed not only the content to `Bananas!`, but also any HTML code included in the item. In this case, you left `<li>` as is, but because you used `.innerHTML`, you needed to specify what the HTML would be.

If you want to change the text of an element without changing the HTML code, you could use code like this:

```
document.getElementById("li3").innerText= "New text here.";
```

Using .innerText (or .textContent) instead of .innerHTML is a better choice because changing the markup code using .innerHTML may lead to human error, makes troubleshooting more difficult, and doesn't maintain the separation of HTML for content and JS for functionality.

You learned that if more than one of something exists it is returned as an array, but how can you change that array? First, use the querySelectorAll( ) method to retrieve all your list items and store the array in a variable named items. For the output of the following code, see Figure 16.2.

```
let items = document.querySelectorAll("li");
```

FIGURE 16.2   Command output

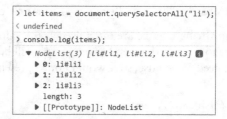

The output shows that three elements were retrieved, numbered 0, 1, and 2, as you would expect. To select a single element, you would use the variable name and element number in square brackets: items[1]. You can use the variable name and number combination to perform actions on that element. And, of course, when you click the arrow next to an item it expands to show you information about that item as can be seen in Figure 16.3 when the arrow under items[1] is clicked.

FIGURE 16.3   Choosing one array element

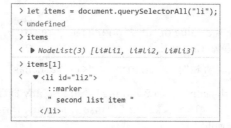

You can also loop through all the items of your array and perform some action on all of them with code. The code shown in the first line of Figure 16.4 simply lists them on the console, but the code between the { } could be replaced with any code.

FIGURE 16.4   Looping through array elements

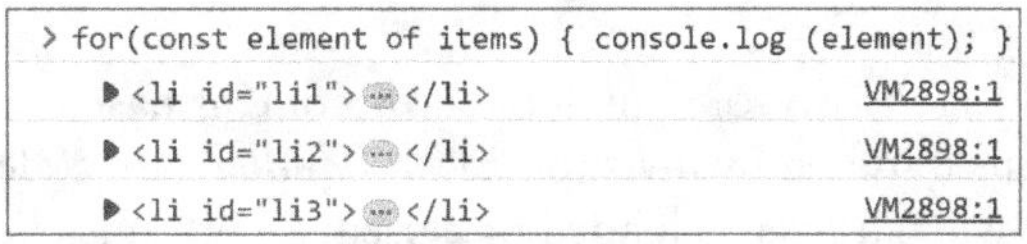

```
> for(const element of items) { console.log (element); }
    ▶ <li id="li1"> ⬤ </li>                          VM2898:1
    ▶ <li id="li2"> ⬤ </li>                          VM2898:1
    ▶ <li id="li3"> ⬤ </li>                          VM2898:1
```

Changing CSS Styling Using the DOM

Although it's possible to change styles in JS, a better way is to create CSS styles for classes and then assign elements to classes as needed. This maintains the separation of style and functionality. If an element needs to be styled differently depending on what's happening, then the class can be changed using the JS classList.add() and classList().remove methods.

Multiple classes can be combined in CSS and JS to achieve the desired effect. Consider the following CSS code that will be used to either show or hide a paragraph depending on the element's group.

```css
p .restrict {
  background-color: white;
  color: white;
  }
p .memberStyle {
  background-color: blue;
  color: yellow;
  }
```

The following JS code adds the memberStyle class or restrict class based on whether the visitor is a member, and would change a paragraph with id="membersOnly" to a blue background with yellow lettering:

```js
if (member = true) {
document.getElementById("membersOnly").classList.add("memberStyle");
} else {
document.getElementById("membersOnly").classList.add("restrict");
}
```

The next section explains using classList.toggle to change which CSS style is applied.

DOM Events

Often you want a web page to do something or show content based on what the visitor is doing. *Events* are actions initiated by a visitor. *Event handlers* are code that runs based on visitor actions, such as when a page is loaded or closed, a button is clicked, a mouse passes over something, or some other event occurs.

Buttons work well as DOM events. Consider the following code that launches a function when a button is clicked, using the onClick HTML attribute:

```
<button onclick="someFunction()"> Click Me. </button>
```

Then JS is used to create the function, and the JS classList.toggle() method toggles the group membership of the object's contents, changing the visibility of the paragraph where the id=membersOnly:

```
function someFunction() {
  document.getElementById("membersOnly").classList.toggle("memberStyle");
  }
```

Code can also be written that will respond to where a mouse is on a page using onmouseover and onmouseout. Notice that the attributes are all lowercase. If you use camelCase for mouseover or onmouseout, your code won't work. The following is written in the JS file:

```
document.getElementById( "specialNotice") .onmouseover = function() {
  show()};
document.getElementById( "specialNotice") .onmouseout = function() {
 hide()};
```

```
function show() {
  document.getElementById( "specialNotice").style.color = "blue";
  }
function hide() {
  document.getElementById( "specialNotice").style.color = "white";
  }
```

You could also use HTML to call the function like this:

```
<p id= "specialNotice" onmouseover= "show()" onmouseout= "hide()">This
paragraph will disappear on mouseout and appear on mouseover. </p>
```

And only the functions (previously shown) would be written in the JS file.

Summary

In this chapter, you learned what the DOM structure is and how to access different elements, which are objects to the DOM, and how to manipulate our page using the DOM and JS. `document.getElementById("idName")` works well for accessing individual objects. `document.getElementByClassName ( "className")` works well when you need to choose multiple objects. Or you can use `querySelector()` and `querySelectorAll()` to use selectors as you do in CSS, and the pseudo-class *element*`:nth-child(9)`, where 9 is any number, lets you choose a specific element when using `querySelector`.

Information from the DOM can be saved in a variable, like an array, and you can choose anything from that list as you would from an array.

DOM methods end with `()` and properties don't. camelCase should generally be used with methods and properties longer than one word, but not with `onmouseover` or `onmouseout`. In HTML, `onmouseover` and `onmouseout` can be used to call functions written in JS. Again, it's a best practice to keep content, style, and function separate in their HTML, CSS, and JS files respectively.

A best practice when styling with CSS is to write styles in the CSS file and have them refer to classes that can be assigned in JS. You can add and remove classes from a JS object using `classList.add()` and `classList.remove()` methods, and `classList.toggle()` is great to toggle between classes using some action like a button click or `onmouseover`.

Using `.innerText` is cleaner than using `.innerHTML` and can save time later when troubleshooting, because changing HTML with JS may make finding problems more difficult.

Exam Essentials

Know the structure of the DOM and how to retrieve information.   Knowing the myriad of ways to retrieve specific information using the DOM ensures that you return the information you expect to get.

Be able to change CSS styling through the DOM.   Changing CSS styling using groups and the style sheet is preferable and will save time in the long run.

Become proficient at changing HTML element properties and contents using the DOM.   This will help you add interactivity to your web page.

Remember the various ways to trigger JavaScript functions using HTML elements.   People expect interactive web pages, and sometimes that functionality is essentially the reason for the web page.

EXERCISE 16.1

Retrieve and Set Values Using the DOM

In this exercise, you change the content and styling of an object using the DOM. Then display the DOM.

1. Open a skeleton HTML file, and save it as **exercise16_1.html**. Open a blank text file and save it as **script16_1.js**, and open a third text file and save it as **styles16_1.css**.

2. In your text editor, open exercise16_1.html and add the following content:

```
<h1> The DOM tree </h1>
  <p> first paragraph </p>
  <p> second paragraph </p>
  <p> third paragraph </p>
```

3. Add a reference to script16_1.js and styles16_1.css to your HTML file. Save the HTML file.

4. Without adding classes or ids to the paragraphs, enter a line in the script file that will retrieve the second paragraph using the DOM, and change only the content to "I like to go fishing" (without affecting the HTML code).

5. Create a style in the CSS file for the group blue that will change the text color to blue and save the CSS file.

6. Add a line to your JS file that will add the first paragraph to the blue group, and add another line that will display the DOM after the HTML file is loaded. Save your JS file.

7. Open the HTML file with a browser, then open the console to verify your code.

ANSWER

Styles16_1.css:

```
.blue {
  color: blue;
  }
```

Script16_1.js:

```
document.querySelector("p:nth-child(3)").innerText = "I like to go fishing.";
document.querySelector("p:nth-child(2)").classList.add("blue");
let body = document.getElementsByTagName("body")[0];
console.log(body.innerHTML);
```

exercise16_1.html:

```html
<!DOCTYPE html>
<html lang="en-us">
<head>
  <meta charset = "utf-8">
  <title> DOM Exercise 16-1 </title>
  <link rel= "stylesheet" href = "styles16_1.css">
</head>
<body>
  <h1> The DOM tree </h1>
  <p> First paragraph </p>
  <p> Second paragraph </p>
  <p> Third paragraph </p>

<script src= "script16_1.js"> </script>
</body>
</html>
```

EXERCISE 16.2

Toggle Content Using a Button

In this exercise, you create a button, and use classList.toggle to change the style of a
<div> element.

1. In your text editor, open exercise16_1.html and save it as **exercise16_2.html**. Do
    the same with script16_1.js and styles16_1.CSS.

2. In your HTML file, change the references to reflect the new filenames, and change the
    <title> to **Exercise 16-2**.

3. After the <h1> heading, add a button whose text says "Click Here!" and that will
    run the function "myFunction()" when clicked.

4. In your HTML file, enclose the three paragraphs in a <div> element.

5. Create the function named "myFunction" in the JS file that will access the <div>
    and use .classList.toggle("funStyle"); to toggle it in and out of the
    funStyle class. Remember that the division is the first one retrieved in the array.

EXERCISE 16.2 *(continued)*

6. In the CSS file, create a style for the `funStyle` class, changing the background color to bright yellow. Add a border or other style if you like (but it's best to make sure your code works first).

7. Save the HTML, CSS, and JS files.

8. Open the HTML file in a browser and test your button.

ANSWER

`Styles16_2.css:`

```
.funStyle{
  Background-color: yellow;
  }
```

`Script16_2.js:`

```
function myFunction() {
  document.getElementByTagName("div")[0].classList.toggle("funStyle");
  }
```

`exercise16_2.html:`

Only affected segments are shown.

```
<head>
  <meta charset = "utf-8">
  <title> DOM Exercise 16-2 </title>
  <link rel= "stylesheet" href = "styles16_2.css">
</head>
<body>
  <h1> The DOM tree </h1>
  <button onClick="myFunction()"> Click Here! </button>
  <div>
    <p> First paragraph </p>
    <p> Second paragraph </p>
    <p> Third paragraph </p>
  </div>
  <script src= "script16_2.js"> </script>
</body>
```

Review Questions

1. Which of these refers to the <head> section of a document?

   A. document.firstElementChild;

   B. document.firstElementChild. firstElementChild;

   C. document.firstElementChild. secondElementChild;

   D. document.secondElementChild;

2. Which of the following are DOM methods? (Choose two.)

   A. getElementsByTagName()

   B. getElementByGroup()

   C. querySelectorAll()

   D. getElementByID()

3. Which of the following can be used to retrieve the entire body of a web page?

   A. document.getElementByTagName("body"){0}

   B. document.getElementByTagName("html")[0]

   C. document.getElementByTagName("body")[0]

   D. document.getElementByTagName("body")[1]

4. From the following code, which of the following options will return only the first paragraph? (Choose two.)

   ```
   <div>
   <p class= "fun" id= "p1"> first paragraph </p>
   <p class= "none" id= "p2"> first paragraph </p>
   <p class= "fun"  id= "p3"> first paragraph </p>
   </div>
   ```

   A. document.getElementById("p1");

   B. querySelector("p");

   C. document.getElementBySelectorAll("p")[1];

   D. document.getElementsByClass('fun');

5. Which of these will change only the content, not the structure of my web page? (Choose two.)

   A. document.getElementById("p1").innerHTML = "What a day!";

   B. document.getElementById("p1").innerText = "What a day!";

   C. document.getElementById("p1").textContent = "What a day!";

   D. document.getElementById("p1") .innerContent = "What a day!";

6. You want to change the wording of the third list item in an ordered list. Which of the following will not work? (Choose two.)

A. `document.querySelectorAll("li:nth-child(3)").innerText= "bananas";`

B. `document.querySelector("li:nth-child(3)").innerText= "bananas";`

C. `document.qetElementsByTagName("li") [3].innerHTML= "<li> bananas! </li>";`

D. `document.qetElementsByTagName("li") [2].innerText= "bananas!";`

7. Which of the following will change the source attribute of a given element?

A. *element*`.setAttribute("src", "elephant.jpg");`

B. *element*`.setAttribute("src = elephant.jpg");`

C. *element*`.setAttribute(src =elephant.jpg");`

D. *element*`.changeAttribute("src" "elephant.jpg");`

8. How can you turn a CSS style named `fun` on and off for a given element, using the DOM and assuming there are functions named on and `off` to add and remove the style?

A. *element*`.onmouseover=function() {toggle fun};`

B. *element*`.onmouseover=function() { on()};` *element*`.onmouseout= function() {off()};`

C. *element*`.onmouseover("on()");` *element*`.onmouseout("off()");`

D. `<p onmouseover= "on()" onmouseout("off()"> content </p>`

9. You want to change the style of an element. What is the best way to do this using the DOM? (Choose two.)

A. *element*`.style( "newStyle");`

B. *element*`.classList.add("newStyle")`

C. *element*`.style( .new {color=red; size = 10px; }`

D. Create `.newStyle {color=red; size= 10px; }` in CSS

10. You want the CSS style of a `<div>` with `Id = "special"` to change to a style called `newStyle` based on a button being clicked. Which two of these do you need? (Choose two.)

A. In HTML: `<button onclick= "myFunction()"> Click here </button>`

B. In HTML: `<button classList.toggle(newStyle);>`

C. In JS: `function myFunction() {documentGetElementById("special") .classList.toggle("newStyle");`

D. In JS: `function newStyle() {.classList.toggle ("special")};`

11. What is the `firstChildElement` of the document?

A. `<head>`

B. `<body>`

C. `<html>`

D. `<title>`

12. You would like to see what classes an element has. How will you do this?

    A. *element*`.show.classList`

    B. *element*`.classList.show`

    C. *element*`.classList.list`

    D. *element*`.classList`

13. Which of the following will ensure that the element in question is *not* hidden?

    A. *element*`.removeAttribute("hidden");`

    B. *element*`.setAttribute("hidden", "");`

    C. *element*`.setAttribute("hidden", "[]");`

    D. *element*`.setAttribute("hidden", "false");`

14. Assuming the following HTML code, what will `document.querySelector` `("p:nth-child(2)")` return?

    ```
    <body>
    <h1> Hello </h1>
    <p> Paragraph 1 </p>
    <p> Paragraph 2 </p>
    </body>
    ```

    A. Paragraph 1

    B. Hello

    C. Paragraph 2

    D. Null

15. Assuming the following HTML code, what will `document.querySelector` `("p:nth-child(1)")` return?

    ```
    <body>
    <h1> Hello </h1>
    <p> Paragraph 1 </p>
    <p> Paragraph 2 </p>
    </body>
    ```

    A. Paragraph 1

    B. Hello

    C. Paragraph 2

    D. Null

16. You no longer want an element to belong to the student class. What is the best option to achieve this?

   A. `element.removeClass("student");`

   B. `element.removeAttribute("class");`

   C. `element.removeAttribute("class" "student");`

   D. `element.classList.remove("student");`

17. Your HTML file has multiple <h3> headings, and you want to access one of them. They don't have ids assigned. Which of the following will help you do that? (Choose two.)

   A. `document.getElementsByTagName("h3")`

   B. `document.getElementsById("h3")`

   C. `document.getElementsByTagName(h3)`

   D. `document.querySelectorAll("h3")`

18. Which of the following could return more than one element? (Choose two.)

   A. `document.getElementById();`

   B. `document.querySelector();`

   C. `document.querySelectorAll();`

   D. `document.getElementsByClassName();`

19. Which method can't be used to change the class of a DOM object?

   A. `classList.toggle()`

   B. `setAttribute()`

   C. `classList.add()`

   D. `changeAttribute()`

20. Which of these is not true of the DOM?

   A. It's a tree structure.

   B. It provides a method to access web page elements.

   C. It's used in JavaScript.

   D. It requires code to start with .DOM.

Chapter

17

NodeJS Basics

LINUX PROFESSIONAL INSTITUTE, WEB DEVELOPMENT ESSENTIALS EXAM 030-100 OBJECTIVES COVERED IN THIS CHAPTER:

✓ **035 NodeJS Server Programming**

- 035.1 NodeJS Basics: The candidate should understand the basics of NodeJS. This includes running a local development server as well as understanding the concept of NPM modules.

    - Key Knowledge Areas:

        - Understand the concepts of Node.js

        - Run a NodeJS application

        - Install NPM packages

    - Files, terms, and utilities:

        - node [file.js]

        - npm init

        - npm install [module_name]

        - package.json

        - node_modules

In this chapter, you'll learn what Node.js is and why you'll want to use it. When you're done, you'll be able to explain what Node.js is, install Node.js, install NPM packages, and run a Node.js application.

What Is Node.js?

When you think of JavaScript (JS), you generally think of the front-end of a website—the browser and the code that the user interacts with. The foundation of websites on the front-end is HTML, CSS, and JS. *Node.js* is a fast runtime environment for programming on the server-side of a web page using the same V8 engine Google's Chrome uses to compile JS code to machine code, so Node.js enables us to run JS programs on a server or on our desktop without a browser. That means you can use it as the back-end of your website, and a programmer familiar with JS on the front-end will be familiar with the JS language on the back-end. Node.js is arguably the most popular back-end solution in use because of its speed and ubiquitous language, along with its other advantages. It's used by big businesses such as LinkedIn, NASA, Netflix, PayPal, and Walmart.

Node.js accepts requests from an event pool on a single thread and passes them to its event listener called Event Loop, which delegates them to a thread pool where a multi-threaded background application picks them up and processes them asynchronously. *Asynchronous processing* means that multiple processes can be running simultaneously in the background while Event Loop continues to accept and delegate requests. Event Loop continuously listens for new requests and completed processes, delegating new requests to the thread pool and passing the results of any completed process back to where it was initiated, where a callback function performs some action based on that result.

Imagine that you're printing a 1,000-page document. You send the document to the printer, and while it's printing you're working on your next assignment. When the document is done printing, you get a message on your screen telling you so that you can pick it up from the printer. Meanwhile, you've completed 10 other tasks that you had to get done. This is asynchronous. If printing your document was a synchronous task, you would need to wait until the printer was finished before you could work on something else. Asynchronous programs are, therefore, much faster and more efficient than synchronous programs.

Other advantages of Node.js are that it is scalable and open source, and that it has the Node Package Manager (NPM), which is a database of thousands of free, open source libraries providing prewritten chunks of code for common functions like file management and networking. It also has a huge community so if you do run into a problem, there is likely someone else who has had the same problem and solved it, or at the very least there are many minds to help you solve it.

Installing Node.js

Node.js needs to be installed before it can be used, regardless of the OS that you're using. A quick search will lead you to `https://nodejs.org/en/download`, where you can download the appropriate version for your OS. Choose the long-term support (LTS) version rather than the current version. An *LTS version* has been out in the wild for months and is known to be stable. In a production environment, you would most certainly want to use the LTS version. Unless you're on a very old machine, you'll choose a 64-bit version, but you should check your operating system to be sure. macOS machines newer than 2007 should be 64-bit, and any Intel-based systems that are Core series will be 64-bit, except for embedded systems.

The files are downloaded in a zip file, so you'll need to extract the files first, and then run the installer.

Alternately, if you're working in Linux Ubuntu, open the terminal and type **sudo apt-get install -y nodejs** and press Enter. Once it's installed, typing **node -v** will display the version of Node.js. At the ~$ prompt, type **node** and press Enter. Your prompt will change to >, indicating that you're now in REPL. *REPL* stands for read, evaluate, print, loop, meaning that Node.js will read our code, evaluate it, and then print it on the screen for us. Let's do some things in REPL.

First, type **process.version** and press Enter. This will (again) show you the Node.js version. It should be at least version 18.16.0.

Now enter a simple equation like **1+100** and press Enter. The screen displays 101. (It performed REPL.) REPL is like the JS code and `console.log` rolled into one. Now here's something a bit more complex. Enter the following:

```
let a=10
let b=15
b-a
let c=b-a
c
```

The output should look like Figure 17.1.

FIGURE 17.1   Code output

Type **.help** to see a list of commands in REPL. Note that they all start with a period before the name such as .exit, which is how you leave REPL and return to the terminal. Exit the terminal now and you're returned to the familiar Linux ~$ prompt. Type **node** and press Enter, and you're back in REPL again. The other options shown by .help are:

.break—Gets you out.

.clear—Same as .break.

.editor—Enter editor mode.

.exit—Exit the REPL.

.help—Brings up this message.

.load—Load JS from a file into REPL.

.save—Saves your REPL session to a file.

Installing a Node.js Module

A *module* is simply a chunk of code that performs a specific function. Node.js modules are akin to the libraries you learned about back in Chapter 1, "Web Development Basics." They can be a part of the program or created by users like you. Creating modules to perform specific, repetitive tasks makes writing the main code easier, more efficient, and cleaner to write. Node.js supports two types of modules. CommonJS modules are packaged specifically for Node.js, and Node.js supports ECMAScript modules that are the standard for other JavaScript runtimes. Node.js has several built-in modules that can be used without any further installation. There are many more CommonJS modules and ECMAScript modules available, as well as many third-party modules that are installed via the Node Package Manager (NPM). The NPM is used to download, install, and manage external packages (those not built in).

The npm init command is used to create a repository for files associated with a Node.js project, and will create a package.json file (more about those later). The npm init command will ask for the following information and provide a guess for default values, which you can overwrite simply by typing something in the space—package name, version, description, entry point (filename.js), test command, Git repository, keywords, author, license (ISC)—and then ask you if all the answers are as intended. For now you can skip all of this with **npm init --yes** to create a package.json file. When you open the package.json file in a text editor, you'll see the answer to all those questions.

To install a module, in the terminal at $ enter **npm install packageName**, and your system will look online for a module with that name to install on your system. When installed successfully, the package will create a package-lock.json file. Opening that in your text editor will show the module installed and its version, and list it as a dependency to your project.

The module installation will have also created a folder called node_modules in the same parent folder as the package.json file. Inside that folder will be a folder for each module installed and a .package-lock.json file.

Once the module is installed, you must assign a variable to it and "require" it so that it will be available wherever you call it in your application. Whatever value the function in the module returns is internal to the function, so by assigning its value to a variable outside of the function, you make it available outside the function by using the variable. This is done with a command such as var colors = require('colors');, where the name of the variable is colors and the name of the required module is colors. It's not required that the variable and the module have the same name, but it does make coding less confusing.

Running a Node.js App

Running an app in Node.js is quite simple, so let's run some code in node! Create a file named **test.js** using your favorite text editor. In that file, enter the code **console .log("Hello World!");** and save the file.

You will want the terminal to be open in the folder where your test.js file lives. To get there, you can right-click the folder and choose Open in Terminal, or back in the terminal, type **cd** at the ~$, then drag the *parent folder* of your test.js file to the terminal. If you saved it in the documents folder, you should see ~$ cd '/home/*yourName*/Documents', except with your username in place of *yourName*, of course. Press Enter and you should see ~/Documents$, if your test.js file was in the documents folder. (Alternately, you can manually enter the path to the file.) Now type **node test.js** to run your code, and Hello World! should appear on your screen. Success!

Summary

In this chapter, you learned why Node.js is so popular and the basics of how it works by using Event Loop to grab a single request and pass it on to the thread pool. There the request is run while Event Loop grabs the next requests and listens for the process to be completed, then sends the results back to the request, where a callback function takes the next steps in processing the results. Then you learned how to use npm init to create a repository for Node.js project files and npm install packageName to install a module. Finally, you ran an app using Node.js.

Exam Essentials

Know the role that Node.js plays and why it is so popular. Node.js is widely used, and understanding and being able to use this tool may be integral to securing that web development position in your future.

Locate and install Node.js modules. Using modules to create your application will save you countless hours of work.

Run an application in Node.js. It's a simple process, but a must-know for any web developer.

EXERCISE 17.1

Install Node.js

In this exercise, you install Node.js. on an Ubuntu-based computer.

1. The exact instructions for installing Node.js will vary depending on the operating system that you're using. We'll assume that you're using a recent version of Linux Ubuntu, but if you're not, start with the download page for Node.js, which can be found at https://nodejs.org/en/download. If you use the download files to install on an Ubuntu machine, you might notice that the Node.js version is around v10. You'll want to update that to the most recent version—continue to step 2.

2. On an Ubuntu machine, open the terminal. You might wish to run **sudo apt-get update** then **sudo apt-get upgrade** to make sure that everything is up-to-date before you install Node.js.

3. While in the terminal, verify that you're at the ~$ terminal. Type **sudo apt-get install -y nodejs** and press Enter to install Node.js The installation should run.

4. Again at the ~$ terminal, type **node**. The resulting message should say "Welcome to Node.js v. 18.16.0." or a newer version, and your command prompt should be the REPL prompt, >.

5. Enter **.exit** to end the Node.js session.

ANSWER

Verify that Node.js is installed by typing **node** at the ~$ prompt and observing the prompt change to >.

EXERCISE 17.2

Install a Node.js Module

In this exercise, you install a Node.js module that adds color to the node.js console.

1. Ensure that your computer is connected to the Internet.

2. Open the terminal.

3. At the `~$` terminal, type **npm install colors** and press Enter. The terminal will access the Internet to find the `colors` module in an online module repository. The message "added 1 package in 665ms" should display, (although the milliseconds might be different) and return you to the `~$` prompt.

4. Type **node** and press Enter to go into REPL.

5. Type **var colors = require('colors');** and press Enter.

6. Now it's time to test the colors. Type **console.log("Sunshine and " .rainbow);** and press Enter. The words "Sunshine and" should appear in rainbow colors. You can use common color names like red, yellow, and so on. Other options include `.inverse`, `.trap`, `.underline`, or simply `.colorName`. When using another option with a color, enter them as `.option.colorName`, such as `console.log("my text here" .underline.red);`.

7. To create a color theme, enter the following, for example:

```
Var colors = require('colors');
Colors.setTheme({
    err: ".underline.red",
    fun: ".rainbow",
    debug: ".orange"
});
```

8. Type a line such as **console.log("let's fix this".debug);** and press Enter. The output (let's fix this) should appear in orange.

ANSWER

Verify that you are able to use colors as explained in the exercise.

EXERCISE 17.3

Run a Node.js Application

On the front side, the browser manages saving files for you, but on the back side, you need tools to help you save a file or save data to a database. In this exercise, you create and run an application to save a file.

1. Open your text editor and enter the following code, replacing *Audrey* with your own name. When you're done, save your file as **nameSave.js**. Note the use of single and double quotes in the last line.

```
const filesystem = require ("fs");
filesystem.writeFile('userLog.txt', "Audrey", (err) => { if (err) throw err;
console.log
("User's name is saved to the file.")});
```

2. In the terminal, navigate to the parent folder of your nameSave.js file.

3. Type **node nameSave.js** and press Enter. The message "User's name is saved to the file." should appear.

4. Close the terminal. Open the folder where you saved nameSave.js. Look for the file named userLog.txt and open it. The name you entered in the code in step 1 should appear in the userLog.txt file.

ANSWER

Verify that the file saved correctly as explained in the exercise.

Review Questions

1. Which of the following is a server-side application?

   A. HTML

   B. CSS

   C. JavaScript

   D. Node.js

2. What are your options for downloading and installing Node.js on a Linux-based computer? (Choose two.)

   A. Use `sudo apt-get install` in the terminal.

   B. Download from the `http://nodejs.org` website.

   C. Go to Programs And Applications in Control Panel.

   D. Download it from the Apple App Store.

3. What does REPL stand for?

   A. Replace, execute, process, load

   B. Read, execute, print, loop

   C. Read, evaluate, print, loop

   D. Read, execute, parse, loop

4. What command is the same as `.break` in Node.js?

   A. `.clear`

   B. `.editor`

   C. `.exit`

   D. `.save`

5. What is a module? (Choose two.)

   A. Code that solves a common issue

   B. Code that can be reused

   C. Any code that executes a function

   D. Only code written by third-party users

6. In Linux terminal, what are two ways to navigate to a folder that contains files you want? (Choose two.)

   A. Drag and drop the parent folder onto the terminal.

   B. Manually type **cd** and enter the path to the parent folder.

   C. Right-click the folder and choose Open in Terminal.

   D. Type **cd** and drag and drop the parent folder onto the terminal.

7. Which of these are advantages of using Node.js? (Choose two.)

    A. It uses familiar JavaScript commands.

    B. It runs in a browser.

    C. It is synchronous.

    D. It is fast.

8. Which of the following statements is *not* true? (Choose two.)

    A. Node.js must be installed in Windows before you can use it.

    B. Node.js is a part of Ubuntu.

    C. Node.js must be installed in Ubuntu before you can use it.

    D. Node.js comes preinstalled in macOS.

9. In REPL, which of these will tell you the version of Node.js that is running?

    A. `process.version`

    B. `.editor`

    C. `.help`

    D. `node`

10. Where does Event Loop send a request when Node.js is being used on the server-side?

    A. The browser

    B. Request pool

    C. Thread pool

    D. Back to the requesting code

11. Which of the following creates a repository for files associated with a Node.js project but requires input from the coder creating the repository?

    A. `npm init`

    B. `create.package.json`

    C. `npm init --yes`

    D. `mpn init`

12. What type of Node.js modules don't require installation before you can use them?

    A. CommonJS modules

    B. ECMAScript modules

    C. Well-known modules

    D. Built-in modules

13. Which of the following will not produce an error message?

   A. At the $ prompt, type **node**.

   B. At the > prompt, type **node**.

   C. At the $ prompt, type **process.version**.

   D. At the > prompt, type **node -v**.

14. What is the data that would be written to a file in the following code?

```
const filesystem = require ('fs');
    filesystem.writeFile('userLog.txt', "123456789", (err)
=> { if(err) throw err;  console.log ("Data is saved.")}); 
```

   A. userLog.txt

   B. Data is Saved

   C. err

   D. 123456789

15. You're in the Linux terminal at a $ prompt. What will happen if you enter the command **node bogus.js** assuming the path to bogus.js is correct?

   A. You'll receive an error message.

   B. The prompt will change to bogus>.

   C. The file bogus.js will run.

   D. A module named bogus will be loaded.

16. You found the perfect Node.js module, named parallelogram, for your program. What will you enter at the $ prompt to install this module?

   A. npm init parallelogram

   B. package.install parallelogram

   C. var parallelogram = require('parallelogram');

   D. npm install parallelogram

17. When is the folder called node_modules created? Choose the best answer.

   A. After npm init --yes is run

   B. When you read the package.json file

   C. When you run npm install *packageName*

   D. When you manually create it

18. Which of the following could be an application file run by Node.js?

   A. `process.js`

   B. `runMe`

   C. `init`

   D. `answer.njs`

19. You're at a > prompt. What will happen if you type **1+3** and press Enter? Choose the best answer.

   A. 1+4 is displayed.

   B. The error `command not found` is displayed.

   C. The number 4 is displayed.

   D. The computer waits for further instructions.

20. What type of Node.js modules will work with other JS runtimes?

   A. CommonJS modules

   B. ECMAScript modules

   C. Well-known modules

   D. Built-in modules

NodeJS Express

LINUX PROFESSIONAL INSTITUTE, WEB DEVELOPMENT ESSENTIALS EXAM 030-100 OBJECTIVES COVERED IN THIS CHAPTER:

✓ **035 NodeJS Server Programming**

- 035.2 NodeJS Express Basics: The candidate should be able to create a simple dynamic website with the Express web framework. This includes defining simple Express routes as well as serving dynamic files through the template engine EJS.

    - Key Knowledge Areas:

        - Define routes to static files and EJS templates

        - Serve static files through Express

        - Serve EJS templates through Express

        - Create simple, non-nested EJS templates

        - Use the request object to access HTTP GET and POST parameters and process data submitted through HTML forms

        - Awareness of user input validation

        - Awareness of cross-site Scripting (XSS)

        - Awareness of cross-site request forgery (CSRF)

    - Files, terms, and utilities:

        - express and body-parser node module

        - Express app object

        - app.get(), app.post()

        - res.query, res.body

        - ejs node module

        - res.render()

        - <% . . . %>, <%= . . . %>, <%# . . . %>, <%- . . . %>

        - views/

The previous chapter introduced Node.js and your entry into the server-side, or programming. Now you'll do even more with Node.js Express. You'll learn how to install it and use it to route requests from your users to the right place on your website, and how to serve static and dynamic files to users. I suggest that you open your Linux machine and work along with this chapter.

Node.js vs. Node.js Express

You've already learned that Node.js provides a runtime that lets you create back-end and other JavaScript (JS) programs that can run outside of a browser, so why do we need Node.js Express? Express is a framework designed specifically for writing the back-end of web pages and mobile applications. You'll soon see that it makes coding much less verbose, and therefore easier to read. Express is free and open source. Like the framework of a house, a *programming framework* provides the structure that a program can be built around. Blocks of code that are needed often are prebuilt into the framework, so the programmer saves enormous amounts of time and energy and is able to focus more on the aspects of their specific project instead of the more mundane coding required to create the server-side. Express is by far the most popular framework for creating websites. It is built using Node.js, so compatibility isn't an issue. Neither is a learning curve because it's all built on the JavaScript language that you're already familiar with.

Installing Express

To install Express, you need root or administrative access, and you must have Node.js installed. We're assuming you're using Ubuntu. First, open a terminal and update your files by typing the following:

```
sudo apt-get update
sudo apt-get upgrade
```

You might want to create your directory on the desktop to make it easier to navigate to it. From ~$ enter **cd Desktop** to navigate there, then continue.

Next, create a separate directory for your server and navigate into it using the following commands:

```
mkdir newserver //creates a directory called newserver
cd newserver //navigates to that directory
```

Keeping the terminal open, from the desktop navigate to the directory you created and open it so that you can see the results of the next steps.

Back in the terminal, create a file that will be your entry point. You can name it anything, but typically it's called `index.js`. You can create a file using your text editor, but since you're already in the terminal try using the `touch` command as follows:

```
touch index.js
```

You should see the file pop into the folder that's open on your desktop. Now it's time to initialize npm, which will create a `package.json` file in your new directory with the following command:

```
npm init
```

You'll be asked a series of questions, and the program attempts to guess what your answers will be. Press Enter to accept the default answers. For the package name it will use the directory name that you created, and it will assume this is version 1.0.0. Give it a description if you like. The entry point will be `index.js` (which is normally used) or whatever `filename.js` you decide upon. Ignore the `test` command, the GIT repository, and keywords for now. Make sure you enter *yourOwnName* next to `author`. The `license` entry defaults to `ISC`, which is fine. Press Enter. When it's done, it will ask you "Is this OK? (yes)." Press Enter to accept the entries. Express will create a `package.json` file in your directory, and you should see it pop into the folder that you have open on your desktop.

Now you're ready to install Express. Enter the following command:

```
npm install express --save
```

As this command executes, you'll see a folder named `node_modules` and a file named `package-lock.json` appear in the folder. If, in the future, you want to find out more, `http:// expressjs.com` is a great resource. The opening page of the website shows you the previous command used to install Express, and there is a plethora of other information available from the menu across the top.

You'll need to make some changes to your index.js file, because right now there isn't anything in it! Right-click index.js and choose Open With Text Editor. Type the following lines at the beginning of your entry file, in this case, index.js:

```
const express = require("express");
const app = express();
const port = 3000;
app.get( "/", (req, res) => {
    res.send ("Request Received")
  });


app.listen(port, function(){
    console.log ( "Server ready!" )
  });
```

Let's break that down line by line:

const express = require("express"); creates a constant named express and runs a built-in Node.js function called require that finds the index.js file you just created and will run a function that creates a new instance of the Express framework when it's called.

const app = express(); creates an object named app that calls the function to create an instance of Express. Essentially, this creates a new application that has all the coding available in the Express module, and going forward you can use the functions and methods of Express by using app, such as app.get and app.listen. The application object (app) is the heart of Express; it *is* the Express application. post and get are used to route HTTP POST and GET requests.

const port = 3000; creates a constant that sets the communication port that the app will listen on. Port 3000 is commonly used for testing, but you can use any number. More often, in a real website setup, you'll use port 80 or 8080 here.

app.get("/", (req, res) => {res.send ("Request Received")}); is a procedure that answers a client's HTTP GET request with the HTTP response "Request Received" from the server. req stands for request object, and res stands for response object. The words *request* and *response* could just as easily be used instead of the shortened version, but using req, res is a common practice. Instead of "Request Received," the server normally responds with an HTML page. res.send assumes this is the last thing you're sending, so if you want to send more than that one line, you can use res.write. For example:

```
app.get("/", (req, res) => {
res.write ("Request Received");
res.write ("Thank you!");
res.send();
});
```

`app.listen(port, function(){ console.log ("Server ready!")});` tells the server to listen on the port specified, and if the server starts without an error, you'll receive the message "Server ready!" in the terminal.

To start the server, in the terminal enter **node index.js**. When the message "Server ready!" appears, your server is running and listening on port 3000. Any time that you make a change to the index.js file, you'll need to stop and restart the server for those changes to take effect. To stop the server, press Ctrl+C. To restart the server, enter **node index.js**.

> If you don't see the "Server ready!" message, make sure you've included the line const port = 3000; in your index.js file, because the server won't start if the port isn't specified. Another line that is normally included in the previous code is const host = "*servername*"; where *servername* is the name of your server. Without defining the host, Express defaults to the value localhost, which in computing terms is the computer you're currently working on. This is fine for our purposes, but when you're setting up a live server, you would use the name of your web server.

Routing and Serving Files

When a user connects to your website, they'll expect to see something other than "Request Received." *Routing* means identifying the path for the user interaction whether sending or receiving, to get the information to or from the right place on your server, and *serving files* means sending users the information that they're requesting.

So far, your users have only been able to get a response from the root of your website with app.get("/", (req, res) => { res.send ("Request Received") });. However, what if you had multiple pages that they might access? You simply specify the path to the different pages in the beginning of the app.get command. For example, if you had a /resources page, you can add the line **app.get("/resources", (req, res) => { res.send ("You've reached the resources page.")});** to your index.js file and tailor the response appropriately. You can add as many paths as needed to your index.js (or other entry) file, and Express will scan the list to send the user's request to the right directory. Figure 18.1 includes three possible paths for the user's requests and varied responses.

FIGURE 18.1 Multiple paths

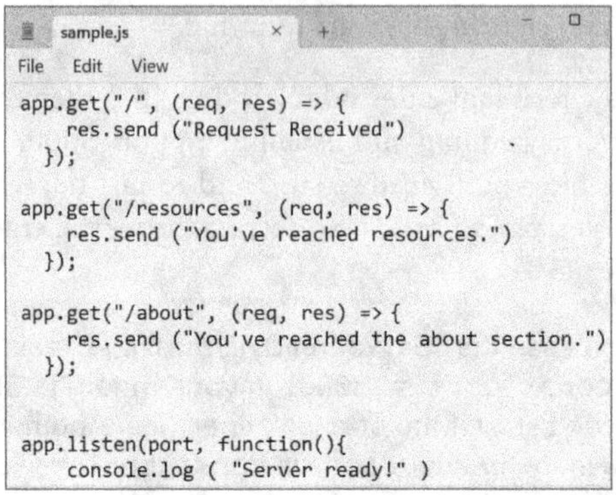

```
sample.js                    ×    +

File   Edit   View

app.get("/", (req, res) => {
    res.send ("Request Received")
  });

app.get("/resources", (req, res) => {
    res.send ("You've reached resources.")
  });

app.get("/about", (req, res) => {
    res.send ("You've reached the about section.")
  });


app.listen(port, function(){
    console.log ( "Server ready!" )
```

If your server will be sending static files such as .css or .jpg types to the visitor, you'll use the built-in express.static function.

 The express.static function is a type of middleware. *Middleware* are functions that can use the request and response objects and access the next function. There are different levels of middleware functions based on whether it's being used at the application-, router-, or error-handling levels. Middleware can also be built-in or from a third party.

As with routing, if there are multiple directories with static files that the server will need to send to users, you must create a line for each directory in your index.js file, such as:

```
app.use(express.static("public")) //for a directory named public
app.use(express.static("images")) // for a directory named images
```

Only the filename needs to be included in a request and not the path unless the resource is in a subdirectory such as /public/images. The files would be loaded using a line, such as http://localhost:3000/lake.jpg.

Express looks in the folders in the order they are listed, so if there might be two different files with the same name, take care in the order you enter them.

So far, you've only looked at a text response and static files, but more often you'll be sending an entire page to a user. To do that, you use the res.sendFile() function. For example, to respond with files named home.html and resources.html, you would include the following code in your index.js file:

```
app.get( "/", function(req, res) {
  res.sendFile("home.html");
  });
app.get( "/", function(req, res) {
  res.sendFile("/resources/resources.html")
  });
```

In the code app.get("/". (req, res) => { res
.send ("Request Received") });, the / refers to the root of the active directory, such
as newserver, but the entire path is actually the /home/*%username%*/Desktop/news
erver directory, where the variable *%username%* is your username. If you were building
a server for someone else, stored on another computer somewhere, you might not know
exactly what that path will be. A way to handle this is to use __dirname in the path. (That's
two underscores and dirname.) This will cause the program to find the file wherever it is,
assuming it's in the same folder as your index.js file. For example:

```
app.get("/", function(req, res) {
  res.sendFile(__dirname + "/index.html");
  });
```

User Input and Validation

Often gathering information is a two-way street, and you'll want to get information from
your users as well as provide information to them. After all, most websites have a database
running on the server-side that users not only retrieve information from, but also provide
input to, such as their names, addresses, and credit card numbers. Let's take a look at how
you'll enable them to do that.

First, you must set up an HTML form to gather information from your users, and then
you'll save it in a file called, for example, **index.html**. Consider the following code, which
gathers a user's first and last name:

```
<!DOCTYPE>
<html lang= "en">
  <head>
  <meta charset= "utf-8">
<title> Input form </title>
</head>
<body>

<h1> Please tell us who you are: </h1>
  <form method= "post">
    <input type= "text" name= "first" placeholder= "First Name">
    <input type= "text" name= "last" placeholder= "Last Name">
    <button type= "submit" name= "submit"> Submit! </button>
  </form>
</body>
</html>
```

In the *<form>* tag, *method="post"* means that the web page user is sending
the information in the form to you. The <form method="post"> line could include the
action= method, which defines where the information is posted, but without it being specified, the program will assume that the information being sent should be saved in the same
directory that you're working in. So, you won't specify it for now, and it will post to your
server folder. Once it's there, how will your server know what to do with it?

Without any instructions for the server to follow, the user will receive a
"Cannot POST /" error and the dreaded 404 Not Found error. To fix that, you must go
back to your index.js file and add the app.post method to tell the server how to handle
the information being posted from the web page. You'll use the format that should be
familiar to you by now with the request and response function as follows:

```
app.post("/", function(req, res) {
  res.send("Thank you for sharing!")
});
```

The previous code will cause the server to respond to the post by sending "Thank you
for sharing!", which will be displayed on the visitor's browser. At this point, you still haven't
done anything with that data. In order to access the data, you need to install the body parser.
To install the body parser, stop the server and enter **npm install body-parser** into the
terminal.

You must require the body-parser module just as you did with the Express
module in the index.js file. In the index.js file, below the line that says
const express = require("express");, you must enter a similar line for the parser
that says const bodyParser=require("body-parser");. To *parse* is to examine
the minutia of something, which is exactly what you want to do with the information
sent to you.

At this point if you restart the server, then right-click the package.json file and choose
Open With Text Editor, you'll see the information that was entered when you initialized npm
and other important information. Under a line that says dependencies, you'll see
"body parser ": and its version and "express": and its version. Any modules you
install and require will show here as dependencies.

Back in the index.js file, you need to tell the program what to do with body parser.
Begin by entering the following code into the index.js file after the constants have been
declared:

```
app.use(bodyParser.urlencoded({extended: true}));
```

The app.use() function binds the body parser to your application.
{extended: true} tells the program to accept any type of data, even if it isn't a string or
array. If {extended: false} is used, then it could only accept a string or array, not our
HTML POST data.

NOTE   Different types of parsers are available. They are raw, text, and URL-encoded, which is the one you're using because the POST method will send information to use in URL format. There are also JSON body parser, body, and co-body types.

You can now change your app.post function to the following, which will pull the user's first name from the parsed input after you save the changes and reload your application:

```
app.post( "/", function(req, res) {
  console.log(req.body.first);
  res.send("Thank you for submitting!")
});
```

With the terminal open, if you reload your application, go to localhost:3000 in your browser, then enter your first and last name and click Submit!, you'll see the first name that you entered in the web page pop up in the terminal, because that's the part that you asked for in the previous code when the data was parsed.

Filling out forms isn't the only data that you can get from your users. The req object holds the HTTP request and has properties for query strings, parameters, body, HTTP headers, and anything else in the HTTP request. Req.ip holds the IP address of the sender, req.query holds a query string, and req.cookies holds information about any cookies sent by the request (but you would need cookie-parsing middleware to access it).

If, for example, you wanted to see the sender's IP address, you could use the following code in your index.js file:

```
app.get( "/", function(req, res) {
  console.log(req.ip);
});
```

Sometimes information is small and sent via the HTTP GET method, such as searching for a particular subject in a website. If you want to pull information from a query, you can use res.query to do so. As you know, a query means you're looking for something. If you had a search box on your website and a visitor searched for spaghetti, the string might look something like this:

```
localhost:3000/search?q=spaghetti & ie=UTF-8
```

Information in the query is stored in name:value pairs, and each pair is separated by the ampersand (&) symbol. The name in the name:value pair can equate to a variable, so in the previous code, q is one variable and ie is another.

To retrieve information from the query, you must set up the route for it:

```
app.get("/search", (req, res) => {
  const what  = req.query.q;
  res.send(q);
});
```

The route `"/search"` matches the route in the URL. It establishes a variable named what, whose value is requested from the query with the named parameter of q. The response (`res.send(q)`) sends the value of q (found in the search string), which is `"spaghetti"`.

Similar to `res.query` is `res.body`, which returns the body of an HTTP request. To view the contents of an HTTP request in Chrome, follow these steps:

1. Open a web page.

2. Click the ellipsis (three dots) at the top right, choose More Tools, then Developer Tools. (Alternatively, press Ctrl+Shift+I.)

3. Reload the page.

4. Click on the Network tab.

5. Click any request on the left in the network window to see its header.

Information in an HTTP request that is located below the headers is considered the payload or body. For example, when information from a form is sent, the contents of the form will be information in the body, but not all HTTP requests have a body.

> **TIP** Sometimes, you'll see code written with the notation JSON, which stands for JavaScript Object Notation. It's a standard way that websites store name:value pairs. JSON objects are surrounded by curly brackets and may have multiple pairs of information in them. They also require double quotes. The following array is an example, but it can also be used for data and objects:
>
> ```
> "Username": [
>   {"first": "Audrey", "last": "Jones" },
>   {"first": "Genvieve", "last": "Dubois"},
>   ]
> ```

Now that you know how to retrieve information from the user, let's discuss validation. *User input validation* means testing the user input to ensure that it meets the specifications you've set. You could use validation methods on your HTML page, but the user can turn them off and put any data in there—perhaps even malicious code—so it's important to establish server-side validation. For now, the objectives merely want you to be aware of server-side validation. (Server-side validation, in fact, could be a book on its own.) Modules are available to help such as `validator` and `express-validator`. The difference is that `validator` works with any framework, and `express-validator` uses the same `validator` library but in the Express framework.

Templates

JavaScript templates are a combination of HTML and JavaScript, where the JavaScript is executed on the server-side in a `.js` file and passes variables to a template file that replaces the HTML file. The page is rendered from the template file for the client. In other words, template files are used to separate HTML from JS when working with dynamic content and presenting it to a user. Using templates to accomplish this avoids having to create repetitive code. For example, if you have 10 possible responses to a single question on your website, you wouldn't want to create 10 different HTML files to send using `res.send()`. So instead you create a template that takes the value of a variable from the JavaScript file and injects it into the embedded JavaScript (EJS) file, which is replacing our normal HTML file.

Template Engines

A quick search shows you several template engines. The default template engine for Express is Jade, but most programmers use the EJS engine. Like any other module, it needs to be installed at the terminal, in this case using `npm install ejs`.

The next step is to require it in your app. Enter the following line of code in your app (`.js`) file, *after* `const app = express();`:

```
app.set("view engine", "ejs");
```

HTML Templates

Inside your root folder (`/`), you must create a `views` directory that will hold your `.ejs` pages. Inside the `views` directory, you'll create a file that will have a name relevant to your project. For now, call it **main.ejs**. The `.ejs` file will contain the HTML information that would have been in your `index.html` file, and a specific tag wherever you need to insert the result of the code from the `index.js` file (your app file). The tag is in the format `<%= variableName %>`, which tells the file to replace the variable with its value from the `index.js` file.

In the `.js` file, after `app.get('/', (req, res) => {` add the command **res.render("main.ejs", {nameOfvalue: variableValue}); });**.

More information about EJS is available at `http://ejs.co`. For now, refer to Figure 18.2 to see how the `index.js` file and `main.ejs` file are related.

FIGURE 18.2   An `index.js` file and related `main.ejs` file

*app.js	*main.ejs
const express = require("express");	<!DOCTYPE html>
const bodyParser = require("body-parser");	<html lang= "en">
	<head>
const app = express();	<meta charset= "utf-8">
	<title> Weather </title>
app.set("view engine", "ejs");	</head>
	<body>
app.get("/", (req, res) => {	<h1> How hot is it? </h1>
var temp =75;	<p> Wow! <%= howHot %>
var message = "";	</p>
if(temp >85 {	</body>
message = "It's too hot!";	</html>
} else {	
message = "Great weather!";	
}	
res.render("main", { howHot:	
message });	
});	
app.listen(3000, function() {	
console.log("Server started	
successfully!");	
});	

Some of the tags used for EJS are shown in Table 18.1.

TABLE 18.1   EJS tag options.

Tag	Purpose
<% ... %>	For control-flow, not output
<%# ... %>	A comment tag
<%- ... %>	Outputs an unescaped value (translates tags)
<%= ... %>	An escaped value (doesn't translate tags)

Security Concerns

Previously user input validation (or lack of it) was mentioned as a concern. It's one way that malicious code can be introduced to your web server. Some other concerns are cross-site scripting and cross-site request forgery.

Cross-Site Scripting

Cross-site scripting (XSS) occurs when someone injects unwanted code into a website. Often it's an unsuspecting person who receives a link that executes the code that causes the problem. It can launch a keylogger, crash the browser, and cause other undesired actions.

Cross-Site Request Forgery

Cross-site request forgery (CSRF) attacks trick an end user into executing malware code on a web application. Some of the negative consequences can be transferring funds, changing the user's email address, or changing the code of the application.

Summary

So much information has been packed in one chapter. You learned to install Express with the npm install express --save command, and how to initialize your server with the npm init command. You also learned how to set up multiple routes using app.get, the importance of request and response, and how to serve static and dynamic files. You then installed and used the body parser to pull information from user input such as forms, and how to use req.query to pull information from a query. Finally, you examined JavaScript templates and used the EJS template engine to make your websites present information to the user by dynamically changing the content of a web page.

Exam Essentials

Know the steps to install a basic web server.   You'll use the same code over and over again, so become very familiar with it and create a skeleton file to start with!

Understand how to define routes in your JS files.   Whether your user needs to access a static or dynamic file, they can't reach it if the route isn't set up correctly.

Remember the standard files and folders to use.   Some setup items, such as the /views folder, are required for the code to work. Others are the way things are typically done, and sticking with those will make it easier for you or others to troubleshoot your website.

Be able to create simple EJS templates. People expect web pages to be dynamic, and to do that you need EJS templates.

Create a Dynamic Website

In this exercise, you use what you've learned to create a website that displays the time.

1. In the terminal, navigate to the desktop. Make a directory (mkdir) called exercise18.

2. Change the focus to the exercise18 directory, and use the touch command to create an app.js file.

3. Initialize npm and accept the default responses.

4. Install npm, express, body-parser, and ejs.

5. On the desktop, open the exercise18 folder and verify that you have the node_modules folder, and the app.js, package.json, and package-lock.json files.

6. Back in the terminal, inside the exercise18 directory, make a directory called **views**, change to that directory, and then create a file called **main.ejs**.

7. Open the main.ejs file and create the skeleton HTML file.

8. Open the app.js file and enter code to:

   - Require express.

   - Require body-parser.

   - Create a constant called app for the Express app.

   - Add the line to set the location of the EJS files.

   - Listen on port 3000 and return "Server started successfully!" when the server starts. (This is akin to the skeleton for HTML files. You'll want to save a copy of this file at this point for future use.)

9. Run the app.js file from the terminal and ensure that the message "Server started successfully!" appears to ensure that your file is correct thus far.

10. You're going to use JS and EJS to display the time. Open the app.js file with the text editor, and enter the following lines of code after app.set and before app.listen.

```
let today = new Date();
let hours = today.getHours();
let minutes = today.getMinutes();
let time = hours + ":" + minutes;
let ampm = "";
```

```
if(minutes < 10) {
  minutes = "0" + minutes;
  };
console.log(time)
app.get("/", (req, res) => {
  if(hours > 12) {
  ampm = hours-12 + ":" + minutes + " PM";
  } else {
  ampm = time + " AM";
  }
  res.render("main", {whatTime:ampm});
  });
```

11. Save the app.js file and open the main.ejs file with the text editor.

12. Set the title to **What time is it?**.

13. In the body, add an <h1> header with the content **The time now is** followed by the appropriate tag to insert the time from the app.js file. Save your work.

14. Restart the app from the terminal. It should display the time in hour:minute format and say "Server started successfully!"

15. Open a browser and navigate to localhost:3000. The time should be displayed on the browser.

ANSWER

The commands to set up the files are:

1. mkdir exercise18

2. cd exercise18, touch app.js

3. npm ini

4. npm install, npm install express, npm install body-parser, npm install ejs (alternatively, npm install express body-parser ejs)

6. mkdir views, cd views, touch main.ejs

8.
```
const express = require("express");
const bodyParser = require("body-parser");
const app = express();
app.set("view engine", "ejs");
app.listen(3000, function (){
Console.log("Server started successfully!");
});
```

9. node app.js

13. Contents of the `main.ejs` file should be:

```
<!DOCTYPE html>
<html lang="en">
<head>
  <meta charset= "utf-8">
   <title> What time is it? </title>
</head>
<body>
  <h1> The time now is <%= whatTime %> </h1>
</body>
</html>
```

The entire `app.js` file should be:

```
const express = require("express");
const bodyParser = require("body-parser");
const app =express();
app.set("view engine", "ejs");
  let today = new Date();
  let hours = today.getHours();
  let minutes = today.getMinutes();
  let time = hours + ":" + minutes
  let ampm = "";
if(minutes < 10) {
  minutes = "0" + minutes;
  };
console.log(time)
app.get("/", (req, res) => {
if(hours > 12{
  ampm = hours - 12 + ":" + minutes + " PM";
  } else {
  ampm = time + " AM";
  }
  res.render("main", {whatTime:ampm});
  });
app.listen(3000, function() {
  console.log("Server started successfully!");
  });
```

Review Questions

1. What type of software provides structure and blocks of code to make programming easier?
   A. Framework
   B. Application
   C. Root
   D. Scripting

2. Which of the following files is created when npm init is run?
   A. index.js
   B. package.json
   C. package-lock.json
   D. index.html

3. Which of these will add Express as a dependency in the .json file?
   A. const app=express();
   B. app.listen(port, function();
   C. const express = require("express");
   D. app.use(express);

4. Which of these lets you read a URL and retrieve information that is not in string or array form?
   A. app.use(bodyParser.urlencoded({extended: true}));
   B. app.use(bodyParser.urlencoded({extended: true});
   C. app.use(bodyParser.urlencoded({extended: false}));
   D. app.use(bodyParser.urlencoded){extended: true});

5. In the following, what part of the code answers a client request with a response to the HTML page?

```
app.get("/", function (req, res) {
    console.log("request received");
    res.send("request received"); });
```

   A. function (req, res)
   B. app.get("/", function (req, res)
   C. console.log("request received");
   D. res.send("request received");

6. You've added another web page, `fun.html`, to your website. It resides as a subdirectory of the main program. What do you need to enter to route traffic to that page and display it in the browser?

A. `app.post("/", (req, res) => {res.send ("received") });`

B. `app.get("fun", (req, res) => {res.send ("fun.html") });`

C. `app.post("/fun", (req, res) => {res.sendFile ("fun.html") });`

D. `app.post("fun", (req, res) => {res.sendFile ("fun.html") });`

7. What is the file extension for an embedded JavaScript engine template?

A. `.js`

B. `.tmpl`

C. `.html`

D. `.ejs`

8. Which tag is used to make a comment in an `.ejs` file?

A. `<%# ... %>`

B. `<%= ... %>`

C. `<%- ... %>`

D. `<% ... %>`

9. You're setting up your website and talking to your security officer about the risks. Which of the following is least likely to be a topic of discussion?

A. XSS

B. User input validation

C. CSRF

D. Using Express

10. You want to retrieve the contents of a field from an input form on your website. Which of the following should you use?

A. `req.query`

B. `req.body`

C. `req.header`

D. `req.form`

11. You're setting up a new web server. Which of the following is *not required* as you set up your site?

A. `const express = require("express");`

B. `const app =express();`

C. `const port = 8080;`

D. `app.listen(8080, function(){`

12. You need to tell your server what to do with information that was *received* from a user interaction with your web page. Which of the following will you use?

A. app.post

B. app.get

C. srv.post

D. ejs.post

13. A form on your website asks for a user's email address and their first name with the following code:

```
<input type= "text" name= "email">
<input type= "text" name= "first">
```

Which of these will you use to retrieve the user's first name from the code?

A. app.get("/", function (req, res) { console.log(req.body.0);});

B. app.post("/", function (req, res) { console.log(req.body.0);)};

C. app.post("/", function (req, res) { console.log(req.body.first);});

D. app.get("/", function (req, res) { console.log(req.body.first);});

14. You're writing code that will send several responses to the web page. Which of these will you use to create each of those responses?

A. res.write("content here");

B. res.sendFile("content here");

C. res.send("content here");

D. write.res("content here");

15. You've set up a repository of .jpg and other static files for your users to download. They're located in the public subdirectory of your application. What do you need to do to enable users to download them?

A. install express.static

B. app.use(express.static("public"))

C. app.use(static("public"))

D. app.use(express.static)(public))

16. You're using a file named mine.ejs for the HTML on your website and app.js for your server application. The variable stuff holds a value that you want to transfer from app.js and have the result displayed on your website. You're using the same name for the identifier in your .ejs file. What will the variable in the mine.ejs file be?

A. res.render("mine", {stuff:stuff})

B. res.render("stuff", {mine:stuff})

C. <%# stuff %>

D. <%= stuff %>

17. Which of the following is *not* needed to use an EJS template?

    A. `npm install ejs`

    B. `const.app=(express);`

    C. `app.set("view engine", "ejs");`

    D. `const app = express ();`

18. What is the correct file extension for a server application?

    A. `.js`

    B. `.app`

    C. `.html`

    D. `.ejs`

19. You want to retrieve data from a user's search box on your website. Which of the following will you use?

    A. `req.query`

    B. `req.body`

    C. `req.header`

    D. `req.form`

20. Which tag will you use when you want to inject a variable into an HTML file from a JS file?

    A. `<%# ... %>`

    B. `<%= ... %>`

    C. `<%- ... %>`

    D. `<% ... %>`

Manipulating SQLite with NodeJS

LINUX PROFESSIONAL INSTITUTE, WEB DEVELOPMENT ESSENTIALS EXAM 030-100 OBJECTIVES COVERED IN THIS CHAPTER:

✓ **035 NodeJS Server Programming**

- 035.3 SQL Basics: The candidate should be able to create individual tables in an SQLite database and add, modify and delete data using SQL. Furthermore, the candidate should be able to retrieve data from individual tables and execute SQL queries from NodeJS. This does not include referencing or combining data between multiple tables.

    - Key Knowledge Areas:

        - Establish a database connection from NodeJS

        - Retrieve data from the database in NodeJS

        - Execute SQL queries from NodeJS

        - Create simple SQL queries excluding joins

        - Understand primary keys

        - Escape variables used in SQL queries

        - Awareness of SQL injections

    - Files, terms, and utilities:

        - sqlite3 NPM module

        - Database.run(), Database.close(), Database.all(), Database.get(), Database.each()

        - CREATE TABLE

        - INSERT, SELECT, DELETE, UPDATE

You've reached the final chapter, so you're almost done! Finish this, review, then practice and study, and you'll be ready for the LPI Web Development Essentials Exam 030-100!

If you have finished Exercise 3.2, "Creating a Relational Database," then some of this chapter will already be familiar to you. Databases are on the back-end of almost every website out there, accepting user input and storing, updating, reading, and eventually deleting data. In this chapter, you quickly review the basics, then focus on working with the database through Node.js, where you enter, update, and query data. Then, you conclude by learning about SQL injections.

Installing the SQLite Module

In Chapter 3, "Database Management Systems," you installed a stand-alone database and created a table into which you entered data. Now you'll interact with SQLite from within Node.js, where installation is similar to installing any other module. In the terminal, navigate to the directory where the server is installed (the `servername.js` file) and enter `npm install sqlite3`. It will take a minute or two to install.

Creating a SQLite Database

Before you can work with a SQLite database, you must require SQLite in your *app.js* file. By now the code to require a module should look familiar:

```
const sqlite3 = require("sqlite3"); //imports the module
```

You can create a new database by entering a line in your *app.js* file as follows, where *customer.sqlite3* is the name and extension of your file:

```
const db = new sqlite3.Database("customer.sqlite3");  //creates a
database object
```

In this example, if `customer.sqlite3` doesn't already exist, it is created in the same folder as the *app.js* file when the server is restarted. *db* is the new object that opens the `customer.sqlite3` file and is used to read and write to the database. db could be anything you choose, such as db1 or database, and *customer.sqlite3* can be any filename and extension you choose.

> There is a way to stop and restart a server that's easier than using **Ctrl+C** and node servername.js. It's called nodemon and whenever there's a change in your source code, it will automatically restart your server. To install it in your server directory, run **npm install -g nodemon** from the terminal. (You may need to do it using **sudo run npm install -g nodemon** instead.) To use it, start your server with nodemon instead of node (i.e., nodemon *app*.js). It will save you a great deal of time and annoyance when you're working on code.

Opening and Closing the Database

Now we'll review how to open and close a SQLite3 database at the terminal, and you'll learn how to do the same in Node.js. Even though you're going to be using Node.js to work with databases, sometimes it's helpful to fall back to a terminal to check your work.

In Terminal

The database can be opened at a terminal prompt, inside the folder where the database resides, with the **sqlite3 *database_name.dbf*** command, where you'll replace *database_name.dbf* with the actual name and extension, such as customer.dbf. Here you're provided with the SQLite version and a message, "Enter '.help' for usage hints." The prompt will now read sqlite>. If you enter **.table** here, it will display any tables that are in the database. If the database is fairly small, you can see what's in it by entering **.dump** at the sqlite> prompt. Nothing will be in it until you add a table and some data.

You read and write to your SQL database using statements and queries. As you learned in Chapter 3, a query asks the database to retrieve information, and a statement is part of the transaction control language (TCL) that tells the database what you want it to do. Both statements and queries consist of keywords (commands) and identifiers like the specific name of something or a group of something. For example, back in Exercise 3.2, the line INSERT INTO birthdays VALUES ("John", 1,2,1990); is a statement that inputs a record (row) of information into the birthdays database. INSERT INTO and VALUES are keywords, and birthdays is the name of the database. ("John", 1,2,1990) are the values of the fields of a single record that is being inserted into the database.

Commands in SQL are not case-sensitive, so INSERT INTO is the same as insert into, but the common practice is to use all caps for SQL keywords. Multiple statements are separated by semicolons. Referring again to Exercise 3.2, each line in the following code is a statement that creates a record in the database, and the statements are separated by semicolons:

```
INSERT INTO months VALUES (1, "January");
INSERT INTO months VALUES (2, "February");
INSERT INTO months VALUES (3, "March");
```

An extensive list of SQL keywords is located online at http://sqlite .org/keyword_index.html. At a minimum, ensure that you know the keywords that are specified on the exam objectives, which you'll find at the beginning of this chapter.

To exit the sqlite> prompt, enter **.exit** in the terminal and then press Enter, which returns you to the usual $ prompt.

In NodeJS

Now you'll learn how to open and close the database using Node.js.

Previously you learned that you can create a new database by entering a line in the *app*.js file as follows:

```
const db = new sqlite3.Database("customer.sqlite3");
```

This same code is used to open an existing database. If the database doesn't exist, the command creates it. If the database exists, the command creates a new database *instance* and passes the path to the database as a parameter (in the last section). Note that the example assumes you're using or creating a database in the same folder as the app.js file.

If you would like a message to notify you that the database was opened successfully, you can use the following instead of the previous command:

```
const db = new sqlite3.Database("customer.sqlite3", (err) => {
  if (err) {
   return console.error(err.message);
  }
  console.log("Successfully connected to the customer.SQLite database.");
});
```

The content of the error message is, if there is an error opening or creating the database, then the SQLite error will display on the screen. If the database opens without incident, "Successfully connected to the *customer.SQLite* database." will be displayed on the terminal.

When you're done using a database, it's a best practice to close it. In Node.js, you do it with the database object (db) and the close() method, as shown in the following command. Again, an option for letting you know that it closed successfully has been included:

```
db.close((err) => {
  if (err) {
    return console.error(err.message);
  }
  console.log(""Database connection closed."");
});
```

Managing SQLite Data with NodeJS

So far, you've learned how to install the SQLite module and require it in your `server`
`.js` file, along with creating a new database, how to open and close the database, and how
to establish an object to use when working with your database. Now you'll learn how to
manipulate some data.

Before you can enter data, you need to create at least one table. Tables are created
with the `CREATE TABLE` command. In Express, you use the database object and
`run()` method (`database.run()`) to execute SQL commands from within the
`app.js` file. However, you'll use `db.run()` because you established the `db` object with
the line `const db = new sqlite3.Database("customer.sqlite3");` in your
`app.js` file, and it's shorter and easier to type!

The following command:

```
db.run("CREATE TABLE IF NOT EXISTS birthdays (
  id INTEGER PRIMARY KEY AUTOINCREMENT,
  first CHAR(18),
  last CHAR(18),
  birthday DATE )");
```

creates a table named `birthdays` with a primary key field called `id` that is an automatically incrementing unique number, and three more fields called `first`, `last`, and `birthday`.
`first` and `last` are character type fields and `birthday` is a date type field in YYYY-
MM-DD format. In Chapter 3, you learned that a primary key is a field whose value is
unique to each record. No two records can have the same value in that field. Each database
table will have a primary key.

Remember that this command will run every time `app.js` is restarted, so it's important to
include `CREATE TABLE IF NOT EXISTS` in the command. Also note that a table must not
be created that begins with `sqlite_` because that is a reserved name for internal use.

The `id` is a whole number (integer) that is unique and increments by 1 each time a new
record is created in the database In addition, because its value is unique to each record, it

will be your primary key. By default, each SQLite3 database contains a 64-bit ROWID (row id) that is unique and serves as a primary key. A column (field) of the type INTEGER PRIMARY KEY is an alias for the ROWID. The primary key can be accessed by ROWID, INTEGER PRIMARY KEY, or id. Databases can also be created specifying WITHOUT ROWID (but why would you?), in which case you must create a field to serve as the primary key.

Notice that each column (field) name (first, last, birthday) is followed by a declaration of the data type that will be stored in that column (that is, DATE, CHAR, and so on.). Other types can be INTEGER, NULL, REAL (floating point), TEXT, and BLOB, in addition to several others. The type can also be followed by a constraint, as in a fixed length of 18 characters for first and last. These constraints are not strictly followed. Types are also not strictly followed. SQLite uses dynamic typing, which associates the data type with the data itself instead of the type of the container that it's in. This allows a user to input a floating point number into a column marked as INTEGER. Dynamic typing allows for some flexibility but can also create problems. As of the end of November 2021, SQLite has a STRICT tables option (keyword) that does enforce rigid types.

Tables can be deleted using the DROP TABLE command, but note that there is no "undo" for it. For example, the command to delete the birthdays table would be DROP TABLE birthdays;.

Entering Data

Once a table is created, you'll want to enter some data into it. As you've seen, the data that the user entered into your form (first, last, birthday) is sent to the server in the body of an HTTP transaction using the POST method. You insert data using the db.run() method and an INSERT command in the syntax db.run('INSERT INTO table_name(column_ name, next_column_name) VALUES(value1, value2);');. The example that follows shows one way that the app.js statement could be written, with the question marks representing variable data:

```
db.run('INSERT INTO birthdays(
  first, last, birthday)
  VALUES(?, ?, ?)',
  req.body.first, req.body.last,
  req.body.birthday);
```

The variable data will be gathered from the body of the HTTP request that was sent to the server from the website user. Note that for each field where data will be inserted, there is a question mark. If you were inserting into two fields, there would be two question marks.

Changing Data

What would you do if a user realized that they had entered incorrect information into the website and wanted to change it? You could have an HTML form built into a website for that, in which case the form POST method would send the information to you in the body of the HTTP packet. In your app.js file, you would use req.body.*fieldname* to find the data. You could again use variables to represent the fields that are gathered from the POST and UPDATE and WHERE clauses to change the value that needs changing. The following code assumes that you have an HTML change form for the birthdays table and that the user wishes to change their last name. The fields are first, last, and birthday:

```
let day = ""; //creates a variable named day
let first= ""; //creates a variable named first
let newLast= ""; //creates a variable named newLast
app.post('/', function (req, res) => { //creates the routing and begins the
function
    day = (req.body.birthday); //gathers data from the body of the POST method
    first = (req.body.first); // gathers data from the body of the POST method
    newLast = (req.body.last); // gathers data from the body of the POST method
db.run("UPDATE birthdays SET last = newLast WHERE first = first AND
birthday = day);
res.send("Dear "  + first + ", your last name has been updated to " + newLast);
}); //updates the database with the new last name and responds to the user
```

Sometimes changing means deleting a record. This can be done in a similar way but using the DELETE clause instead of UPDATE as follows:

```
let day = "";
let first= "";
let last= "";

app.post('/', function (req, res) => {
    day = (req.body.birthday);
    first = (req.body.first);
    last = (req.body.last);
db.run("DELETE FROM birthdays WHERE first = first AND last=last AND
birthday = day);
res.send("Number of records deleted: " + result.affectedRows);
});
```

There are other ways these changes can be made, depending on the individual style of the programmer, as each person chooses their preferred ways of achieving the desired outcomes.

Running Queries

Sometimes, you'll want to simply retrieve existing information from a database. There are three main methods to retrieve data from a database:

db.each()   Runs a query and applies the callback to each of the results.

db.all()   Retrieves all records, then applies the query from the callback only to those records that meet the criteria.

db.get()   Selects only the first record that matches the criteria and applies the callback to that record.

db.each() will likely be the method that you'll use the most. Continuing with the birthdays table example, assume your database stores the birthday as three fields: month, day, and year. The following is a query to find everyone born in December and list their names in the console log:

```
db.each("SELECT * FROM birthdays WHERE bMonth = '12'",
  (err, row) => {
  if (err) {
  throw err;
  }
  console.log(row);
  });
```

The SELECT clause chooses which rows will be affected based on what follows the WHERE clause. The * is shorthand for all. bMonth is the fieldname for the birth month. (err, row) are the parameters for the function (=>), and console.log(row) tells the program to print all the fields for each row (record) to the console. console.log(row.first) only prints the value of the field named first.

Wildcard characters are often used with the LIKE clause in searches. The underscore (_) represents only one character, while the percent sign (%) takes the place of 0 to infinity characters. Table 19.1 shows examples of searching with LIKE and wildcards.

TABLE 19.1 Using LIKE and wildcards.

This code...	... will find any value that ...
WHERE firstName LIKE 'J%'	starts with "J" (example: Johnny)
WHERE lastName LIKE '%a'	ends with an "a" (example: O'Shea)
WHERE firstName LIKE '%ll%'	contains "ll" anywhere in it (example: Allen)
WHERE lastName LIKE 'O%a'	is any length that starts with an O and ends with an a, (example: O'Shea)
WHERE firstName LIKE '_b'	the second letter is "b" (example: Abraham)
WHERE lastName LIKE 'O_%_%_%'	any value that starts with an O and is at least four characters long (example: O'Shea)

Some characters need to be *escaped*, meaning that something must be done to tell the program to see them as a character and not a part of the program. One such character is the single quote, as in the name O'Shea. To see that quote as a character, you would use two single quotes instead of one—not a double quote, but two single quotes, such as O''Shea, or o''clock. You could also use a backslash before the special character such as O\'Shea. To include a backslash, enter it twice. For example, white\blue would be entered as **white\\blue**.

When using the LIKE clause, if you wanted to retrieve a record (row) where a string begins or ends with an underscore (_), for example, you'll need to escape the underscore, which is normally read as a wildcard. Instead of writing the code as follows:

```
SELECT * FROM birthday WHERE name LIKE '%_'
```

write it like this:

```
SELECT * FROM birthday WHERE name LIKE '%\_'
```

so that the underscore will be interpreted correctly. \% would be used where you need a percent sign in a string.

Security Concerns

You may be wondering why you use question marks in a statement, then reference the data after, as in the statement that follows:

```
db.run('INSERT INTO birthdays(first, last, birthday) VALUES(?, ?, ?)',
req.body.first, req.body.last, req.body.birthday);
```

The reason is to avoid a SQL injection. A *SQL injection* occurs when malicious code is entered into a data field of a SQL (or SQLite) database and automatically run. If malicious code was in one of the data entries and it was in the run part of the statement, then it may be executed when the run command runs. By separating the data from the run section, the code would still be inserted into the database but not run.

Summary

Understanding databases is an important part of being a back-end web designer. In this chapter, you installed SQLite3 and created an application that required it with the lines const sqlite3= require("sqlite3"); and const db = new sqlite3 .Database("filename.ext");. You opened and closed databases from the terminal where you used .table and .dump to see the contents of the database.

You learned the syntax of statements such as INSERT INTO databasename VALUES (value1, value2, ...valueX), where X is any number of values. Next, you opened and closed the database using Node.js, and learned the importance of `CREATE TABLE IF NOT EXISTS`.

The `db.run()` method is used both to create a new database and to create tables. By default, `ROWID` exists in every table and identifies each record. It can also be accessed through assigned aliases. And you learned that `DROP TABLE tablename;` is used to delete a table.

`INSERT INTO tableName` is used to add records, but instead of the values you use question marks to prevent SQL injections from causing problems. `req.body.fieldname` is used to find the data again so you can update it. Both updating and deleting use `app.post` and `db.run` to achieve results.

There are three basic kinds of queries: `db.each()`, `db.all()`, and `db.get()`, and although you'll normally use `db.each`, the other two are used from time to time so you need to know them.

There are two types of wildcards: the underscore (_) replaces one character and the percent sign (%) replaces any number of characters. The underscore and percent sign wildcards are often used with the `LIKE` clause in searches.

Some characters will confuse the program because they mean specific things, so they need to be "escaped." Normally a \ goes before the character that you want to escape.

Exam Essentials

Understand how to connect to and retrieve data from a database. You'll need to remember how to get data from a `POST` using references such as `req.body.firstName` and the `db.run()` method so that you can pull data into your app and manipulate it there.

Be able to create tables. A database is no good without tables in which to store the data.

Remember the little things. Avoid hours of troubleshooting by remembering the escape character and how each type of query (`.get`, `.all`, or `.each`) chooses its data.

Be conscious of SQL injections. Ensure that your code is using `?` instead of inserting the actual contents of a `POST` method into a `run` command to avoid inadvertently running malicious code.

EXERCISE 19.1

Create SQLite Tables

In this exercise, you'll create two SQLite tables. You'll use them in the next two exercises, so make sure you save them!

1. Use the instructions in Exercise 18.1, steps 1 through 9, substituting **exercise19** in place of `exercise18` to set up the basic files you'll need for this exercise.

2. Make the title of your exercise19 HTML file "User Contact List", and insert an `<h1>` heading that says, "Enter Your Information".

3. Create a form in the `main.ejs` file that has `<form method= "POST">` and the fields `first`, `last`, `email`, `frequency`, and `item`. All the fields can be `text` types for this exercise. Use appropriate placeholders. For frequency, the user will choose monthly or yearly. Between `email` and `frequency`, use a `<br>` and add a `<p>` that says What would you like a subscription for? and insert another `<br>`. At the end of the form, insert a `<br>` and add a submit button that says Submit Here! on it.

4. Install `sqlite3` and create an entry in the `app.js` file to require `sqlite3` (put it just after the other `require` entries), then write another entry that will create a database named `customers.dbf`. Test your entries by running the app. If no error messages are presented, you're ready to continue.

5. Open your `app.js` file again and enter the lines to create two tables in the `customers.dbf` database, one named `users` and the other named `subscriptions`. Each table will have an `id` field that is autoincrementing and the primary key. The `users` table will have the fields `first`, `last`, and `email`. Ensure that the field names exactly match the name= entries on your input form. The `subscriptions` table will have an `email` field, a `frequency` field, and an `item` field. All the fields can be CHAR type for this activity.

6. Stop/restart the `app.js` application to create the tables.

7. Close the application. Type **sqlite3 customers.dbf** and press Enter to open your database and the `sqlite>` prompt. At the `sqlite>` prompt, type **.database** and press Enter to see the name and path of your database. Type **.table** and press Enter to see the two tables you created. Press Ctrl+D to exit the `sqlite>` prompt.

ANSWERS: Exercise 19.1:

Contents of `app.js`:

```
const express = require("express");
const bodyParser = require("body-parser");
const sqlite3 = require("sqlite3");
const app =express();
app.set("view engine", "ejs");
const db = new sqlite3.Database("customers.dbf");
db.run("CREATE TABLE IF NOT EXISTS users (id INTEGER PRIMARY KEY
AUTOINCREMENT, first
CHAR, last CHAR,email CHAR )");
db.run("CREATE TABLE IF NOT EXISTS subscriptions (id INTEGER PRIMARY KEY
AUTOINCREMENT, email CHAR, frequency CHAR, item CHAR)");
app.listen(3000, function() {
  console.log("Server started successfully.");
  });
```

Contents of `main.ejs` (placeholder values may vary):

```html
<!DOCTYPE html>
<html lang="en">
  <head>
    <meta charset= "utf-8">
    <title> User Contact List </title>
  </head>
  <body>
    <h1> Enter Your Information </h1>
    <form method=POST>
      <input type= "text" name= "first" placeholder= "first name">
      <input type= "text" name= "last" placeholder= "last name">
      <input type= "text" name= "email" placeholder= "you@whatever.com"> <br>
      <p> What would you like a subscription for?</p><br>
      <input type = "text" name= "frequency" placeholder= "M = monthly,
        Y = Yearly">
      <input type = "text" name= "item" placeholder= "what item?"><br>
      <button type = "submit" name= "Submit Here!" </button>
    </form>
  </body>
</html>
```

EXERCISE 19.2

Use SQL to Input Data

In this exercise, you'll add data to your tables, then in Exercise 19.3 you'll perform queries on your data. It's advisable to make a copy of your `exercise19` folder and name the copy **exercise19_1backup** before you begin Exercise 19.2. Use the files in the `exercise19` folder for the following instructions.

1. Open the `app.js` file in the `exercise19` folder, and after the `app.set` command, add a line to bind the `bodyParser` to the application and accept any type of data. (Hint: It starts with `app.use`. See Chapter 18, "NodeJS Express," if you don't remember how.)

2. After the app.use command, declare the following three variables: let first= ""
    and let last= "" and let email= "". These variables are created outside the
    functions, so you'll be able to use them anywhere in the program.

3. Next enter a line that will display the main.ejs file when localhost:3000 is opened
    in a browser. (Hint: It starts with app.get.)

4. Now, you'll insert some lines *after* the two that created the tables. This entry will pull
    the data from the form. Enter the following:

```
 app.post("/", function (req, res) {
first=(req.body.first);
last=(req.body.last);
email=(req.body.email);
res.send ("Thank you for your order, " + first + "!")
;})
```

5. Finally, you'll add the two lines that will insert data into the database. The first is as
    follows:

```
db.run("INSERT INTO users (first, last, email) VALUES (?, ?, ?)", req.body
.first,
req.body.last, req.body.email);
```

Now it's your turn to figure out the second one to insert email, frequency, and item
into the subscriptions database. After the second entry remember to put }); to
end the app.post method.

6. Save your app.js file. Run it from the terminal. You should receive a message that the
    server started successfully.

7. Open a browser and navigate to localhost:3000. Your form should pop up. Enter
    information into the form. When you click the Submit Here! button, you should receive
    the "Thank you for your order, *firstname*!" message in the browser.

8. Open the terminal. Exit the app. Open the sqlite3> prompt with the command
    sqlite3 customers.dbf to access your database. Enter **.tables** (This command works
    whether you type **.table** or **.tables**). It should display the names of your two tables.
    Now enter **.dump** to see the contents of the tables.

9. Restart the server and go back to your browser to access the localhost:3000 page
    and make additional entries to your database. Don't hit Refresh—instead, enter the
    URL again.

ANSWER: Exercise 19.2:

```
const express = require("express");
const bodyParser = require("body-parser");
const sqlite3 = require("sqlite3");
const app =express();
app.set("view engine", "ejs");
app.use(bodyParser.urlencoded({extended: true}));
let first= ""
let last= ""
let email= ""
app.get("/", (req, res) => {
  res.render("main.ejs");
});
const db = new sqlite3.Database("customers.dbf");
db.run("CREATE TABLE IF NOT EXISTS users (id INTEGER PRIMARY KEY
AUTOINCREMENT, first CHAR, last CHAR,email CHAR )");
db.run("CREATE TABLE IF NOT EXISTS subscriptions (id INTEGER PRIMARY KEY
AUTOINCREMENT, email CHAR, frequency CHAR, item CHAR)");
app.post("/", function (req, res) {
  first=(req.body.first);
  last=(req.body.last);
  email=(req.body.email);
  res.send ("Thank you for your order, " + first + "!")
db.run("INSERT INTO users (first, last, email) VALUES (?, ?, ?)",
req.body.first,
req.body.last,
req.body.email);
db.run("INSERT INTO subscriptions (email, frequency, item) VALUES(?, ?, ?),
req.body.email, req.body, frequency, req.body.item);
});
app.listen(3000, function() {
  console.log("Server started successfully.");
  });
```

EXERCISE 19.3

Use NodeJS to Execute SQL Queries

In this exercise, you'll execute queries on the data in the tables created in Exercise 19.1, to view, change, and delete data.

1. In your exercise19 folder, copy app.js and save the copy as **myQuery.js**.

2. In Exercise 19.2, step 9, the instructions asked that you make several entries into your database. If you haven't, please go back and do that now. When you're ready, use the following instructions to create a query.

3. Open myQuery.js with the text editor. In the myQuery.js file, just above the app .listen(3000, function() { line, enter the following:

```
const query = "SELECT * FROM users';
db.all(query, [], (err, rows) => {
        if (err) {
        throw err;
        }
          rows.forEach((row) => {
          console.log(row.first, row.last, for.email);
          });
        });
```

4. Save your myQuery.js file.

5. Open the terminal to the folder where your myQuery.js file is.

6. Enter **node myQuery.js** and press Enter. You should see all the records that you entered into the users table of the customers.dbf database.

7. Now it's your turn to look back in the chapter and use db.each to select just some of your data.

ANSWER: Exercise 19.3:

6. The answer is in the exercise.

7. Answers will vary, but the base code is as follows:

```
db.each("SELECT * FROM database.dbf WHERE fieldname = 'value'",
  (err, row) => {
  if (err) {
  throw err;
  }
  Console.log(row);
  });
```

Review Questions

1. Which of the following commands is used to install the current version of SQLite on a Linux computer?

   A. `npm install sqlite`

   B. `install sqlite3`

   C. `npm install SQLite3`

   D. `npm install sqlite3`

2. Your *app.js* file is in a folder called `inventory`. You want to create a new SQLite3 database in `inventory`. The database will be called `products.dbf`. What command will you enter in your `app.js` file in the `inventory` folder to do this?

   A. `const sqlite3 = require("sqlite3")`

   B. `const sqlite3 = require("products")`

   C. `const db = new sqlite3.Database("products.dbf");`

   D. `const db = new sqlite3.Database("/inventory/products.dbf");`

3. You're working at a terminal and need to start your SQLite3 database named `inventory.dbf`, which is located in the `working` folder. Which command will you use to open your database here?

   A. `sqlite3 inventory.dbf`

   B. `sqlite3 .inventory.dbf`

   C. `.table`

   D. `.dump`

4. You're building an application that will use a SQLite3 database. Which of the following will you need to enter in your *application.js* file to establish a connection to the database? (Choose two.)

   A. `const db = new sqlite3.Database("databaseName.ext");`

   B. `db.open = new sqlite3.Database("databaseName.ext");`

   C. `const sqlite3 = require('sqlite3') ;`

   D. `npm install sqlite3`

5. The following code is in your `app.js` file. What will happen when it is executed? (Choose two.)

```
db.close((err) =>
  if (err) (
    return console.error(err.message);
  {
  Console.log ("Database connection closed.");
  });
```

A. The currently open database will be deleted.

B. The currently open database will be closed.

C. If an error occurs, the database will be deleted.

D. If an error occurs, the error will be displayed on the console.

6. What will the following code in an `app.js` file do? (Choose two.)

```
db.run ("CREATE TABLE IF NOT EXISTS postal (
  zip INTEGER,
  city CHAR,
  state CHAR )");
```

A. Create a database named `postal`.

B. Create three tables in the `postal` database.

C. Create a table name `postal`.

D. Create three fields in the `postal` table.

7. You're working within an `app.js` file. You have a database named `postal`, with a table named zips, and three fields in the table named `zip`, `city`, and `state`. You're using an HTML input form to add a record for zip code 13212 that is in Syracuse, NY. Which of the following commands are the best to have in your `app.js` file to perform the insert? (Choose two.)

A. `db.run("INSERT INTO zips (zip, city, state) VALUES (req.body`
`.zip, req.body.city, req.body.state);`

B. `db.run("INSERT INTO zips (zip, city, state) VALUES (?, ?, ?)",`
`req.body.zip, req.body.city, req.body.state);`

C. `app.post('/', function (req, res) => {`
`  let zip = (req.body.zip);`
`  let city = (req.body.city);`
`  let state = (req.body.state);`
`  res.send( );`
`});`

D. `db.insert(TABLE zips, VALUES (`
`req.body.zip, req.body.city, req.body.state);`

8. Which of the following clauses will you use to add new data to an existing database?

A. `app.post`

B. `CREATE`

C. `ADD`

D. `INSERT`

9. Which of the following clauses will you use to change a record that already exists in an existing database?

A. UPDATE

B. CREATE

C. CHANGE

D. INSERT

10. Which clause chooses the row or rows in a database that an action will be applied to, based on provided criteria?

A. WHERE

B. GET()

C. SELECT

D. RETRIEVE

11. You need to query and find a person in your database with the first name of Ariel. You happen to know that there is only one. What partial command that follows will find that record for you? (Choose two.)

A. db.get("SELECT * FROM people WHERE first = "Ariel",

B. db.find("Ariel" FROM people),

C. db.get("CHOOSE * FROM people WHERE first = "Ariel",

D. db.each("SELECT * FROM people WHERE first = "Ariel",

12. You're trying to find a record where the value you're searching for is 100%, but you're not able to retrieve it from the database. In fact, your database is acting strangely. How can you change the WHERE profit = "100%" clause so that the record can be found?

A. WHERE profit = "%100%"

B. WHERE profit = 100%

C. WHERE profit = "100\%"

D. WHERE profit = "100/%"

13. You've finished working with your database named joe.dbf. What command must be next in your *app.js*?

A. db.close(joe.dbf)

B. db.close( )

C. db.() (CLOSE joe);

D. CLOSE joe;

14. The following shows a partial command. Based on this information, which of the records listed will the following code retrieve? (Choose two.)

db.each("SELECT * FROM contacts WHERE area LIKE "13_01"

A. 13a01

B. 1301

C. 130101

D. 13401

15. You have the following records in a database. Based on the information provided, what is the primary key for this database?

Cust#	RecNo	Customer	Total
1	234	Johanna	$100
2	536	Johanna	$500
3	427	Malaki	$100
1	555	Elangovani	$450

  A. Cust#

  B. RecNo

  C. Customer

  D. Total

16. You want to run a query that will list all the purchases that are over $100. The field name is total in the sales database. Based on the following partial code, which of the following will do that for you?

  A. `db.all("Select * FROM sales WHERE total LIKE "1_ _ %";`

  B. `db.all("Select * FROM sales WHERE total LIKE "1_ _";`

  C. `db.all("Select * FROM sales WHERE total LIKE "1\%";`

  D. `db.all("Select * FROM total WHERE sales LIKE "1%"`

17. Given the code that follows, which of the following is not a valid value for location?

```
db.run("CREATE TABLE IF NOT EXISTS headcount (id INTEGER PRIMARY KEY
        AUTOINCREMENT, location CHAR(5), employees INTEGER(3))");
```

  A. 6

  B. 12578

  C. NYC

  D. Atlanta

18. Which of the following will create a table called sales in a database called profits?

  A. `db.run("CREATE TABLE IF NOT EXISTS sales {dollars INTEGER, invoice CHAR}");`

  B. `db.run("create table if not exists sales dollars INTEGER, invoice CHAR");`

  C. `db.run("create table if not exists sales (dollars INTEGER, invoice CHAR)");`

  D. `db.run("create table if not exists sales (dollars INTEGER, invoice CHAR)');`

19. Which of the following fields exists by default in a SQLite database?

    A. `first`

    B. `id`

    C. `recordNumber`

    D. `rowid`

20. Which of the following clauses will you use to permanently remove an existing database?

    A. `DROP`

    B. `DELETE`

    C. `CHANGE`

    D. `INSERT`

Appendix

Answers to Review Questions

Chapter 1: Web Development Basics

1. B. The part of a website that a user interacts with is known as the front-side or client-side.

2. A. The broad definition of software is lines of instruction for a processor to follow. Software includes many specific categories beyond that.

3. D. Writing pseudocode is the way that most programmers begin to write. It helps them to think through the process that they want to accomplish *before* they start the actual coding. Pseudocode is written in a human-readable language.

4. A. After a programmer has completed their pseudocode and understands what they want a program to do, they will begin writing the source code in a programming language.

5. A. Source code is written in human-readable language, following the rules of the particular programming language that is being used.

6. B, D. CSS and JavaScript are used on the front-end of a website, the part that a user interacts with. PHP and Ruby are often used on the back-end of the website where a server is working to answer requests and manipulate data.

7. C. Syntax in programming languages is similar to grammar and human languages. Depending on the language, types of words or commands may be in different order, and different punctuation marks can be used.

8. B, C. `for` and `while` are keywords used often in programming to control the number of times a section of code is run. These words are combined with a logic statement and possibly a counter so that the program knows when to stop.

9. C. Libraries are pieces of code that have been written to solve a specific programming problem or for a task that is often repeated and then shared for others to use. Libraries are essential for the modern programmer as they save time and frustration.

10. B. Before you do anything else, you will determine if the code is correct. Often a program will have parts that are written in a different language than the main program.

11. A, B. Computing devices only understand whether a particular circuit is off or on, which is denoted as a 0 or 1. This is called binary, and machine language is written in binary.

12. D. Notepad, Notepad++, TextEdit, and Vim are examples of popular text editors that are used to write code. This code is later compiled or interpreted to be displayed to a user.

13. B. `.cpp` is the file extension used with C++ programming. The `.c` extension can be used with C or C++. The extension for Python files is `.py` and for Perl it's `.pl`.

14. A, C. Keywords have different types such as operators (`and`, `not`), iteration control (`for`), and to control program flow (`if`), among others.

15. C, D. Pseudocode is written when determining what you want a program to do. Source code is the actual code that you write, which is later compiled, or interpreted. A compiler can output machine language, bytecode, or both.

16. C. The programming paradigms that this certification wants you to understand are functional, object-oriented, and procedural. The procedural paradigm executes lines of code in order but may call procedures to run, then return to the lines of code.

17. A. Each programming paradigm has its advantages and disadvantages. The advantage of procedural programming is that you can program more quickly because repeated lines of code (procedures) can be called and reused. A program can be written using more than one paradigm.

18. D. Version control systems (VCSs) are specialized software that is used to track changes made to computer programs and manage those changes. Git is one example of a VCS.

19. B. The place where a version control system (VCS) holds copies of all the iterations of a program is called a repository.

20. C. In the procedural paradigm, procedures (subroutines) can be called and ran from the main program.

Chapter 2: Client/Server Computing

1. C. The term *client* can refer to either a hardware device or software. Client software can be found on a multitude of local computing devices, such as your laptop, smartphone, or tablet. Choice D is incorrect because a client can be software, not just hardware.

2. B. The client is responsible for initiating the conversation between the client and the server. The client will request information from a URL. The URL request goes to a DNS server, which translates the URL to an IP address and sends that IP address to the client. The client will then request information from the server at that IP address, and if the request is appropriately formatted, the server will respond.

3. B, C, D. An application server is only needed if the website is interactive and will provide the behind-the-scenes processing of information. For a static website, the application server isn't needed at all, but a web server is. A web server is sometimes provided by an application server. APIs are needed so that the client will know how to format the request to the server.

4. A, C. Progressive web applications (PWAs) and web applications are both accessed using a browser, whereas native applications and hybrid applications are downloaded from an app store to the computing device. With hybrid applications, the majority of their work is done on a server to which they connect.

5. C. Browsers are by far the most common type of client used to access a web server.

6. C. Chrome can be downloaded on almost any platform, Edge and Internet Explorer are Microsoft products, and Safari is included on Apple devices. Firefox is the browser that is most often included in Linux distributions, but it can also be downloaded to other platforms.

7. A. Rendering engines are responsible for drawing text and images on a screen. Single-page applications (SPAs) update only the part of a web page that changes, rather than reload an entire page. Virtual machines (VMs) are used to execute a web page's code and may be specific to the language used to create the code. Application programming interfaces (APIs) assist in the communication between two different systems, and Opera is simply a type of browser.

8. D. WebKit is the rendering engine used with Safari. Blink is used with Chrome, Opera, and other browsers. Quantum is used by Firefox, and a rootkit is a type of malware.

9. D. Minification is the process of removing whitespace and characters that aren't needed so that the code is smaller, sometimes even 60 percent smaller, thus allowing a requested web page to load more quickly. Debugging and testing code are types of tooling that are often included in a browser. Frameworks are a tool to make web page development faster and easier. Linters alert a programmer if something in their code doesn't match predefined rules.

10. A, B, D. The term *server* is used to refer to both the hardware and software used to respond to client requests. In web communications, the client initiates a request to which the server responds.

11. D. A browser interprets HTML and other code and displays it for a user. A browser is a type of client. Clients connect to servers and request data, but before they can get what they want, they need to format the request properly. The server that the client contacts shares an API with the client, so the client will be able to properly formulate requests to the server.

12. A. Parts of a URL are `scheme://host:port/path?query`. In the example, `https` is the scheme, i.e. the protocol; `cliffjumpertek.com` is the host (the domain); and `binary-is-fun` is the path. The path could also have a filename at the end such as `binary.html`. There is no query because there is no ? after the path.

13. C. The HTTPS protocol uses Transport Layer Security (TLS) to encrypt transmissions between a client and host, adding security to the transaction. Transmission Control Protocol (TCP) is a transport layer protocol that guarantees delivery of packets. File Transfer Protocol (FTP) can use a graphical user interface (GUI) or command-line interface (CLI), and is used specifically for fast and efficient file transfers. Search engine optimization (SEO) is a set of practices companies use to have a website featured more prominently when searching in a browser.

14. A. An application server provides the business logic that you interact with through a client. A web server dishes out the HTML and other files that make a web page, and can be part of an application server. A file server provides access to files, and may be simply a server on a local area network (LAN). A domain name server (DNS) translates domain names to IP addresses.

15. A, D. Apache HTTP Server (HTTPD) and NGINX are by far the most popular web servers, although there are many others available, including Microsoft IIS, Cloudflare, node.js, LiteSpeed, and others.

16. A, B, D. Most modern websites are created using HTML, CSS, and JavaScript. HTTP is a protocol used to communicate between a client and a server.

17. B. A single-page application is one that will rewrite only content changes when interacting with a website. Content management systems allow a user to create a website without knowing how to code. Web application packaging is the process of putting all the files needed to

install a web application into a single, downloadable ZIP file. WebAssembly is a new standard being developed to improve the performance of applications running in a browser.

18. C. In the URL schema, the protocol used for communication is the scheme, in this case, `https`. The domain, also called the host, is `grammarly.com`, and `/business/ learn/business-communication-etiquette` is the path to the information on the host's server.

19. A. A website that changes what is shown based on who accesses it is a dynamic website. A static website displays the same information regardless of who accesses it. A web application accesses data and programming on a server via a browser, and although this could be done through a web application, that's not in the description of the question. TLS is the protocol used to secure HTTPS and again, although this could be an HTTPS website, that's not part of the description.

20. C. The client is responsible for initiating the conversation between the client and the server. The client will request information from a URL. The URL request goes to a DNS server that translates the URL to an IP address and sends that IP address to the client. The client will then request information from the server at that IP address, and if the request is appropriately formatted, the server will respond.

Chapter 3: Database Management Systems

1. A. A database management system (DBMS) is a great way to store large and complex amounts of data that are all similar in nature.

2. B. Information that identifies a type of information that can be specified for each entry is called a field. Fields are often the column headings in a flat-file database. In this example, each product would be a record, and each record would minimally contain the fields SKU Number and Price.

3. C. You would use a NoSQL database, also known as a nonrelational database. A filing cabinet won't let you search electronically, and the items are too different to use SQL. GraphQL is for creating APIs to use with data.

4. A, C, D. PostgreSQL, MySQL, and SQLite are all open source DBMS. GraphQL is a programming tool for getting only the right information from a web-based database.

5. D. A key in a table that you're connecting to with the currently active table is known as a foreign key. The main key in the table you're working with is known as a primary key.

6. C. When a database has multiple tables that are linked together through common fields, this is known as a relational database. (The databases are related to each other.) Nonrelational databases may be NoSQL or simply flat-file databases, and a schema describes the characteristics of a database such as the fields in a table, what format they must be in, and how different tables relate to each other.

7. A. A schema describes the characteristics of a database such as the fields in a table, what format they must be in, and how different tables relate to each other.

8. A, B, C. Any key field is used to sort and find records in a database. Key fields can also be a primary key or a foreign key, depending on whether they're in the table you're working with or the one to which it is connecting. The main key is not a valid term.

9. C. REST, or representational state transfer, is an architecture used when a client downloads all the information from a particular URL. GraphQL is a query language where the programmer specifies the schema of the data, and it will download only the data that is needed. SQL (Structured Query Language) is also used to retrieve data from a database. A DBMS (database management system) enables users to create and modify databases.

10. C. The set of information about each specific visitor is known as a record. In this example, Name and Email Address are fields. Schema is a description of the database, and data definition language (DDL) consists of commands for controlling a schema such as creating, removing, and renaming tables, and changing columns, fields, and so on.

11. C. When you're granting or revoking access to a database, you're using data control language (DCL). DDL (data definition language) encompasses the commands used to change the schema of a database. DML (data manipulation language) are the commands for adding, removing, or modifying the actual data in the database. TCL (transaction control language) is the set of commands such as `commit` or `rollback` that ensure the integrity of data being entered. After all, you wouldn't want just half of an accounting transaction to be entered!

12. D. TCL (transaction control language) is the set of commands such as `commit` or `rollback` that ensure the integrity of data being entered. DDL (data definition language) encompasses the commands used to change the schema of a database. DML (data manipulation language) consists of the commands for adding, removing, or modifying the actual data in the database. When you're granting or revoking access to a database, you're using data control language (DCL).

13. B. The fields being described in the question have a one-to-many relationship. There will only be one customer record in the first database, but there will be many transactions in the second database that are related to each customer through the customer's account number. Primary-to-secondary is not a term used to explain the relationship between tables.

14. A. Forms are commonly used for entering data into a database. Queries, SQL, and reports are used for retrieving data from a database.

15. D. SQLite is faster than MySQL, but only on small databases, and it doesn't guarantee referential integrity. MariaDB is a free DBMS from Oracle, PostgreSQL is open source and cross-platform, and Access is not free and is a Microsoft product.

16. B, C. Documents that have different identifiers or data that doesn't easily fit into the same fields are known as unstructured data. CouchDB is a NoSQL database that will work well for unstructured data.

17. B. Forms are typically used to enter, modify, and view information, whereas reports are used to print out information, whether to a PDF file or a hard copy (printed on paper). A query is how one would find the specific information they're looking for, and NoSQL refers to an unstructured database, not a structured one.

18. B, D. MongoDB and Redis are databases for unstructured data. SQLite and MariaDB are for structured data. Couch DB, although not in the choices, is another DBMS for unstructured data.

19. A. Structured databases are used for information where records are similar and contain the same type of information for each record, such as name, date of birth, address, account number, blood type, and so on. Unstructured databases are for keeping records that don't necessarily fit into neat fields, such as images and handwritten reports. Modified is not a DBMS type, and NoSQL databases are unstructured.

20. D. GraphQL is a query language and a runtime for APIs. It enables a programmer to specify a schema.

Chapter 4: Client/Server Communication

1. A, C. Hypertext Transfer Protocol (HTTP) is a communication protocol that is used to facilitate communication between a web browser and a web client. It isn't secure unless it's HTTPS. It is not a markup language.

2. A. Communication between a web server and web client is started by the client. Sometimes the client is a web browser but not always. A web server can send a push notice when WebSockets is being used, but not when HTTP is being used. Even then, a client initiates the initial connection.

3. C. Status codes in the 4XX range indicate a client error. The codes 2XX are success codes, 3XX are redirection codes, and 5XX are server error codes.

4. B. Virtual hosts (vhosts) is a service on some server software that allows for more than one domain on a single server. WebSocket API and HTTPS are protocols. HTML is the language used to mark up a web page.

5. D. Like HTTP, WebSocket API is a protocol and an API used to transfer data between a web server and a client. SSL and TLS are security protocols, and HTML is a markup language.

6. C, D. WebSockets keeps the connection open until one party or the other closes it. HTTP closes after each request/response cycle.

7. A. A cache stores previously downloaded information about a website such as text and images, which makes subsequent visits to the website load more quickly. Cookies store information about the client like shopping cart contents and login information. WebSockets facilitates real-time communication between clients and a server.

8. D. HTTP is not secure, so it is vulnerable to being intercepted and read. SSL and TLS are encryption protocols used to secure communications. HTML is a markup language, not a communication protocol.

9. B. The `accept:` entry of a header tells the receiving party what type of information can be understood or accepted by the party sending the header such as `text/html`. The authority is the domain receiving the request, the method is either GET or POST, and the scheme is the protocol, which is either HTTP or HTTPS.

10. B. Status code 301 is the status code given when a resource has been permanently moved and is able to be located. Code 200 means all is OK. Code 401 means the client is not recognized by the server, and 403 means that the server knows the client but the client failed to provide credentials.

11. B, C. Hypertext Transfer Protocol Secure (HTTPS) is a secure protocol for transferring data between a web browser and client. What makes HTTP secure is the Transport Layer Secure (TLS) protocol. It's the improved version of Secure Sockets Layer (SSL) protocol, and some people still refer to TLS as SSL. TCP is the protocol used to make a connection from one computer to another.

12. D. A server status code, such as 401, is supplied by the server once it has been contacted by a client. The authority is the domain receiving the request; the method is either GET or POST, and the scheme is the protocol, which is either HTTP or HTTPS.

13. C. Code 404 is not an error that you want your visitors to get, because it means that they can't reach your web page.

14. A, B. Virtual hosts are easier to maintain, and they cut down on hardware and software costs. They may not work well with older browsers, and they can be dynamic.

15. D. HTTPS and WebSocket Secure are both secure, but HTTPS is half-duplex, and WebSocket is full-duplex.

16. A. A GET request is sent as a part of a URL, so it is unencrypted, available in browser history, and should never include password information. A POST request sends information in the body of a packet. A status code wouldn't contain password information, and TLS is an encryption protocol.

17. B, C. Shared cache and private cache will both use less bandwidth and lower latency because the bulk of information needs to be downloaded only one time. Shared cookie is not a valid term, and a virtual host is the feature of a web server supporting more than one domain.

18. B. Port 80 is used for HTTP. The port number for HTTPS is 443. Port 22 and 995 are not discussed in this chapter, but 22 is used by SSL, and 995 is used by the POP3 protocol.

19. C. Transport Layer Security (TLS) is an encryption protocol. HTTP and HTTPS are communication protocols, and OSI is a framework for networking.

20. C. The port number for HTTPS is 443. Port 80 is used for HTTP. Port 22 and 995 are not discussed in the chapter, but 22 is used by SSL, and 995 is used by the POP3 protocol.

Chapter 5: HTML Introduction

1. B, C. In Linux Ubuntu 20.04.2, you can use the included program text editor or install Vim to create an HTML file. Firefox is a browser that will interpret an HTML file, and Notebook++ is, as far as I know, a fictitious program name, although there is a Notepad++ program that is used with Microsoft Windows.

2. D. Meta tags are included in the head section of an HTML page. They are not a part of the skeleton. The skeleton consists of `<!DOCTYPE html>`, `<html>`, `<head>`, `<title>`, `<body>`, and associated end tags.

3. A. `<!DOCTYPE html>` is used to declare that this is indeed an HTML file. `<title>` and `<b>` are tags, and `style="background-color:blue;"` is an attribute with property:value pair.

4. A. The `charset` attribute is used to declare the character set to be used with a web page. It should always be included in the head section close to the top.

5. C. The only properly nested statement is `<p> My text is bold. </b> </p>` because the nested tag must end before the tag it is inside of. Option A does not have a nested tag. Option B ends the first tag before the nested tag, and option D is not correct because comments must not be nested inside other elements.

6. B, C. In the given code snippet, `src`, `width`, and `height` are attributes of the `img` tag. `mountains.jpg` is the content.

7. B, D. Options B and D are correct. Option A is incorrect because the # symbol is omitted. Option C is incorrect because the "s around the content are missing, and the # should not be there when using the color name instead of numbers.

8. B. The correct answer is B, use the `<br>` tag. This tag will act like a carriage return in a Word document and continue text on the following line. Pressing Enter in the HTML file will show a break in that file, but will have no effect on the web page that is rendered. The `<p>` tag inserts a blank line between what is before it and what comes after. There is no `<enter>` tag.

9. A. Option A is not an important use of a `<meta>` tag. Meta tags don't set the site's displayed date and time (yet). Yes, it is possible to use them to identify the date the site was created but not the current date and time. Meta tags are great for search engine optimization (SEO) and providing information such as the copyright and which character encoding should be used.

10. A, C. Option A is correct because it's the language used to format elements of a website. Option C is correct because by definition, a markup language is used to format how data is to be displayed. HTTP is a protocol used to move information from one place to another. A programming language is incorrect because HTML is a markup language, not a programming language.

11. A. Option A is correct. Start tags are used to identify the beginning of an HTML element. Empty elements are those that don't have any contents. There is no `</start>` tag. `</html>` is an end tag, not a start tag.

12. B, C. Options B and C are correct. The `<br>` tag inserts a carriage return and is an empty element because it has no content. It does not insert a blank line, and it is a complete element because it doesn't require an end tag in HTML.

13. B, D. WHATWG and W3C are the two groups that have been involved in maintaining the HTML standards. CompTIA is a provider of technology certifications. Intel is a processor manufacturer.

14. A. Option A is correct. `<h1>` provides the largest heading. Options C and D are not valid code entries.

15. C. Option C is correct. `script` is the tag. `type` and `src` are attributes, and `module` and `new_page.js` are values. Attributes are entered in name:value pairs.

16. A. Option A is correct. An element consists of a start tag, some content, and an end tag. There are a few exceptions known as empty elements, because they don't have any content and don't need to be closed.

17. B. Option B is correct. `<hr>` stands for horizontal rule. It is an empty tag that will place a line across the page horizontally. `<br>` inserts a carriage return, and `<area>` makes a spot clickable. They are both empty tags, but they don't draw lines across the page. `<p>` identifies a paragraph and is not an empty tag.

18. D. Of the choices given, D, `<!DOCTYPE html>` is the only one that should not be in the head section. It should be the first thing in the HTML file.

19. D. Option D is the only one that will display on the HTML page when rendered by a browser, even though all the lines will likely be there. It will display the text `"Color=blue"`, because that is the content between the two paragraph tags.

20. A. Option A is correct. An attribute provides additional information about the contents of an element and will be interpreted by a browser. An element consists of a tag, any attributes, and contents. Comments may be put into HTML code as information for the coder to remember why something was done as it was or to identify sections of code.

Chapter 6: Content Markup

1. A. The blockquote heading is a level 2 heading, so its parent is the level 1 heading.

2. C. The horizontal rule is a block element because it takes the entire width of the screen, regardless of how wide it is.

3. A, D. An `<h6>` tag is a block element, so it will add a line between it and other contents. It's also a heading tag and not intended to format content in the middle of a paragraph as bold.

4. B, C. The lines in the unordered list are indented because the ordered list is not ended, so the browser thinks that they are to be nested. To fix this issue, place an `</ol>` at the end of the second thing line. And, to be correct, each `<li>` should be ended with `</li>`.

5.   C, D. The preferred way to style multiple paragraphs is to use CSS. While you could enclose multiple paragraphs using `<span>`, it's actually an inline element and the code as entered with it in the question is *not* correct. The `<div>` element is a block element and the preferred way to choose multiple paragraphs that will be formatted the same way, if not using CSS.

6.   A. `<article>` is the tag you use for content that can stand on its own and be reused independently from the rest of its web page. The `<main>` tag encompasses *all* of the content. A `<section>` can't stand on its own without its web page, and an `<aside>` is additional, loosely related information about what is on the page.

7.   C. Bold , break `<br>`, and computer output `<samp>` are all inline elements. Paragraph `<p>` is not, because it adds an empty line and takes an entire horizontal line. The `<br>` element inserts a line feed, moving what follows it to the next line, but it doesn't add blank lines.

8.   A. The `<body>` tag contains the contents of a website, so it will always be an ancestor to any other tags that are used in the content.

9.   A, B. The `<h1>` and `<div>` tags are block elements. The `<span>` tag can be used to group multiple paragraphs, but it is intended to identify part of a line so it's an inline element. The `<tt>` tag is for teletype font—it's an inline element.

10.   C. Hierarchical means that the structure can be represented in a pyramid shape with a single object located at the top. A hierarchy is structured, but the question given is not the definition of structured.

11.   A, B. At a minimum, to have a numbered list you would need to start it with ordered list `<ol>` and have list items `<li>`.

12.   D. Although styles such as text color, size, and font can be defined in several places, they should be defined in a CSS file to which an HTML file refers. Coding can become very messy if the formatting is defined in the HTLM file.

13.   C. The `<aside>` element is a semantic element used for information that is indirectly related to other content located on a web page. `<nav>` is used for hyperlinks to other places, `<main>` is akin to `<body>` and contains the rest of the web page content, and `<note>` is not a semantic structural element.

14.   A. The paragraph `<p>` tag inserts a blank line. The `<div>` and `<br>` tags move content to the next line but do not insert a line. The horizontal `<hr>` tag inserts a horizontal line across a page.

15.   A. Although technically you could put many `<h1>` headings on a page, it isn't recommended. There should only be one `<h1>` heading per page. If you find that there is more than one "main idea" on the page, consider using multiple pages.

16.   C. Either `<span>` or `<div>` could be used, but `<div>` is the best tag to use with multiple paragraphs. It is a block element and `<span>` is an inline element.

17.   D. The `<blockquote>` tag indents each line of its content and allows you to cite the quote, although the cite won't show in the browser.

18. B. Although you could change the style with CSS to make your headings stand out, using appropriate heading levels is important because search engines use headings to index pages.

19. D. The largest heading is level 1. As the level numbers get larger, the font gets smaller.

20. B, C. Ordered lists <ol> and unordered lists <ul> can have nested items. Description lists <dl> do not have nested items, and the <q> tag is for quotes.

Chapter 7: References and Embedded Resources

1. A. The anchor tag <a> defines a hyperlink. id, href, and alt are all attributes, not tags.

2. A. An absolute URL reference includes the full path, so you would use this when linking to a different domain. A relative URL does not include the full path; it is relative to the folder you're in. A domain is a location, not a type of URL, and semantic refers to a type of element.

3. D. All four of the options are common attributes of the <img> tag, but src is the only required one.

4. A, B. When using an image to create an image map, the first thing to do is to identify the source image and the name of the map to use, which is option A, and the next is to name the map, option B. After that you specify the area and shape that will be clickable.

5. D. SVG is a vector file format. GIF, JPG, and PNG are all raster files.

6. C. The <iframe> tag is used to specify a window to another HTML page within the current HTML page. href is an attribute, not a tag. window is not an HTML tag, and <style> is used to define attributes applied to a page or element such as color.

7. A. To get a background image for the page, the code needs to go between <style> </style> tags in the <head> section of the web page.

8. B. Global attributes can be used with any element. Absolute and relative refer to URLs. Semantic refers to elements whose name describes what they are.

9. A. In this example, page2 is inside the pages folder, and the pages folder is a subfolder of the folder that the file we're working on is in. That is, if we're working on page1.html, which is in the mysite folder, then pages is a subfolder of mysite, and page2.html is in the pages folder.

10. B, D. Width and height are expressed in pixels by default. The alt attribute provides alternate text that will show if the image won't load for any reason, and src identifies the file that is the source of the image.

11. B. Option B, href, is an attribute, not a tag. The other options are all elements (tags) and are all required to create an image map.

12. B, C. PNG and JPG files both can use over 16 million colors. GIF files are limited to 256 colors and SVG files are limited to only 147 colors.

13. B, D. You can put an image at the end of a line of text. The text will be the size specified, but the height of the image will determine how far above this line of text that the previous line is.

14. C. The `target` attribute of the `<img>` tag determines where an embedded external link will open, if it is specified. The `href` attribute specifies what is to be opened. `frames` and `pages` are not attributes of `<img>`.

15. B, D. You would first create an id at paragraph 4 with `<a id="paragraph4"></a>`, then create the link to it with `<a href="#paragraph4"> [Go to paragraph4]</a>`. `<a href="#pageAnchors">[Go to paragraph4]</a>` won't work because it doesn't have the right name for the `href`, and `<a href="#paragraph 4"> [Go to paragraph4]</a>` won't work because there can't be a space in the `id` name.

16. B. Option A will not work because it doesn't include the `target` attribute. Option C has a blank space in the filename. Option D uses the wrong `target` attribute value.

17. B, C. Options B and C are the same except that B includes alternate text. Option A won't work because the source reference is incorrect. Option D won't work because `width` and `height` should come after the `src` attribute of the `<img>` tag.

18. A. To identify the area of an image that will be used for the clickable link, you need to provide outlining coordinates of the area in pixels, in x,y format.

19. B. JPG and PNG files both can use over 16 million colors, but PNG files are larger so they load more slowly than JPG files. GIF files are good for animation, but only have 256 colors available, and SVG files are better at scaling up and down, but they only have 147 colors available.

20. D. The code shown will create a window in the current HTML page. Since no border is specified with the `style` attribute, the default border is used.

Chapter 8: Creating HTML Forms

1. C. The `name` attribute identifies data to the server. `for` is used to link the `<label>` to the data in the `<input>` element, and `<label>` is the tag used to create a label that explains the purpose of a text box or other input area. `for`, `id`, and `name` are all attributes of the `<label>` tag.

2. B. The `value` attribute sets a default value that can be changed by the site visitor, and the value in this line of code is 21.

3. A. Of the choices given, only `<input type="submit">` will show text without specifying it. The button will say "Submit."

4. B. The POST value of method is used to send large amounts of data when submitting a form. The GET method is only suitable for small amounts of data because it sends data as a URL addendum. POST is not a value for type, and the action attribute tells the browser where to send the data, such as a file on a server.

5. C. The <label> tag tells the browser and the user the purpose of the referenced input field. The other two main tags for a form are <form> and <input>. <display text> is not valid.

6. B. The <textarea> element creates a text box that can be resized and hold copious amounts of text. <form> tells the browser that this section is grouped together. <label> does not accept user input. <legend> labels a list of check boxes or radio buttons.

7. D. The for attribute is used with the <label> tag to link the human-readable label to the input box. The for= value of the <label> tag must equal the value of the id= attribute in the <input> line.

8. C. To automatically enter information based on previous information input on a form, the autocomplete="on" attribute needs to be in the <form> element.

9. D. Either <input type="reset"> or <button type="reset"> will create a reset button that will clear form data when clicked. <input type="clear"> and <button="submit"> are invalid, but <button type="submit"> will create a submit button. The action of <button type="button"> depends on what it is programmed to do.

10. A. If a form is sending information to another file where it will be read by humans, like an email, then <form enctype="text/plain"> should be used. enctype="email" is not a valid encoding type. enctype="application/s-sss-form-urlencoded" is the default, and enctype="multipart/form-data" would be used for sending a file with the form data.

11. C. If the type of input isn't specified, the default is text, which will provide a text entry box.

12. D. The password type of <input> is the only type value that will obscure what is being entered with a dot instead of the character.

13. B. To send information from a form to someplace else, you would enter the instructions in the <form> element using action= to tell it where and method= to tell it how.

14. C. The type="checkbox" attribute:value is used with the <input> tag when there will be multiple options and the visitor can choose more than one.

15. A, B. The <fieldset> element is used to group <input> elements together in a list. The <legend> element is used to describe the list that follows it, and each choice in the list will be an <input> element with a <label> element to identify it.

16. C. The "range" value for <input type= will provide a slider bar. Minimum and maximum values must be entered.

17. C, D. <input type="file" id="yourfile" accept="*.pdf"> will allow the user to update only one PDF file. Adding the multiple attribute will enable the user to upload more than one PDF file.

18. B. To enter a date in mm/dd/yyyy format, the `type="date"` attribute and value would be used with the `<input>` tag. `"week"` and `"month"` are also valid values, but the dates chosen with them would not be in mm/dd/yyyy format.

19. A, B. The hidden button type will not be visible to website visitors, but you can make it take action based on several events, including `"onmouseover"`. It can be used for anything you like, and it can react to what the user does.

20. D. If a form is sending a file along with form data, then `enctype="multipart/form-data"` would be used. If sending information to another file where it will be read by humans, like an email, then `<form enctype="text/plain">` should be used. `enctype="email"` is not a valid encoding type. `enctype="application/s-sss-form-urlencoded"` is the default and for sending a file with the form data.

Chapter 9: Introducing CSS

1. A. The `<style>` tag is used in the `<head>` of an HTML document. The `style` *attribute* is used at individual elements.

2. C, D. Using the `<style>` tag in the `<head>` section of an HTML file and using the `style` attribute in the opening tag of an element are both valid ways to embed styles in an HTML document. The option `<body><link rel="stylesheet" href="css/styles.css" />` would have been correct if it had been in the head of the document and the CSS file were in a subfolder called CSS from the folder the HTML file is in. The option `<head><link rel="styles.css" href="styles" />` is the wrong syntax.

3. A, B. A selector tells the browser what you want the style applied to. Headings and paragraphs are just two of several selectors.

4. D. Anything between `/*` and `*/` in CSS is considered a comment and is ignored by the browser.

5. B. The proper syntax for a CSS rule is `selector{property:value;}`. The style in the question won't be applied because the semicolon is missing.

6. B. The `<link>` tag is used to reference a style sheet from an HTML page.

7. C. `rel` and `href` are attributes of the `<link>` tag, so `<link rel="stylesheet" href="style1.css" />` is the correct way to link the HTML file with the style sheet. `<link rel="stylesheet" href="/style1.css" />` is incorrect because the `/` before `style1.css` indicates the root of the folder and the question indicates that `style1.css` is in the same folder as our HTML file.

8. C. To temporarily keep a style from being applied, put it between `/*` and `*/`. If you forget the ending comment mark, the browser will ignore everything after the open comment.

9. B. Using the wrong color combinations can make reading a website difficult. Alternate text for images and semantic elements for creating the website are important because screen readers use these. Only the topic of the website isn't an important concern for accessibility.

10. B. The `<link>` tag belongs in the `<head>` section of your HTML file. It references the CSS style sheet.

11. A. The proper syntax for a CSS rule is `selector {property:value;}`.

12. D. The `<link>` tag is used to connect an HTML file to an external CSS file. The `href` attribute is used to indicate the name and location of the external file.

13. A, B. The `type` attribute of the `<style>` tag is used to tell the browser what media type is being used for the file. Currently, `"text/css"` is the only available option.

14. C. The syntax for a CSS rule is selector`{property:value;}`. The selector is not written with the `< >` brackets surrounding it. It must have the colon and semicolon in the right spots. Extra spaces do not affect how the code works.

15. D. CSS selectors are a part of a CSS rule. CSS rules can be in the `<head>` section of an HTML file by using the `<style>` tag, or they can be in a CSS file. They are not used with the `style` attribute.

16. A, C. The `style` attribute and the `<style>` tag are used to apply styles within the HTML file. The `<link>` tag and the `href` attribute point to external file sheets.

17. B. A selector can be a semantic tag, written without the angle brackets.

18. D. There are several advantages of using CSS files. The styles are created and maintained in one file. Many files can use the CSS file without having to duplicate the code. CSS files can provide a cohesive look for a website and cut down on human error and programming and troubleshooting time.

19. A, B. Ignoring accessibility options can make it impossible for some people to use your website, and depending on where you live, you might have to pay fines or face legal consequences.

20. A, D. Using CSS for formatting styles makes your job easier, and using semantic elements will help with SEO and accessibility. Colors too close together make reading your website difficult. You should use headings instead of trying to make plain text look like a heading.

Chapter 10: Applying CSS Styles

1. D. Only an `id` requires a hashtag before it when identifying it in a style sheet.

2. D. Using a type selector means that you're using an element to specify where a style belongs. Descendant selectors specify child elements of an `id` to be styled.

3. D. The syntax for applying the same style to only elements that are in two classes is `.class1.class2 {property:value;}`.
Although `.class1 .class2 {property:value;}` is very similar, the space between the first class and second class means they would be applied to an element in either class, not both.

4. B. Using classes and ids makes code less cluttered in the body of the web page, helps prevent human error, and saves time because you only enter them once, not multiple times.

5. D. The pseudo-class :hover takes the specified action whenever a mouse hovers over the specified selector, in this case, any anchor (a), which is used to specify a hyperlink.

6. A, B. :hover and :focus are pseudo-classes. The other two choices are related to id selectors.

7. B. When specifying a style, an id has a hashtag (#) before it, a class has a period (.) before it, and an element is written without its brackets, such as simply p. To be correct, a colon must be between property and value.

8. C. The three ways that styles can be created are in a separate CSS style sheet, in a <styles> section within the HTML <head>, or using the styles attribute at the beginning element tag.

9. A, D. To style just one paragraph and not the others, you could create an id that would be assigned to the paragraph <p id="mammals">, then specified in the style sheet #mammals{property:value;}.

10. A. If no style has been specified for an HTML file, it will get its style from the browser's default style.

11. B. The entry near the bottom of a style sheet that styles ordered lists <ol> takes precedence over the style at the top of the sheet. If no style was specified for <ol>, it would get its style from the <body> of the web page, but because it is specified, any conflicting styles between the <body> and <ol> will be styled as the <ol> specifies. How the paragraphs are styled is irrelevant.

12. A, C. To style several but not all paragraphs the same, you would use a class. The two steps you need to do are assign the class to each paragraph using <p class="className">, then enter the style either in the HTML file's <head> or a CSS style sheet. This example is using the <style> element within the <head> element, <style> .className {property:value;}. You would not use #className because the hashtag identifies an id, not a class.

13. A. When specifying a style, a class has a period (.) before it, an id has a hashtag (#) before it, and an element is written without its brackets, such as simply p.

14. B. In this scenario, the body style will override the default browser style, and then the paragraph's style color will override the body's style color. More specific styles override more general styles.

15. D. A link that has been visited is one that has been clicked on. The proper syntax is a:visited {property: value; }.

16. B. The syntax for applying the same style to two selectors is selector1, selector2 {property:value;}, as in p, #footer {property:value;}.

17. B. Elements within the division will be styled the same as the division, as long as no conflicting styles have been applied to those elements. The child elements inherit styles from their parent.

18. B, C. The currently selected item, (such as a window being opened) on a web page is said to be in focus, so to modify its appearance you must use the pseudo-class :focus.

19. B. A style with the !important rule will always override any previous styles for that property, even if the other style is more specific. p is more specific than div but is overridden by the !important rule of the division.

20. A. li.fun {color: orange;} causes any list items in the fun class to have the font color of orange. .li is how a class would be written, not an element. Entering <li color="orange"> at each list item would work, but that's not the best way to achieve the result.

Chapter 11: CSS Styling Fundamentals

1. C, D. Of the options given, only em and % are relative. em is a multiple of the current element's size, and % is relative to the size of the parent object. An inch (in) is always an inch, and in CSS a pixel (px) is always 1/96 of an inch.

2. B. Colors can be expressed in a keyword, rgb value, or hex number. With either hex or rgb, the last value is blue, so option B contains no blue.

3. A, C. fit is not a valid value for background-size, and the proper format for repeating a background is background: repeat-y; or background-repeat: repeat-y;. In either case, the word repeat must follow the colon.

4. C. To put a box around an element, we use the border property. There are several styles including solid and dashed, but only border-style: solid; has both the correct property name and the semicolon at the end.

5. B, D. Fonts are applied in the order specified. If a font is not available on the computer where a web page is opened, the page will use the default of the browser, in this case, Times New Roman.

6. B, C. The text-emphasis-style property is used to put an emphasis above a span of text. The text-decoration-style property is used to specify a style for an underline. In one of the two correct options, the dot is colored blue. In the other, it is the default color.

7. C, D. When using a keyboard character as an unordered list style, the character must be surrounded by quotes as in list-style: ""x""; and an image can be specified as in list-style: url("mypic.gif"); where the image is in quotes and the URL with its path is between brackets. While disc is a valid value, colors for bullets can't be specified this way.

8.   D. The types for ordered lists are i = lowercase Roman numerals, I = uppercase Roman numerals, a = lowercase alpha, and A = uppercase alpha.

9.   A, C. Viewport width (vw) and viewport height (vh) are relative measurements that will adjust the content to the size of the screen it's being viewed on. Inches (in) and pixels (px) are absolute measurements that stay the same regardless of the device they're being viewed on.

10.   D. The option body { background: url("myimage.png") 50% 50% ; } specifies that the image should be 50 percent down the page and 50 percent between left and right—in other words, centered in the page. body { background: "myimage.png" ; } is not the right syntax. The other two choices use the default and the image will be placed top left.

11.   B. To make an element resize based on what it is being viewed on, you need to use relative units. Inches and pixels are absolute units.

12.   B. Opacity ranges in a number from 0.0 to 1.0, with 1.0 being the most opaque (solid), so 0.2 is the most transparent that still has some of the color. There must be a colon between the word opacity and the number.

13.   A, D. By default, a specified image will repeat as many times as needed to fill the screen, so background: url("image.png"); will work and background is a shorthand for several background properties, including repeat, so background: repeat -x; will work. When added after a line specifying an image, background: repeat -y; will repeat the image vertically on the screen and background-repeat: l,r; contains an invalid value.

14.   A. If no position is specified, an image is placed in the top left of the web page.

15.   A. Relative font sizes can be specified from xx-small to xxx-large. font-weight is a density from 100 to 900, with 100 being the lightest and 900 being the most thick and dark, but it doesn't change the size of the font. The oblique font style changes the font's angle but not the size.

16.   B. When three values for border-style are specified, the order is top, right and left, bottom. So, for the example given, the top will have a double line, the left and right will be dotted, and the bottom will be solid.

17.   A, D. text-orientation and text-decoration are block elements, so they can be inherited, while text-shadow and text-emphasis are inline elements that are not inherited.

18.   A, D. If two values are specified for border-style, the first applies to the top and bottom of the border, and the second value applies to the right and left borders.

19.   C, D. The upper-alpha value and type="A" will both result in an ordered list that uses uppercase letters. An unordered list (ul) will not have uppercase alphabet letters for numerators, and type="I" will result in uppercase Roman numerals.

20.   C. One point (pt) is equal to 1/72nd of an inch. There are 2.54cm in an inch, a pica (pc) is 1/6th of an inch, and a pixel (px) is 1/96th of an inch.

Chapter 12: CSS Layout and Box Model

1. A. The CSS box model includes the padding, border, and margin layers around an HTML element.

2. C. The dimensions of an element include the size of the content all the boxes around it, on all sides, so in this example it would be 100 + 10 + 10 + 3 + 3 + 5 + 5 for a total of 136 pixels high.

3. B, D. `<p class="middle">` would be placed in the HTML document, and `.middle { margin: auto; }` would be placed in the style sheet, and together they would center the paragraph.

4. C. In normal flow, block elements will be stacked on each other from top to bottom in the same order as the web page hierarchy. Inline elements flow from left to right, with any overflow going to the next line.

5. B. The CSS flexbox model causes elements to be arranged horizontally instead of vertically. The CSS box model refers to content and the layers around it. Normal flow puts objects vertically.

6. A. The CSS grid layout creates rows and columns, making placement of elements much simpler.

7. D. Parts of the CSS Box model include the margin, border, padding, and content.

8. C. Even though the first paragraph has no margin, the second paragraph has a margin of 10px, so that space exists around the second paragraph on all sides, including between it and the first paragraph.

9. B. `#item4 { grid-column-start: 4; grid-column-end: 6; }` sets the style to start a block at column 4 and ends it when it reaches column 6, so it would combine columns 4 and 5.

10. C. Padding is the space between the content and the border in the CSS Box model. It has the same background color as the content.

11. D. When giving measurements for parts of the CSS Box model, if there are four of them they start with the top and go clockwise around the box. In this case, top = 20, right side = 30, bottom = 40, and left side = 10.

12. A. Viewport is the term given to describe the area that an HTML page is being rendered in, whether it's all of a smartphone or a browser taking half of a screen (or the whole screen) on a desktop computer.

13. D. A box's width is the sum of all of the components of the box, including left and right sides. In this case, however, the margin is set to `auto`, which means that the margin will automatically adjust to a changing viewport to keep the content centered on the screen. The box will be taking up the entire width of the screen regardless of the screen's width.

14. B, D. `@media` will cause the browser to read the size of the viewport and respond appropriately by choosing how to display the page based on the size of the viewport.

15. A. Margins are designed to add space between elements in a CSS Box layout.

16. D. `{ clear:both ; }` means that the object it is applied to will ignore any floated elements that are above it in the hierarchy and will position itself below them as it would in normal flow.

17. A. The `absolute` value places a box relative to the `<body>` element or relative to a parent that is not static, so it will follow the parent as it moves. `fixed` places a box relative to the viewport. `relative` places a box relative to its original position, and there is no `follow` value for the `position` attribute.

18. C. A CSS flexbox container was created with the style sheet entry and the style applied to the ordered list. Flexboxes put immediate child items in a horizontal row rather than stacked vertically. The code has nothing to do with viewports.

19. D. The `grid-template-columns: 200 200 200;` line tells the browser to display three columns that are each 200 pixels wide, assuming that above the code is a line that says `display: grid;`. There is no `display: pattern;`, and the two gap entries define the space between columns and rows respectively.

20. B. Media queries cause a browser to react differently (that is, respond) based on what they read, so media queries are a part of responsive web design.

Chapter 13: JavaScript Essentials

1. C. `//` is used for a comment that is only on one line. Any JavaScript comment that is going to span multiple lines needs to be commented out with `/*` at the beginning and `*/` at the end.

2. D. The option `<script> src = "scripts/anyName.js" </script>` is invalid because when using the `src` attribute, it must be included in the opening `<script>` tag, like `<script src = "scripts/anyName.js" > </script>`. The other options are all valid.

3. A. The code `<script type= "text/javascript">` is the correct option. Option C is missing the quotes. Options B and D use the wrong terminology.

4. A, C. Each answer is a statement; however, although code may work without a semicolon because automatic semicolon insertion (ASI) may intervene and put one there, it is not dependable or recommended. JavaScript syntax rules dictate adding a semicolon at the end of every statement.

5. D. You may put as many `<script>` tags in an HTML page as you need.

6. B. JavaScript syntax requires a semicolon at the end of each statement, and although automatic semicolon insertion (ASI) might work, it isn't always dependable.

7. A, B. Identifiers cannot start with a number or use dashes. They can use capitalization as long as it is used consistently—JavaScript is case sensitive. And although dashes can't be used to separate words, underscores can be.

8. D. Only current and current are the same identifier. JavaScript identifiers are case sensitive, and numbers are not allowed as the first character of an identifier, nor are dashes (but underscores are).

9. A, C. The two attributes of src, async and defer, will both download a script in the background while a page is parsing. async will load the script when it's available, and defer will load the script after the page is parsed. The other two options are fictitious.

10. A, C. JavaScript syntax dictates that either single or double quotes may be used, but double quotes are used more often. Parentheses ( ) must enclose the value of alert, and there should be a semicolon at the end of each statement. Extra spaces are allowed.

11. B. The <script> tag is used in HTML, not in a JavaScript file. The default value can be omitted when using prompt.

12. A, D. Options A and D are correct. <script src= "scripts/myScript.js"> </script> gets the script locally from a subfolder called scripts, and <script src= "https://yourDomain.com/scripts/MyScript.js" > </script> gets the script from a specific URL. Option B is invalid because it's missing the quotes around the URL, and option C is invalid because the src attribute must be part of the first <script> tag.

13. B. Entering document.write ( ) will clear everything on the HTML page you're working with. Using console.log will show your work in the console. The other two options do not clear the screen.

14. D. Both of these express a value, so they are expression statements. Boolean and logical both mean a statement would equate to true or false, and conditional statements start with if.

15. C. The two attributes of src, async and defer, will both download a script in the background while a page is parsing. The difference is that async will run the script as soon as it's available, but defer won't run the script until the page is finished parsing. The other two options are fictitious.

16. B. Any JavaScript comment that is going to span multiple lines needs to be commented out with /* at the beginning and */ at the end. // is used for comments that are only on one line.

17. C. Expression statements assign a value. Conditional statements will perform an action if the condition is met, and declaration statements are used to create variables and functions. Variable is not a type of statement.

18. D. The correct way to declare a function is function myFunction ( );. The let keyword is used to declare a value. isFunction is not a keyword. function myFunction ( ) is missing the semicolon at the end.

19. C. The `type= "importmap"` is used to create a list of shorter references to a group of long URLs.

20. A. Without any other attributes, the page will be parsed and the script will be downloaded and run when the page reaches it, causing the parsing to stop momentarily. Adding the `defer` or `async` attribute causes the script to be downloaded in the background and run after parsing or when available, respectively.

Chapter 14: JavaScript Data

1. B, C. The two keywords used to define a variable are `let` and `var`. The `const` keyword defines a constant.

2. B. The result will be 2,6 because c=2, d as declared = 3, and d*=c means to get the value of d, multiply d by c, which is 6. If the third line were c*=d, then the result would be an error because c is a constant whose value cannot be changed.

3. D. This code returns an error because b was defined inside a block of code and can't be used outside of the code block.

4. B, C. Data conversion and data coercion are both terms used to identify when JavaScript automatically interprets one type of code as another.

5. B. Where the plus sign is used with numbers in quotes, JavaScript will coerce the numbers to string values. The result of a = "5" + "3" will be 53, not 8. When only one of the two is in quotes, it will assume that the number in quotes was intended to be a number and treat it as such.

6. C. Of these, only a = 0 - null; is equal to 0. Null, unless used in an equation, is the absence of value, not a value of 0. Undefined is declared but not defined, and let a; equates to undefined.

7. C. In an equation, the Boolean `true` equates to the number 1; however, "true" is treated as a string.

8. A. An error message will result because c was declared as a constant, and a constant can't be changed.

9. C. Boolean, numeric, undefined, and null types are converted to a string when used with the + sign AND a string. "3" is a string because it is in quotes and isn't used with another number.

10. A. Non-numeric strings with *, /, or - in an equation result in NaN.

11. B. A string such as '10' is converted to a value when used with the -, /, or * operator.

12. D. A Boolean will be converted to a number when used with a number: true = 1, false = 0.

13. D. When used in an equation with a number, null will be converted to 0.

14. C. Boolean, numeric, undefined, or null are converted to a string when used with the + sign and a string.

15. A. A string such as "50" is converted to a number when used with the /, *, or − operator.

16. B. Undefined in any equation with a numeric value equates to NaN.

17. D. push( ) and unshift( ) add items, whereas pop( ) and shift( ) remove them. shift( ) and unshift( ) affect the beginning of the list, and push( ) and pop( ) affect the end of the list.

18. C. The const keyword creates a value that can't be changed through a program. Option B is incorrect because it would result in an error message, and if "Pi" were used instead of Pi, it wouldn't cause an error but p would equate to a string.

19. B. The symbol data type is a guaranteed unique identifier for a value within a program.

20. A. console.log(typeof x) will display the type of data that x is, such as Boolean, BigInt, number, and so on.

Chapter 15: Functions and Control Structures

1. B. A method is a type of function that is tied to a specific object. Other functions can be used anywhere in a program. A function starts with the function keyword.

2. C, D. Falsy values are NaN, 0, -0, 0n, " ", and document.all. They will equate to Boolean false. All other values are truthy, meaning they will equate to Boolean true.

3. B. In this situation, you would use !==, which is a strict comparison operator. != would not work because the string "1" and the number 1 would equate as true because the string will be coerced into being the number 1 even though it is a string. === is strictly equal, you want the code to execute only if they are unequal. <> is not a valid comparison operator.

4. D. A simple if statement works best in this situation. The premise said that you don't want the code to do anything if the equation is false. And while it may be tempting to choose if (x=y) {//code;} else {'';}, the result of that is an empty string, which is a falsy value and would return false, not nothing if x did not equal y.

5. B, C. switch/case will compare a value (in this case, the value of day) and run the code immediately following the case that matches the value, then exit the conditional statement.

6. A, C. The code will not run once a = 100, so 100 is the final value of a. The value of b is 2, because the formula does not change b. The value of c will be 198, because the last time the program runs the value of a will be 99. The program stops when a = 100 and multiplication is done before addition, so the last value of a that will be multiplied is 99. 99 * 2 = 198. Then a will be incremented, its value becomes 100, and the program no longer runs.

7. C. The <= comparative operator means less than or equal to. ==> is not a comparative operator. In z += a, the value of a would be added to z. += is not a comparative operator, and z >= a is the opposite of what we want.

8. A, B. !== and === are strict comparison operators, while == is a loose comparison operator. Strict comparison operators do not allow coercion, so 99 !== "99" is a true statement because, strictly speaking, the number 99 does not equal the string "99". However, 99!==99 (99 does not equal 99) is a false statement because 99 is equal to itself. In 99=="99", the string will be coerced into a number, so they are equal.

9. A. The function statement in the question declares the function, but a function can be invoked by writing the function name and any parameters to be used, as in total(100,5);.

10. B, C. The for and while keywords are used to create program loops. The if and switch keyword are used to create conditional statements.

11. A, C. The value of x starts at 0, and as long as x is less than 10, it will perform the action between the curly brackets {console.log(x);} and then increment x by 1. The last line will print 9 because when x is incremented to 10, the code, which prints the value of x to the console, will no longer occur because the condition (x <10) will be false. The code will execute 10 times; the first when x is 0, and nine more. x=0 will only run once.

12. A. switch (siteNo) { case 1: city = "New York"; break; case 2: city = "Tokyo"; break; } is the proper syntax. The other options have colons where there should be semicolons or are missing a break.

13. C. The syntax for a function is function name (parameter1, parmeter2) { code to run;}. The first doesn't separate the parameters with a comma. The second doesn't use the parameters in the calculation, and the last is missing the semicolon.

14. D. The empty string (' ') is a falsy value, so the result will be undefined. Because the if statement is false, the code after it will not execute, so the answer will not be 5, and null must be declared.

15. B. You would use == because using it, the string "5" would equal the number 5. The single equal sign (=) is used to assign a value, not to compare values. Using === would stop the coercion of a string to a number, and != means "not equal to."

16. D. x would remain undefined because perfect is not enclosed in quotes, so the program thinks that perfect is the name of an undefined variable, not a string, and consequently it doesn't know what value to assign to x.

17. C. Using if, else if will enable you to create multiple conditions and options with a default one if none of the other conditions apply. The if, else statement would only allow for two outputs, and you want three. A switch/case statement is only appropriate where there are a limited number of specific values that can be input.

18. B. The option function mySquare(a) { return a*a; } is correct. The others are incorrect because one asks for two parameters to multiply, another is missing the semicolon, and the other incorrect answer doesn't include return or calculate a square.

19. B, D. Alert() is a predefined function that is invoked by using the function name and putting the contents of the alert between the ()parentheses. let a = mine(1,2,3); is invoking the function named mine with the parameters 1, 2, and 3, and will return the value of the function's calculation to a. Option C is declaring a function.

20. B, D. The line let x = total (2,4); is providing the parameters 2 and 4 to the function named total, which will return the result of its calculation (2 * 4) to the letter x.

Chapter 16: The DOM

1. B. The <head> section of an HTML page is the firstElementChild of the HTML document. HTML is the firstElementChild of the document, so document.first ElementChild.firstElementChild refers to the <head> section of the HTML page.

2. A, C. getElementsByTagName() and querySelectorAll() are DOM methods. getElementByGroup will return an error because Element must be plural, and getElementByID()must be written as Id, or you'll get an error stating this is not a DOM method.

3. C. The DOM returns lists of items in an array-like structure, and because there is only one <body>, it will be first in the array, which always starts at the number [0]. Retrieving the "html" would give both the <head> and <body> sections. The other options have syntactical errors.

4. A, B. document.getElementById will always return only one value because Ids must be unique on a web page. querySelector("p") will always return the first instance of the selector given. document.getElementBySelectorAll("p")[1] is incorrect syntax, and document.getElementsByClass('fun'); will return the first and third paragraphs. Classes are not assigned uniquely.

5. B, C. Using .innerText or .textContent enables changing the text without changing the HTML structure. .innerHTML changes the HTML too, so you need to include the HTML in the new text. innerContent is invalid.

6. B, D. When using document.querySelector, the result will be the first of that type of selector, so in this case, the first list item, not the third. Document .getElementsByTagName("li")[2]... will not work because we want the third item in the list.

7. A. The `element.setAttribute("src" "elephant.jpg");` option will change the `src` attribute of the `element`. `changeAttribute()` is not a valid method, and the other options have syntactical errors.

8. B. One way this could be done using the DOM is to set `onmouseover` and `onmouseout` functions, assuming you want it to turn on and off as a mouse goes over the object. Calling the functions from HTML (`<p onmouseover= "on()" onmouseout= "off()" content </p>`) would also work, but the question specifically asks how to do it using the DOM.

9. B, D. The preferred way to change CSS styling using the DOM is to create the class and its style in CSS, then add the element to the class using `.classList.add`.

10. A, C. You would add the `onclick` attribute to the button and have it call the function that you created in JS, which will find the content and use `classList.toggle` to alternate between adding and removing the new style.

11. C. `<html>` is the first child element of the DOM, then the `<head>` is the first child element of `<html>`, and the body is the second child element of `<html>`. The `<title>` would likely be the second or third child element of the `<head>`, depending on web page layout.

12. D. All you need is the element and `.classList` to retrieve the list of classes that element belongs to.

13. A. When working with Boolean attributes, if the attribute is in the code, it is considered to be true. If it does not exist, then it's false. A falsy value does not equate to false.

14. A. Because the paragraphs are not enclosed in a division, the parent of the paragraphs is the body. The first child of the body is the `<h1>`, the second child of the body is paragraph 1. Because it is the second child and a paragraph, that is what will be selected.

15. D. Because the paragraphs are not enclosed in a division, the parent of the paragraphs is the body. The first child of the body is the `<h1>`. Because it is the first child but not a paragraph, there is nothing to select, so the value is null.

16. D. The `element.removeAttribute("class");` will remove the class list in its entirety, so there won't be any classes associated with this element. It would work but uses a tank to kill a mosquito. The `element.classList.remove("student");` option will remove only the `student` class and leave others intact. The other two options have invalid syntax.

17. A, D. `document.getElementsByTagName("h3")` and `document .querySelectorAll("h3")` will both return all of the `<h3>` headings, but for either option you'll need to know the number in the array of the one you want and would put it in square brackets at the end, that is, `[5]`. Searching by `Id` won't work because `id`s haven't been assigned, and the other option has syntactical errors.

18. C, D. The `document.querySelectorAll()` and `document.getElementsByClass()` options will return all the elements that fit those criteria, whether it is one or many. `getElementById` and `querySelector` will always return only one element.

19. D. The changeAttribute() option doesn't exist. classList.toggle() can be used to add and remove a class from an object repeatedly. setAttribute() can be used to change the class to a new value, and classList.add() is used to add a class to an object's class list.

20. D. The Document Object Model (DOM) is a hierarchical tree structure that is used in JavaScript to access elements of a web page. Accessing an element starts with .document, not .DOM.

Chapter 17: NodeJS Basics

1. D. Node.js runs on the server-side. HTML, CSS, and JavaScript are all client-side languages.

2. A, B. You can either download the Node.js application from the http://nodejs.org website or install it from the terminal using **sudo apt-get install**. Control Panel is a Windows utility and App Store is for macOS computers.

3. C. REPL stands for read, evaluate, print, loop, because that's what happens when you enter a command in the Node.js runtime.

4. A. .clear is an alias for .break, so they both do the same thing, which is terminate the running process. .editor opens editor mode, .exit closes REPL, and .save will save the REPL session to a file.

5. A, B. Modules are code that can be reused, and the reason you would reuse them is that they solve problems that are common to multiple coders. Modules often contain functions, but not all code that contains a function is a module. Some modules are built into Node.js.

6. B, D. In the Linux terminal, you can type **cd** and the path to a folder or type **cd** and drag and drop the parent folder onto the terminal. While it's true that you can right-click a folder and choose Open in Terminal, that isn't done from within the terminal so it is an incorrect choice here, and simply dragging and dropping the folder without entering cd first will produce an error message.

7. A, D. Node.js works outside of a browser so applications can be built using it on a desktop or server computer. It uses the familiar JavaScript commands, and it's a very fast, asynchronous environment.

8. B, D. Regardless of the operating system, Node.js must be installed before it can be used.

9. A. Once you're in REPL, entering **process.version** will tell you the version of Node.js that is running. Typing **node** in RPEL will give an error message that node is not defined. .editor opens editor mode, and .help lists available commands.

10. C. Requests that are received by the server go first to a request pool where Event Loop will pick them up and pass them to a thread pool. A multithreaded application then picks them up, processes them, and when they're done, Event Loop returns them to the application that made the request.

11. A. The `npm.init` command will create a repository and ask for information about the repository, while `npm init --yes` will create a repository but use default entries. The other two options are simply not valid commands.

12. D. Built-in modules for Node.js don't require installation. Node.js also supports CommonJS modules and ECMAScript modules. Well-known modules is not a valid term.

13. A. Of the choices given, only typing **node** at the $ prompt will not produce an error; it opens Node.js.

14. D. The first line assigns a variable to the module, so its results can be used outside of the module. `userLog.txt` is the filename where the data will be stored and `123456789` is the data that will be stored there. The callback is what happens with the information when it is returned to the code that called it. In this case, the code will send an error message if there's a problem, and if not, it will print `Data is saved`.

15. C. The $ is the normal terminal prompt.

16. D. For any module that isn't a built-in module, type **npm install** *moduleName* at the $ prompt to install it.

17. C. A folder called `node_modules` is created when the first module is installed using npm `install` *packageName*. This does occur after `npm init --yes` is run, but not as a result of running that code.

18. A. The most likely choice is `process.js`. `.njs` is not a valid file extension, `init` is used to create a repository, and `runMe` would likely produce a `runMe is not defined` error message.

19. C. You're at the REPL prompt, so the statement is read, evaluated, and printed, and because `1+3=4`, the number 4 is displayed. Then the computer waits for more instructions.

20. B. ECMAScript modules are a standard that can be used by other JS runtimes and Node.js. Built-in modules for Node.js don't require installation. Node.js also supports CommonJS modules.

Chapter 18: NodeJS Express

1. A. A programming framework provides the structure that a program can be built around, such as blocks of reusable code.

2. B. The only file created when `npm init` is run is `package.json`.

3. C. `const express = require("express")` imports the Express module into the code and creates a dependency that appears in the `.json` file as soon as the server is restarted.

4. A. `app.use(bodyParser.urlencoded({extended: true}));` is the correct command and syntax to read and use data that is not in string or array format. `extended: false` only reads strings and arrays.

5. D. The first part of the first line, `app.get`, tells the program to use the GET method, then sets up the route for the request. The function `(req, res)` is the callback function. `res.send("request received");` will send a response to the HTML page, and `console.log` displays what follows in the terminal.

6. B. `app.get("/fun", (req, res) => {res.sendFile ("fun.html") });` is the proper command and syntax to route the request to the page and load it in the browser. If on any server other than your localhost, you would change `("fun.html")` to `(__dirname + "fun.html")`.

7. D. `.ejs` is the file extension used for template files. `.js` is the file extension used for app files, `.html` is used for web pages, and `.tmpl` isn't used in web pages.

8. A. `<%# ... %>` is a comment. `<%= ... %>` will inject a variable, `<% ... %>` and `<%- ... %>` are for flow control and unescaped values, respectively.

9. D. Using Express most likely isn't a security discussion as it is what the website is built on. XSS, CSRF, and user input validation are all security concerns.

10. B. Although your first instinct might be to use `req.form`, it is invalid. The data from the form's input will be in the body of the HTTP request, not the header, so you must use `req.body`. The other option you'll use often is `req.query`, which is used to gather information that appears after the `?` in a URL.

11. C. It isn't required that the port be assigned to a variable (`const port = 8080;`) as long as the port number is entered in the `app.listen` entry. All the other lines of code are necessary.

12. A. `app.post` is used to define a route handler that tells a server what to do with information that it *receives* from user interaction (HTTP POST) with a web page. `app.get` is used to route user requests (HTTP GET) to the right place in your website. `srv.post` and `ejs.post` are not valid.

13. C. `app.post("/", function (req, res) { console.log(req.body.first);` displays the data from the field named `first` in the console. The other options either have the wrong command (`app.get`) or the wrong identifier (0).

14. A. You can enter many responses with `res.write ( );` but it will not write to the web page until you use `res.send` which is the "final" entry.

15. B. The proper way to route users to the `public` subdirectory is `app.use(express.static("public"))`. One of the other choices has a `)` in the wrong place, and `express.static` is a built-in function of Express that doesn't need to be installed separately.

16. D. `<%= stuff %>` is correct. In option C, `<%#` is a comment, and `res.render` (options A and B) would appear in the `app.js` file.

17. B. The syntax `const.app=(express);` is incorrect. It is needed, but the syntax should be `const app = express()`. All the other options are needed as written to use Express. Additionally, you need to require Express with the line `const express = require("express");`.

18. A. `.ejs` is the file extension used for template files. The file extension `.js` is used for app files and `.html` for web pages, and `.app` isn't used in this setting.

19. A. `req.query` is used to gather information that appears after the ? in a URL. `req.form` is invalid. `req.header` and `req.body` are used to get information from an HTTP request.

20. B. `<%= ... %>` will inject a variable. `<%# ... %>` is a comment. `<% ... %>` and `<%- ... %>` are for flow control and unescaped values, respectively.

Chapter 19: Manipulating SQLite with NodeJS

1. D. `npm install sqlite3` is used to install SQLite on a Linux computer. Linux commands are case-sensitive, so `SQLite3` will not work and both `npm` and the 3 need to be there, which means the other options are all incorrect.

2. C. To create a new database, the line `const db = new sqlite3.Database ("databaseName.ext");` needs to be entered in the *app.js* file for your application. You would not need to include the path `/inventory` because you're creating it in the same folder where your *app.js* file is. The command `const sqlite3 = require("sqlite3");` would need to be in your *app.js* file, but that's not what the question is asking about.

3. A. To open your `inventory.dbf` database from the terminal, when you're in the working directory that contains the database, you simply type **sqlite3 inventory.dbf**. There is no period before `inventory`. The other options, `.table` and `.dump`, will provide information about what's in the database once you have accessed it.

4. A, C. To make a connection with a database from Node.js, you would first need to enter the command **const sqlite3 = require('sqlite3');** and then **const db = new sqlite3 .Database("databaseName.ext");**. `npm install sqlite3` is needed, but it is run from the terminal to install SQLite3 before you can use it. `db.open` is not a valid command.

5. B, D. The referenced code is designed to close the open database and provide an error if it was not successful or a message that it closed successfully. The database will not be deleted.

6. C, D. The code as written will create a table (`CREATE TABLE`) named `postal`, and the items in parentheses are the field names followed by their types.

7. B, C. First you would need to gather the data from the POST method of the form with the app.post command; then you would need to insert it into the database using the db.run command. However, VALUES should be (?, ?, ?), not the data directly from the POST, to avoid a SQL injection.

8. D. The INSERT clause is used to insert a new record into a database. ADD is Boolean logic. The CREATE clause is used to create a table, and app.post is used when retrieving data from a POST from an HTML page.

9. A. The UPDATE clause is used to change an existing database record. The INSERT clause is used to insert a new record into a database. The CREATE clause is used to create a table, and CHANGE is not a valid SQLite3 clause.

10. C. The SELECT clause is used to choose rows in a database to apply an action to. WHERE is the clause that supplies the criteria. GET() and RETRIEVE are invalid.

11. A, D. db.get(SELECT * FROM people WHERE first="Ariel", will select only the first instance of what is specified in the WHERE clause, and because we know it is the only record with that first name, this will work. db.each( ) will find all records that match the criteria, so that will also work. db.get(CHOOSE... is not valid; neither is db.find.

12. C. The percent sign character must be "escaped" from the program so that it will be treated like any other character. The way to escape anything in SQLite is to precede the character with a backslash.

13. B. The close method of the database object is used to close a database as in db .close( ). A callback function can be used with the close method, but it's not required.

14. A, D. The underscore wildcard represents one character; therefore, anything that starts with 13 and ends with 01, and that has a single character between, will be selected. 1301 is too short. 130101 is too long.

15. B. From the information shown about this database, you can tell that RecNo is the primary key because it is the only field that doesn't have any duplicate values.

16. A. FROM must be followed by sales, as that is the name of the database. You may be tempted to choose the line that ends with " 1_ _" (one and two underscores); however, that won't find all the sales over $100 if any of them are greater than $999. Because each under-score only represents one character, "1_ _ %" works because the value needs to be at least three characters long and can be any number above that because of the percent sign wildcard. "1%" will find all values over 1, and "1\%" will see the % sign as a character, not a wildcard.

17. D. The number (5) after location CHAR is a constraint for how long the field can be, not a numeric value. Atlanta is the only field value that is longer than five characters. However, SQLite uses dynamic typing so it associates a type with the value, not the container. It also does not strictly enforce the constraints.

18. C. Commands in SQL aren't case sensitive, so although common practice is to put the com-mands in all caps, they will still work fine in lowercase. The correct code is db .run("create table if not exists sales (dollars INTEGER, invoice CHAR)");. The other entries all have small syntax errors.

19. D. An autoincrementing field named `rowid` is always created by default in a SQLite database, even if it is not declared. A database can be created without a `rowid` field if the phrase `WITHOUT ROWID` is at the end of the `CREATE TABLE` statement.

20. B. The `DELETE` clause is used to delete an existing database. The `DROP` clause is used to delete an existing table. The `INSERT` clause is used to insert a new record into a database, and `CHANGE` is not a valid SQLite3 clause.

Index

Online Test Bank

To help you study for your LPI Web Development Essentials certification exams, register to gain one year of FREE access after activation to the online interactive test bank—included with your purchase of this book! All of the practice questions in this book are included in the online test bank so you can study in a timed and graded setting.

Register and Access the Online Test Bank

To register your book and get access to the online test bank, follow these steps:

1. Go to www.wiley.com/go/sybextestprep. You'll see the "**How to Register Your Book for Online Access**" instructions.
2. Click "here to register" and then select your book from the list.
3. Complete the required registration information, including answering the security verification to prove book ownership. You will be emailed a pin code.
4. Follow the directions in the email or go to www.wiley.com/go/sybextestprep.
5. Find your book on that page and click the "Register or Login" link with it. Then enter the pin code you received and click the "Activate PIN" button.
6. On the Create an Account or Login page, enter your username and password, and click Login or, if you don't have an account already, create a new account.
7. At this point, you should be in the test bank site with your new test bank listed at the top of the page. If you do not see it there, please refresh the page or log out and log back in.